Namaste Nanny

Simple Indian Home Cooking

By Natasha Khanna

Family Edition

To Justine & the team, Congratulations! With love, Natasha & Annelis x

*Thank you to Nick England for his exceptional patience
with the typesetting and layout.*

1st edition
Copyright © Namaste Nanny Ltd, 2023
The moral right of this author has been asserted.
All rights reserved.
No part of this publication may be reproduced, stored in a retrieval system, or transmitted, in any form or by any means, without the prior permission in writing of the publisher, nor be otherwise circulated in any form of binding or cover other than that in which it is published and without a similar condition including this condition being imposed on the subsequent purchaser.
Editing and publishing by UK Book Publishing
www.ukbookpublishing.com
ISBN: 978-1-916572-54-6

Every effort has been made to trace any copyright holders and obtain permission to reproduce this material. Please get in touch with any enquiries for future print editions via the publisher.

*For Indian Nanny...
And of course, Big Dada!*

INDIAN NANNY
Mediterranean Cruise April 2011

BIG DADA
100th Birthday Celebration 11th April 2017

Dedicated to
all creatures great and small

THE KHANNA COOKBOOK
by Natasha

The majority of this book covers authentic Indian home cooking taught by Indian Nanny. The Khanna household is a multi-generation home, renowned by friends and family for offering a hearty meal with a few good bottles of wine. The environment is energetic and entertaining as children, adults and animals share the house and there is always someone popping in. I have included some family favourite recipes, which adds variation to this cookbook.

All the recipes are really easy and include fresh vegetables, I would encourage you to use organic and non-GM where possible.

I would also suggest using vegetables that are in season. I have a veg box delivered from Riverford every week and we are also lucky enough to get fresh quality produce from a local source. I love my veg boxes. It has encouraged me to use local, organic, seasonal veg, but also understand a little more about ethical farming, and Riverford also have a zero-airfreight policy. Indian Nanny taught me some classic vegetarian dishes which include ingredients grown in the Asian climate, so sometimes veggies like okra and aubergine have to be sourced from further afield.

Once cooked most dishes can be kept in the fridge for 24/48 hours and be reheated or eaten cold and used for lunches and dinners.

Enjoy! x

CONTENTS

INTRODUCTION

Authentic Indian Home Cooking	13
Uncle Gigi's History Lesson	18
The Spice Rack	31
Helpful Info & Tips	37

PURE VEGETARIAN

Starters & Snacks	57
Dry Veggie Dishes	93
Veggie Curries	147
Paneer	161
Dahl	183
Rice	219
Bread	239

NON - VEGETARIAN

Non-Vegetarian Starters & Snacks	265
Non-Vegetarian Curries	279

ACCOMPANIMENTS

Sauces & Sides	299
Salads	317
Desserts	347
Fruit Desserts	369
Drinks	379
Thank you	400

INTRODUCTION

AUTHENTIC INDIAN HOME COOKING BY INDIAN NANNY

Indian Nanny was head of our family. She lived for nearly 91 years.

I feel blessed that during my 20s, after work, we snatched pockets of precious time, where she taught me to cook authentic, Indian home cooking.

During this time, as well as the time that I then visited her with my young children during my 30s, Indian Nanny told me many stories about India, cooking and our family. Some I will relay during this very special cookbook which is dedicated to her; other stories, I continue to smile about, however... keep to repeat only on exceptional occasions!

I have been a vegan since 2018 and before that I was a vegetarian from the age of four! My mum and dad tell the story that they were cooking and I was sitting by the side of the hob. I asked, "what's the red juice coming from the meat?" and they told me, "it's blood from the animal". I told them that I didn't want to eat meat anymore. For a child growing up in South London in the 80s, this was an unusual choice; however, luckily for me, it was a choice that many of my ancestors had made. Vegetarianism was popular in India. Hindus do not eat beef, as cows are a sacred animal. This is evident when you visit India and you can see cows sitting in the middle of very busy roads! No one moves them and the cows are left to their own devices. The other fact that I have learned from my recent trips to India is I grew up as a "pure vegetarian" – I did not eat meat, fish or eggs. Indian Nanny taught me that most elderly Hindus are largely vegetarian. My Great Grandmother was also a pure vegetarian – she wouldn't even boil an egg! If anyone wanted to cook meat, this had to be done outside of the home. We now tend to do this too and most of the meat cooked in our house is grilled on the barbecue. Indian vegetable dishes go very well with this style of cooking. Therefore, most of my cooking follows the path of vegetarian-style cooking and in fact, most of the dishes are vegan or can be slightly adjusted (i.e. using dairy-free yogurt) to be plant-based. Luckily for our family, she also taught us a few non-vegetarian recipes which we will be happy to share with you. In addition, I am very pleased to be able to include other dishes by my mum, dad, aunties, uncles and family, which will add variety and completion to what Nanny taught me. She probably taught these dishes to them too!

There is healthy competition in the cookery department for the Khanna family – we are always looking to taste one another's beautiful cooking at our family get-togethers.

Family Portrait 1980
Rita, Veena, Vipen, Big Dada, Mahesh, Nanny & Madhu (from the left)

Ebony

Freddie

Snowy

Uncle Gigi's
HISTORY LESSON

Indian Nanny told me a bit about her history, the family and India while we were cooking, but Uncle Gigi loved to tell me about India. He told me stories about our family history on our extensive trip to India when he showed me where our family grew up in Amritsar; we also visited the foothills of the Himalayas and Delhi. He then regularly followed these history lessons up with more information over a few glasses of wine. On one occasion, he disappeared to call a few Indian cousins to make sure he had his facts straight!

In addition, Ravi (1st cousin, once removed – whom I share 25% of my genes with) used to visit Indian Nanny and Big Dada regularly. Always delighted to hear stories of the family's past as his own mother and father had passed away. He would often enquire about the family history over a cup of tea and a pakora!

I then asked the brothers and sisters (Mahesh, Vipen, Veena, Madhu & Rita) to help me with this information. Well, there were some fond memories revived, photos found and naturally between brothers and sisters some disagreements about the matters!

Ok, so here we go...

Pushpa Mehra was born 11th January 1924 in the industrial town of Batala; this is in the state of Punjab, Northern India. Batala is the 8th largest city in Punjab and the second oldest. It is 109 years older than Amritsar! Pushpa was an only child and grew up spending lots of time with her cousins. I am told that she was thoroughly pampered, being the only child. She attended primary school for a few years but was largely uneducated.

Pushpa was very close to her mum and dad, known to us as "Biji and Bouji" (Kamala and Ram Kumar Mehra). Her parents gave her the "nickname" of Bimla. Her father, Bouji, had a fabric business in Amritsar and was a tailor. It is said that they all travelled a bit due to his job. The cities of Lucknow and Kanpur (famous for leather and textiles) were both mentioned as places where they stayed.

Krishan Khanna was born 11th April 1917, in Lahore. Prior to the partition, this was also in Northern India. He had one elder brother called Dharam Prakash (born 1913) and a sister called Shukuntala. I do not know very much about her, except that she was married young (about 15 years old) to a gentleman called Mulkh Raj Kapoor, who worked on the Indian Railway. Soon after her marriage she became pregnant, but at childbirth both mother and the baby sadly died. I have been unable to confirm Shukuntala's date of birth or when she passed away; we think that she was born in 1915 and passed away 1931. Both brothers had accountancy/commercial qualifications and they both worked in National Bank of Lahore. Their father, Hira Lal, was a Bank Manager and their mother was called Lajwanti. During this generation mostly the women were homemakers. Hira Lal and Lajwanti were married before she was 16 years old. Lajwanti had three brothers and was the only girl in her family. We suspect that her dad had a soft spot for her as she was allowed to attend senior school. She was a bright cookie; she could read and write, which was very unusual for women at that time.

When Krishan was in his early 20s, the Khanna family started to look for a wife for him. In India it was normal practice for the families to decide who their children would marry; this is known as an arranged marriage. Krishan was working and had a secure job with good prospects of being a Bank Manager. It is said that the Khanna family had connections in Amritsar, friends and family that knew of a Punjab family who were looking for a husband for their 15-year-old daughter. So, the families were introduced and it was decided that Krishan would be a suitable match for Pushpa.

On 31st January 1940, Krishan Khanna and Pushpa Mehra were married in Lahore; she had just celebrated her 16th Birthday. Weddings in India have always been a big celebration, lasting days and sometimes a week! Krishan and Pushpa met for the first time on their wedding day – Indian Nanny told us, that she did not see Krishan's face for days. This was quite normal in India at this time because the groom would be wearing a heavy flower garland covering his face and she would have been wearing a veil. Big Dada said that when he did see her "she was just beautiful".

Pushpa and Krishan started their married life in Lahore as it was also tradition that the son and his wife would stay where his parents were established. The girl moves in with the family, it would be their responsibility to look after them and offer support. Indian Nanny told me that they took time to get to know one another.

Krishan enjoyed his career in the National Bank of Lahore. Like his father, he quickly climbed the career ladder to Bank Manager. They were posted in various locations in both Pakistan and India, as the bank often switched staff between cities. One location they lived in was Ketal. The National Bank of Lahore was later renamed Punjab National Bank when the partition took place.

In total, Krishan and Pushpa had five children, all born in India; two sons, Mahesh, Vipen and three daughters, Veena, Madhu and Rita.

Each time Pushpa had a child she would go back to her parents to deliver the child and stay for 40 days; this was also an Indian tradition.

Their first child Mahesh was born in October 1942, Pushpa was still a child herself, so her mother and father took responsibility for Mahesh and bought him up.

Veena was born in August 1944 and in July 1946, Vipen was born. The family lived in Lahore; however, they were aware that the partition was coming. Nanny said that there was divide between Hindus and Muslims, they lived in an enclosed Hindu colony, she told me at night fighting and unrest could be heard outside of their colony walls.

In 1947, the Partition of India took place. This was the division of British India into two independent dominion states, India and Pakistan. Vipen was a year old. Lahore became the capital of Pakistan and a Muslim-dominated city. Luckily, Krishan and Dharam were still close to the widower of their sister, Mulkh Raj Kapoor, who worked on the railways. Whilst lots of people were helpless, Mulkh Raj Kapoor helped the family escape and facilitate the rail tickets to Amritsar; this quickly got Krishan and Dharam's families out of Lahore. So, the family fled to Amritsar and were taken in by cousins who had a jewellery business. This was a tough time for all the families too, living together in cramped conditions.

Krishan and Pushpa soon built up home here with their family, living above a chemist with "Biji and Bouji". There was also a heavy hardware shop next door and a book shop close to their home. It was a bustling and busy street in Hall Bazaar, Amritsar.

Krishan continued to work on his career and Nanny learnt to be what would now be called "a stay-at-home mother", looking after the house, cooking and bringing up the children.

After the partition, in addition to working for the bank, Krishan and Dharam decided to open a tea plantation business. Indian Nanny sold most of her jewellery to get money and they nearly lost everything; this business did not take off.

In 1948 Dharam Prakash Khanna (Krishan's brother) anticipated the chaos that might envelop India post-partition. He managed to obtain a passport and with two other friends made a plan to set up a carpet export business to England with the belief that England, post-war, was a business hotspot. The friends pulled out at the last minute, but Dharam was always an adventurer and was given his mother's blessing – she told him "Take your chance and travel to England". So, he came with half a dozen carpets by cargo boat.

On arriving in England, Dharam was surprised that it wasn't as affluent as he had been led to believe. He struggled and was taken in by a kind English family who let him store the carpets in their living room! Unfortunately, the carpet business never took off.

The Indian High Commission opened up in London and Dharam obtained a job in the accounts department. With this role he started to build up a circle of Indian friends and widening his contacts, they helped one another to get established and move to a house in Brixton.

In 1950, Dharam was able to bring his family to London by small cargo boat; like Krishan, he also had two sons and three daughters. He continued to work for the Indian High Commission and live in Brixton. Life was difficult.

Despite the struggles in London, Krishan constantly asked his brother to organise for him to also come to London. Dharam Prakash said that when established, he would organise things.

At this time back in India, Bebe, my grandfather's cousin, lived with Nanny and Big Dada for about ten years. This was in between Madhu being born in July 1949 and Rita being born in November 1959. Bebe as a young girl had been engaged to a boy when she was just 11 years old to be married at 14. Before they were married, sadly the boy drowned in an accident, so Bebe was left as a "widow" at just 12 years old. In those days she was seen as an outcast and could never marry "again", so she was taken in originally by Krishan's mother. Bebe was very religious, a strict and pure vegetarian; she also did not eat onions or garlic. She would not allow meat to be cooked in the home and Nanny adapted to these habits and looked after her wishes carefully. A vegetarian diet was quite popular in India at this time and still is, for religious reasons as well as cost and the issue of storing meat in the heat.

When Big Dada's father Hira Lal passed away, his mother Lajwanti and Bebe moved to an ashram in Haridwar, where the families regularly sent money to finance their stay. Traditionally an ashram was a spiritual hermitage or a monastery in Indian religions. All this family history is written in scripts by holy men in Haridwar! Later Bebe unfortunately died and Lajwanti moved to Rishikesh, a sacred city on the banks of the river Ganges. The city is traffic-free, alcohol-free and vegetarian. She lived here for the last ten years of her life, she was content and had a simple life being vegetarian. Meditation and yoga were also daily habits. It is said that she had a bench made here, with her late husband's name on it. Rishikesh is now famous for these practices as well as traditional medicine and the beautiful temples. It received worldwide media attention when The Beatles travelled here to attend a meditation course. It is now also known for white water rafting!! Gigi once told me of a trip he took to this city with a Canadian Diplomat. He always travelled with a bottle of whiskey and in the hotel, requested some soda to mix with it. The waiter explained that this was profoundly not allowed. Gigi asked if there was any diplomatic exemption to this law? The diplomat showed his card and the soda was brought out straight away!

In 1952 Indian Nanny, Big Dada and the family moved to Delhi because of his job. The bank was very centrally located in a place called Korah Bagh; they were also given a house by the bank that was conveniently located right next door. Madhu told me that it had a large veranda with a small brick wall and a paddling pool. When there was heavy rain, the pool would fill up with water. Krishan would go shopping and buy lots of mangoes, and he would throw them into the water for the children to catch and suck their delicious juice in the heat. Veena also remembers delicious mangoes in Delhi; however, she recalls climbing trees with her school friends and using a stick to get the really high ones down. They would fill their skirts up with mangoes and run off home, sometimes being chased by whoever the mango tree was owned by! Again, Krishan and Pushpa built up their circle of friends. Life was good, with the Bank House. They were given a servant to help with the children, collecting them from school on a bicycle and carrying out chores as well as shopping. It was also customary for business people and friends to pop in, Nanny would not let them leave without having a drink and something to eat. My dad recalls his father lending customers and friends his personal money when he couldn't lend the bank's money. He also remembers dinner parties nearly every night and lots of whiskey drinking! There was always something cooking, Pushpa was renowned for being an excellent cook – the bank head office employees would often visit, delighted to feast on her delicious cooking.

My dad remembers his childhood in India as being happy; hanging out with his siblings and cousins, kite flying, bike riding and catching flies in match boxes! He recalls visiting Jalandhar on holiday and staying with family. As well as looking after his grandparents – Biji and Bouji.

Vipen's business mentality started from a young age when his grandmother (Biji) used to ask him daily to go and get her pills from the chemist. He soon realised that he could purchase them in bulk, at a discount and sell them on to her daily at a profit, saving him time and money! He was about 12 years old at this point.

Bouji, at a similar time, had retired from his tailoring business, which he had in Hall Bazaar, Amritsar. He spent the days reading the newspaper, visiting his friends and shop keepers in the large market as well as smoking a hashish pipe, which again was a common tradition at this time in India.

During the hot summers, it was custom for families to holiday in the Hill Stations nestled in the Himalayas. They travelled by train as Mulkh Raj Kapoor continued to work for Indian railways and remained a close family friend – he was able to facilitate favourable family travel rates! Nanny mentioned Mussoorie as her favourite and Big Dada liked Shimla, as well as some other places including the lake at Kashmir. Nanny also said that Kanyakumari, was a nice place to go and that it was the Indian equivalent of Land's End. India is really vast so it's interesting to know that they travelled.

In 1956 Dharam and his wife made their first joint trip back to see the many Indian relatives. Apparently, he made a point of visiting everyone all over India. Krishan continued to press his older brother about his family joining them in London.

In July 1957 Krishan's older brother, Dharam Prakesh Khanna, sadly passed away at the age of 44. He left his wife aged 39 and five children. It is said that she cried every day for three years.

It was Krishan's duty to look after his brother's family, so he resigned from his position as Bank Manager in Delhi and moved his family back to Amritsar to live with Pushpa's mum and dad. He came to England to check on his older brother's wife and family. He was also curious as to what England could offer his family. He arrived with £3 in his pocket, taking the boat from Bombay and arriving at Tilbury Docks, Essex.

He spent some months caring for his brother's family. Regular trips to the shops and markets I am told put him off food shopping! He also explored the possibility of moving his family here. He originally worked for the board of trade, then an import / export clothing business and finally a petticoat business on Petticoat Lane.

In November 1960, Krishan sent for his wife, and she travelled by boat with Madhu and Rita. The journey was a month-long and Rita celebrated her first birthday on the boat to England. Madhu recalls arriving in England in December 1960 – she said it was cold, foggy and hard to see any daylight. A real contrast to the warm and sunny Amritsar they'd left behind.

Vipen recalls arriving in August 1961, when he was 15 years old and Veena thinks it was 1964, when she was 16 years old. They travelled by boat for 17 days with Rajan (Mulkh Raj Kapoor's son). They definitely remember travelling together!

Mahesh's memory is that he came in 1961 by air with Vipen, then Biji and Bouji last in 1964.

The Khanna family established home in South London. Originally, in the Brixton and Peckham area, then Krishan set up home in Beatrice Avenue, Norbury. They moved a few times including Arragan Gardens, Streatham, Pollards Hill, Rosebury Avenue, Thornton Heath and then Norbury Crescent, Norbury.

Indian Nanny got a part-time job working for the electric company Philips on the Purley Way, Croydon on the assembly line, putting together television sets, and the family adapted to Western life. Indian Nanny continued with her excellent Indian home cooking when she was in the UK. She taught her girls to cook; they cooked for family weddings, dinner parties, they regularly all ate together on a Friday night inviting friends and family to feast on the simple delicious Indian home cooking and she often sent them home with content full bellies and a container or two for the following days!

Mahesh and Vipen both married European girls at a joint wedding in the hot summer of 1976.

My grandfather, we named as Big Dada. His name comes from his love of Wrestling in the 80s, when he would look after the grandchildren while watching the wrestling on a Saturday afternoon. Indian Nanny would make milky cups of tea, while our dads were working and our mums were out shopping.

When they moved here, Indian Nanny told me that she recalled they enjoyed the holidays driving to North Wales, Cornwall, Littlehampton, Bognor Regis and the Isle of Wight.

In 1981 Rita and Gigi got married in India. Nanny and Big Dada decided to move back to Delhi, India with them. Rita was grateful to have the support of her mum and dad living nearby. Rita told me that they went on holiday to Kashmir all together. Nanny had been delighted to visit the area as it was beautiful. Previously there had been lots of unrest due to fighting over whether it would be owned by Pakistan, China or India, and her memories of gunfire could be replaced by calm, tranquillity and beauty. Nanny and Big Dada lived in Delhi from 1982 to 1994, when Big Dada had a heart attack and his health suffered so they decided to come back to London. Their last years were spent together living in Shirley, Croydon.

I clearly remember, Nanny always loved to feed whoever popped in. This is when she taught me to cook simple Indian home cooking. She always had a fridge full of exciting goodies, Indian homecooked food, Indian snacks, chocolates on the table, Kit-Kats and biscuits in the cupboard for delighted children! There were flowers on the table from cousins, friends and daughters on their weekly visits. Pink roses were her favourite, especially if they were from Marks and Spencer!

Pushpa passed away on New Year's Day 2015 and Krishan passed away in April 2017, 16 days after his 100th Birthday.

The legacy continues – Nanny and Big Dada have five children, eleven Grandchildren, eighteen Great-Grandchildren and two Great-Great-Grand Children, which is correct as of 2021!

THE BIG DADDY
ANNUAL 1983

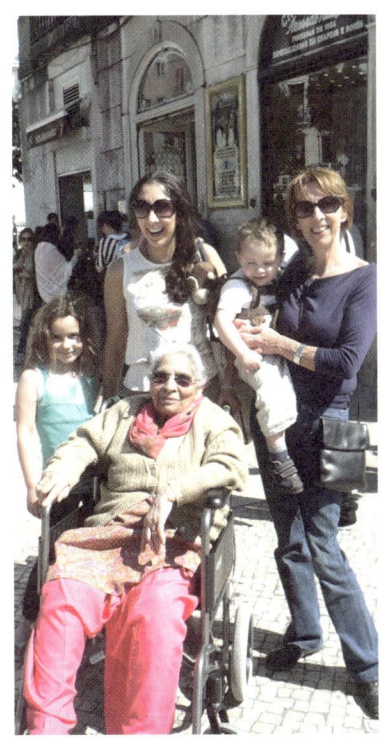

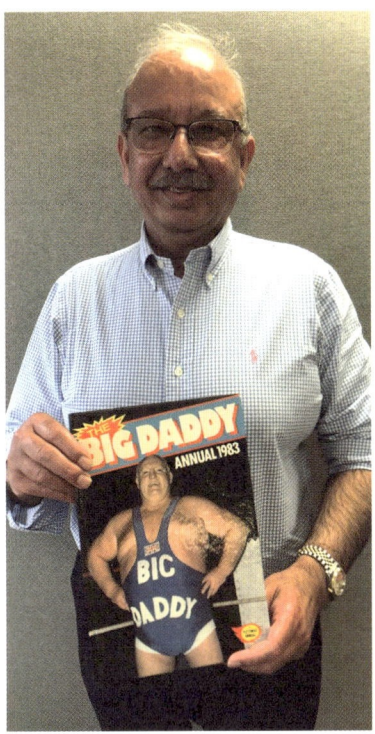

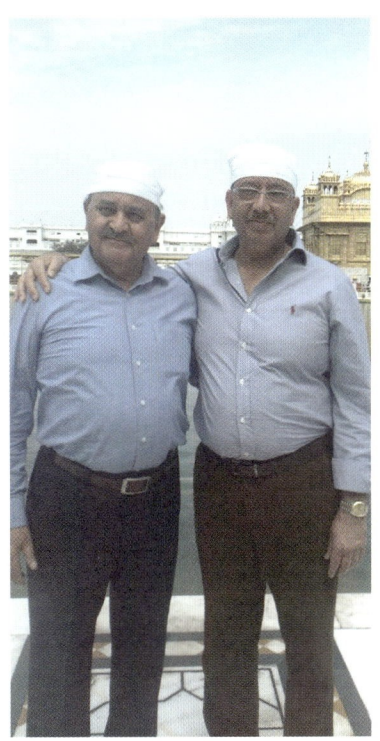

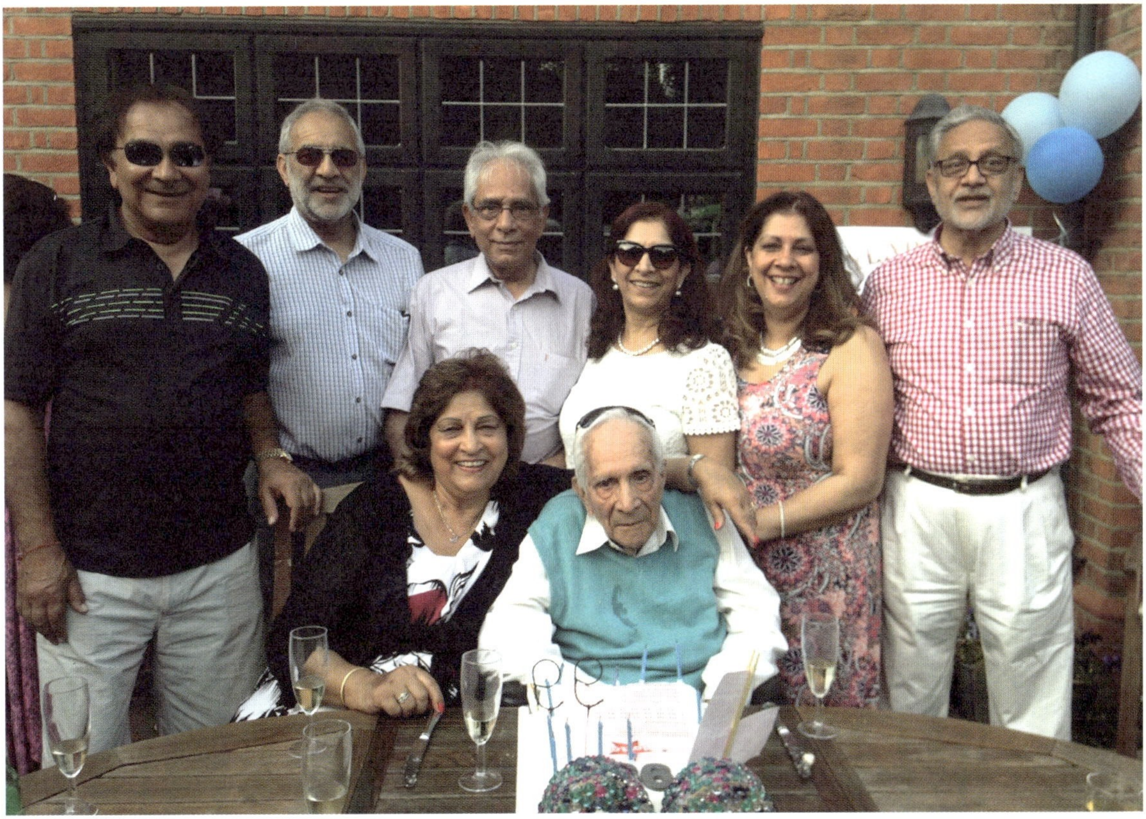

Krishan Khanna
Photo sent to Pushpa's family in 1939

Pushpa Khanna
Photo sent to Krishan's family 1939

To Dear Brother

Lest you forget. London

Lahore 1946

THE SPICE RACK

Our Indian food is easier to cook than most people think!

Our family recipes are mainly cooked using seven different spices plus salt.

Fresh garlic, onions, ginger and coriander are also commonly used within most of the dishes.

The Spice Tin

I would suggest investing in an Indian spice tin. This will keep your spices fresh and at hand for when you want to cook. This is what I recommend that you have in your spice tin:

- **Jeera** (cumin seeds)
- **Paprika powder**
- **Haldi** (turmeric powder)
- **Chilli powder** – you may want to change this to chilli flakes; however, in our Punjabi cooking we tend to keep it quite mild for the children and also so you taste the flavour of the food as opposed to HEAT! (Except in the case of Uncle Gigi who loves a hot chilli.)
- **Coriander powder**
- **Mango powder**
- **Garam Masala** – shop bought or you can buy the spices whole & grind yourself in a coffee grinder – see Garam Masala recipe

THE SPICES

Jeera
Cumin seeds (jeera in Hindi) come from small plants, they are from the same family as parsley and fennel. Jeera is said to be packed with health benefits and contain antioxidants. It has a strong flavour. We usually fry the seeds in oil for a few seconds at the beginning of cooking a dish. They are a key ingredient in Garam Masala. My dad also likes to sometimes use ground jeera, so you will find this mentioned in a few of his recipes. You can buy ground jeera in the powder form, or grind it yourself in a spice grinder or pestle and mortar.

Haldi
Turmeric powder (haldi in Hindi) comes from a flowering plant, which is part of the ginger family, and the roots are used in cooking. Heating it with oil could be the best way to get the most from the spice. Turmeric has an ancient history of uses including fabric dyeing, cosmetics and traditional medicine. Reported health benefits are anti-inflammatory, antioxidant, anti-cancer, skin conditions and brain food. Curcumin gives turmeric its bright yellow colour and be warned it is practically impossible to get out of clothing!

Paprika powder
Paprika is a key ingredient in Indian cooking as it gives great flavour and colour to our dishes. The powder is made by drying particular sweet red peppers, then grinding them to a fine, rich, red powder. It has a high vitamin A content, and the flavour can vary from sweet and mild to strong and hot. Paprika is commonly used in food from many countries including Spain, Morocco, India and Austria.

Chilli powder
There are a variety of chilli powders, it is produced by drying chilli peppers then reducing it to a fine powder. Indian chilli powder is named after the Kashmir region of India, the spice is bright red and mild in flavour. We use chilli powder in our cooking for heat as well as the colour that it brings to dishes and curries. Sometimes, fresh chillies are used during the cooking as well as chilli powder if an extra kick of heat is required.

Garam Masala
Garam masala is widely used in Indian cooking, it is a key ingredient in marinades and in our family recipes it is normally added at the end to a dish or curry; it has a fantastic aroma. Garam Masala translates to "hot spices"; however, it is not usually a spicy combination. It is a blend of several spices and the recipe varies according to region of India as well as personal taste. Our family recipe for garam masala contains 8 different spices and can be found on page 35.

Coriander powder
Coriander powder (dhaniya in Hindi) is made by roasting and grinding the seeds from coriander plants. Coriander contains a variety of vitamins and minerals associated with health benefits including controlling blood sugar levels and skin conditions as well as acting as an anti-inflammatory. Earthy, floral and citrus flavours are all words used to describe this lovely spice, which is widely used in our cooking.

Mango powder
Mango powder (amchur in Hindi) gives dishes a tangy and distinct taste. It is produced mainly in India and Pakistan by drying slices of unripe green mangoes in the sun, then grinding them to a fine powder. It can provide the nutritional benefit of mangoes when the fresh fruit is out of season. It is a popular spice especially in Northern India, where our family originate from.

SPICE RACK

Make your own
Garam Masala

I would highly recommend making your own garam masala, just for the smell of grinding the spices – the aroma that it creates in the kitchen is stunning.

From the Indian shop you can buy a bag of spices ready to grind for a couple of pounds.
This is Indian Nanny's special garam masala recipe, which she taught to her daughters.
A coffee grinder is good, easy, cheap and fun to use. You can pick one up for less than £20 online.

INGREDIENTS

- 6 tablespoons cumin seeds
- 6 tablespoons whole dried coriander seeds
- 2 tablespoons whole black peppercorns
- 6 bay leaves

- 1 tablespoon whole cloves
- 2 tablespoons whole black cardamoms pods
- 1 tablespoon green cardamom pods
- 3 cinnamon sticks

METHOD

Put all of the above into a (coffee) grinder, pulse until it is a fine powder. This powder has an intense flavour, so we would now add an equal quantity of shop bought garam masala and mix the two together.

If you do not want to use shop bought, reduce the amount of homemade garam masala to half in the recipes.

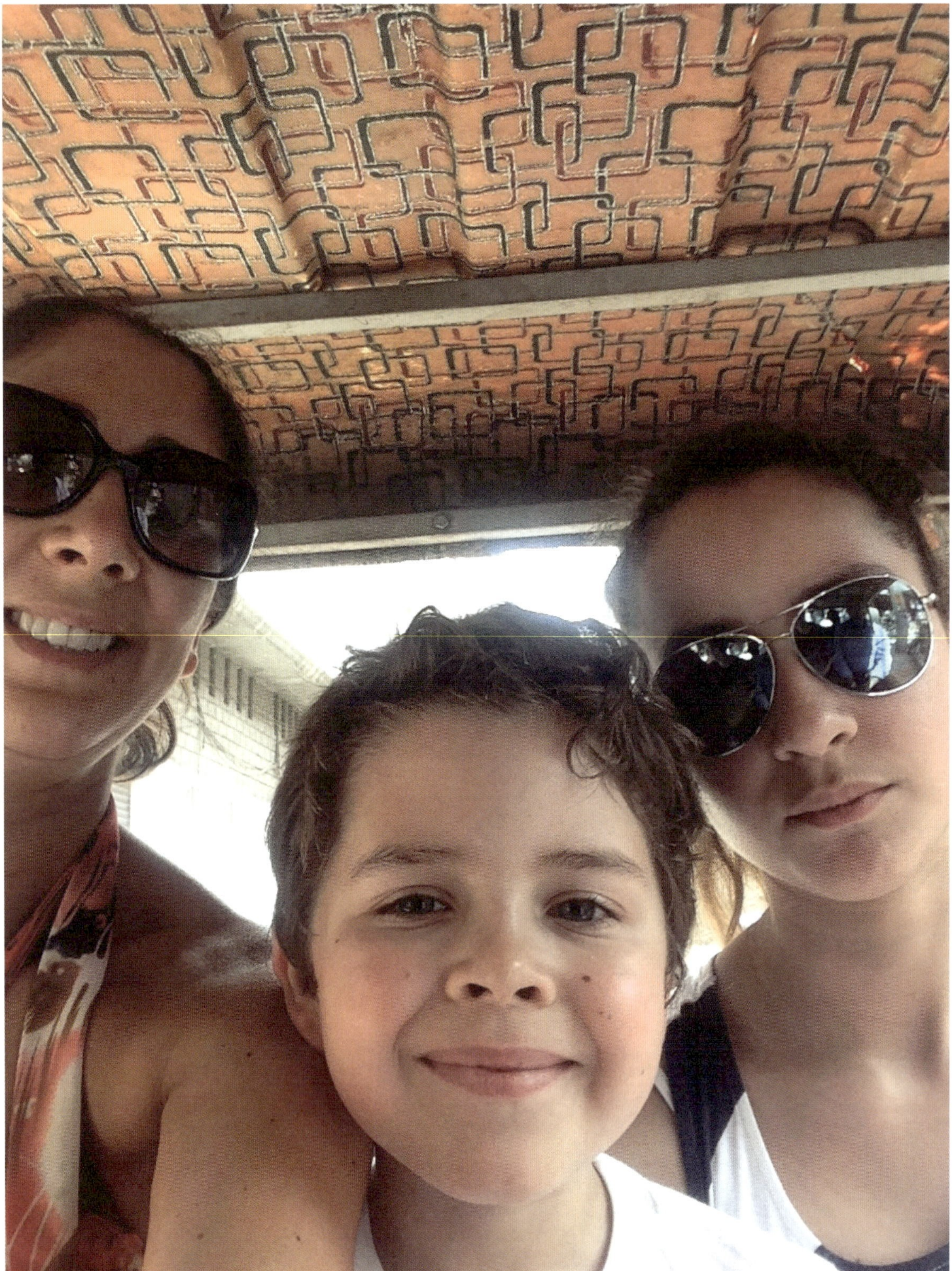

HELPFUL INFO & TIPS

The Bare Necessities

Wok
I love a wok! Easy to use and clean, with a lid that fits. My friends laugh but I do often take it on holiday if I'm planning to do any cooking...

Note, if you use a hob with a "wok" burner, make sure you turn the heat right down as the high heat will be far too strong and you will risk burning your spices or the water evaporating before the potatoes are cooked.

Pressure Cooker
A pressure cooker (yes, I am still scared of the noise it makes) needed for dahl and lentils as well as some non-veg dishes. I have a pressure cooker that my Nanny bought for me from an Asian Supermarket. I also inherited hers (they are both fairly scary to cook with!). Now, you can purchase a modern pressure cooker – my dad loves his Kuhn Rikon Swiss pressure cooker, and I understand that you can buy digital pressure cookers which are exceptionally easy to cook with (and not so scary!).

Food Processor
Large & mini, both really useful and relatively cheap. Although (buy cheap buy twice!) I would suggest Kenwood as a great brand.

MultiPro Compact Food Processor by Kenwood is a fantastic kitchen appliance, great for cooking and baking.

The Mini Chopper by Kenwood, small, easy to clean and store. A real kitchen must have! Perfect for chopping garlic, ginger and onions, as well as herbs.

Saucepans
A small saucepan is great for making tarka. I also have a medium size saucepan for cooking rice and a heavy pan for making curries. I would suggest a good fitting lid for all saucepans.

Cup or mug?
The recipes refer to a "cup"; however, this is not the metric cup. It's a mug! Now I know that mugs come in many different sizes, so for the purpose of this book I measured my "mug" against the metric cup; my mug is very slightly bigger than a metric cup but not so much that it would really matter or make a difference. It's 210g if you want to be exact...

Wooden spoon & silicone spatula
A wooden spoon is great for stirring your curries and tarka. A silicone spatula is brilliant for turning veg dishes as it will reduce the chance of mashing up the potatoes or vegetables.

Meal Planning

What goes with what?

If you ask the Aunties this question, there will definitely be some quarrelling!

I believe that a rice, veg dish and either a dahl or paneer or meat dish accompanied by yogurt or / and salad is a really lovely, satisfying meal.

Rita's Indian dinner party suggestion would be a lentil dish, meat dish, 2 x vegetable dishes, paneer dish, rice and either chapati or naan with a yogurt.

Indian Nanny & the Aunties enjoy putting on a lavish spread, which may mean you will cook for days (remember most of the dishes will taste better the following day or day after that, as they have marinated in the spices).

Rice, I believe, is best cooked fresh and warm just before serving; everything else can be cooked beforehand. Curries I warm on the hob and vegetables I pop in the microwave.

Simple and quick!

- Chana mushroom and fluffy white rice
- Peas and potato rice with yellow dahl
- Puri aloo, white rice and puris
- Nanny's Paneer and fluffy white rice

A feast...

- Mince & peas, dahl, aloo gobi, puri aloo, rice, chapatis
- Pumpkin, chana, puri aloo, rice, puris
- Paneer, two different vegetable dishes, dahl, rice, chapatis
- Red beans, aubergine partha, biryani rice, chapatis
- Black eye beans, peas & potatoes, bhindi, Veena style rice, chapatis

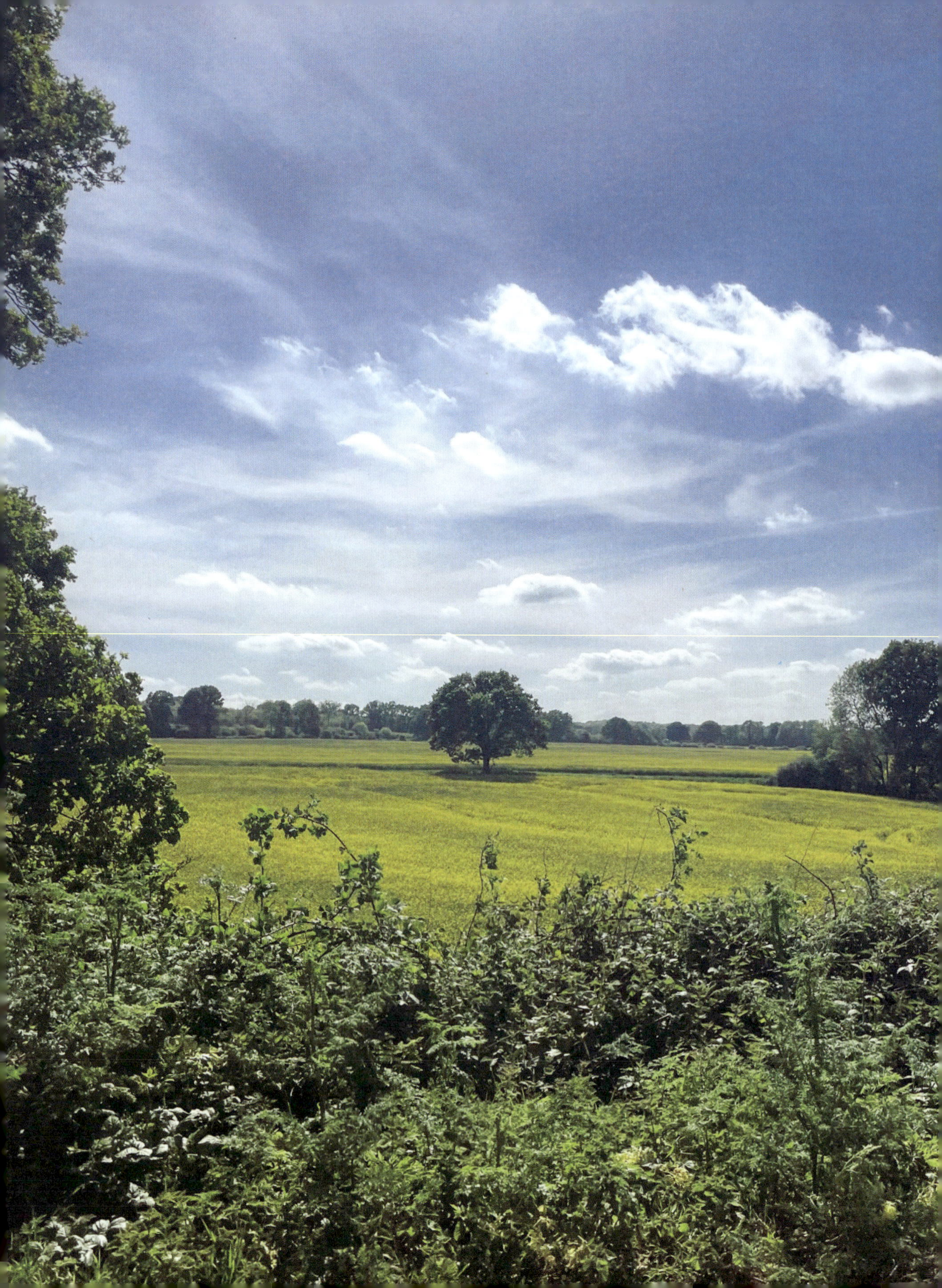

HELPFUL INFO & TIPS

General note about quantities
When baking, exact quantities are needed because a chemical reaction will take place during the baking process, so measurements in grams and litres is the metric unit that is commonly used in the Western world. With cooking it is slightly different, the most important point is the cooking process and when to put the ingredients in, how long to cook things for and at what heat. In time, you will vary the spices slightly to the taste of your family or guests, and if you only have two small potatoes rather than three the dish will still come out well. So, what I'm saying is, don't get too hung up on measurements or quantities, I have added them to help you cook, not hinder you!

Salt and Oil
The recipes are exactly as my Indian Nanny taught me, plenty of salt and oil! My grandad lived on her food daily from when they married at 16 and lived until he celebrated his 100th Birthday. Most Western families would probably want to reduce the salt and oil to the taste of their own family.

You can probably reduce both the salt and oil slightly without affecting the flavour too much. However, if you reduce it right down, it will have an impact on the flavour. Ok, so you can add salt at the table; however, I was taught that especially with potatoes, if you add the salt during cooking, the flavour will be within the ingredients and actually require less salt than if you add it once cooked – I hope that makes sense!

What Oil?
Indian Nanny always used a light olive oil, unless stated in the recipe (i.e. she would use Sunflower oil for frying). My mum prefers Sunflower oil as she finds it easier to digest. My brother and Sarah (who was one of the guinea pigs for this recipe book!) prefer Rapeseed oil as its local. The long and short of it is, you can cook Indian food using your preferred oil.

Auntie Madhu taught me to use "Crisp n' Dry Rapeseed oil" for frying, I have found that it does give pakoras a delicious, crispy finish!

I have written these recipes using Nanny's preferred oil.

Chillies

My Uncle Gigi loves a chilli! A chilli plant makes a colourful addition to the kitchen windowsill, they grow well, and the chillies can be frozen if the supply outweighs the demand...

Red chillies are generally hotter than green ones, also small ones are more potent than large ones.

If you cut off the stalk of the chilli and roll it between your fingers, this is an easy way to remove the seeds which again are full of heat and power.

Alternatively, if you leave the chilli completely whole within the dish, this will reduce the heat but give you the flavour.

You can substitute the chilli powder with a fresh chilli in the recipes within this book. Chilli flakes also can give you a good kick if that's what you are looking for.

Generally, our home cooked Indian food is full of flavour but not heat, so if you want to turn up the heat you will need to increase the chilli in our family recipes.

43

Garden herbs

I love growing herbs in my garden and on our kitchen windowsill. Dani, my Swiss cousin, once told me that he enjoys cooking with all sorts of fresh herbs. I guess sometimes they can be a bit underrated, but herbs are fantastic. In Indian cooking, fresh coriander finishes off the curries and some vegetable dishes really nicely. They're also great in a salad. Coriander will grow nicely in the garden during spring and summer or on the windowsill in a sunny spot all year round. Alternatively, if you do not like coriander, it's fine to leave it out of the recipes.

Packets of coriander can be picked up fairly cheaply from the supermarket or even cheaper (and without the plastic packaging) from an Asian store, if you have one locally.

Frozen herbs

Whilst one of these packets or bunches will not last long enough to wilt if you are cooking a few Indian dishes per week, you can also freeze the herbs and use straight from the freezer to decorate vegetable dishes or add to curries. The best way to do this is wash and chop the coriander, fresher the better. Pop in a freezer bag and freeze. Use within 1-2 months.

Store cupboard & freezer

For me, it's really important and makes cooking easier if you have a few ingredients always in reserve. In your store cupboard I would suggest tinned tomatoes, a couple of tins of chickpeas or other lentils, and some shop bought naan as they do save time. Dried lentils also can be quickly soaked the night before and again will make the prep time quicker. Potatoes and onions are a principal ingredient in lots of Indian dishes, they keep well and are fairly cheap to buy, so worth having a stash. I always have a bag of rice; fluffy white rice can be cooked in just over ten minutes.

There are a few veggies that you can wash and cut then bag in the freezer to reduce cooking time to minutes – Bhindi (okra), grilled aubergines, carrots to name a few. I would also recommend a bag of petit pois as a staple freezer item, quick to cook and versatile, used in many Indian dishes.

As you wish!

Indian food definitely becomes tastier if you leave it a few hours or a day or two to absorb the flavours of the spices, so it's great as you do not need to cook it to serve. You can cook it the day before, pop it in the fridge then reheat it when you are ready to eat (this can be done in a microwave or on the stove; you may need to add a little water to curry dishes). The only exception to this I believe is rice – there is nothing better than warm fluffy rice served fresh!

Language

Some of the spices and vegetables are called different things, just to confuse you! The spices section has the English version. Here are some of the other items that may cause confusion:

- Aloo - potato
- Chana – chickpeas
- Dahl – dal or lentils
- Gobi – cauliflower
- Paneer – Indian cheese
- Bhindi – lady's finger or okra

HELPFUL INFO & TIPS

Garden Herbs with Petal and Rosie (who love a bit of coriander too!)

Give a gift
Indian Nanny would always have leftovers in the fridge for unannounced children and grandchildren that turned up hungry. For meals, we tend to cook a few dishes, put them in the middle of the table and let everyone help themselves. We do not cook portions per person; there are a few reasons for this. Indian food tastes great the next day and can be heated up quickly on a plate when you are in a hurry. Dry vegetable dishes go well in a sandwich, a wrap with some salad, or as part of a salad. You can freeze some of the dishes and defrost at a later date. Great if you batch cook a dahl or curry. Lastly, give as a gift.

Neighbours and friends love a little takeaway container or two filled with delicious Indian cooking.

Potato size!
An odd thing to mention but this is really important! If you cut the potatoes too big, the vegetables will overcook, too small and the potatoes will become like mash! So, 2cm to 3cm cubes are about perfect. Remember I told you so...

An inch of ginger
An inch of ginger is about the size of the top part of your thumb. You can also measure the water over a dahl recipe with the top part of your finger as an inch or two inches to the second knuckle!

The easiest way to peel ginger is with the side of a teaspoon as there is minimum waste (thank you, Lisa).

Wash your onions
Cutting onions make you cry? Not anymore! Skin the onion and quickly run it under the tap. You'll never cry over an onion again.

To peel or not to peel, that is the question?
Indian Nanny would always wash the fruit and vegetables before putting them in the fridge when she bought them home. She would also peel most fruit and vegetables before cooking them. I have also been taught to wash fruit, veg and salad. These habits were to remove dust, dirt and pesticides.

Now that there is more thought towards food waste and the health of our planet, you may choose to wash vegetables and not peel them if you do not need to, for instance potatoes and carrots. In this instance give them a good scrub and they may take a little longer to cook. We will have to carry on peeling the onions but remember to wash them too!

HELPFUL INFO & TIPS

Cheats!

Garlic Naan
Garlic naan or plain naan from one of the large supermarkets can be frozen and toasted straight from the freezer, with a spread of butter or vegan spread is a great accompaniment to an Indian meal.

Chopped Ginger and Garlic
You can chop a large batch, then freeze in foil or pots. A great way to speed up cooking curries and one less thing to wash up!

Pickle
There are a variety of Indian pickles that a spoon on the side of your dinner plate gives a tangy flavour to Indian everyday meals (the Indians' version of mayonnaise, ketchup or brown sauce!). Nanny's lemon pickle and carrot pickle recipes are in this book. If you have the delight of visiting an Indian shop – which is like an Aladdin's cave – you can buy every type of pickle: mango, lime, lemon, carrot, mixed vegetable. Our favourite is green mango, which is a green sauce rather than a red one; green is from northern Indian and red is typically from southern India.

Samosas
When Milly was small, we used to bake a lot. She baked cake, after cake, after cake. Some of her cakes were amazing. She baked cakes for model homework and friends' birthdays. I cleared up… a lot! Icing sugar and flour made our worktop white when it was black granite! One day we decided to make samosas, it was good fun but they were not a patch on the shop-bought ones. Our family always get our samosas from the Indian shop, Hounslow or Tooting. A must and mighty fine with ketchup. Varieties include veggie or meat.

Uncle Prem's masala tip
Uncle Prem's handy tip is to make the tomato, onion and spice masala in batches and freeze it. You can then use this as a base for various Indian dishes which speeds up the cooking time.

HELPFUL INFO & TIPS

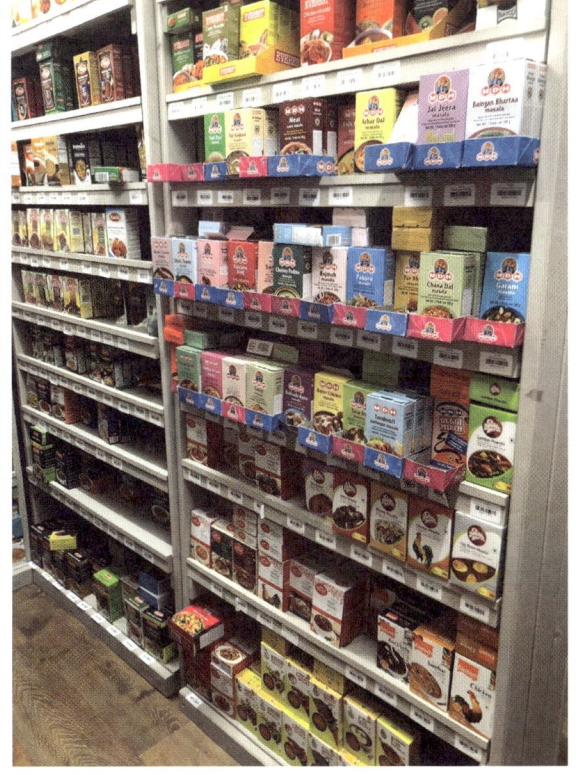

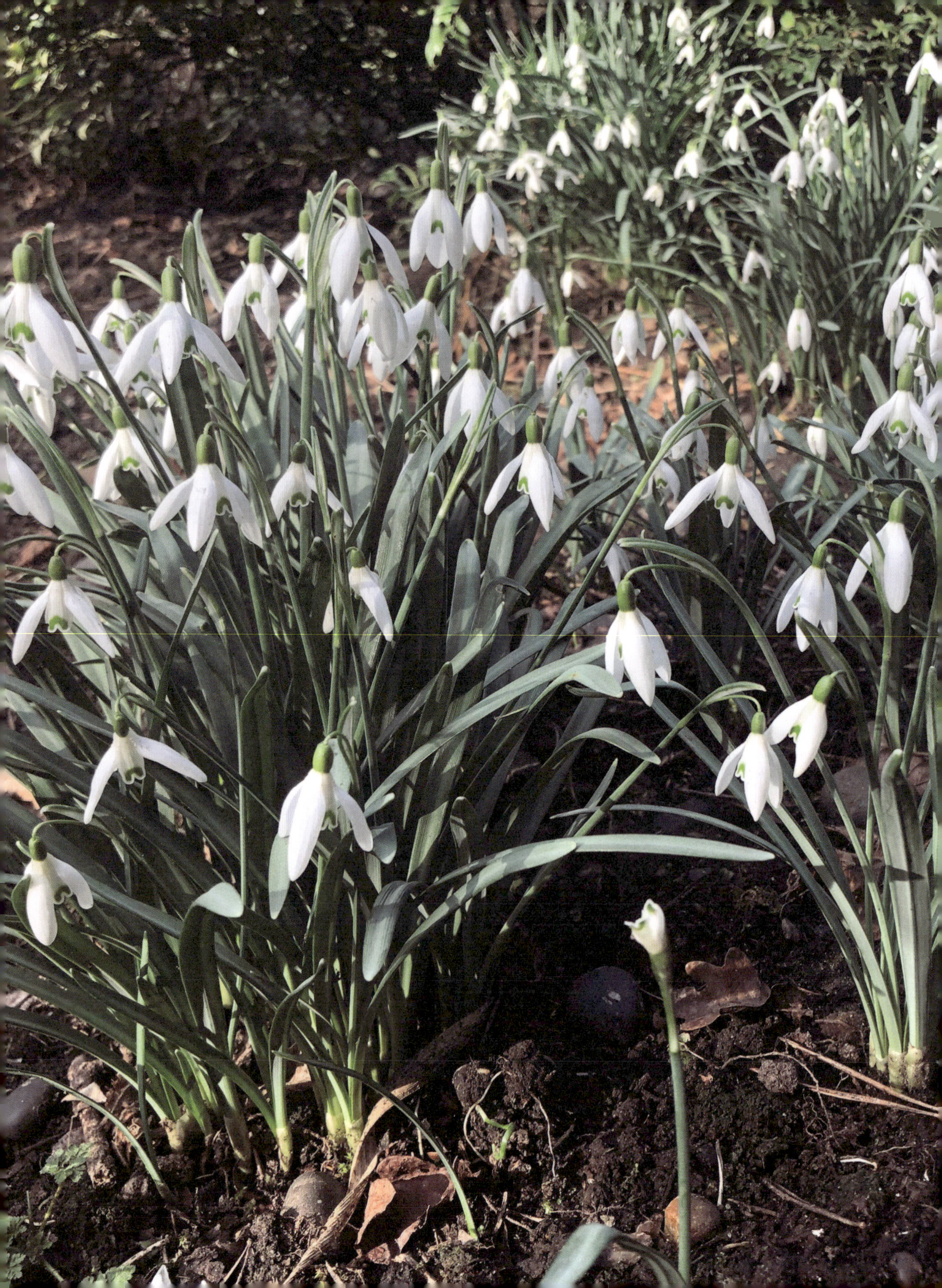

Climate change

A simple and very effective change we can all make to positively impact climate change is to reduce our intake of animal products and support sustainable, higher welfare farming practices.

As of the early 2020's, I was surprised to discover that industrial agricultural animal farming is one of the leading causes of global warming. Would you believe it is responsible for 24% of greenhouse gases produced in the world? That's nearly the same volume released by drilling for oil and harvesting fossil fuels (25%).

So, the rearing of animals and production of animal products is responsible for almost a quarter of all greenhouse gas emissions.

Climate change will affect hundreds of millions of human beings, unfortunately the worst affected will probably be those in third world countries. I am told that if we stop intensive farming, it would give those poorer countries the grain and water to live a life free from famine. It's an interesting thought.

From a health perspective, many studies have shown that eating higher quality meat (e.g. organic) and reducing overall intake is beneficial. An added benefit of this is that widespread uptake of this practice will reduce the strain placed on the environment. Could you contribute to this by carrying out small actions like reducing or leaving out meat, dairy and your consumption of animal products? If so, it will help the future of the planet and our children.

Fortunately eating a nutritionally balanced plant-based diet is now easily accessible, as there are many different meat-free options available. Indian food is a fantastic choice, as the spices give food an incredible flavour. Tofu as an alternative to paneer (cheese) or meat is a great substitute and really easy to cook. Lentils, beans and pulses are also a really nutritious form of protein.

52

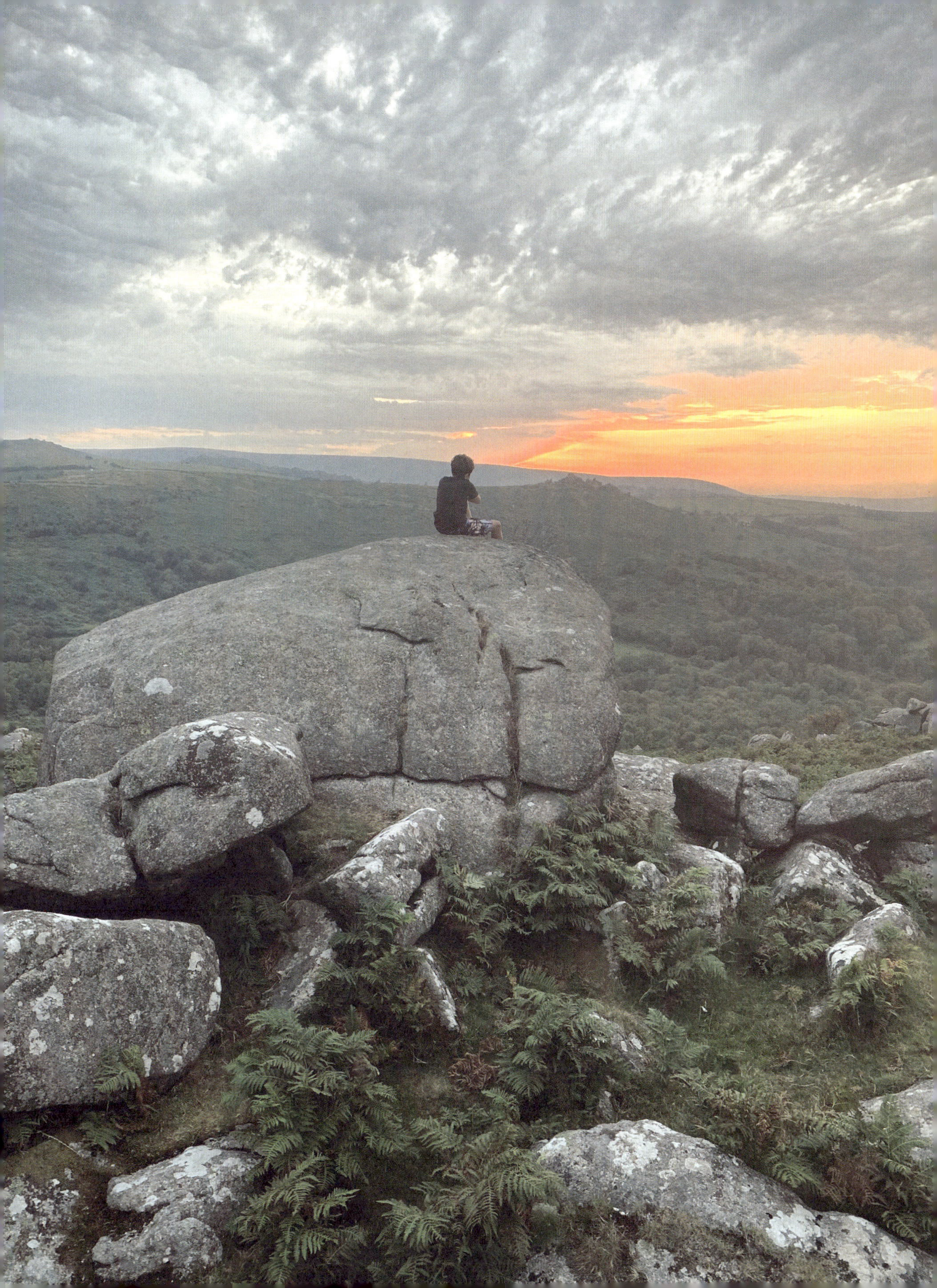

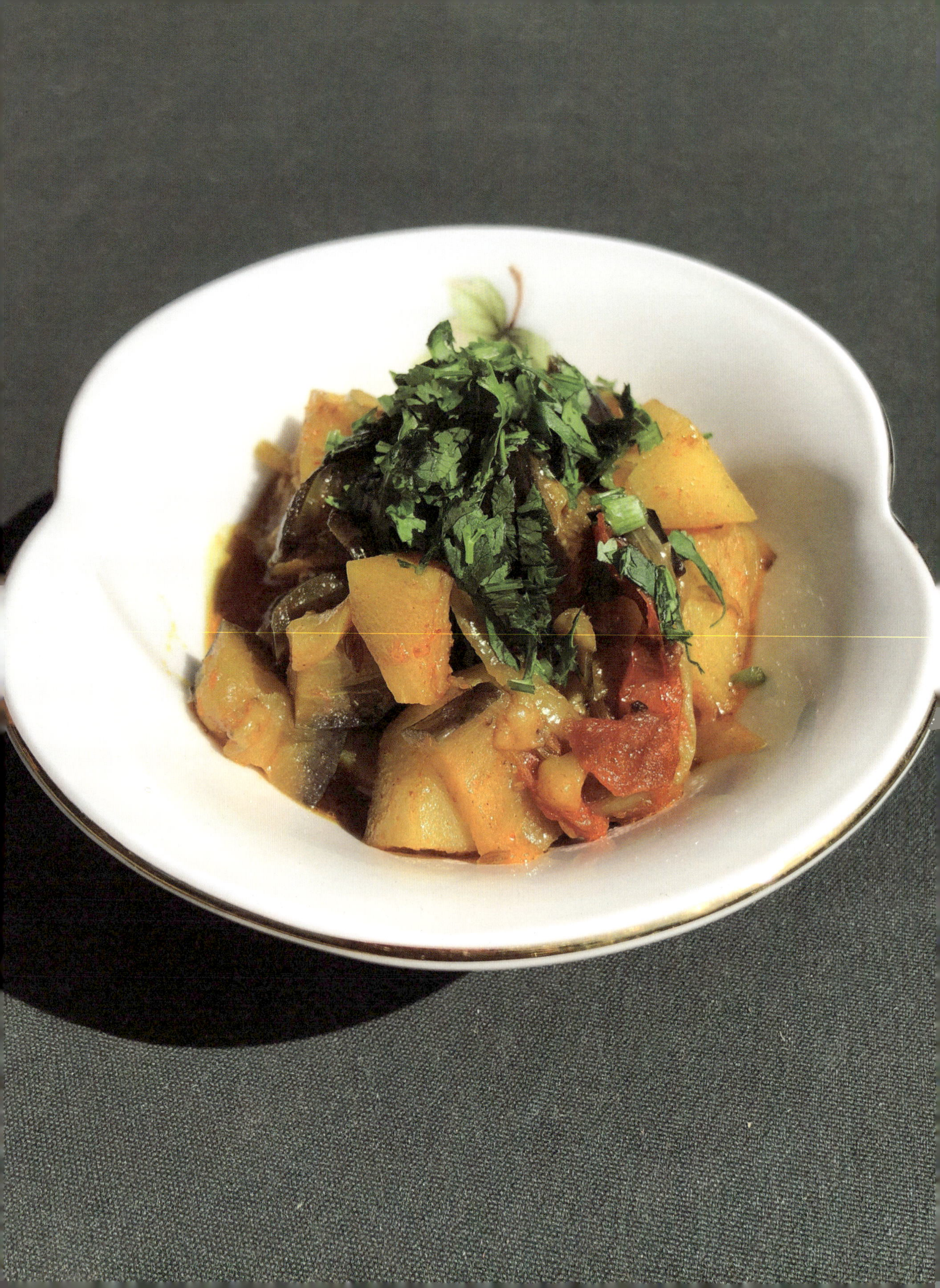

PURE VEGETARIAN
Simply the best!

INDIA

INDIA

STARTERS & SNACKS

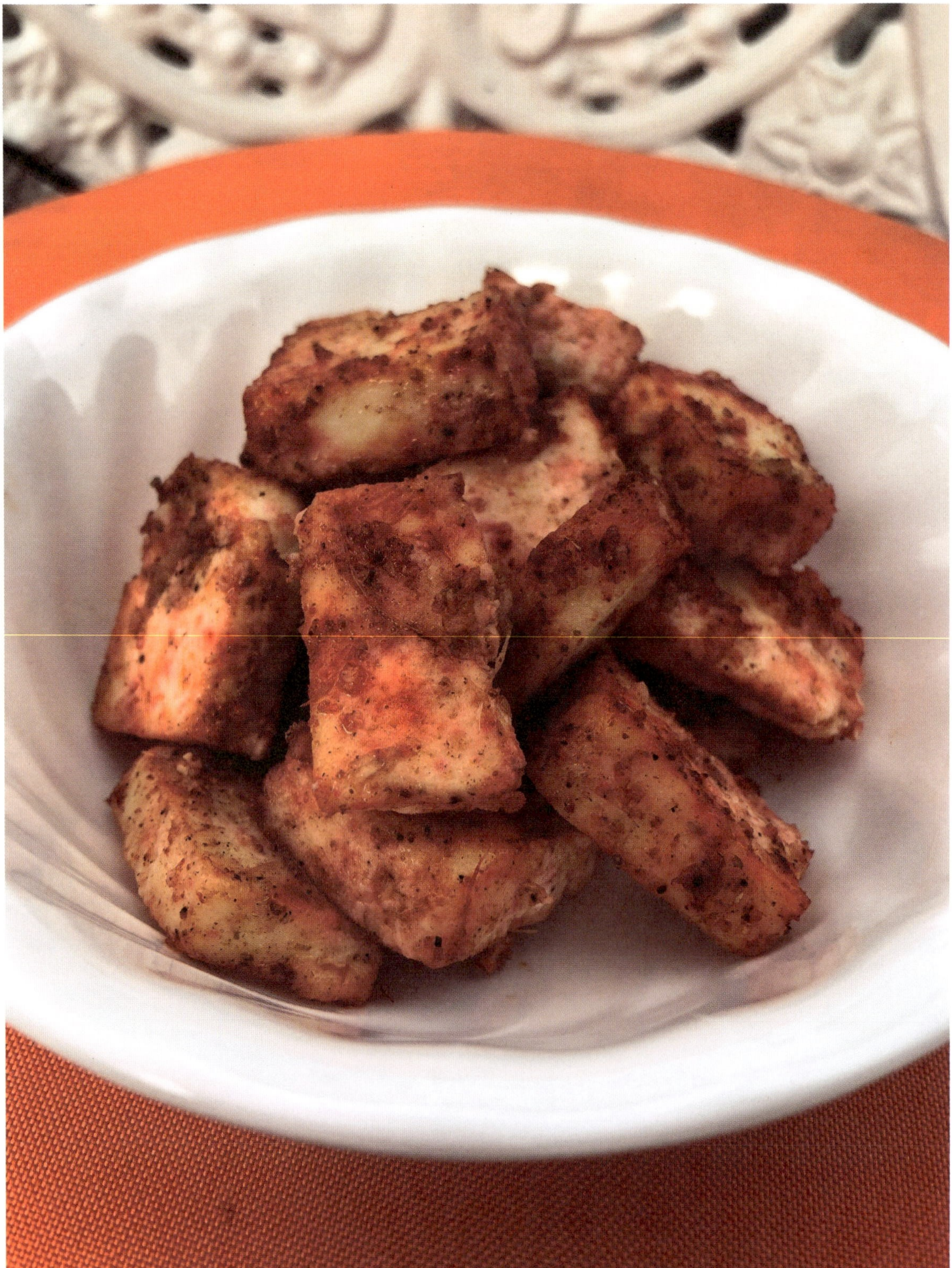

STARTERS & SNACKS

Paneer Tikka

READY IN
20 MINS
+ MARINATING

SERVES
3-4

My dad taught me to make tikka, so this is one of my dad's home-made recipes! Once he'd mastered the chicken tikka, he decided to make paneer tikka, which had everyone's mouths watering.

INGREDIENTS

2 tablespoons light olive oil

2 blocks paneer (250g each)

1 inch ginger, peeled

3 cloves garlic, peeled

Small handful fresh coriander

SPICES

1 teaspoon salt

1 teaspoon tandoori masala (available from Indian supermarkets)

Pinch of food colouring powder if you like (optional) - red or green

1 heaped teaspoon garam masala

METHOD

1. In the mini chopper put the ginger, garlic and small handful of coriander. Blitz until finely chopped and put in a large bowl.

2. Cut the blocks of paneer into pieces 2cm x 1cm approximately.

3. Add this to the bowl with the salt and 2 tablespoons of olive oil, give it a gentle stir.

4. Then add to the bowl 1 teaspoon of tandoori masala, pinch of food colouring powder (if you are using it) and 1 heaped teaspoon of garam masala. Gently mix it. Cover the bowl with cling film and marinate in the fridge for a minimum of 1 hour or so; you can leave it overnight if you prefer. The longer you leave it, the better.

5. Once marinated, the paneer is ready to cook.

6. Preheat the oven to 180°C, lay the paneer out on a foiled baking tray and once the oven is hot, put the paneer in for 12 minutes. It will be cooked to perfection. You do not need to turn it over... the result is beautiful, tasty paneer!

STARTERS & SNACKS

Tofu Tikka

READY IN 30 MINS + MARINATING

SERVES 2

I felt wildly jealous that the family (Milly and Jude included) were all raving about my dad's chicken and paneer tikka! I almost went back to vegetarian (from vegan) to try one piece of paneer. So, I asked Dad if he could make his famous recipe with tofu. It came out fantastically! The only difference to chicken or paneer is tofu needs a bit more salt.

INGREDIENTS

1 tablespoon light olive oil

300g plain tofu (1 packet)

½ inch ginger, peeled

1 clove garlic, peeled

Small handful fresh coriander

SPICES

1 teaspoon salt

½ teaspoon tandoori masala (available from Indian supermarkets)

Pinch of food colouring powder if you like (optional)

½ teaspoon garam masala

METHOD

1. In the mini chopper put the ginger, garlic and small handful of coriander. Blitz until finely chopped and put in a large bowl.

2. Drain the tofu and cut into 2cm x 1cm pieces.

3. Add this to the bowl with the salt, olive oil, ½ teaspoon of tandoori masala, pinch of food colouring powder (if you are using it) and ½ teaspoon of garam masala. Give it a gentle stir, mix thoroughly.

4. Cover the bowl with cling film and marinate in the fridge for a minimum of 1 hour or so; you can leave it overnight if you prefer. The longer you leave it, the better.

5. Once marinated, the tofu is ready to cook.

6. Preheat the oven to 180°C, lay the tofu out on a foiled baking tray and once the oven is hot, put the tofu in for 20 minutes, turn occasionally. If you are in a hurry it will cook on 220°C in 15 minutes! Either way it will be cooked to perfection.

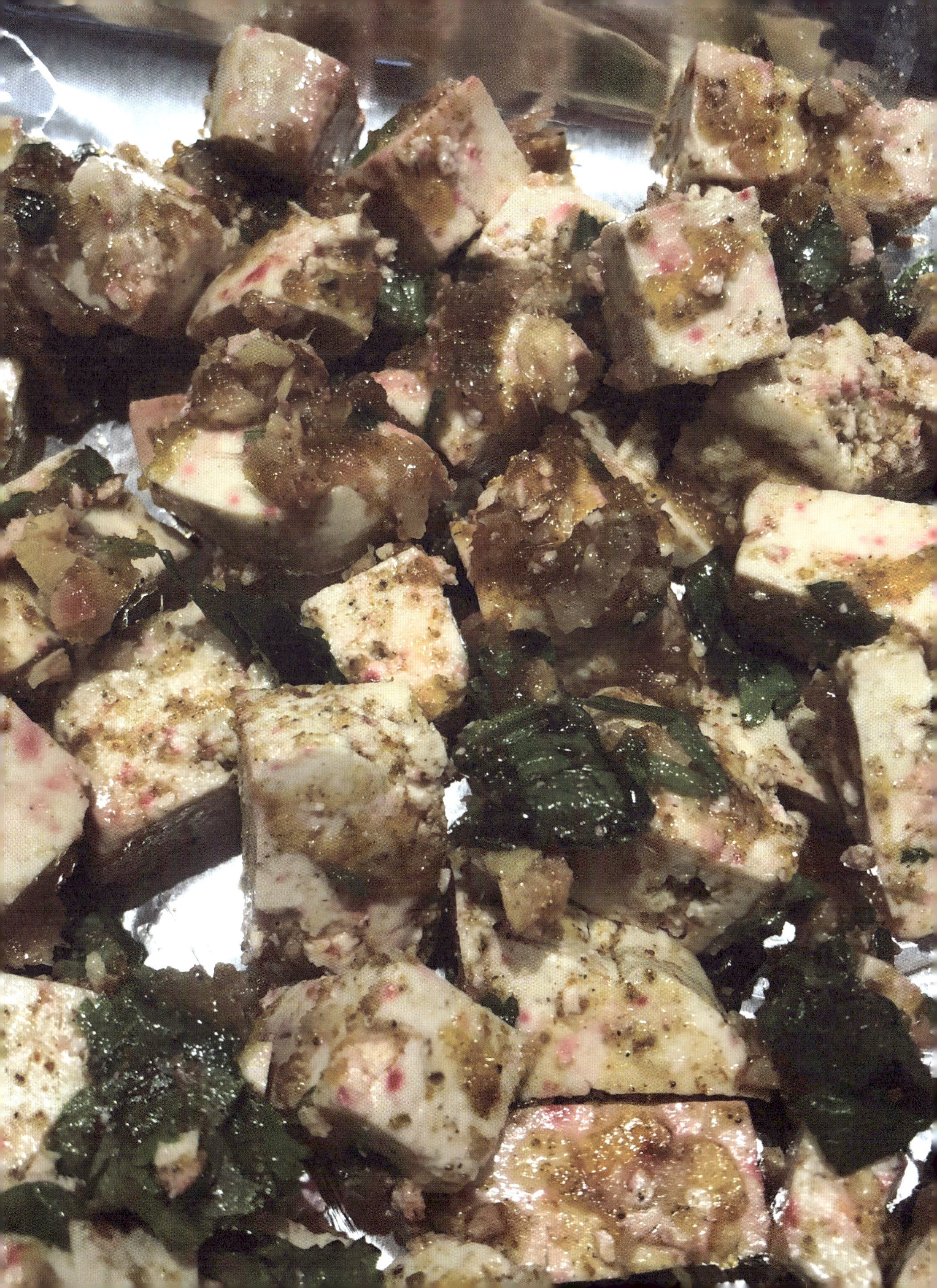

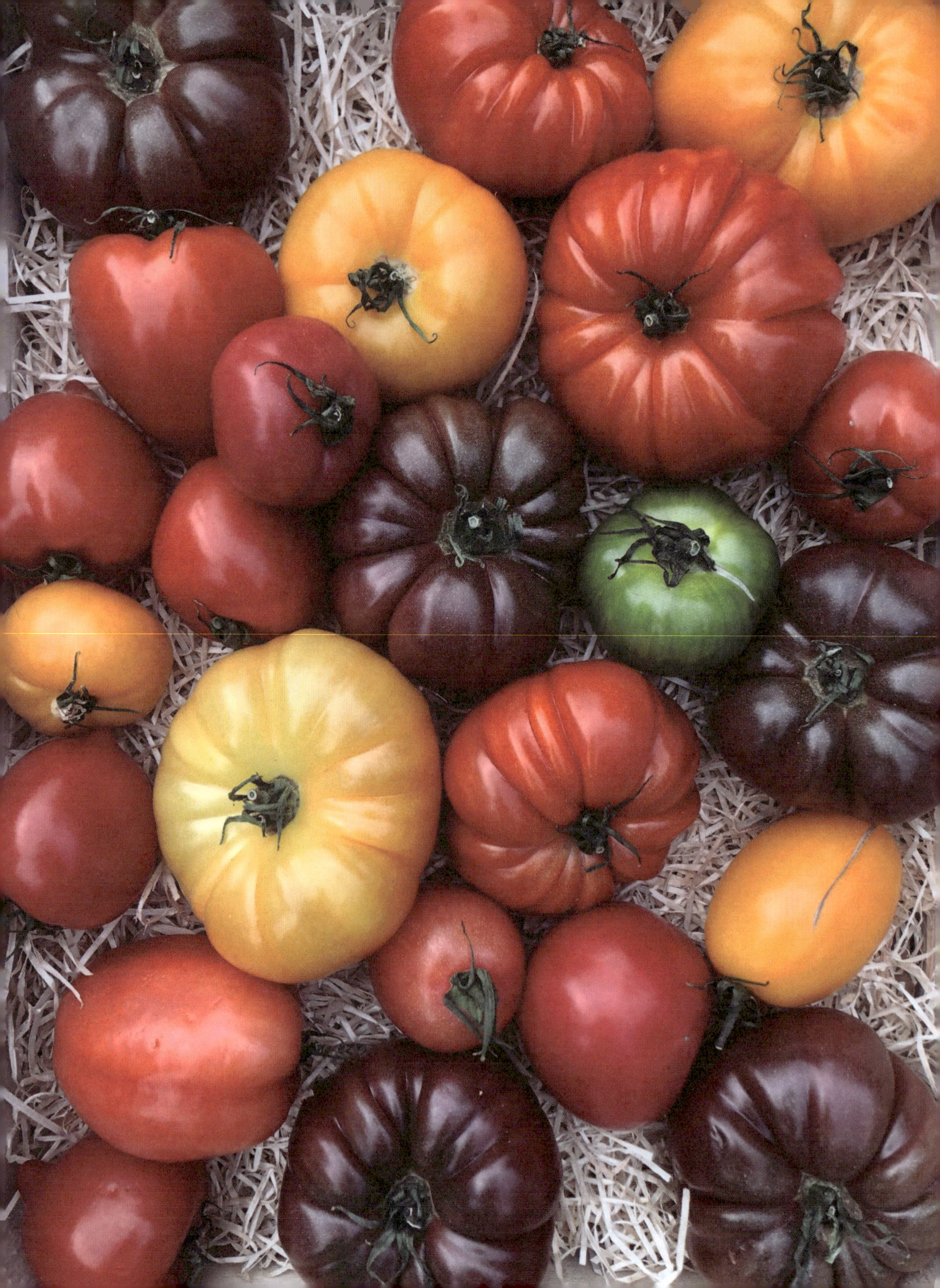

STARTERS & SNACKS

Paneer Shashlik

READY IN
30 MINS
+ MARINATING

SERVES
3-4

This is really easy! The recipe is the same as paneer tikka but with some vegetables too.

INGREDIENTS

2 tablespoons light olive oil

1 block paneer (250g)

1 inch ginger, peeled

1 clove garlic, peeled

Small handful fresh coriander

One pepper (red, green or yellow) deseeded and cut into pieces

2 tomatoes cut into quarters or a handful of cherry tomatoes

1 medium onion, peeled & cut in quarters (red or white)

SPICES

1 teaspoon salt

1 teaspoon tandoori masala (available from Indian supermarkets)

Pinch of food colouring powder if you like (optional)

1 teaspoon garam masala

METHOD

1. In the mini chopper put the ginger, garlic and small handful of coriander. Blitz until finely chopped and put in a large bowl.

2. Cut the paneer into cubes. Add this to the bowl with 1 teaspoon of salt and 2 tablespoons of olive oil, give it a good stir.

3. Then add to the bowl 1 teaspoon of tandoori masala, pinch of food colouring powder (if you are using it), 1 teaspoon of garam masala and mix thoroughly. Cover the bowl with cling film and marinate in the fridge for a minimum of 1 hour or so; you can leave it overnight if you prefer. The longer you leave it, the better.

4. Once marinated, the paneer is ready to cook.

5. Preheat the oven to 180°C, remove the paneer from the fridge and add the peppers, tomatoes and onions, give it a stir to mix the ingredients.

6. Then put this on a foiled baking tray and once the oven is hot, put the paneer in for 12 minutes. It will be cooked to perfection. You do not need to turn it over.

STARTERS & SNACKS

Tofu Shashlik

READY IN 30 MINS + MARINATING

SERVES 3-4

This is great and encourages everyone to try a bit of tofu. The recipe is the same as tofu tikka but with some vegetables. It is fantastic cooked in foil on a barbecue too.

INGREDIENTS

2 tablespoons light olive oil

300g tofu

1 inch ginger, peeled

1 clove garlic, peeled

Small handful fresh coriander

One pepper (red, green or yellow) deseeded and cut into pieces

2 tomatoes cut in quarters or a handful of cherry tomatoes

1 medium onion, peeled & cut in quarters (red or white)

SPICES

1 heaped teaspoon salt

1 teaspoon tandoori masala (available from Indian supermarkets)

Pinch of food colouring powder if you like (optional)

1 heaped teaspoon garam masala

METHOD

1. In the mini chopper put the ginger, garlic and small handful of coriander. Blitz until finely chopped and put in a large bowl.

2. Drain the tofu and cut into 2cm x 1cm pieces.

3. Add this to the bowl with the salt and 2 tablespoons of olive oil, give it a gentle stir.

4. Cover with cling film and marinate this in the fridge for 30 minutes.

5. Then add to the bowl 1 teaspoon of tandoori masala, pinch of food colouring powder (if you are using it), 1 heaped teaspoon of garam masala and mix thoroughly. Cover the bowl with cling film and marinate in the fridge for a minimum of 1 hour or so; you can leave it overnight if you prefer. The longer you leave it, the better.

6. Once marinated, the tofu is ready to cook.

7. Preheat the oven to 180°C, remove the tofu from the fridge and add the peppers, tomatoes and onions, give it a stir to mix the ingredients.

8. Then put this on a foiled baking tray and once the oven is hot, put the tofu in for 20 minutes. Turn it over occasionally. It will be cooked to perfection.

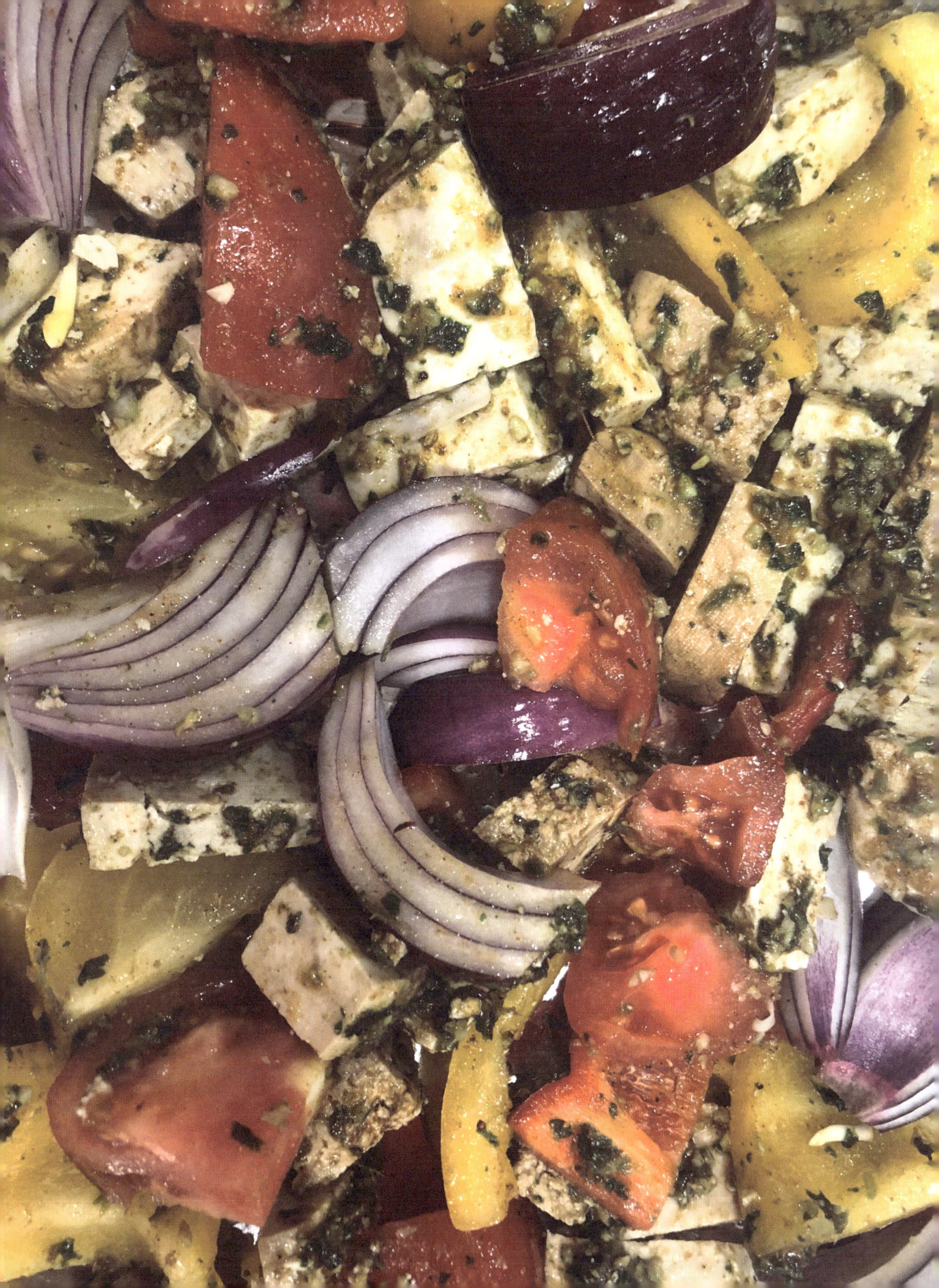

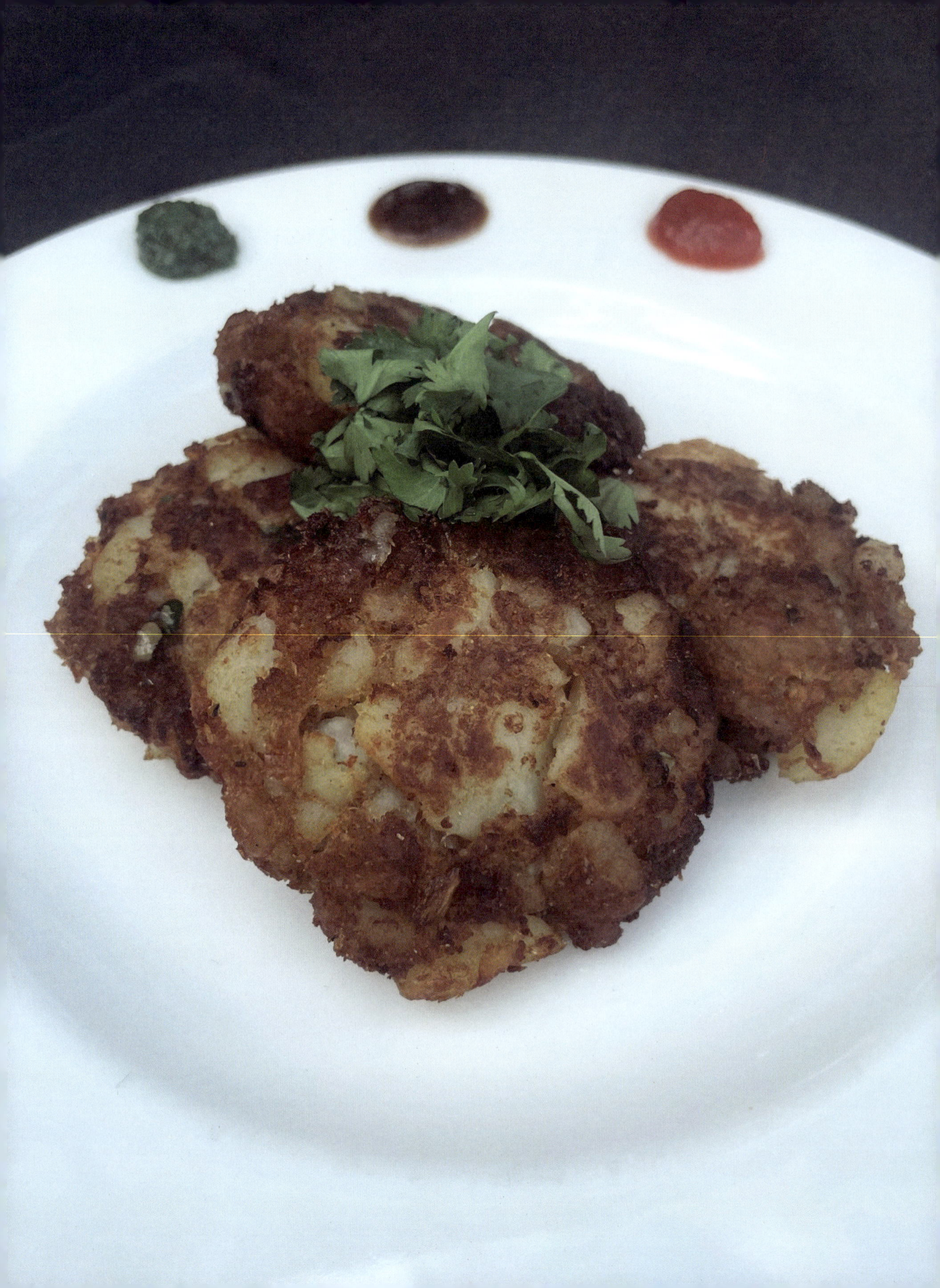

STARTERS & SNACKS

Aloo Tikki

READY IN
45 MINS

SERVES
4-6

My Auntie Rita taught the grandchildren this recipe on a Zoom call during the Covid-19 lockdown in 2020. They were an instant hit! Great as a snack or starter. With salad or on their own. In India these are traditionally a street food, fried in massive, big pans at the side of the road.

INGREDIENTS

1kg potatoes – Charlottes, new or salad are a good variety, you need a "waxy potato". Do not use Maris Piper as they are too fluffy and do not stick together well

1 green chilli, finely sliced (optional)

3 cloves garlic, crushed

½ medium onion, peeled and finely chopped

1 - 2 slices white bread

Oil for frying

SPICES

2 teaspoons salt

1 heaped teaspoon paprika

1 heaped teaspoon garam masala

1 heaped teaspoon coriander powder

METHOD

1. Boil the potatoes, skin on until they are soft. Drain and leave to cool on the side.

2. Once cool, remove the skin with your fingers / side of a teaspoon. Put the potatoes into a large mixing bowl and mash up using your hands. This will give your tikkis a chunky look.

3. Add the chilli (if using), garlic, onion and all the spices.

4. Add 1 slice of bread by crumbling it in with your fingers.

5. Knead or mix this with your hands for a few minutes to mix it evenly. If you feel it is sticking together, carry on; if not add some more bread. This will help to bind the ingredients. Jude says "you get potato hands"!

6. Make small little patties with the mixture. Jude called them flattened snowballs, Mia said mini hamburgers. Each about 2 inches in diameter, smooth the edges nicely so they are round and smooth.

7. To a wok or frying pan, add about an inch of oil for frying on a high heat. After a few minutes, test the heat of the oil by dipping the edge of a patty in the oil. If it sizzles then the oil is hot enough. Add the patties, 4 or 5 at a time to the pan, cook for a few minutes on each side before turning over. They should be golden brown.

8. Remove with a spatula / slotted spoon and drain on a plate covered with kitchen towel.

9. Serve with mango sauce, tamarind sauce, mint sauce, ketchup or on their own.

STARTERS & SNACKS

Aloo Tikki Surprise!

READY IN 45 MINS **SERVES 4-6**

Hiding the vegetables… Yes, they even do this in India! My children ate them without worrying about the vegetables as they are so delicious. You can also put cooked mince in the middle (veggie or meat) for a tasty alternative.

INGREDIENTS

1kg potatoes – Charlottes, new or salad are a good variety, you need a "waxy potato". Do not use Maris Piper as they are too fluffy and do not stick together well

1 green chilli, finely sliced (optional)

3 cloves garlic, crushed

½ medium onion, peeled and finely chopped

1 - 2 slices white bread

Oil for frying

½ cup chopped cooked vegetables (any / or all of carrots, sweetcorn, green beans, peas)

SPICES

2 teaspoons salt

I heaped teaspoon paprika

I heaped teaspoon garam masala

I heaped teaspoon coriander powder

METHOD

1. Boil the potatoes, skin on until they are soft. Drain and leave to cool on the side.

2. Once cool, remove the skin with your fingers / side of a teaspoon. Put the potatoes into a large mixing bowl and mash up using your hands. This will give your tikkis a chunky look.

3. Add the chilli (if using), garlic, onion and all the spices.

4. Add 1 slice of bread by crumbling it in with your fingers.

5. Knead or mix this with your hands for a few minutes to mix it evenly. If you feel it's sticking together, carry on; if not, add more bread. This will help to bind the ingredients.

6. Make small little patties with the mixture. Each about 2 inches in diameter, smooth the edges nicely so they are round and smooth.

7. In the middle make a hole with your thumb (not all the way through), add a little of the veggie mixture then cover again with a little potato.

8. To a wok or frying pan, add about an inch of oil for frying on a high heat. After a few minutes, test the heat of the oil by dipping the edge of a patty in the oil. If it sizzles then the oil is hot enough. Add the patties, 4 or 5 at a time to the pan, cook for a few minutes on each side before turning over. They should be golden brown.

9. Remove with a spatula / slotted spoon and drain on a plate covered with kitchen towel.

10. Serve with mango sauce, tamarind sauce, mint sauce, ketchup or on their own.

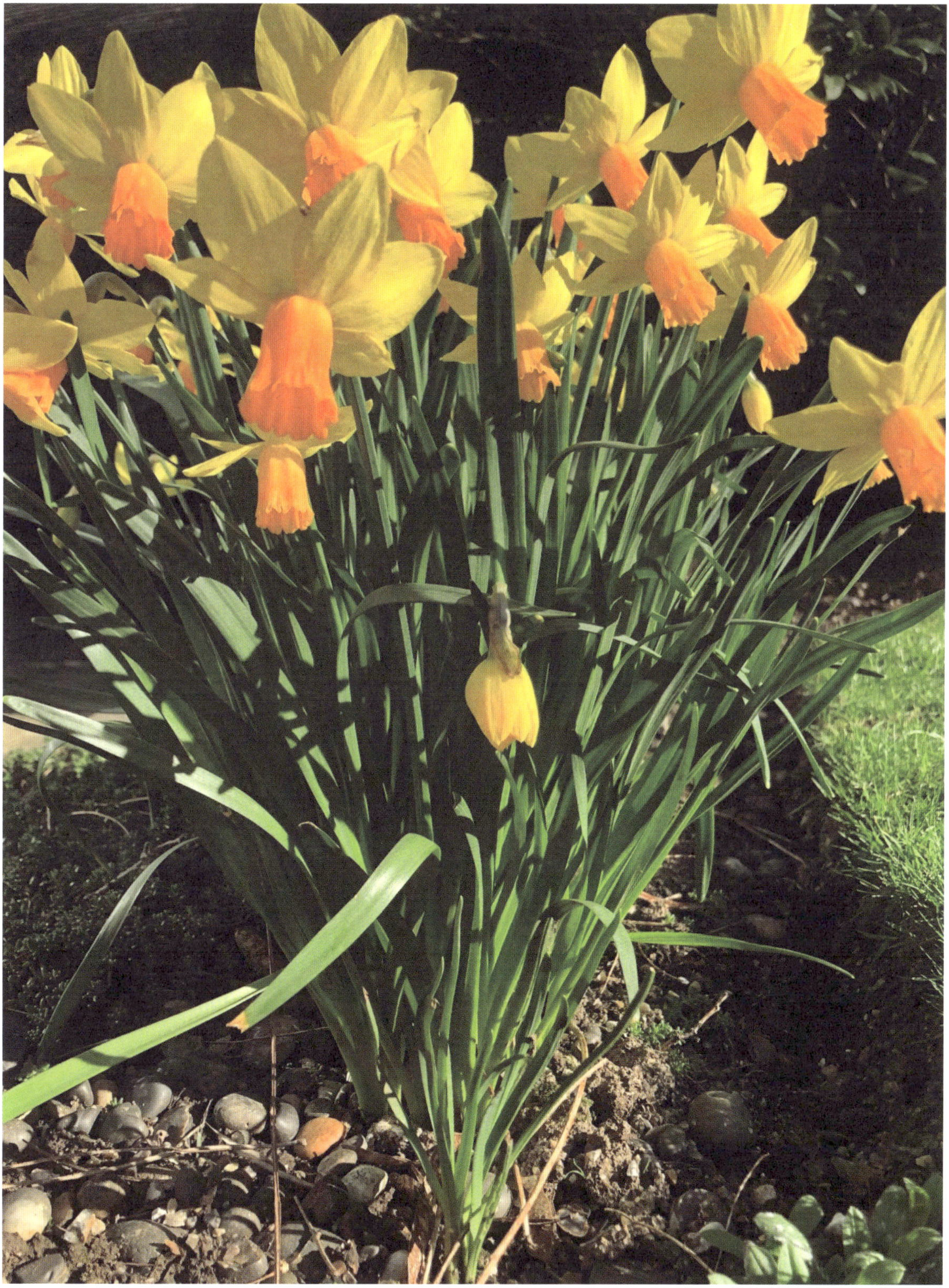

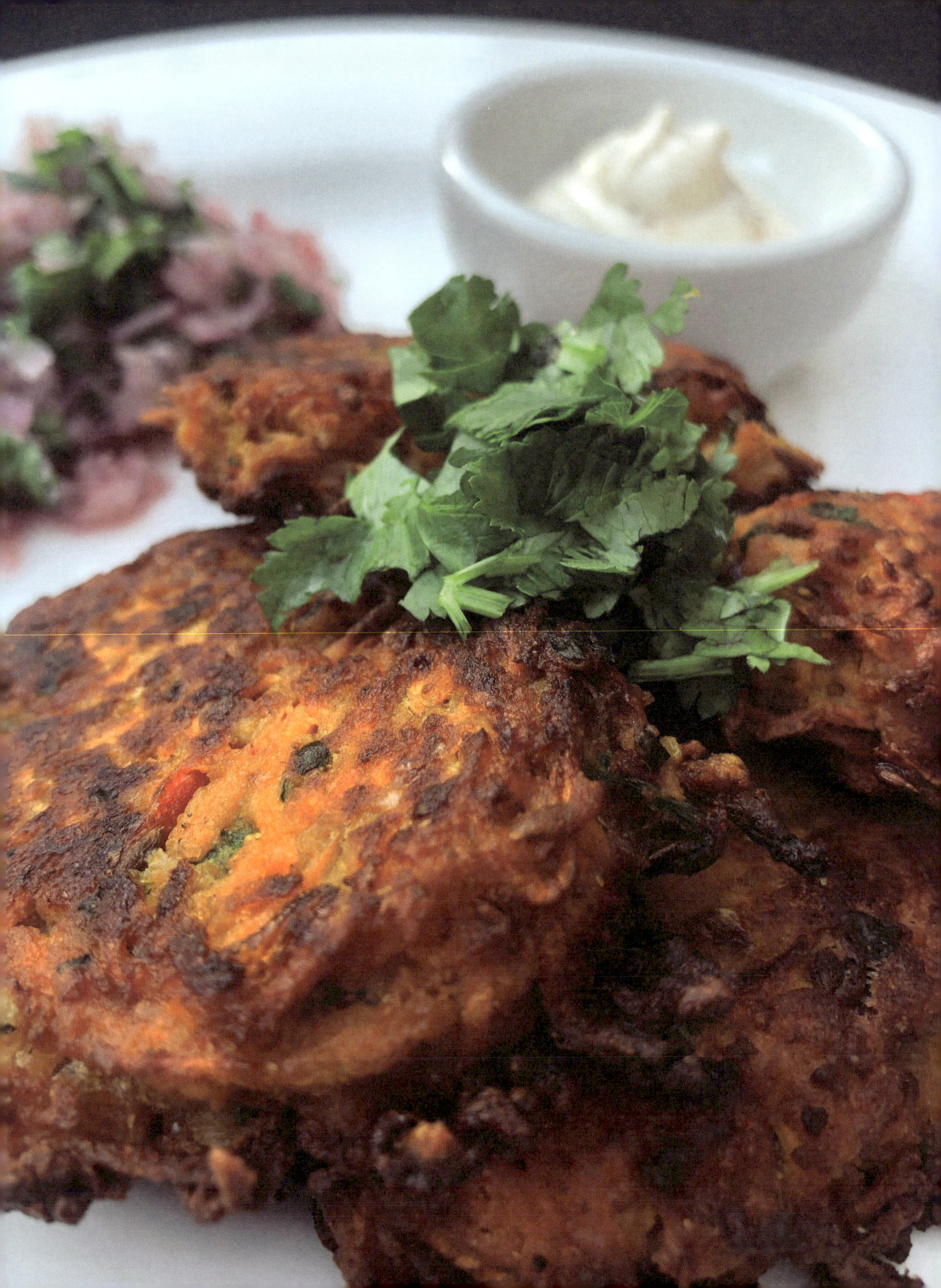

STARTERS & SNACKS

Carrot Pakoras

READY IN
30 MINS

SERVES
3-4

INGREDIENTS

2 large carrots, grated

1 small red onion, finely chopped

1 lemon

3 heaped tablespoons gram (chickpea) flour

Rapeseed or sunflower oil for frying

3 tablespoons of water

½ fresh red chilli, thinly sliced

Handful fresh chopped coriander / more for decoration

SPICES

1 teaspoon jeera

pinch chilli powder

1 teaspoon coriander powder

½ teaspoon garam masala

1 teaspoon paprika

1 teaspoon salt

½ teaspoon haldi

I would like to take credit for these delicious carrot pakoras; however, I have to thank Riverford for I have slightly modified their recipe. These are actually the first pakoras I learnt to cook; I promise you they are quick and easy to make!

METHOD

1. Mix the carrot and the onion together in a bowl with 2 tablespoons of lemon juice, add all the spices and chilli.

2. Leave this to sit for about 10 minutes, then add the gram (chickpea) flour and chopped coriander.

3. Add enough water to make a sticky batter (approx. 3 tablespoons depending on the amount of water released by the salt).

4. Add a shallow layer of oil to a wok or frying pan. Bring it to a medium / high heat.

5. Dollop dessertspoons of the carrot mix into the pan and flatten them out with the backside of the spoon.

6. Fry until golden, flip them gently and repeat on the other side. Do this in batches of no more than four at a time. Use a slotted spoon to drain and remove from the oil.

7. If serving immediately, keep the cooked pakoras on a tray in a medium oven to stay warm while you repeat.

8. Delicious served with either cucumber raita or mint yogurt, chopped onion salad and coriander for decoration.

STARTERS & SNACKS

Leek Pakoras

READY IN 30 MINS

SERVES 3-4

Annually during the hunger gap (after the winter harvest ends, but before all the new season's crops have arrived), we seemed to get an abundance of leeks in our UK veg box! So, I was willing to try anything with these beauties. Leeks I'm told are a great substitute for onions, so I braved the leek pakora, not to be disappointed: these are fabulous.

INGREDIENTS

2 leeks

2 large new potatoes, boiled and cooled

½ lemon

3 heaped tablespoons gram (chickpea) flour

Rapeseed or sunflower oil for frying

3 tablespoons of water

½ fresh red chilli, thinly sliced

Large handful fresh chopped coriander / more for decoration

SPICES

1 teaspoon jeera

pinch chilli powder

1 teaspoon coriander powder

½ teaspoon garam masala

1 teaspoon paprika

1 ½ teaspoon salt

½ teaspoon haldi

METHOD

1. Remove the outer leaves of the leeks, cut off a little from both ends and discard. Finely chop the leeks and wash well. Add to a large bowl with all the spices, chilli and ½ squeezed lemon.

2. Leave this to sit for about 10 minutes. Peel the potatoes with your fingers or the back of a teaspoon, roughly mash them with a fork, then add to the bowl with the gram (chickpea) flour and chopped coriander.

3. Add enough water to make a sticky batter (approx. 3 tablespoons depending on the amount of water released by the salt).

4. Add a shallow layer of oil to a wok or frying pan. Bring it to a medium / high heat.

5. Dollop dessertspoons of the leek mix into the pan and flatten them out with the backside of the spoon. Fry until golden, flip them gently and repeat on the other side. Do this in batches of no more than four at a time. Use a slotted spoon to drain and remove from the oil.

6. If serving immediately, keep the cooked pakoras on a tray in a medium oven to stay warm while you repeat.

7. Delicious served with cucumber salad and coriander for decoration. We love them with ketchup too!

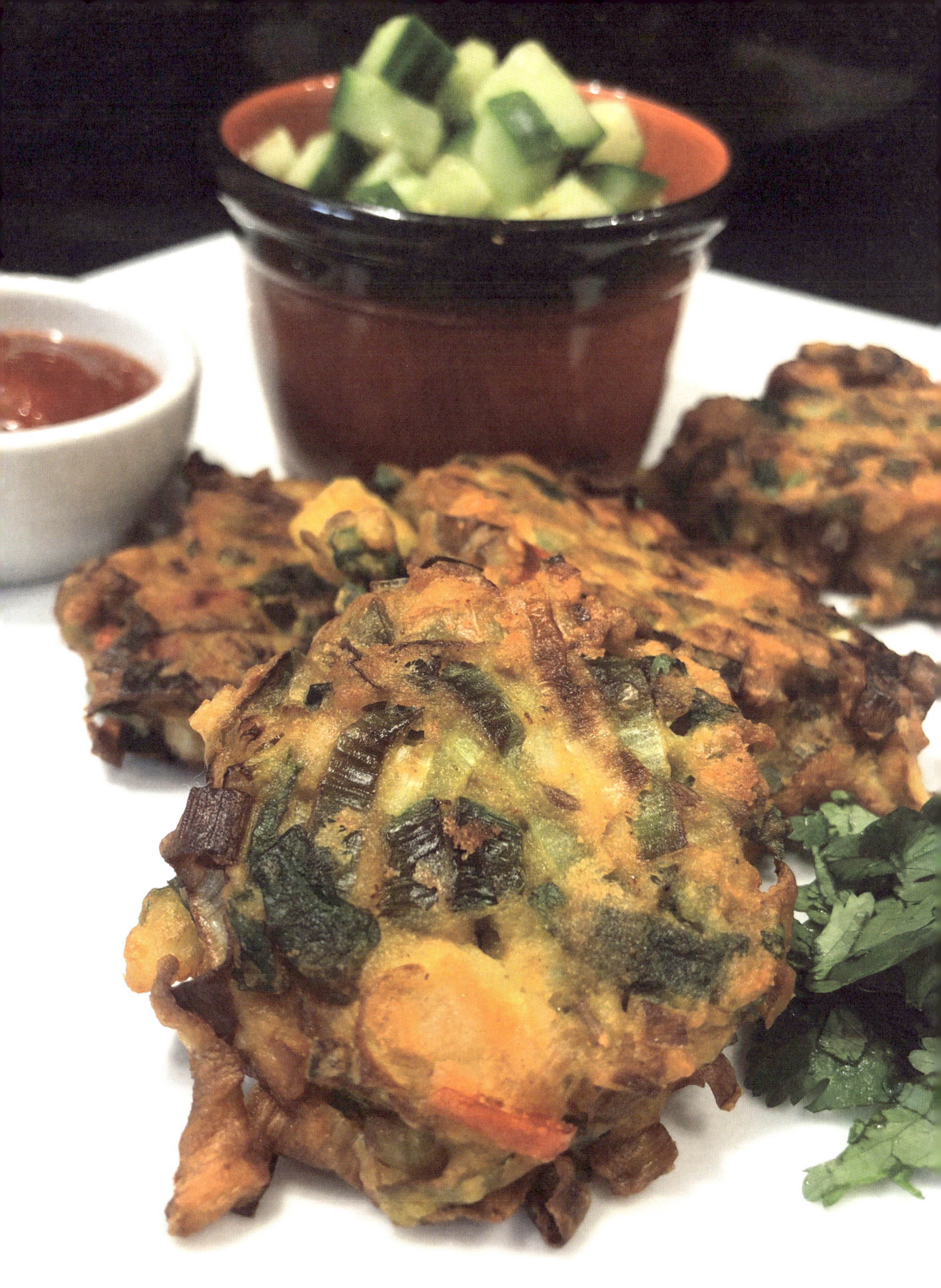

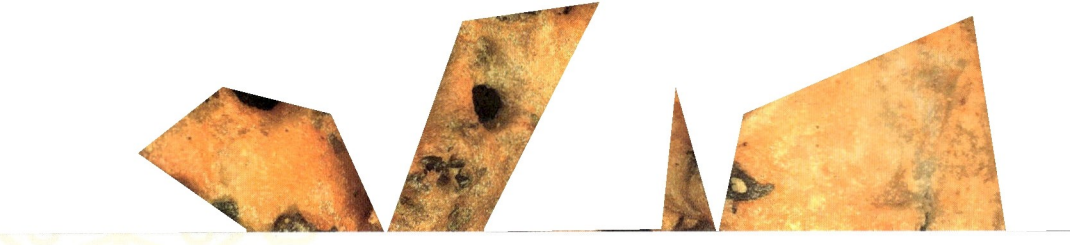

INGREDIENTS

1 large onion, coarsely chopped

3-4 medium sized potatoes (350g) boiled with the skin on (a firm potato, Rita likes duchy salad potatoes)

200g spinach leaves, washed and finely chopped

1 aubergine, washed and cubed

1 litre oil for frying

Coriander (optional)

1 or 2 green chillies, finely chopped (to taste)

500g gram flour (chickpea flour)

600ml water (approximately)

SPICES

2 teaspoons salt

2 x 1 heaped teaspoon coriander powder

2 x 1 heaped teaspoon paprika

2 x 1 teaspoon chilli powder

2 x 1 heaped teaspoon garam masala

Sprinkle mango powder, if required, as a garnish

STARTERS & SNACKS

Mixed Vegetable Pakoras

READY IN 60 MINS

SERVES 10

Pakoras are a firm favourite in the Indian starter department. Traditionally, Indian Nanny would make pakoras for an afternoon teatime snack, especially if she had guests coming. We eat them with ketchup!

This is Rita's recipe; she says you can vary the vegetables with whatever you have in your fridge. Simply potatoes and onions work well too – see Madhu's quick pakora recipe, page 86.

Note, pakoras are quite fiddly to make! The batter needs to be of the correct consistency to get it right. It may take two or three attempts, but I promise it will be well worth it.

Note – You can freeze pakoras once cooled. I would suggest putting them in freezer bags, they will last up to three months and can be oven cooked from frozen in about 15 minutes.

METHOD

1. Once you have boiled the potatoes, let them cool then remove the skin with your fingers and coarsely chop them into a large bowl.

2. Then add the onion, spinach and aubergine. If adding green chilli and fresh coriander do this now.

3. Season with 2 teaspoons salt, 1 heaped teaspoon each of coriander powder, paprika, garam masala and a level teaspoon chilli powder. Mix together gently with a wooden spoon.

4. In another bowl add the gram flour and another 1 teaspoon of the core spices. Add about 1 cup of water and beat vigorously to remove any little lumps and get lots of air through it. You can use a fork, or a silicone spatula is great for this. Keep adding water until you have a smooth but thick batter. The liquid needs to be a thick pouring consistency.

5. Pour the batter over the vegetables and mix together gently with a wooden spoon.

6. Half fill a large wok or a deep frying pan with the oil and heat it up. After a few minutes add ½ teaspoon of the mixture to test the temperature, when it sizzles the oil is hot enough to start cooking your pakoras.

7. Using a dessert spoon, add spoonfuls of the vegetable mixture to the oil. If you start adding the first one at 12 o'clock, then add them clockwise as you go round so you will remember where you started. Usually you can add 8 or so to the oil and cook in batches. The pakoras should be floating on top, not sitting at the bottom of the pan. If they are at the bottom, unstick them – either you need more oil in your wok or the oil isn't hot enough.

8. After a minute or so start with the pakora at 12 o'clock and flick them over to let both sides brown. You may need to lower the heat slightly so they cook in the middle too once the oil gets really hot.

9. Turn regularly.

10. Fry for 3-4 minutes until crispy brown on both sides. Once they are a nice golden colour, using a slotted spoon, bring them to the edge of the pan and hold on one side to remove the excess oil. Remove from the pan and lay them on a plate covered with kitchen towel, again this will help to drain the oil from the pakoras.

11. Sprinkle with a little dried mango powder if you wish and serve immediatley OR wait for them to cool and store in the fridge. To heat up, pop them in a warm oven for 5 minutes or so to heat through.

12. Serve with ketchup, tamarind sauce or chilli sauce.

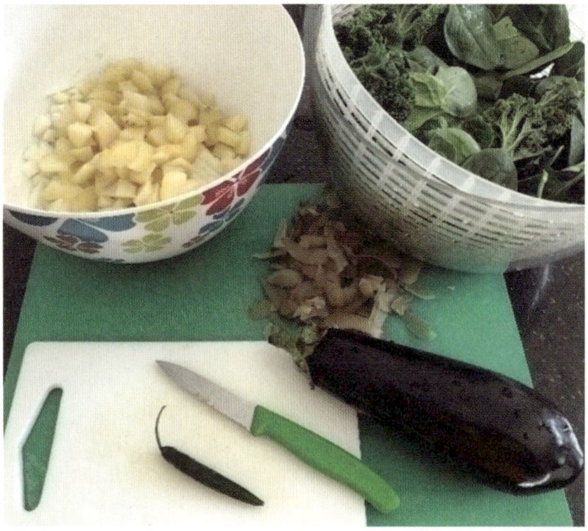

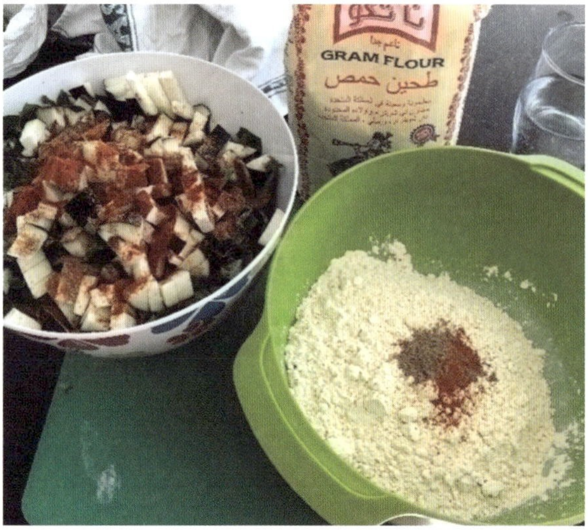
GRAM FLOUR
طحين حمص

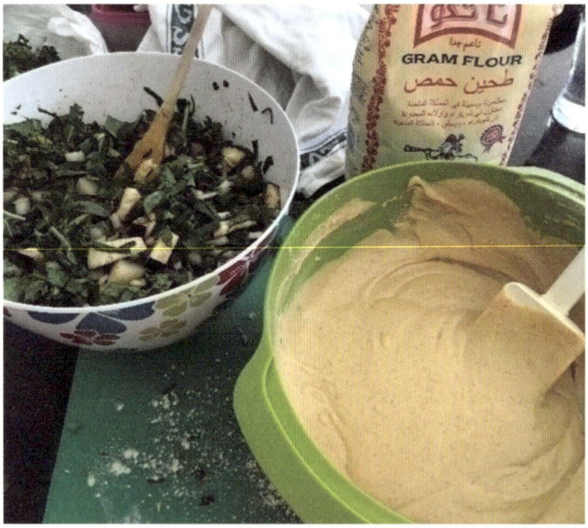
GRAM FLOUR
طحين حمص

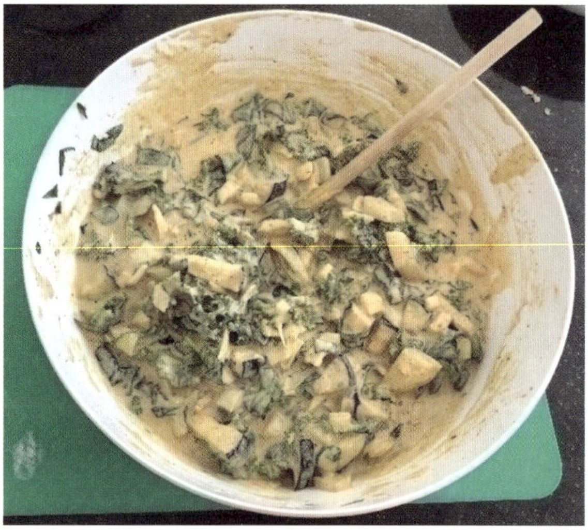

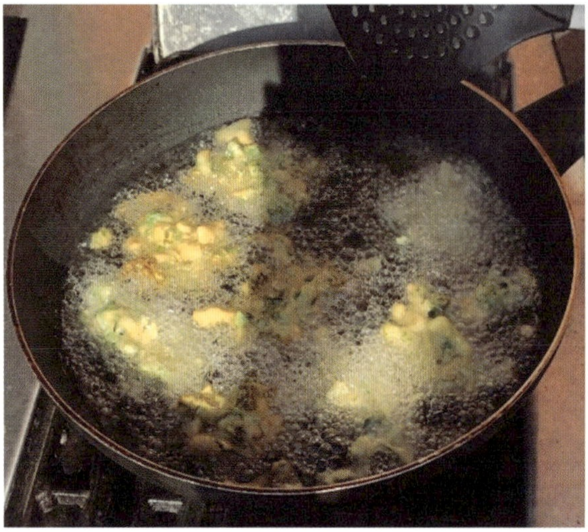

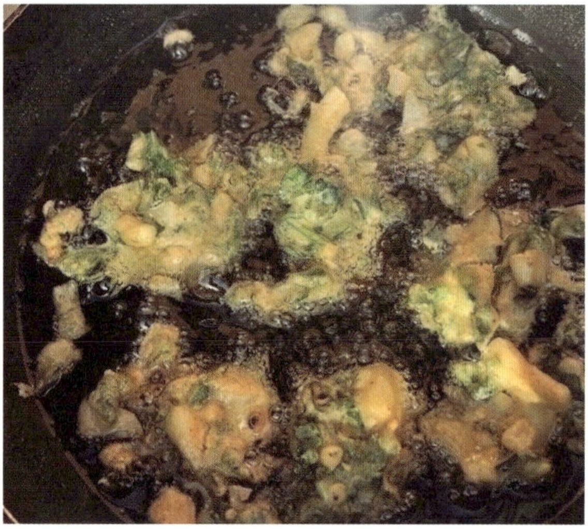

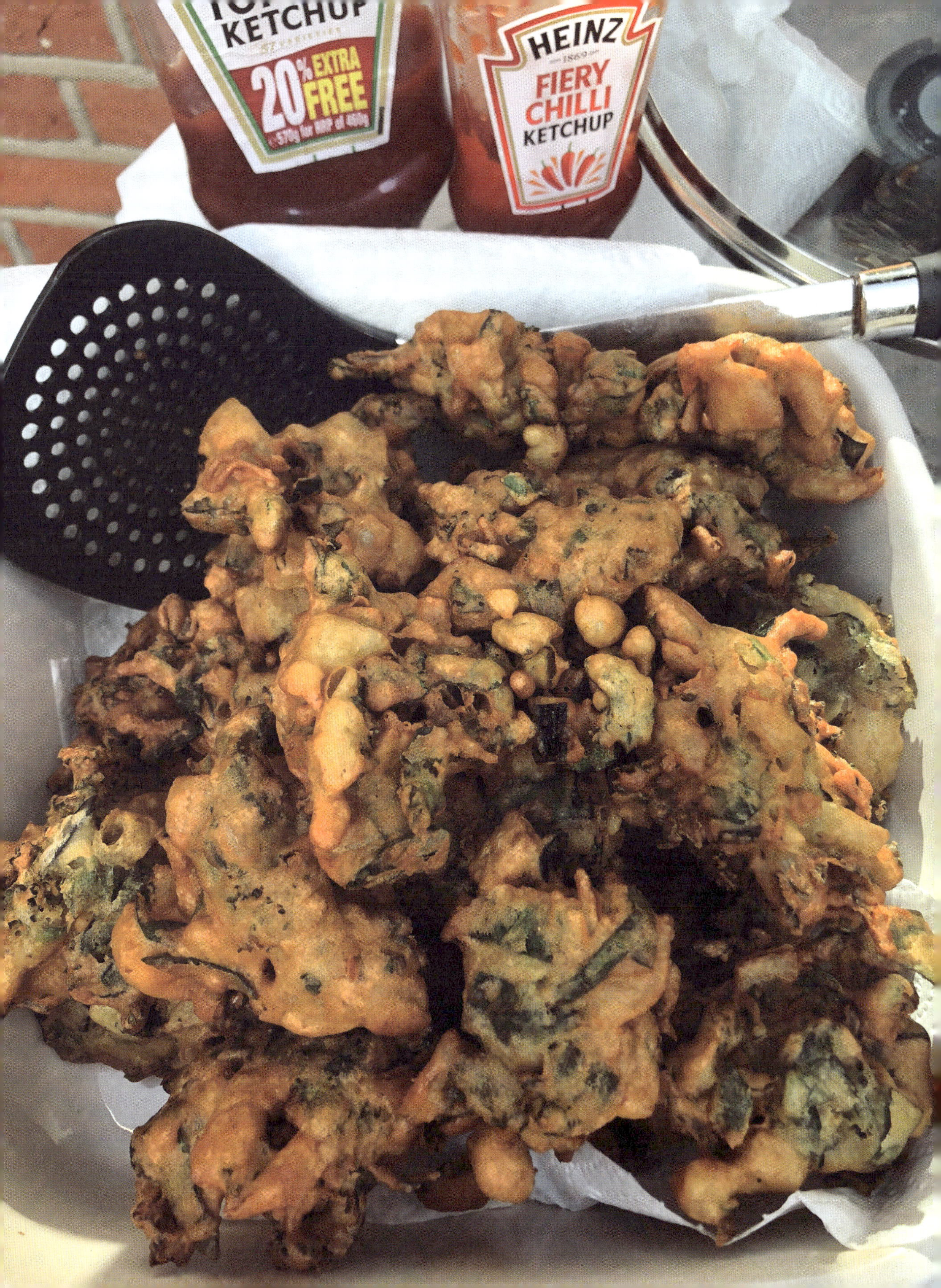
KETCHUP
20% EXTRA FREE
HEINZ
1869
FIERY CHILLI
KETCHUP

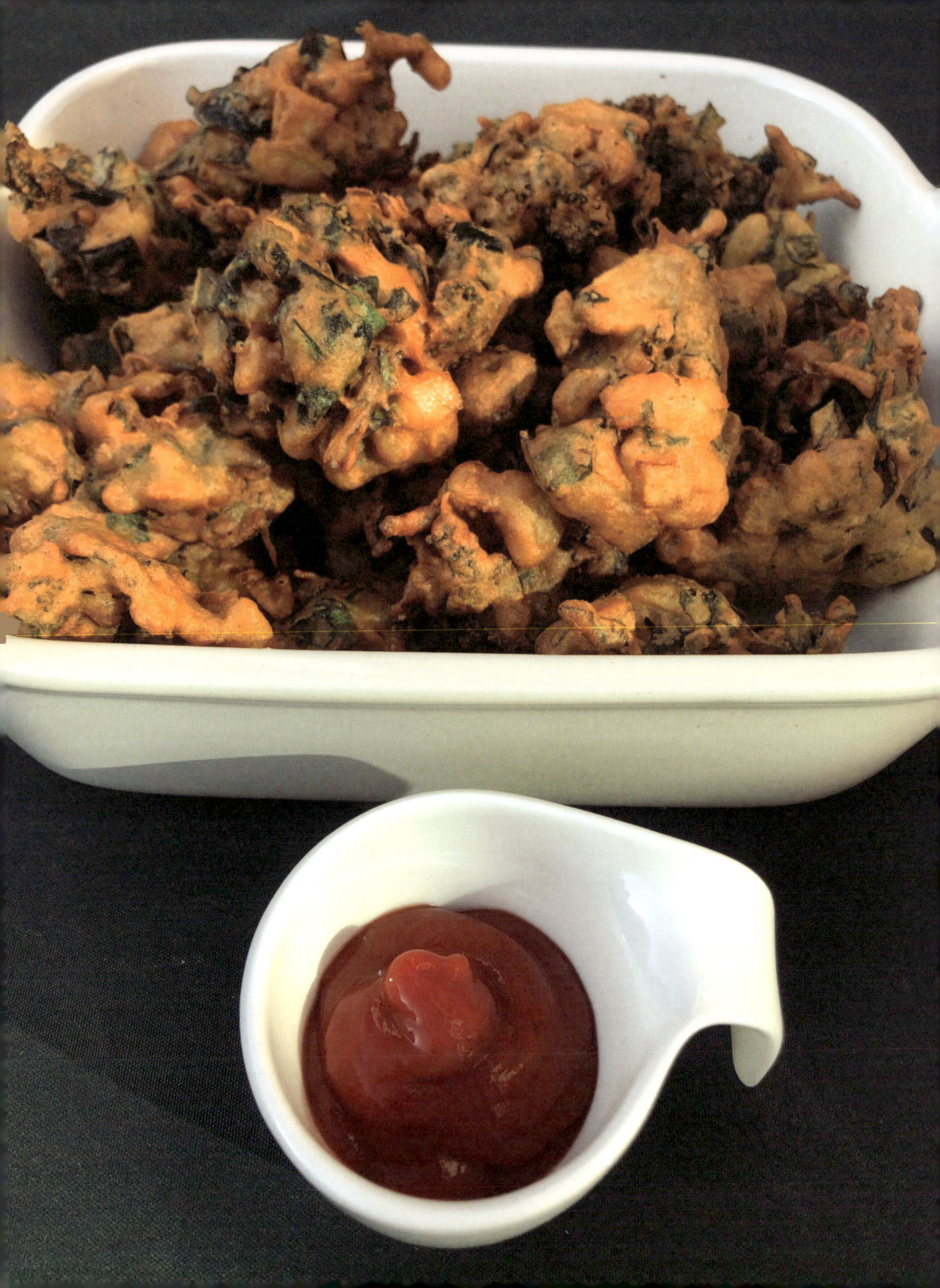

Just Pakoras

Ok, so once you get the hang of making pakoras, you can cook variations including paneer or parboiled parsnips, cauliflower or carrots. Any vegetable works, for instance peppers or other vegetables you have in your fridge, so Rita tells me!

Next are a few Rita showed me when I was learning to cook pakoras (it took me a few attempts...).

If you would like a chilli "kick" add a chopped red or green chilli to the batter.

STARTERS & SNACKS

Potato Pakoras

READY IN 30 MINS

SERVES 3-4

INGREDIENTS

2 medium sized potatoes, peeled and thinly sliced (or you can use boiled if you prefer)

Approximately 100g gram flour (chickpea flour)

½ - 1 cup water

1 litre oil for frying

SPICES

2 x ½ heaped teaspoon coriander powder

2 x ½ heaped teaspoon garam masala

2 x ½ heaped teaspoon paprika

2 x ½ teaspoon salt

2 x ¼ teaspoon chilli powder

METHOD

1. Into a bowl make your batter, add the gram flour and 1 x all the core spices. Add about ¼ cup of water and beat vigorously trying to remove any little lumps and get lots of air through it. Keep adding water until you have a smooth but thick batter. The liquid needs to be a thick pouring consistency.

2. In another bowl add your pototoes plus another 1 x all the core spices. Mix together gently with a wooden spoon and drop the potatoes into the batter. Again mix gently with a wooden spoon.

3. Fill a large wok or a deep frying pan ½ full with oil and heat it up. After a few minutes add ½ teaspoon of the mixture to test the temperature, when it sizzles the oil is hot enough.

4. Take a slice of potato, make sure it's coated in batter and gently lower into the oil. You can usually add 8 or so to the oil to cook in batches. The pakoras should be floating on top, not sitting at the bottom of the pan. If they are at the bottom, unstick them – either you need more oil in your wok or the oil isn't hot enough.

5. After a minute or so flick them over to let both sides cook and lower the heat slightly so they cook from the middle too.

6. Turn regularly.

7. Fry for about 5-7 minutes and turn regularly until crispy brown. Once they are a nice golden colour, using a slotted spoon, bring them to the edge of the pan and remove from the oil, this will help to remove excess oil. Lay them on a plate covered with kitchen towel, again this will help to drain the oil from the pakoras.

8. Serve immediately OR wait for them to cool and store in the fridge. To heat up, pop them in a warm oven for 5 minutes or so to heat through.

STARTERS & SNACKS

Cauliflower Pakoras

READY IN
30 MINS

SERVES
3-4

INGREDIENTS

1 cauliflower

Approximately 250g gram flour (chickpea flour)

1 - 2 cups water

1 litre oil for frying

SPICES

2 x 1 heaped teaspoon coriander powder

2 x 1 heaped teaspoon garam masala

2 x ¼ teaspoon chilli powder

2 x 1 teaspoon salt

2 x 1 heaped teaspoon paprika

METHOD

1. Cut the cauliflower into very small florets, parboil for a few minutes, then drain. Leave to cool, then using your hands gently squeeze the water out of the florets. Set to one side.

2. Into a bowl make your batter, add the gram flour and 1 x the core spices. Add about ½ cup of water and beat vigorously, trying to remove any little lumps and get lots of air through it. Keep adding water until you have a smooth but thick batter. The liquid needs to be a thick pouring consistency.

3. In another bowl add your cauliflower florets plus another 1 x all the core spices. Mix together gently with a wooden spoon and drop the vegetables into the batter. Again mix gently with a wooden spoon.

4. Fill a large wok or a deep frying pan half full with oil and heat it up. After a few minutes add ½ teaspoon of the mixture to test the temperature, when it sizzles the oil is hot enough.

5. Using a dessert spoon, add spoonfuls of the vegetable to the oil or you can pick up the florets with your hands and gently add them. You can usually add 5 or so to the oil to cook in batches. The pakoras should be floating on top, not sitting at the bottom of the pan. If they are at the bottom, unstick them – either you need more oil in your wok or the oil isn't hot enough.

6. After a minute or so flick them over to let both sides cook and lower the heat slightly so they cook from the middle too.

7. Turn regularly.

8. Fry for about 3-5 minutes, turn regularly until crispy brown. Once they are a nice golden colour, using a slotted spoon, bring them to the edge of the pan and remove from the oil, this will help to remove excess oil. Lay them on a plate covered with kitchen towel, again this will help to drain the oil from the pakoras.

9. Serve immediately OR wait for them to cool and store in the fridge. To heat up, pop them in a warm oven for 5 minutes or so to heat through.

STARTERS & SNACKS

Onion Pakoras
(commonly known as onion bhajis!)

READY IN 30 MINS **SERVES** 3-4

INGREDIENTS

2 large onions

Approximately 250g gram flour (chickpea flour)

1 - 2 cups water

1 litre oil for frying

SPICES

2 x ½ heaped teaspoon coriander powder

2 x ½ heaped teaspoon garam masala

2 x ½ heaped teaspoon paprika

2 x ½ teaspoon salt

2 x ¼ teaspoon chilli powder

METHOD

1. Remove the skin from the onions and cut them either into onion rings, or slice. Set to one side.

2. Into a bowl make your batter, add the gram flour and 1 x all the core spices. Add about ½ cup of water and beat vigorously trying to remove any little lumps and get lots of air through it. Keep adding water until you have a smooth but thick batter. The liquid needs to be a thick pouring consistency.

3. In another bowl add your onion rings / slices plus another 1 x all the core spices. Mix together gently with a wooden spoon and drop the onions into the batter. Again mix gently with a wooden spoon.

4. Fill a large wok or a deep frying pan half full with oil and heat it up. After a few minutes add ½ teaspoon of the mixture to test the temperature; when it sizzles the oil is hot enough.

5. Using a dessert spoon, add spoonfuls of the onions to the oil or you can pick up the onion rings with your hands and gently add them. You can usually add 5 or so to the oil to cook in batches. The pakoras should be floating on top, not sitting at the bottom of the pan. If they are at the bottom, unstick them – either you need more oil in your wok or the oil isn't hot enough.

6. After a minute or so flick them over to let both sides cook and lower the heat slightly so they cook from the middle too.

7. Turn regularly.

8. Fry for about 3-5 minutes, turn regularly until crispy brown. Once they are a nice golden colour, using a slotted spoon, bring them to the edge of the pan and remove from the oil, this will help to remove excess oil. Lay them on a plate covered with kitchen towel, again this will help to drain the oil from the pakoras.

9. Serve immediately OR wait for them to cool and store in the fridge. To heat up, pop them in a warm oven for 5 minutes or so to heat through.

STARTERS & SNACKS

Spinach Pakoras

READY IN
30 MINS

SERVES
2

INGREDIENTS

1 bag spinach leaves (200g)

Approximately 200g gram flour (chickpea flour)

1 – 1 ½ cups water

1 litre oil for frying

SPICES

2 x ½ heaped teaspoon coriander powder

2 x ½ heaped teaspoon garam masala

2 x ½ heaped teaspoon paprika

2 x ½ teaspoon salt

2 x ¼ teaspoon chilli powder

METHOD

1. Wash, dry and chop your spinach leaves. Set to one side.

2. Into a bowl make your batter, add the gram flour and 1 x all the core spices. Add about ½ cup of water and beat vigorously trying to remove any little lumps and get lots of air through it. Keep adding water until you have a smooth but thick batter. The liquid needs to be a thick pouring consistency.

3. In another bowl add your spinach leaves plus another 1 x all the core spices. Mix together gently with a wooden spoon and drop the spinach leaves into the batter. Again mix gently with a wooden spoon.

4. Fill a large wok or a deep frying pan ½ full with oil and heat it up. After a few minutes add ½ teaspoon of the mixture to test the temperature; when it sizzles the oil is hot enough.

5. Using a dessert spoon, add spoonfuls of the vegetable to the oil or you can pick up the leaves with your hands and gently add them. You can usually add 5 or so to the oil to cook in batches. The pakoras should be floating on top, not sitting at the bottom of the pan. If they are at the bottom, unstick them – either you need more oil in your wok or the oil isn't hot enough.

6. After a minute or so flick them over to let both sides cook and lower the heat slightly so they cook from the middle too.

7. Turn regularly.

8. Fry for about 3-5 minutes, turn regularly until crispy brown. Once they are a nice golden colour, using a slotted spoon, bring them to the edge of the pan and remove from the oil, this will help to remove excess oil. Lay them on a plate covered with kitchen towel, again this will help to drain the oil from the pakoras.

9. Serve immediately OR wait for them to cool and store in the fridge. To heat up, pop them in a warm oven for 5 minutes or so to heat through.

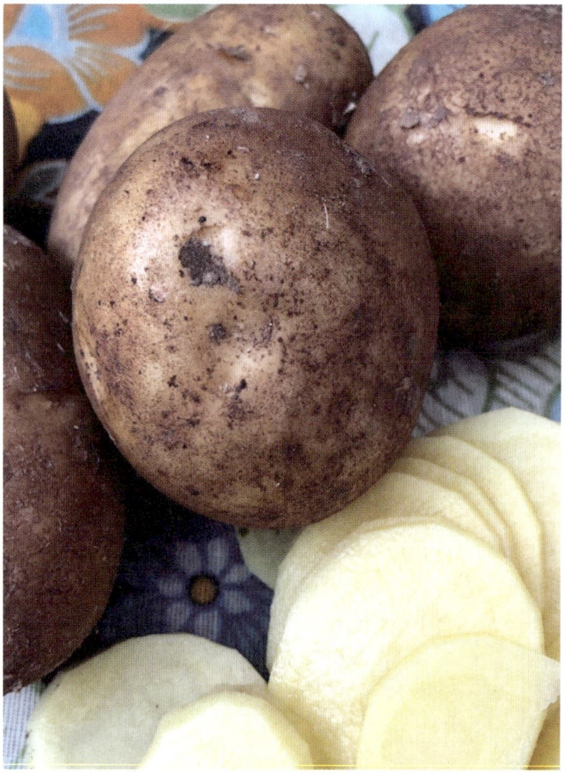
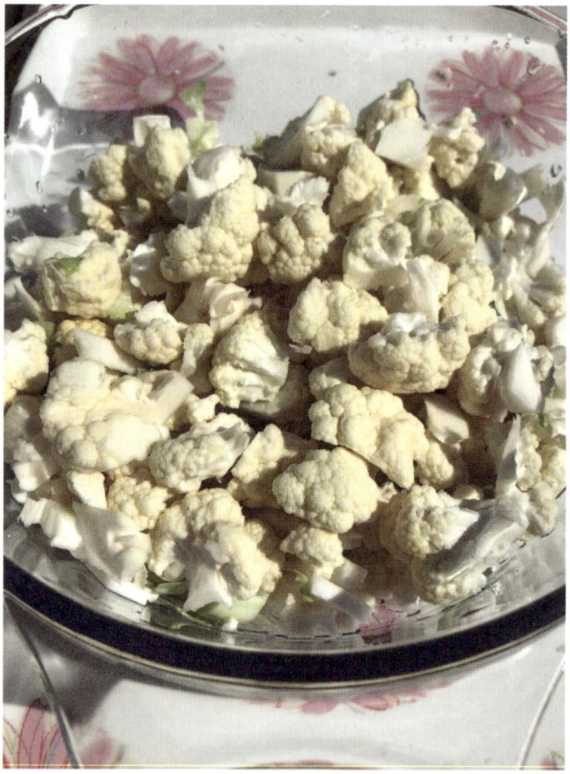
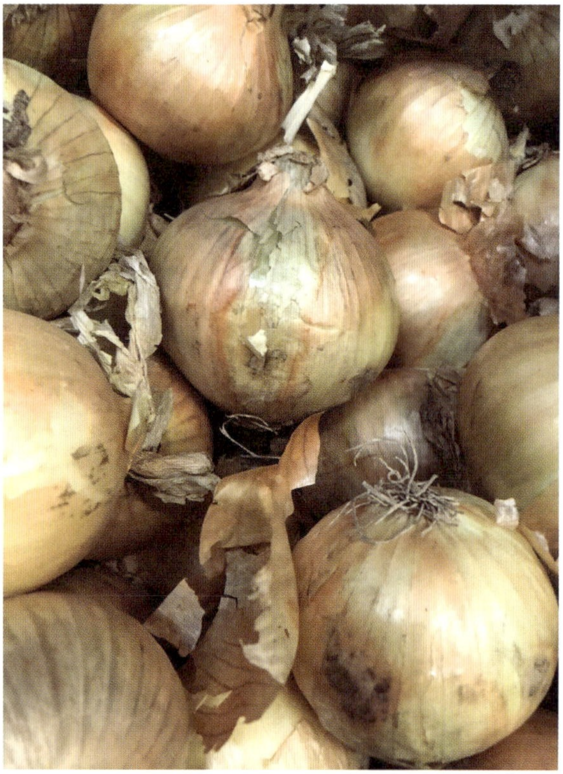
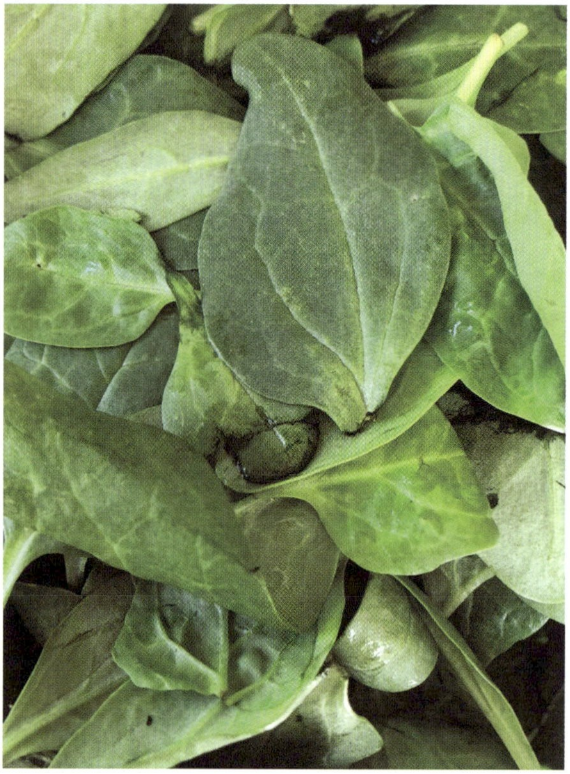

85

STARTERS & SNACKS

Quick Pakoras

READY IN 30 MINS
SERVES 3-4

This is a lovely pakora recipe from Auntie Madhu. Even the children like these as there are no surprises with vegetables, just potatoes! It's also great if you would like to cook for 1 or 2 people. Auntie Madhu likes to serve her pakoras with chilli sauce, which is great if you like it hot – Nando's chilli sauce is a good one.

INGREDIENTS

4 medium size potatoes

Thinly slice 1 medium onion

2 cloves garlic, peeled, finely chopped in the mini chopper, add a tablespoon of water so it's liquidised or use ½ teaspoon of garlic paste as an alternative

250g gram flour

1 - 2 cups water

1 litre oil for frying – Madhu recommends Crisp N' Dry, or use sunflower oil / preferred oil

SPICES

1 teaspoon salt

1 teaspoon coriander powder

1 teaspoon garam masala

¼ packet Pakora mix masala (from the Indian shop), optional

¼ teaspoon chilli flakes

If you prefer, you can shallow fry in an inch of oil instead.

METHOD

1. Boil the potatoes whole, with the skin on in a saucepan of water until parboiled.

2. Drain the potatoes, allow to cool and cut into round thin slices or little squares. Put the potatoes and finely sliced onions in a bowl on the side.

3. Sieve the gram flour into another bowl and add some water. Mix gently with a tablespoon and make it into a batter – this needs to be quite runny, similar consistency of a cheese sauce! Then beat it for a few minutes to get some air through it.

4. Put the salt, spices and garlic into the gram flour mix and give a stir. Add the potatoes and onion and stir well.

5. Into a wok add the oil; you need the wok half full of oil*. Heat on a medium to high heat. To test the heat of the oil, add a 5p size of the mixture to the wok – once it sizzles it's ready for you to deep fry your potatoes.

6. Using a dessert spoon, collect small flat balls of the potato and onion mix. Slowly lower these balls into the hot oil one at a time.

7. You can fry 4 or 5 at a time. Turn after a few minutes.

8. Once crispy and brown, remove from the pan using a slotted spoon and place on a plate, with a sheet or two of kitchen towel to remove the excess oil.

9. Serve immediately OR wait for them to cool and store in the fridge. To heat up, pop them in a warm oven for 5 minutes or so to heat through.

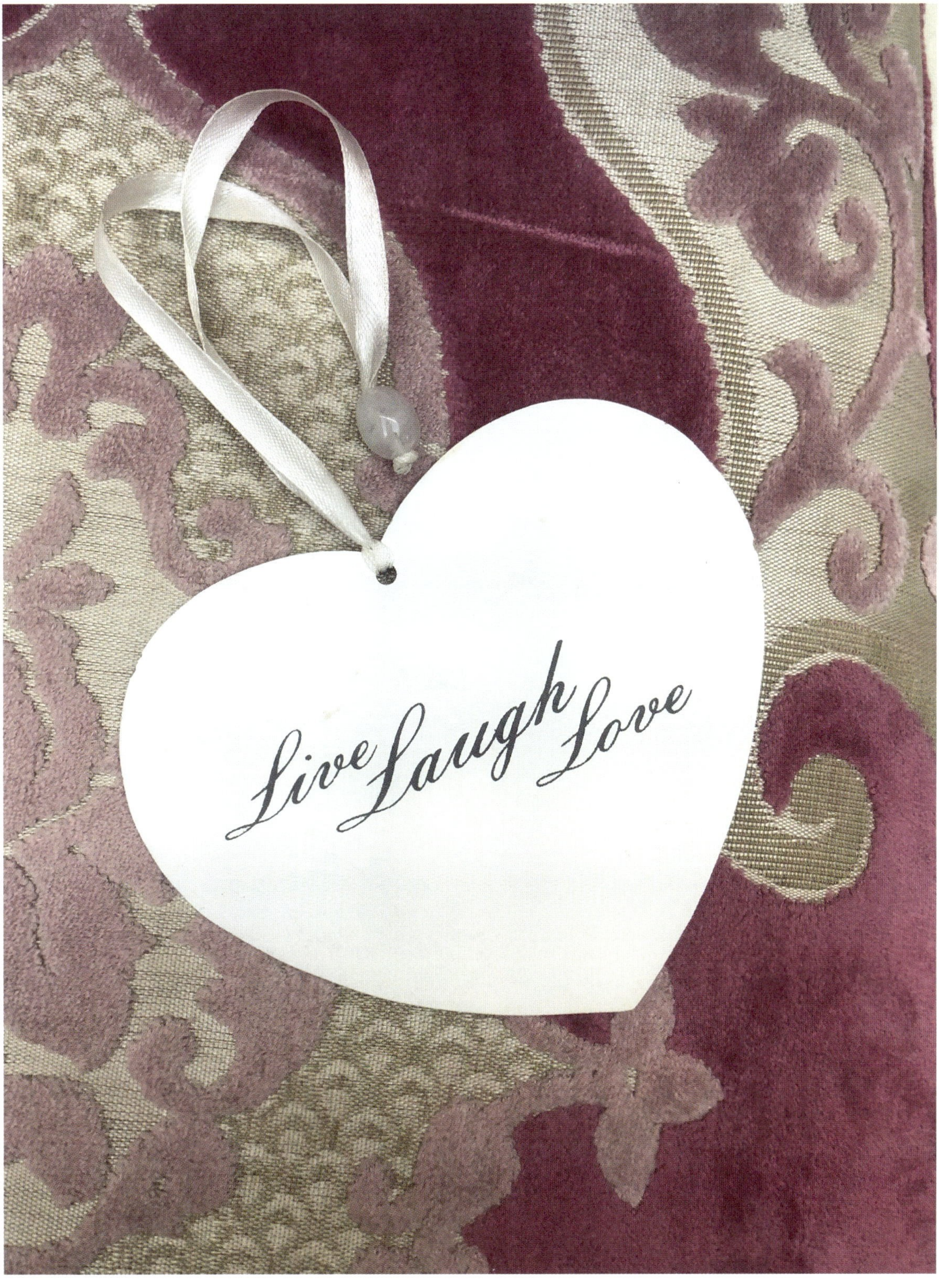
Live Laugh Love

INGREDIENTS

1 tablespoon oil

2 - 3 eggs

1 tablespoon finely chopped onion

1 tablespoon finely chopped tomato

Fresh green chilli, ginger & coriander to taste, chopped

SPICES

½ teaspoon salt

¼ teaspoon paprika

¼ teaspoon coriander powder

¼ teaspoon garam masala

STARTERS & SNACKS

Indian Omelette

READY IN
10 MINS

SERVES
1

A lovely brunch or lunch recipe from Auntie Rita. With lunch I would serve with a fresh mixed leaf salad.

This is not a pure vegetarian recipe as it contains egg.

METHOD

1. In a bowl, crack the eggs and whisk. Add all the ingredients and mix together.

2. In a frying pan, heat the oil, add the egg mixture and cook as you would normally make an omelette.

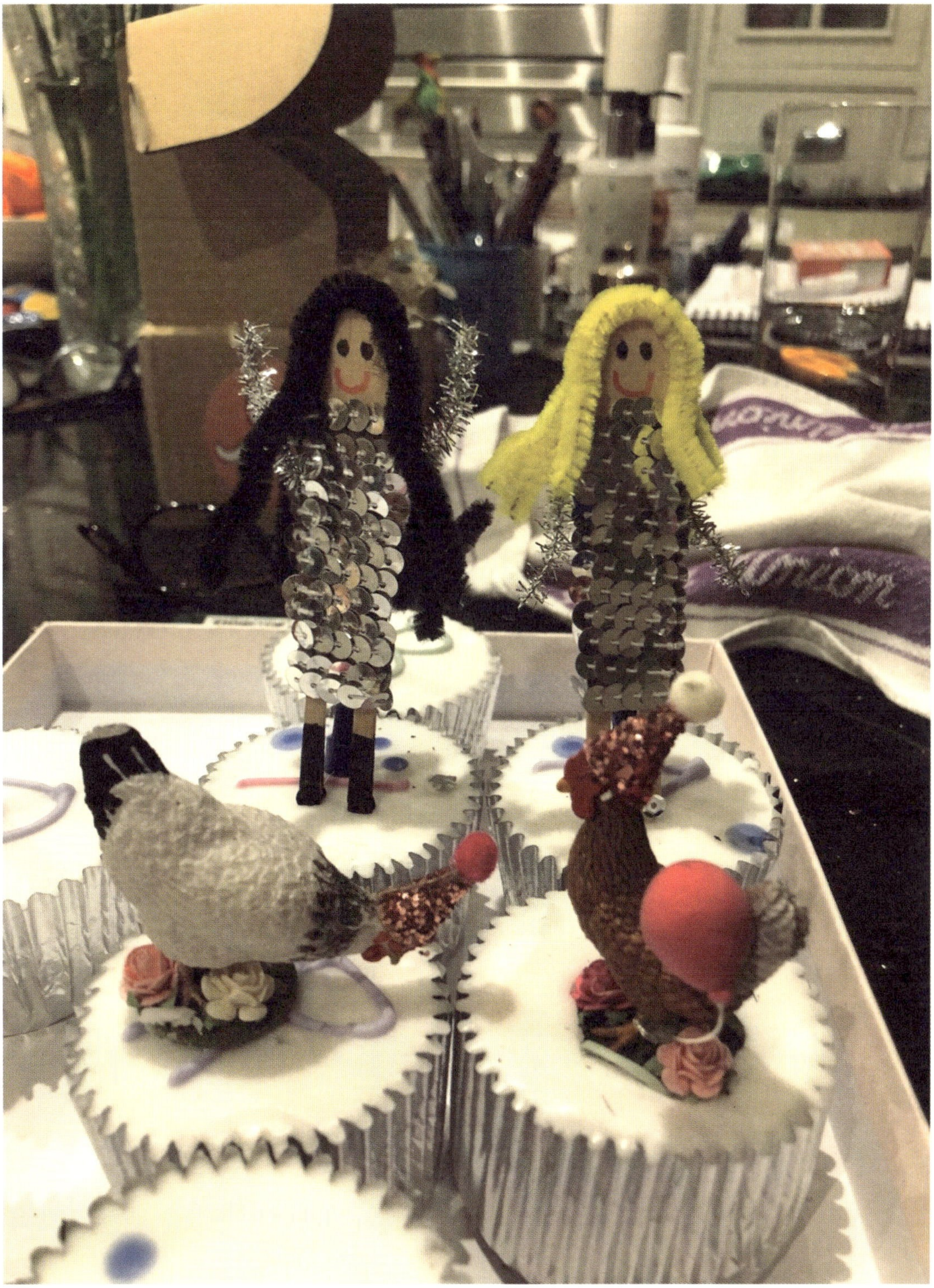

Connor & Milly
Celebrating Holi

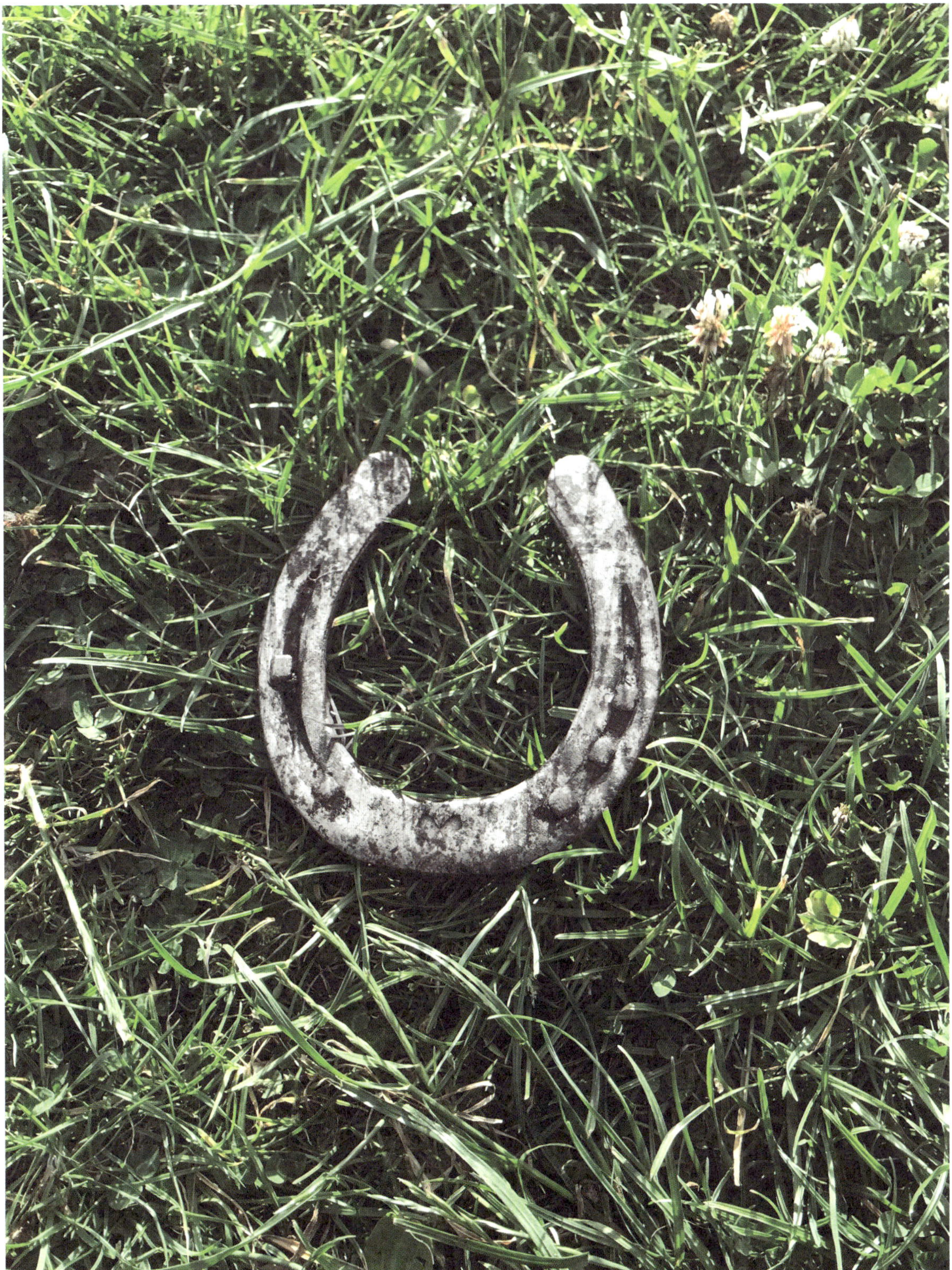

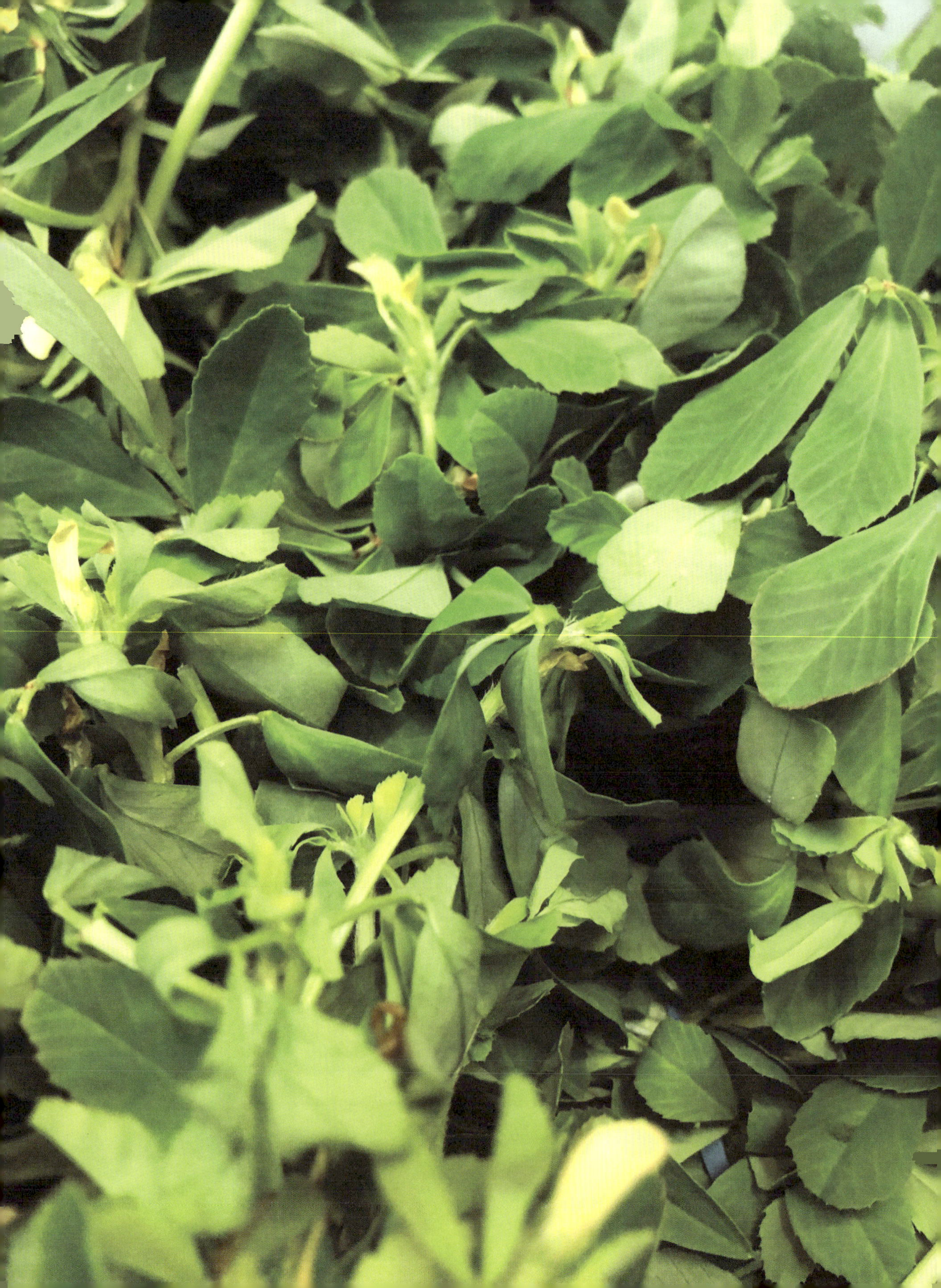

DRY VEGGIE DISHES

DRY VEGGIE DISHES

Flat Beans & Aloo

READY IN 30 MINS   **SERVES** 3-4

This is the first dish Indian Nanny taught me to cook. It is a great veggie dish, simple to make and can be eaten hot as part of an Indian meal or cold. It's a favourite at a barbecue too. If you do not have runner beans, you can use any other green beans.

INGREDIENTS

1 packet runner beans

2 medium potatoes

2 medium onions

4 tablespoons light olive oil

1 tomato

SPICES

1 teaspoon jeera

2 teaspoons salt

½ teaspoon haldi

½ teaspoon paprika

¼ teaspoon chilli powder

½ teaspoon garam masala

METHOD

1. Top and tail the beans, run a peeler down each edge if necessary. Slice into 2cm pieces & put in a bowl of cold water to wash them.

2. Peel and chop the potatoes into 2-2.5cm cubes, add them to the bowl of water.

3. Peel, wash and thinly slice 2 medium onions, put them into the wok and add 4 tablespoons of oil on a high heat for 10 minutes (no need to go very brown). Add 1 teaspoon of jeera.

4. Cut the tomato into 8 segments and add straight to the wok. Give it a quick stir and then add the drained beans and potatoes. Lower the heat and stir (a lower heat is better as they cook in their own juice and is more flavoursome); if the heat is higher, you'll need to add more water.

5. Add 2 teaspoons salt, ½ teaspoon haldi, ½ teaspoon paprika, pinch of chilli (¼ teaspoon), stir and cover with a lid. Simmer on a low heat.

6. After 5 minutes give the vegetables a gentle stir. Only stir a few times during cooking to avoid the potatoes going mushy. The aim is to have the veg cooked and little or no juice left.

7. After 15-20 minutes, check the potatoes are cooked. If they're a little hard, add some water if necessary and cook for a little longer. If cooked but there's still juice in the pan, cook with the lid off for a few minutes.

8. Finally, add ½ teaspoon garam masala, turn off the heat and the dish is ready.

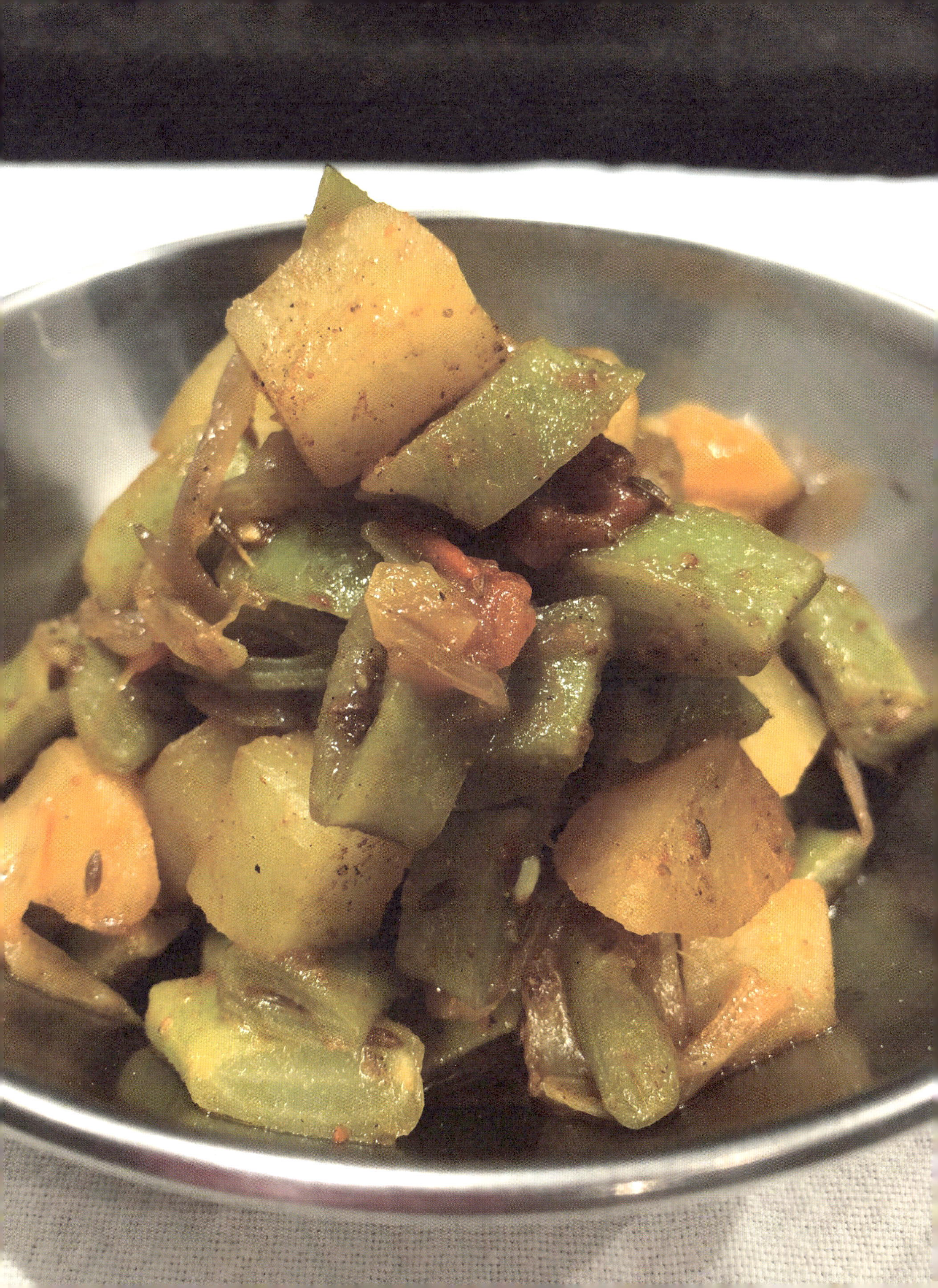

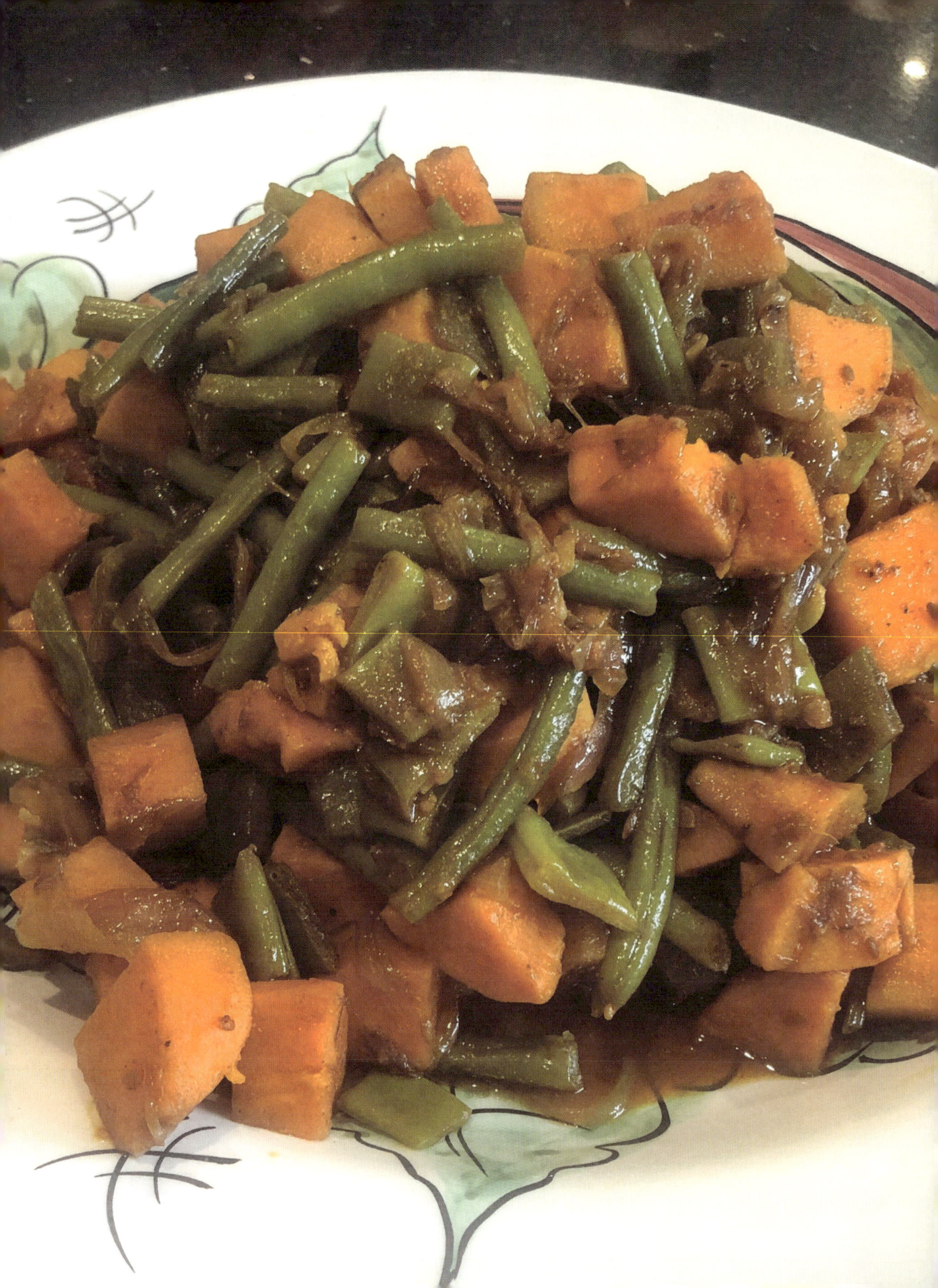

DRY VEGGIE DISHES

Sweet Potato & Three Bean Aloo

READY IN
45 MINS

SERVES
10

I cook this dish when I am cooking for a large party. It brings great colour to the table and a variety of flavours.

INGREDIENTS

4 tablespoons light olive oil

1 packet stringless green beans (200g)

1 packet French beans (200g)

1 packet pre-cut finely sliced runner beans or cut yourself (200g)

3 medium onions

2 tomatoes or 10 cherry tomatoes

3 medium size sweet potatoes

SPICES

1 ½ teaspoons jeera

3 teaspoons salt

1 teaspoon haldi

1 heaped teaspoon paprika

½ teaspoon chilli powder

1 heaped teaspoon garam masala

METHOD

1. Top and tail the stringless green beans, chop into 1-inch pieces, the French beans into 2-inch pieces & put the pre-cut runner beans all in a bowl of cold water to wash them.

2. Peel and chop the sweet potatoes into 1-inch cubes, add them to the bowl of water.

3. Peel, wash and thinly slice 3 medium onions, put them into the wok. Add 4 tablespoons of oil and put on a high heat for 10 minutes (no need to go very brown). Add 1 ½ teaspoons of jeera. Stir regularly.

4. Cut the tomatoes into 8 segments (if using cherry tomatoes leave whole) and add straight to the wok. Give it a quick stir and then add the drained beans and cubed sweet potatoes. Lower the heat (a lower heat is better as they cook in their own juice and is more flavoursome); if the heat is higher, you'll need to add more water.

5. Add the salt, haldi, paprika and chilli powder. Stir, lid on and simmer on a low heat.

6. After 5 minutes give the vegetables a gentle stir. Only stir a few times during cooking to avoid the sweet potatoes going mushy. The aim is to have the veg cooked and little or no juice left.

7. After 15-20 minutes, check the potatoes are cooked. If they're a little hard, add some water if necessary and cook for a little longer. If cooked but there's still juice in the pan, cook with the lid off for a few minutes.

8. Finally, add 1 heaped teaspoon garam masala, turn off the heat and the dish is ready.

DRY VEGGIE DISHES

French Bean & Aloo

READY IN
40 MINS

SERVES
3-4

This dish is very similar to flat beans & aloo; however, you add a chopped red pepper and an inch of ginger at the same time as the tomato. It gives the dish a bit of colour and the ginger gives it a zingy flavour. I'm pretty sure Auntie Veena taught me this dish!

INGREDIENTS

4 tablespoons light olive oil

1 packet French beans

2 medium potatoes

2 medium onions

1 tomato

1 red pepper

1 inch ginger, peeled, finely chopped

SPICES

1 teaspoon jeera

2 teaspoons salt

½ teaspoon haldi

½ teaspoon paprika

¼ teaspoon chilli powder

½ teaspoon garam masala

METHOD

1. Top and tail the beans, chop into 3cm pieces & put in a bowl of cold water to wash them.

2. Peel and chop the potatoes into 2-2.5cm cubes, add them to the bowl.

3. Wash, deseed and chop the pepper into 3cm pieces. Set to one side.

4. Peel, wash & thinly slice the onions, put them into the wok with 4 tablespoons of oil on a high heat for 10 minutes (no need to go very brown). Add 1 teaspoon of jeera and the ginger.

5. Cut the tomato into 8 segments, add straight to the wok. Give it a quick stir and then add the peppers, give it another stir and cook for a few minutes. Drain and rinse the beans and potatoes, add to the wok. Lower the heat and stir (a lower heat is better as they cook in their own juice and is more flavoursome); if the heat is higher, you'll need to add more water.

6. Add 2 teaspoons salt, ½ teaspoon haldi, ½ teaspoon paprika, pinch of chilli (¼ teaspoon), stir and cover. Simmer on a low heat.

7. After 5 minutes give the vegetables a gentle stir. Only stir a few times during cooking to avoid the potatoes going mushy. The aim is to have the veg cooked but little or no juice left.

8. After 15-20 minutes, check the potatoes are cooked. If they're a little hard, add some water if necessary and cook for a little longer. If cooked but there's still juice in the pan, cook with the lid off for a few minutes.

9. Finally, add ½ teaspoon garam masala, turn off the heat and the dish is ready.

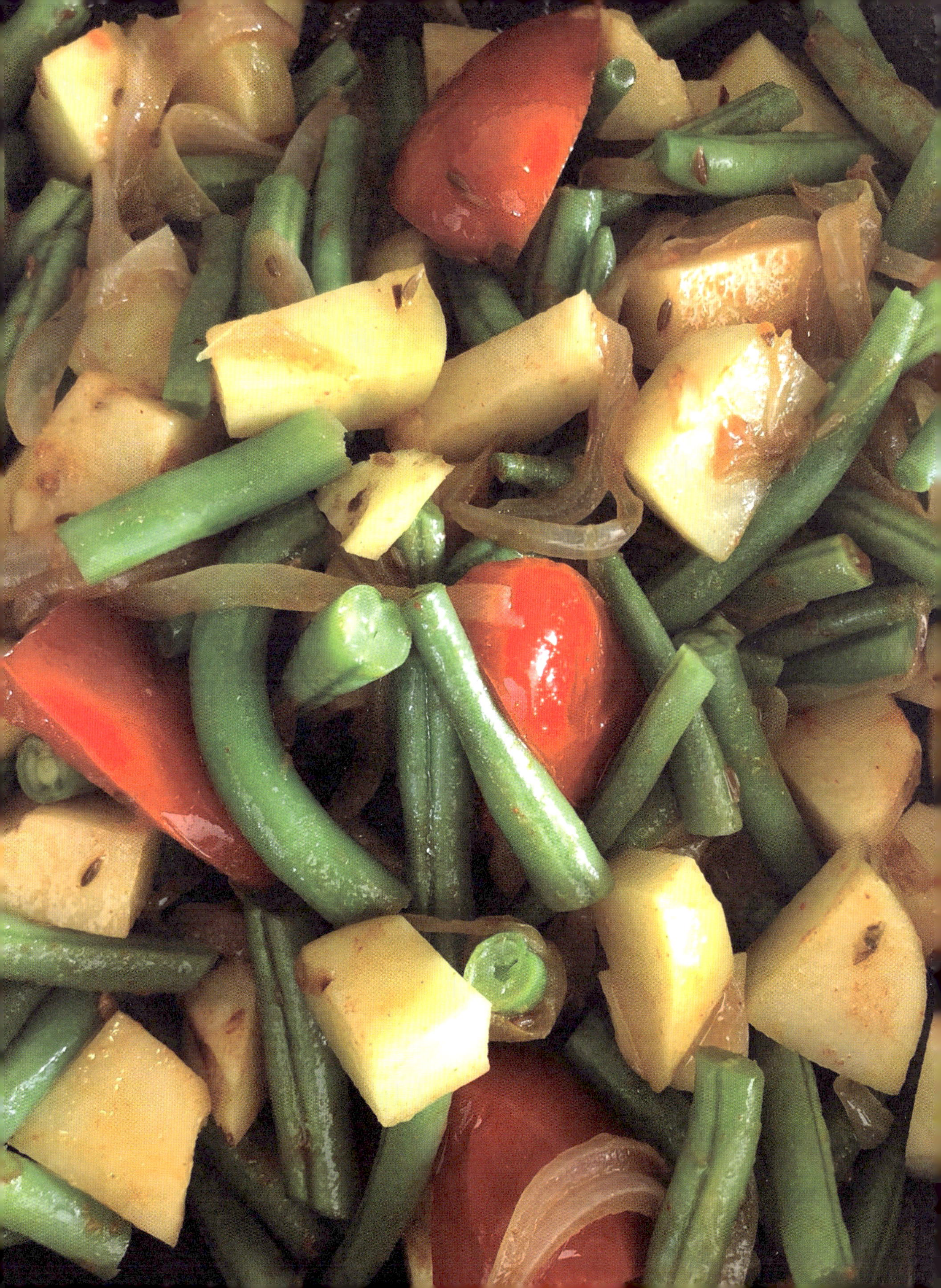

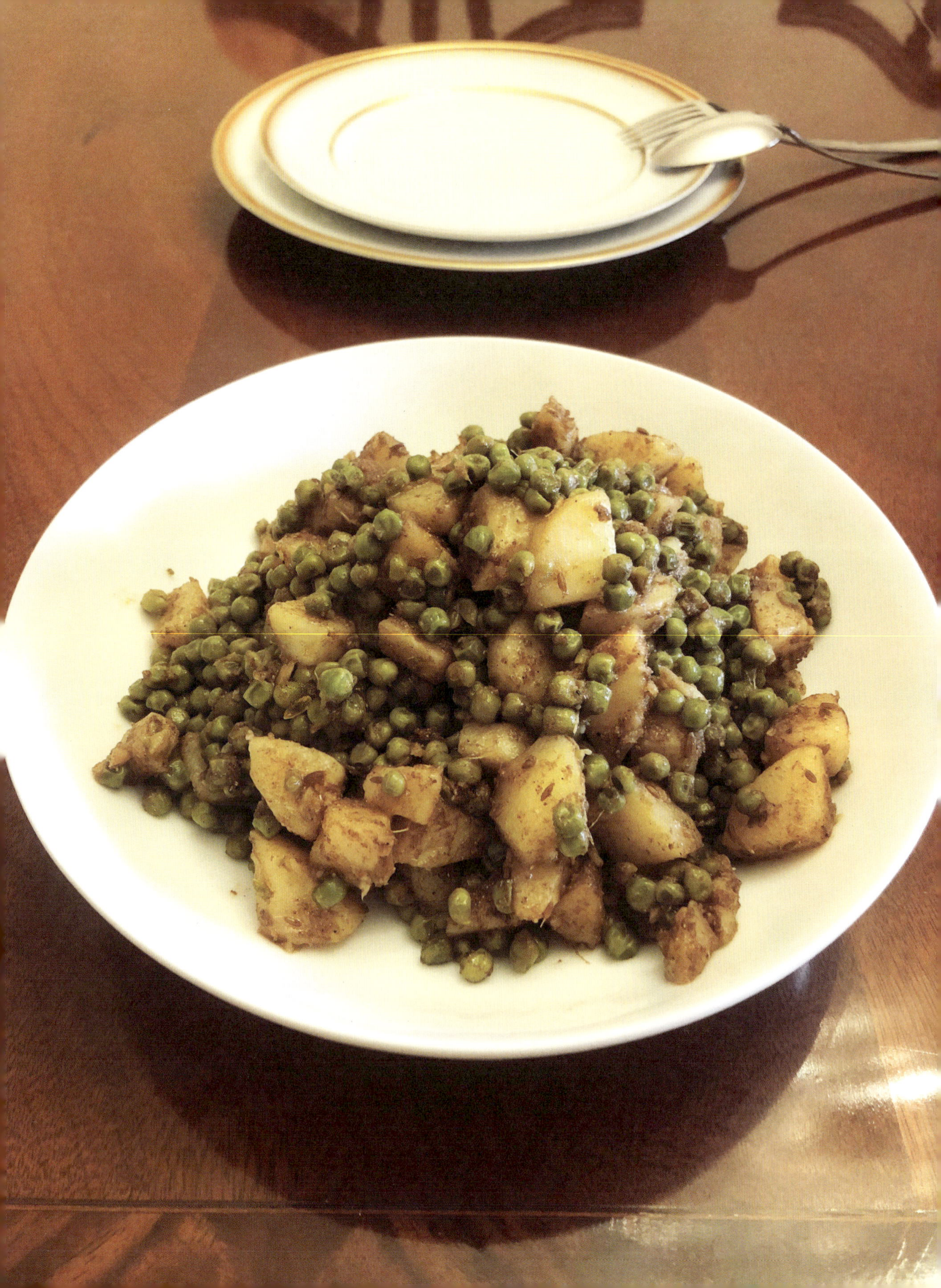

DRY VEGGIE DISHES

Peas & Potatoes

(No tomato or onion in this dish)

READY IN 30 MINS

SERVES 3-4

Indian Nanny's recipe. This is my brother's favourite vegetable dish. If he ever asks me to cook Indian for him, this is top of the list! It's handy that I usually have potatoes in my home and peas in the freezer. It's simple and easy to cook, one that my friends also usually request the recipe for.

INGREDIENTS

4 tablespoons light olive oil

5 medium white potatoes or new potatoes (approx. 700g)

450g frozen peas or petit pois

1 inch ginger, peeled & finely chopped

SPICES

1 ½ teaspoons jeera

1 teaspoon coriander powder

1 teaspoon paprika

¼ teaspoon chilli powder

4 teaspoons salt (reduce if wish)

2 teaspoons garam masala

2 heaped teaspoons mango powder

METHOD

1. Peel and chop the potatoes into 2cm cubes.

2. Put peas and potatoes into a bowl of cold water, then rinse under a cold tap and drain into a colander.

3. Put 4 tablespoons oil into a wok and heat. Add 1 ½ teaspoon jeera, 1 teaspoon coriander powder, 1 teaspoon paprika, ¼ teaspoon chilli powder. Add the ginger.

4. Give it a stir then add peas and potatoes. Add 4 teaspoons salt.

5. Give it a stir and put the lid on.

6. Simmer for 20 – 25 minutes over a medium heat until the potatoes are soft. Only stir once or twice.

7. Add 2 teaspoons garam masala and 2 heaped teaspoons mango powder.

8. Stir and turn off the heat, the dish is ready.

DRY VEGGIE DISHES

Aloo Gobi

READY IN 30 MINS **SERVES 3-4**

One of the most famous Indian vegetable dishes. This is Indian Nanny's special recipe. My friends love this one. It can be eaten hot, traditionally as part of an Indian meal, or we also like it cold or as part of a fantastic barbecue spread. Aloo gobi sandwiches or served with a salad, this veg dish is fantastic!

It's important that both the potatoes and the cauliflower florets are cut quite small. The reason for this is there will be more masala (spice) around each of the pieces, offering a more intense flavour.

Once you have mastered cooking this simple Indian vegetable, it will become a mealtime favourite.

INGREDIENTS

1 cauliflower cut into florets (it's best if you let the florets naturally break away from one another, then cut them smaller if necessary)

2 or 3 medium potatoes, peeled, cut into 2cm chunks, washed in a bowl of cold water

1 inch ginger, peeled and chopped

4 tablespoons light olive oil

Handful chopped fresh coriander for decoration (optional)

SPICES

1 heaped teaspoon jeera

¼ teaspoon chilli powder

½ teaspoon paprika powder

2 teaspoons salt (reduce if you wish)

½ teaspoon haldi

½ teaspoon garam masala

METHOD

1. Wash and cut the potatoes and cauliflower. Rinse in a colander and set to one side to drain.

2. Add the 4 tablespoons of oil to a wok on high heat. Add 1 heaped teaspoon of jeera, ¼ teaspoon of chilli powder, ½ teaspoon of paprika. Heat this for 30 seconds.

3. Add the ginger, give it a quick stir, then add the potatoes and cauliflower. Add 2 teaspoons of salt and the ½ teaspoon of haldi. Quick stir, low heat and lid on so the vegetables are simmering in the juice of the dish.

4. Cook until the potatoes are soft (approximately 20 minutes); do not stir the dish too often or vigorously as the vegetables will mash up.

5. Add ½ teaspoon garam masala and turn off the heat. Add a handful of chopped fresh coriander for decoration (optional).

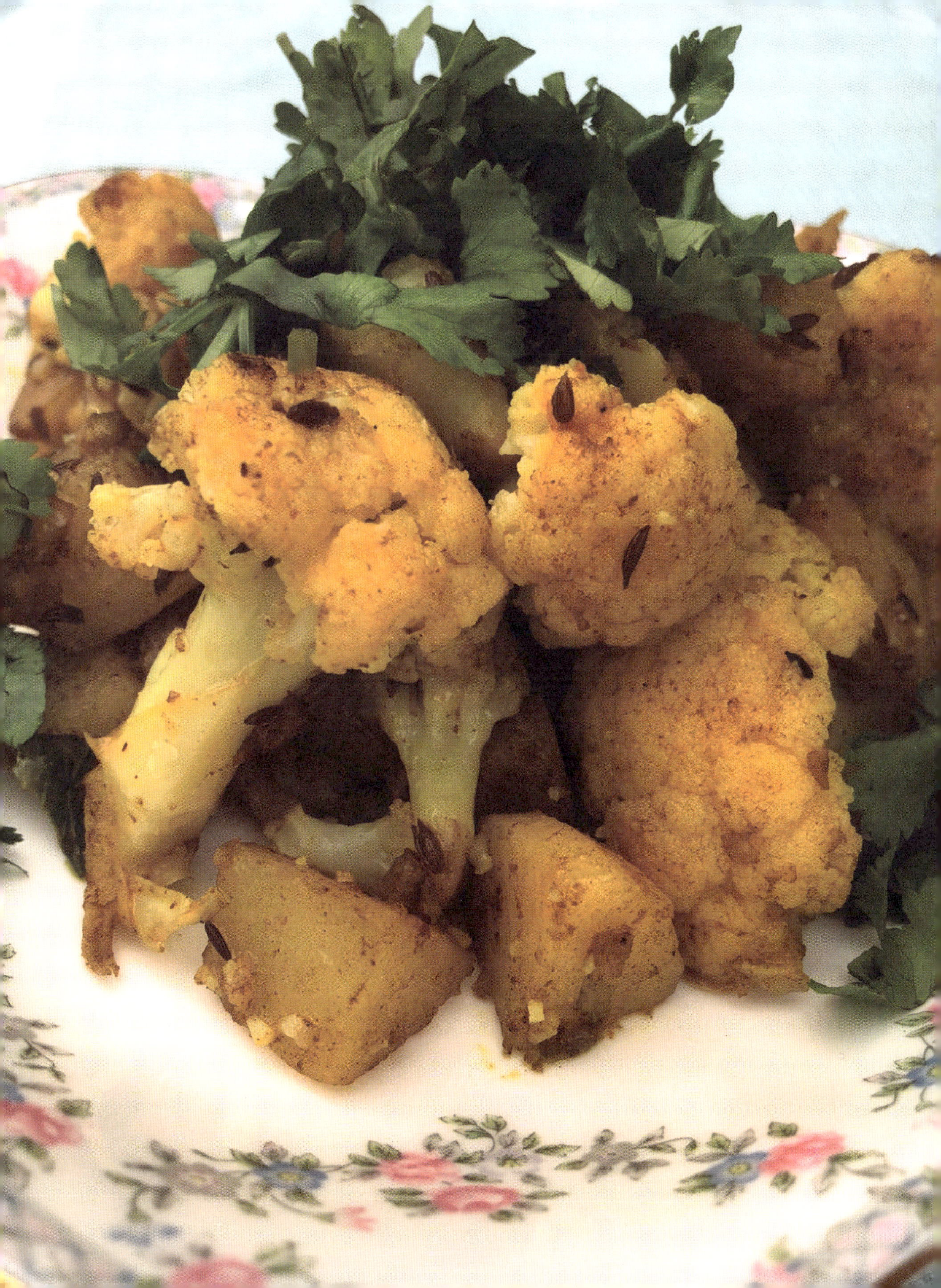

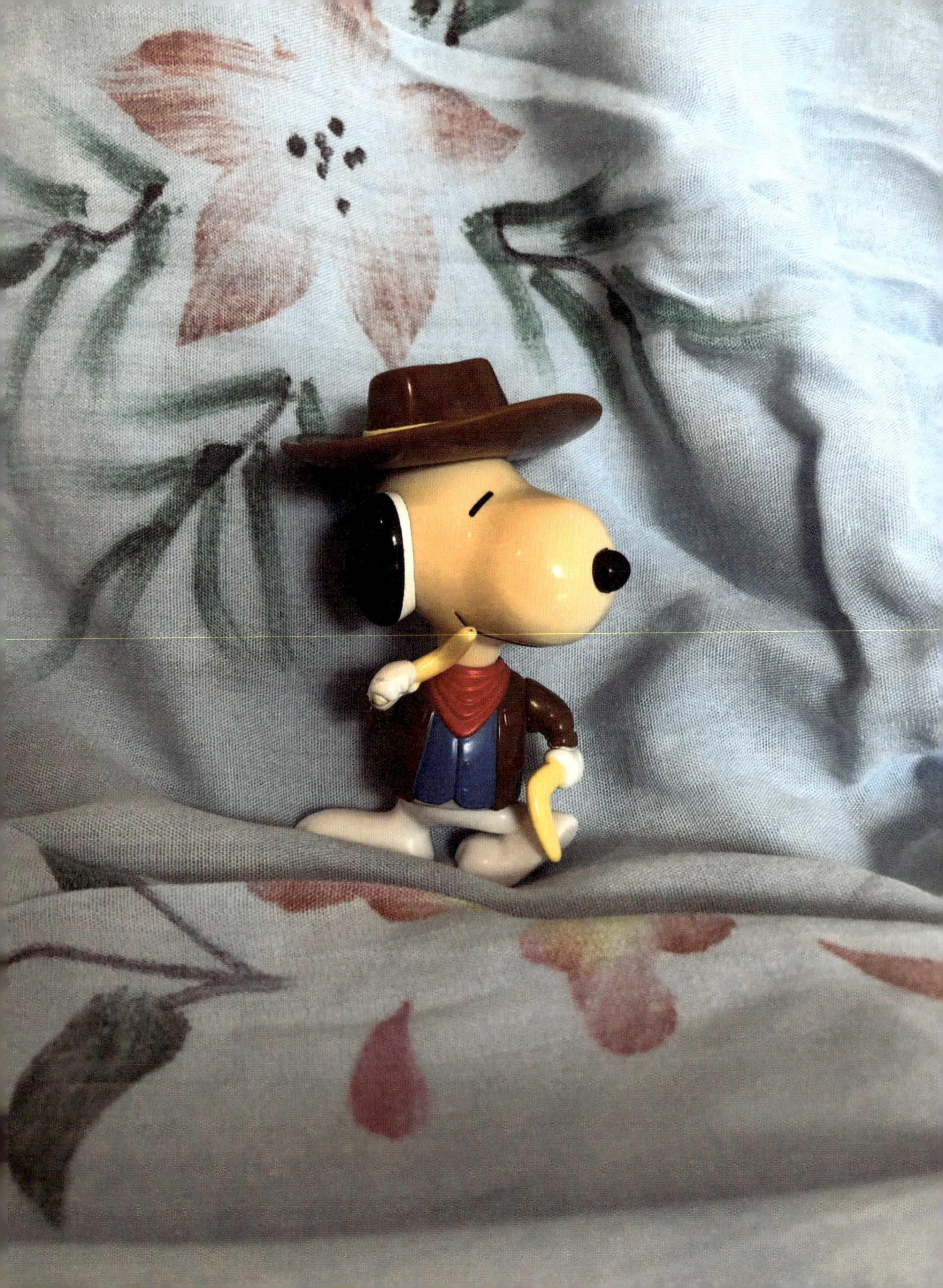

DRY VEGGIE DISHES

Aussie Auntie's Aloo Gobi

READY IN
30 MINS

SERVES
3-4

On one of our trips to Australia, an Indian Auntie living over there told me that she likes to cook Aloo Gobi with black mustard seeds as well as slightly less oil and salt. It is a nice variation.

METHOD

1. Wash and cut the potatoes and cauliflower. Rinse in a colander and set to one side to drain.

2. Add the 1 tablespoon of oil to a wok on high heat. Add 1 teaspoon of jeera, 1 teaspoon black mustard seeds, ¼ teaspoon of chilli powder, ½ teaspoon of paprika. Heat this for 30 seconds.

3. Add the ginger, give it a quick stir then add the potatoes and cauliflower. Add 1 teaspoon of salt and the ½ teaspoon of haldi. Quick stir, low heat and lid on so the vegetables are simmering in the juice of the dish.

4. Cook until the potatoes are soft (approximately 15-20 minutes); do not stir the dish too often or vigorously as the vegetables will mash up.

5. Add ½ teaspoon garam masala and turn off the heat.

6. Handful of chopped fresh coriander for decoration (optional).

INGREDIENTS

1 tablespoon light olive oil

1 cauliflower cut into florets (it's best if you let the florets naturally break away from one another, then cut them smaller if necessary)

2 or 3 medium potatoes, peeled, cut into 2cm chunks, washed in a bowl of cold water

1 inch ginger, peeled & chopped

Handful chopped fresh coriander for decoration (optional)

SPICES

1 teaspoon jeera

1 teaspoon black mustard seeds

¼ teaspoon chilli powder

½ teaspoon paprika powder

1 teaspoon salt (level)

½ teaspoon haldi

½ teaspoon garam masala

DRY VEGGIE DISHES

Auntie Veena's Aloo Gobi

READY IN 30 MINS

SERVES 3-4

Auntie Veena likes to use up whatever's in her fridge! So, to this traditional dish she will often add a sliced carrot and a cup of peas. It's great as it adds some extra colour to this beautiful dish.

METHOD

1. Wash and cut the potatoes, cauliflower, carrot and peas. Rinse in a colander and set to one side to drain.

2. Add the 4 tablespoons of oil to a wok on high heat. Add 1 heaped teaspoon of jeera, ½ teaspoon of chilli powder, 1 teaspoon of paprika. Heat this for 30 seconds.

3. Add the ginger, give it a quick stir then add the potatoes, cauliflower, carrot and peas. Add 2 teaspoons of salt and the 1 teaspoon of haldi. Quick stir, low heat and lid on so the vegetables are simmering in the juice of the dish.

4. Cook until the potatoes are soft (approximately 20 minutes); do not stir the dish too often or vigorously as the vegetables will mash up.

5. Add 1 teaspoon garam masala and turn off the heat. Handful of chopped fresh coriander for decoration (optional).

INGREDIENTS

1 cauliflower cut into florets (it's best if you let the florets naturally break away from one another, then cut them smaller if necessary)

2 or 3 medium potatoes, peeled, cut into 2cm chunks, washed in a bowl of cold water

1 carrot, peeled and sliced

1 cup peas

1 inch ginger, peeled & chopped

4 tablespoons light olive oil

Handful chopped fresh coriander for decoration (optional)

SPICES

1 heaped teaspoon jeera

½ teaspoon chilli powder

1 teaspoon paprika powder

2 teaspoons salt

1 teaspoon haldi

1 teaspoon garam masala

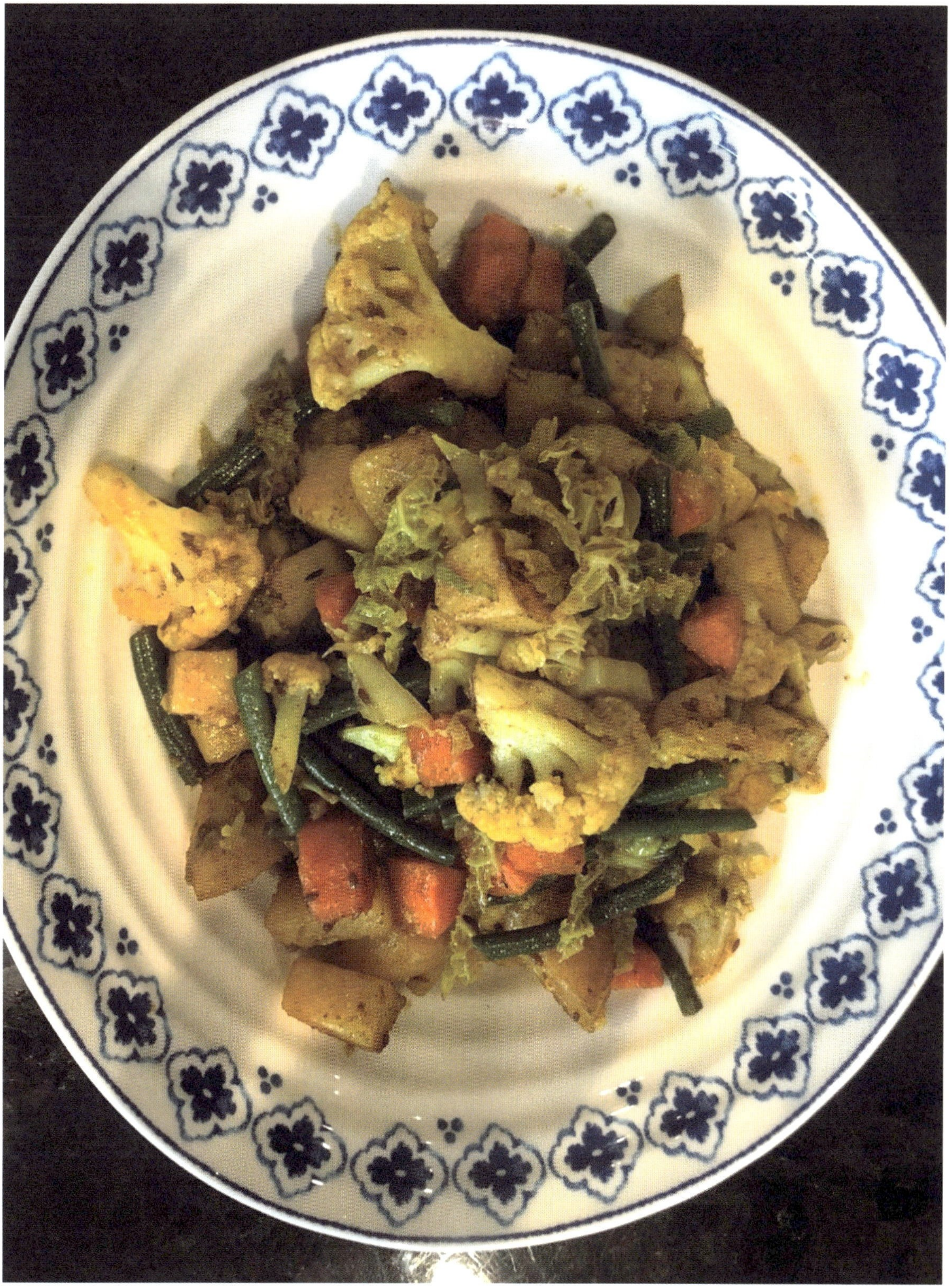

DRY VEGGIE DISHES

Methi Aloo

READY IN 30 MINS
SERVES 3-4

As a child this was a popular dish at Indian Nanny's house, this is her recipe. Be warned methi or fenugreek leaves are potent – the smell can come out in your pores for days after eating this delicious dish!

India is a large producer of methi due to the warm climate. This herb plant is known as a traditional and powerful natural remedy used all over the world for treating a wide variety of conditions.

This recipe also works well if you want to swap the methi for a bag of spinach leaves.

INGREDIENTS

2 tablespoons light olive oil

2 bunches of methi (fenugreek) leaves

450g potatoes

SPICES

1 teaspoon jeera

Pinch chilli powder

¼ teaspoon paprika

1 teaspoon salt

1 teaspoon garam masala

METHOD

1. Peel and chop the potatoes into 2cm cubes, put in a bowl of cold water.

2. Wash and chop the methi leaves, removing any wilted / discoloured leaves.

3. Add 2 tablespoons of oil to a wok on a medium heat for a few minutes. Add 1 teaspoon jeera, pinch chilli powder, ¼ teaspoon paprika.

4. Rinse the methi and potatoes in a colander, then add the methi and the potatoes with 1 teaspoon salt to the wok.

5. Stir and cover, cook on a medium to low heat until the potatoes are soft (approx. 20-25 minutes); remove the lid towards the end of this time so the water can evaporate.

6. Add 1 teaspoon of garam masala and continue to cook for a few minutes until the vegetable is dry, then turn off the heat. It is important that there isn't any water left as it will make the vegetable taste bitter.

Note – Auntie Veena's secret is to add a teaspoon of oil once cooked to make the veg look shiny.

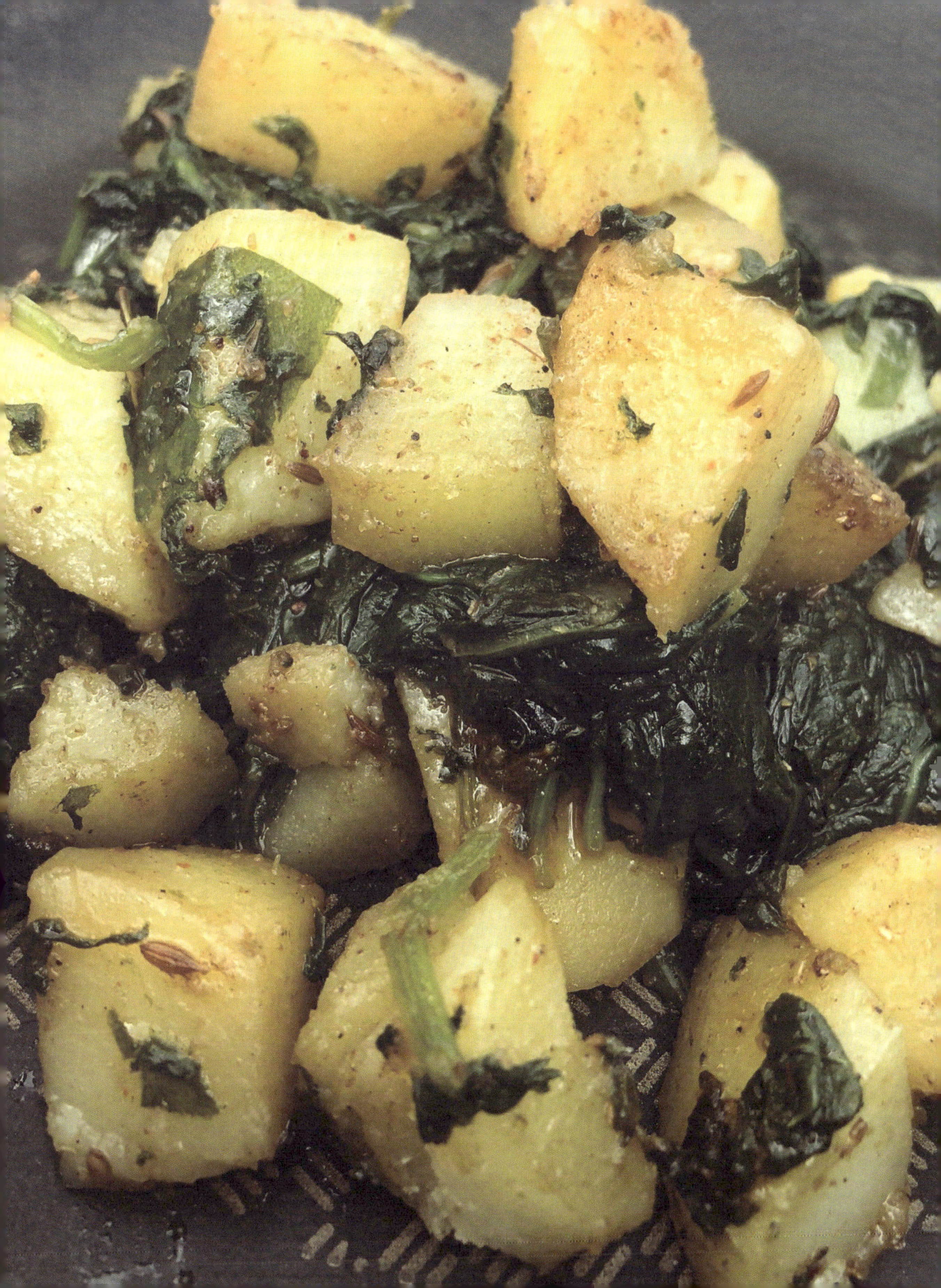

DRY VEGGIE DISHES

Dundal Aloo

READY IN 30 MINS **SERVES 3-4**

One of my grandad's favourite vegetable dishes, this is Indian Nanny's recipe. It's great not to waste the beautiful leaves of the cauliflower by using them in this dish.

INGREDIENTS

2 tablespoons light olive oil

2 medium potatoes

Root & leaf of 1 whole cauliflower, washed (not the actual cauliflower)

SPICES

½ teaspoon jeera

Pinch chilli powder

¼ teaspoon paprika (for colour)

1 teaspoon salt

1 teaspoon mango powder

½ teaspoon garam masala

METHOD

1. Peel, wash and chop the potatoes into 2cm cubes, put in a bowl of cold water.

2. Chop the very end bit off the stalk and discard as well as the very outer leaves of the cauliflower, if worse for wear or anything slightly brown. Chop the rest up and rinse through a colander with the potatoes.

3. Add the oil to a wok on a medium heat, add the jeera, chilli powder and paprika. Heat the spices for 30 seconds.

4. Add cauliflower leaves, root and potatoes, 1 teaspoon of salt, give it a stir. Then simmer on a low / medium heat with the lid on until the potatoes are cooked, approximately 15-20 minutes.

5. Stir a few times during cooking.

6. Add 1 teaspoon mango powder and ½ teaspoon garam masala once the dish is done. Stir and turn off the heat.

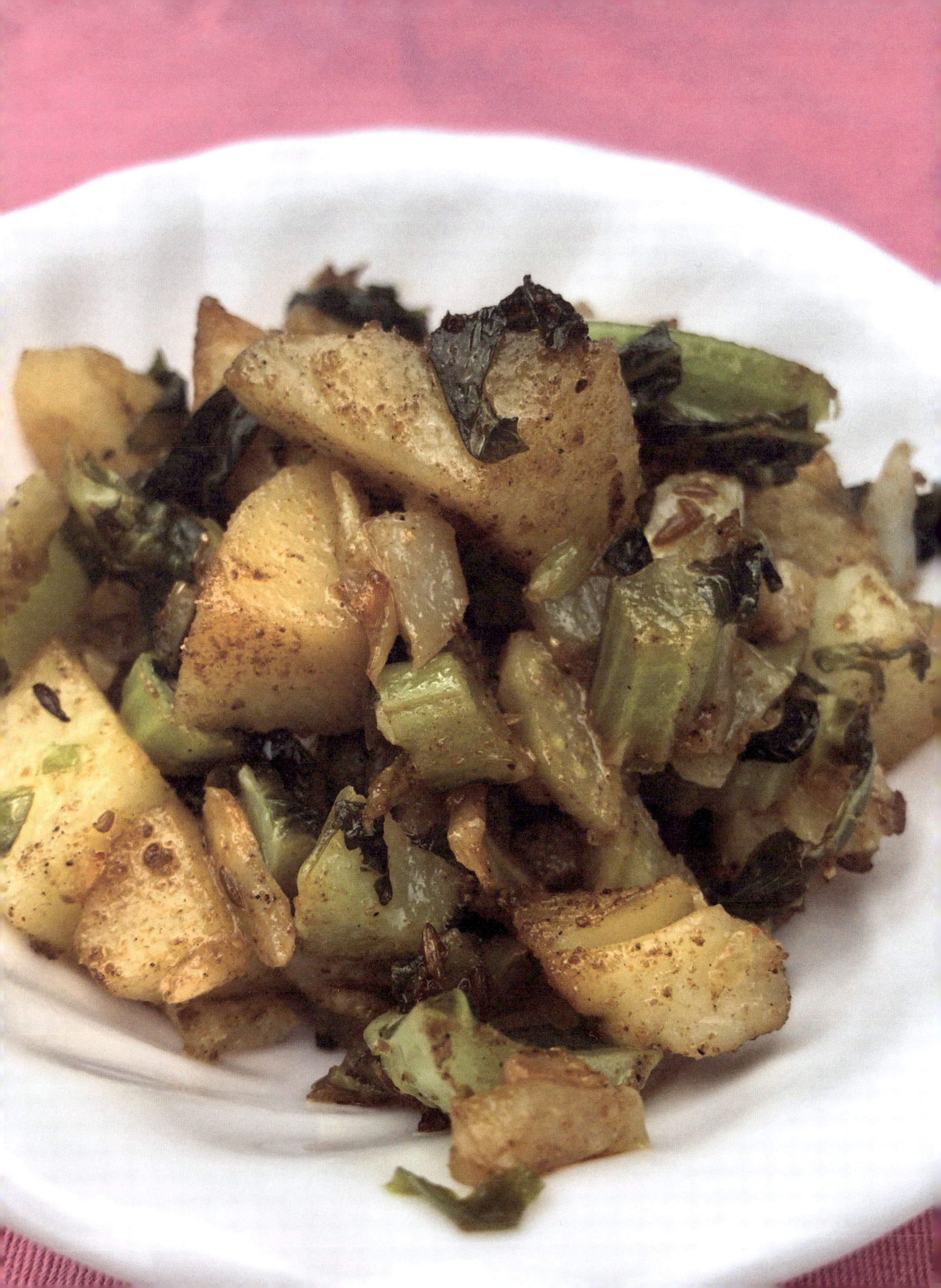

DRY VEGGIE DISHES

Shell of Peas or Sugar Snaps & Aloo

READY IN 30 MINS   **SERVES** 3-4

I never knew about this dish! Traditionally, this is cooked using the shell of peas and potatoes. My Auntie Veena talked me through it and I find it amazing how great it is not to waste any veg – even if we would usually put the shells on the compost! She explained that Seema used to shell the peas for Biji to cook this dish in the 80s.

I also vary this dish, using sugar snaps rather than shells of peas and it works very well.

INGREDIENTS

3 tablespoons light olive oil

1 medium onion, peeled and sliced

2 medium potatoes – washed and chopped into 2cm cubes

200g shells of peas or sugar snaps; if they are big cut them in half

SPICES

1 teaspoon jeera

¼ teaspoon chilli powder

½ teaspoon paprika

1 ½ teaspoons salt

1 teaspoon mango powder

1 teaspoon garam masala

METHOD

1. Add the oil to a wok on a medium heat, add the jeera, chilli powder and paprika. Heat the spices for 30 seconds.

2. Add the onion, give a stir and cook until the onions are pink.

3. Add the potatoes and the salt. Cook on a low to medium heat with the lid on for 5 minutes, then add the shell of the peas or sugar snaps.

4. Gently stir a few times during cooking.

5. Cook for 15 – 20 minutes until the potatoes are cooked.

6. Add 1 teaspoon mango powder and 1 teaspoon garam masala once the dish is done. Turn off the heat.

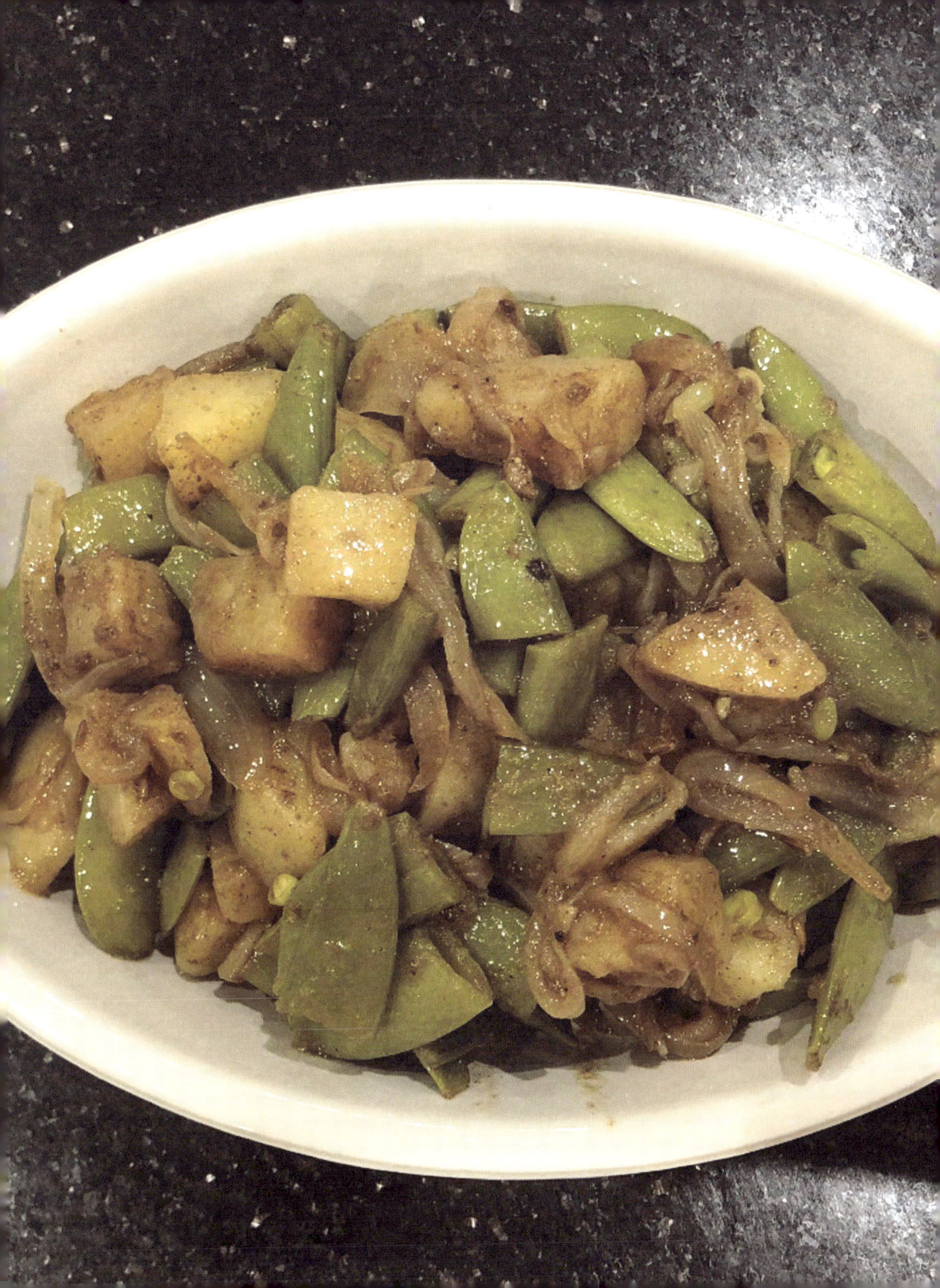

DRY VEGGIE DISHES

Natasha's Mixed Veg

READY IN 30 MINS

SERVES 4-6

The good thing with this veg dish is that you can use whatever you have in the fridge!

INGREDIENTS

½ cauliflower cut into small florets (it's best if you let the florets naturally break away from one another, then cut them smaller if necessary)

2 or 3 medium potatoes, peeled, cut into 2cm chunks, washed in a bowl of cold water

1 carrot, peeled and sliced

Cup peas or handful green beans, chopped

½ cabbage

4 tablespoons light olive oil

1 inch ginger, peeled & chopped

Handful chopped fresh coriander for decoration (optional)

SPICES

1 heaped teaspoon jeera

1 teaspoon paprika powder

½ teaspoon chilli powder

2 teaspoons salt

1 teaspoon haldi

1 teaspoon garam masala

METHOD

1. Wash and cut all the vegetables. Rinse in a colander and set to one side to drain.

2. Add the 4 tablespoons of oil to a wok on high heat. Add 1 heaped teaspoon of jeera, ½ teaspoon of chilli powder, 1 teaspoon of paprika. Heat this for 30 seconds.

3. Add the ginger, give it a quick stir then add all the veg. Add 2 teaspoons of salt and the 1 teaspoon of haldi. Quick stir, low heat and lid on so the vegetables are simmering in the juice of the dish.

4. Cook until the potatoes are soft (approximately 20 minutes); do not stir the dish too often or vigorously as the vegetables will mash up.

5. Add 1 teaspoon garam masala and turn off the heat. Handful of chopped fresh coriander for decoration (optional).

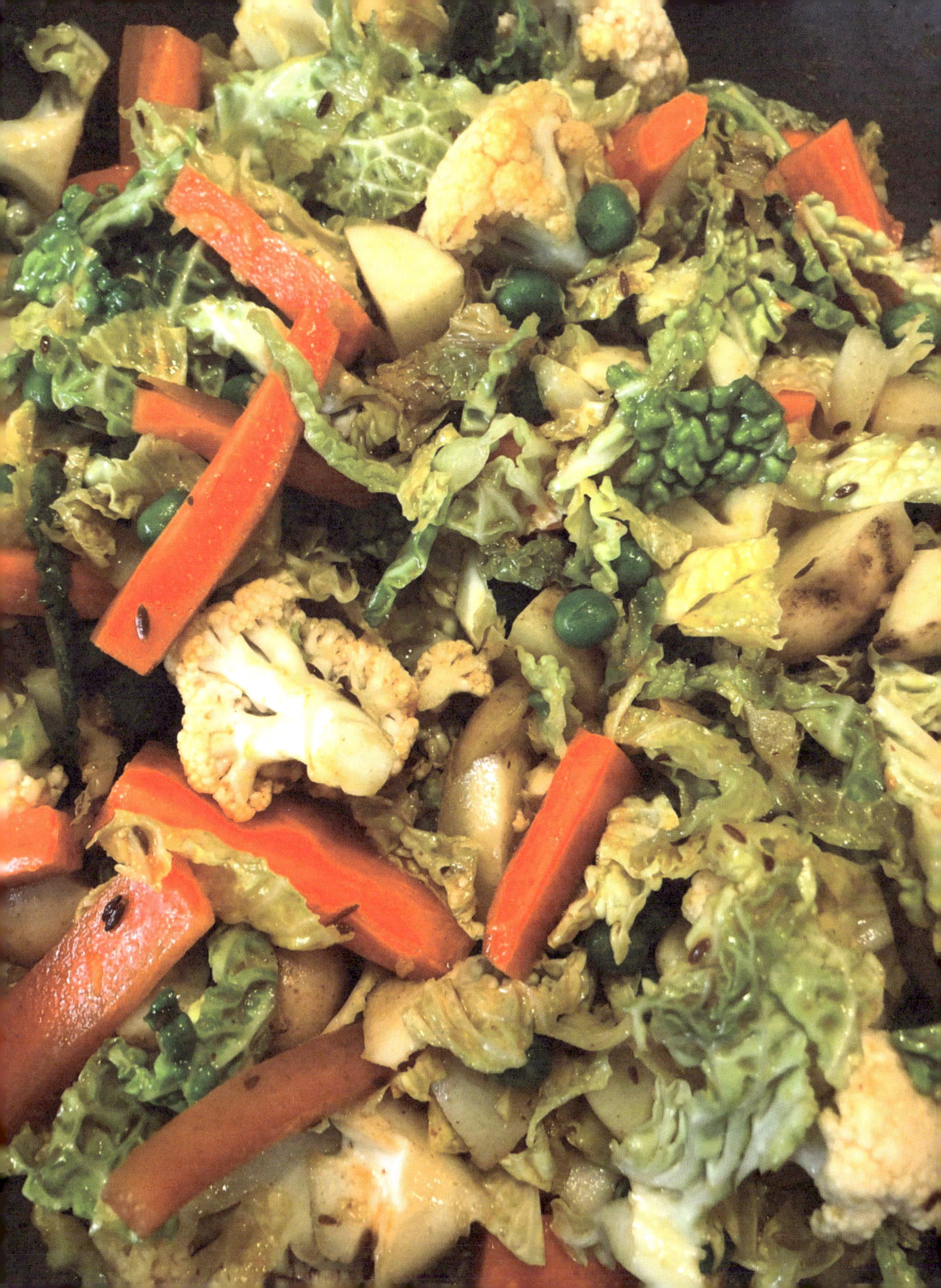

DRY VEGGIE DISHES

Carrots & Peas

READY IN
30 MINS

SERVES
3-4

INGREDIENTS

6 carrots, peeled & sliced in circles (about 0.5cm thick)

2 cups frozen peas or petit pois

3 tablespoons light olive oil

4 teaspoons sugar

SPICES

1 teaspoon jeera

2 teaspoons salt

¼ heaped teaspoon haldi

½ heaped teaspoon coriander powder

½ heaped teaspoon paprika

¼ teaspoon chilli powder

½ heaped teaspoon garam masala

2 heaped teaspoons mango powder

Indian Nanny's recipe – A simple and quick Indian veg to cook. This is Rakhee's childhood favourite. We usually always have carrots in our fridge (thanks to having ponies) and peas in the freezer. My grandad always preferred petit pois as they are slightly smaller, sweeter and he said they taste better with the Indian veg dishes.

I think it's interesting that the traditional Brit dish is also an Indian classic!

METHOD

1. Wash the peas and carrots in a colander, set aside to drain.

2. Heat the oil in a wok over a medium heat with the jeera until warm (30 seconds), add the peas and carrots.

3. Add the salt, haldi, coriander powder, paprika and chilli powder.

4. Give a gentle stir, put on a low heat, cover with a lid and cook for about 15 minutes until vegetables are cooked.

5. Add the sugar, garam masala and mango powder. Give it a gentle stir.

6. Turn the heat off and leave for a few more minutes with the lid on before serving.

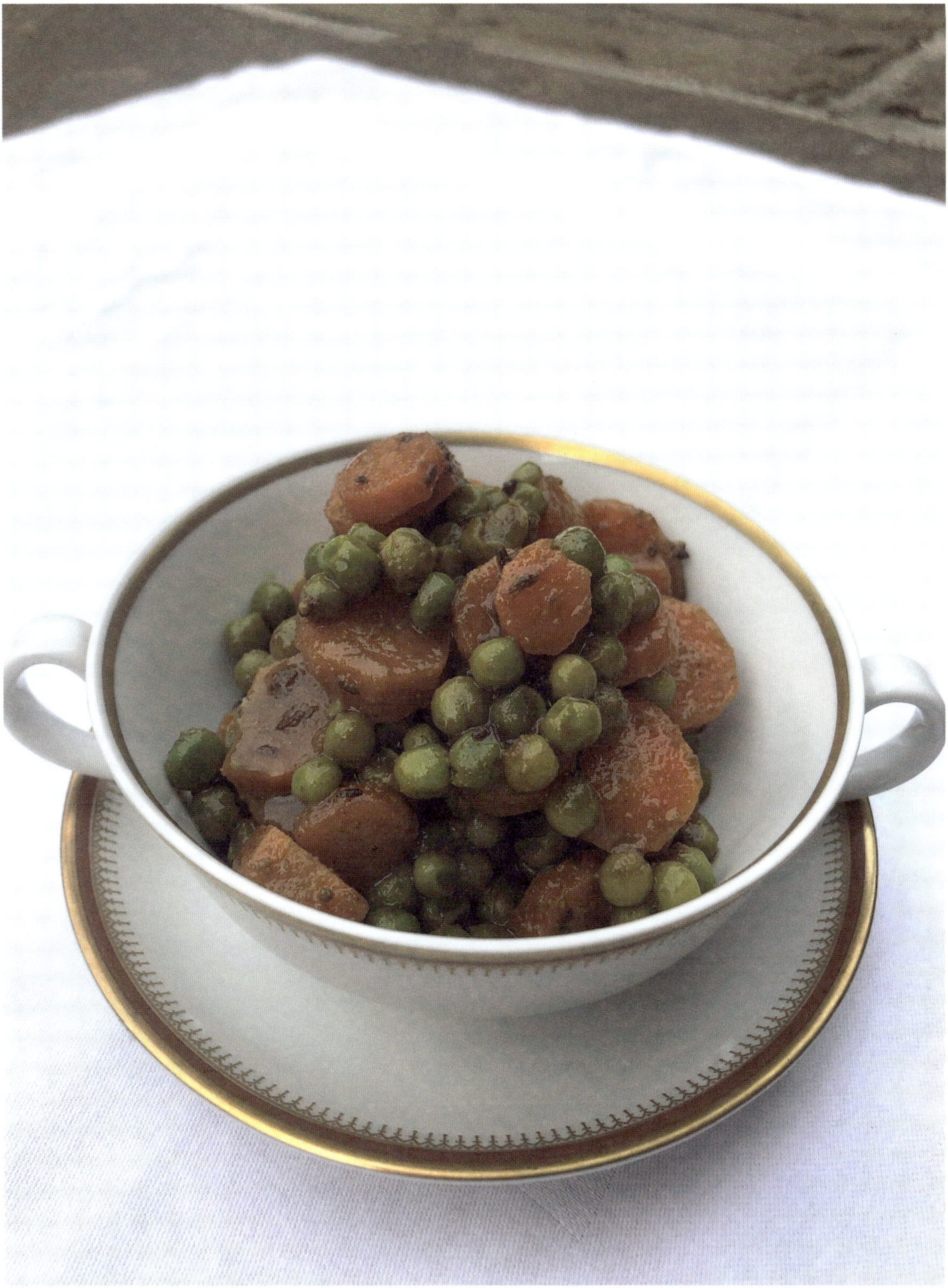

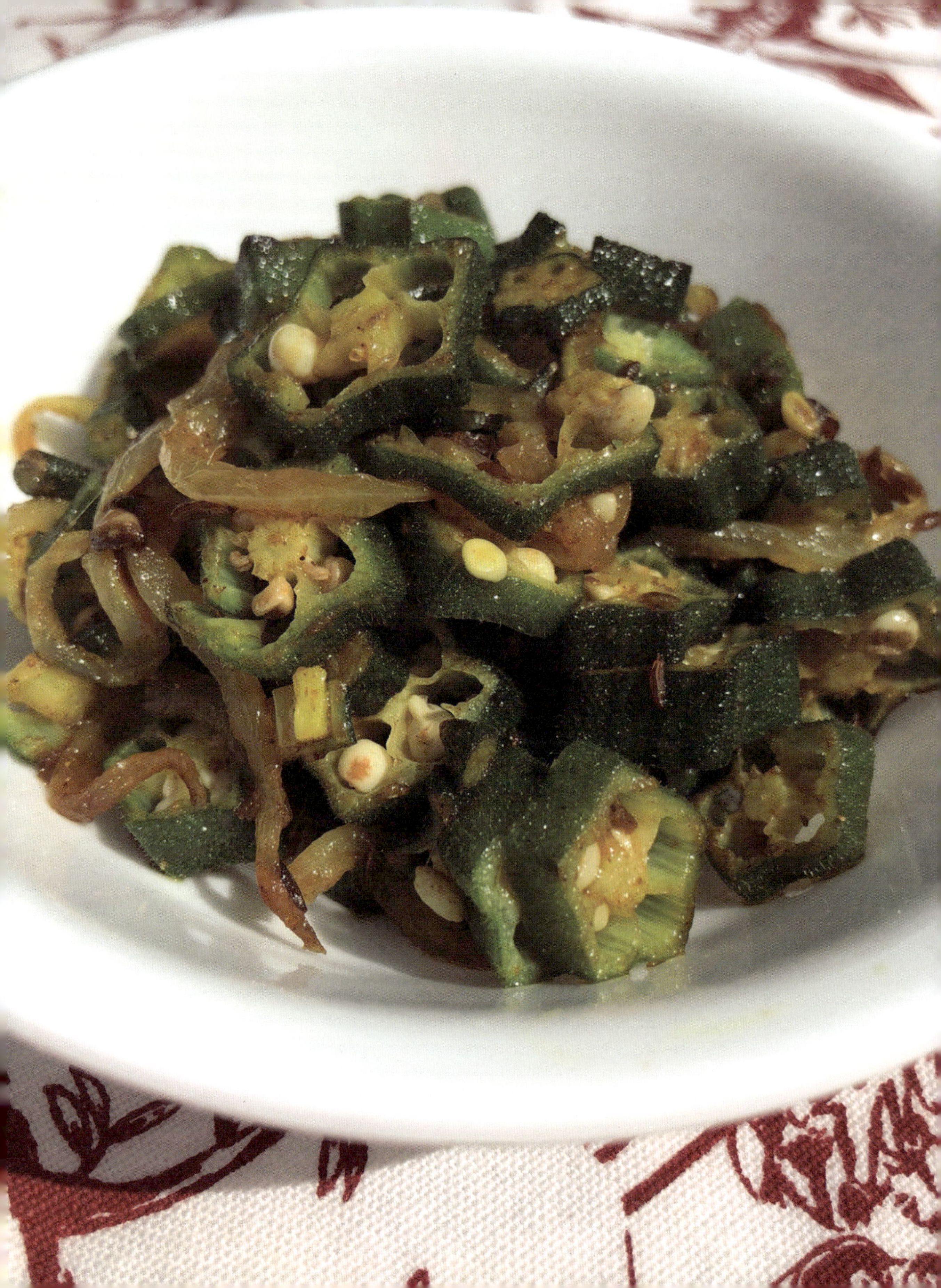

DRY VEGGIE DISHES

Bhindi

READY IN 20 MINS

SERVES 3-4

Bhindi, lady's finger or okra as it is more commonly known. This is a quick dish to cook. Lady's finger again is one of my dad's favourite vegetables, so I was delighted when Indian Nanny showed me how to cook it; however, totally disappointed when I cooked it for Dad and it turned out slimy. It took me at least 3 or 4 attempts at trying to cook these as my Nan had showed me before I worked out what was wrong!

Indian Nanny would always wash the vegetable in the morning, then leave it to dry in a colander until the evening. That way the vegetable was totally dry. I didn't see this as I was at work in the day and pitched up to see the cooking process. The key is to make sure you wash and DRY the okra prior to cooking otherwise it becomes slimy when you start to heat them and not as appetising at all. Therefore, I usually wash them and either dry them using kitchen paper or wash them and leave them to dry in the colander for a few hours.

You can buy the okra, then wash, dry, cut it and freeze it in a bag. You can then cook this dish really quickly from frozen.

INGREDIENTS

3 tablespoons light olive oil

2 medium onions – peeled and thinly sliced

350g / approx. 4 handfuls of bhindi

SPICES

1 teaspoon jeera

1 teaspoon coriander powder

1 teaspoon salt

¼ teaspoon haldi

½ teaspoon paprika

Pinch chilli powder

½ teaspoon garam masala

METHOD

1. Wash and thoroughly dry the bhindi. Top and tail, then chop them horizontally so they are little circles and look like stars!

2. Heat the oil in a wok on a medium heat, add the onions and fry until soft (approximately 5 minutes).

3. Add 1 teaspoon of jeera, give it a stir and cook for another couple of minutes.

4. Then add 1 teaspoon coriander powder, 1 teaspoon salt, ¼ teaspoon haldi, ½ teaspoon paprika and the pinch of chilli powder.

5. Add the chopped bhindi, stir a few times, cover and simmer over a low heat for approximately 5-10 minutes until the vegetable is soft.

6. Once cooked, turn off the heat and add ½ teaspoon garam masala.

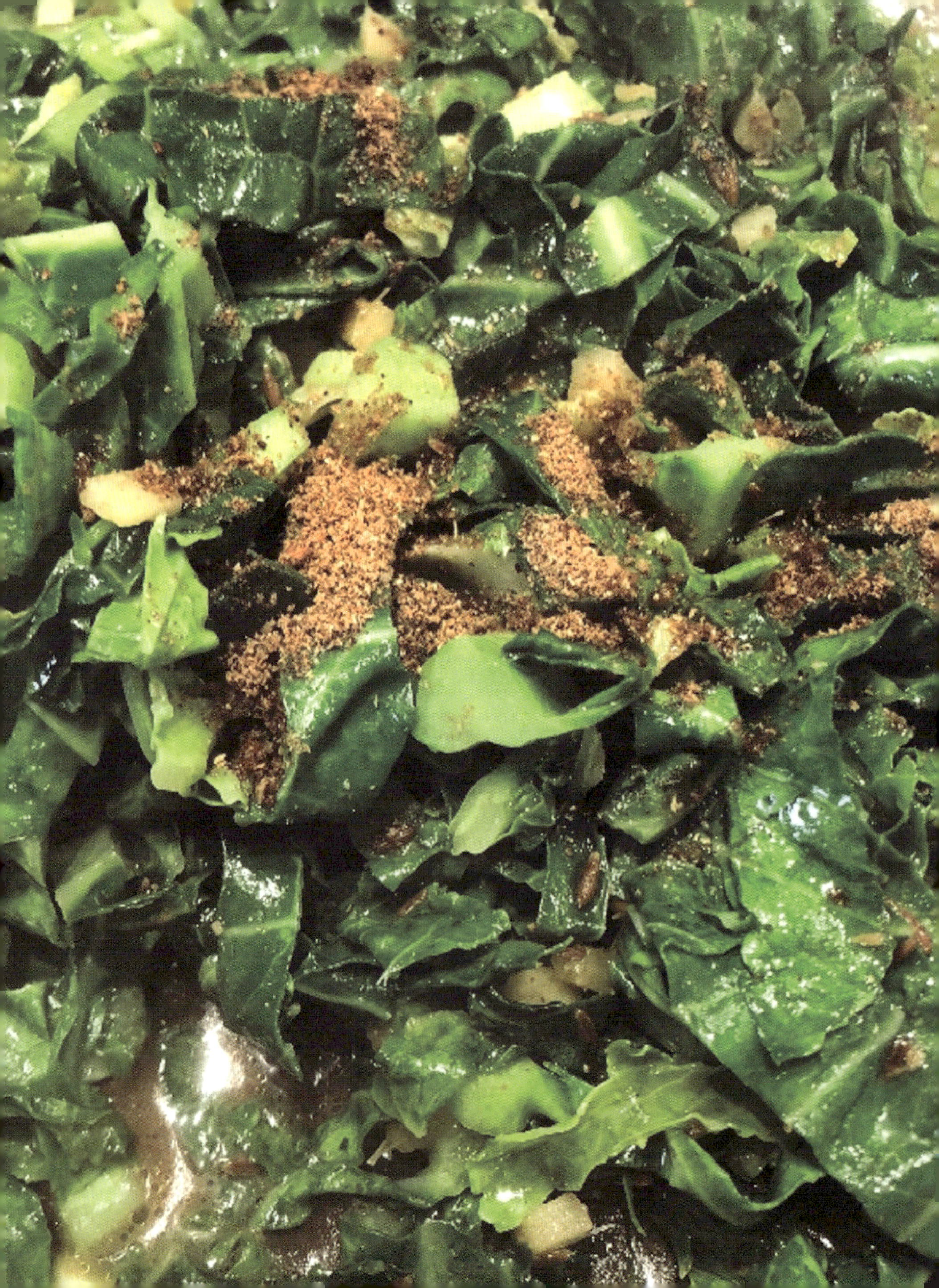

DRY VEGGIE DISHES

Spring Greens

READY IN
20 MINS

SERVES
3-4

Quick to cook as it will steam through in a matter of minutes. All green vegetables, especially dark green veg, are packed with vitamins. Indian Nanny taught me to cook this one.

INGREDIENTS

1 packet spring greens (approx. 200g), washed and chopped

2 tablespoons light olive oil

1 inch ginger, peeled and finely chopped

SPICES

1 teaspoon jeera

1 teaspoon coriander powder

1 teaspoon salt

½ teaspoon paprika

¼ teaspoon chilli powder

½ teaspoon garam masala

METHOD

1. Add the jeera and coriander powder to the oil in a wok on a medium to high heat.

2. Once these spices are warm, add the greens, ginger, the salt, paprika and chilli powder.

3. Cover and cook over a medium heat. The vegetable will cook in its own water in about 7 minutes.

4. Once the water has dried, take the lid off, add the garam masala and the dish is ready.

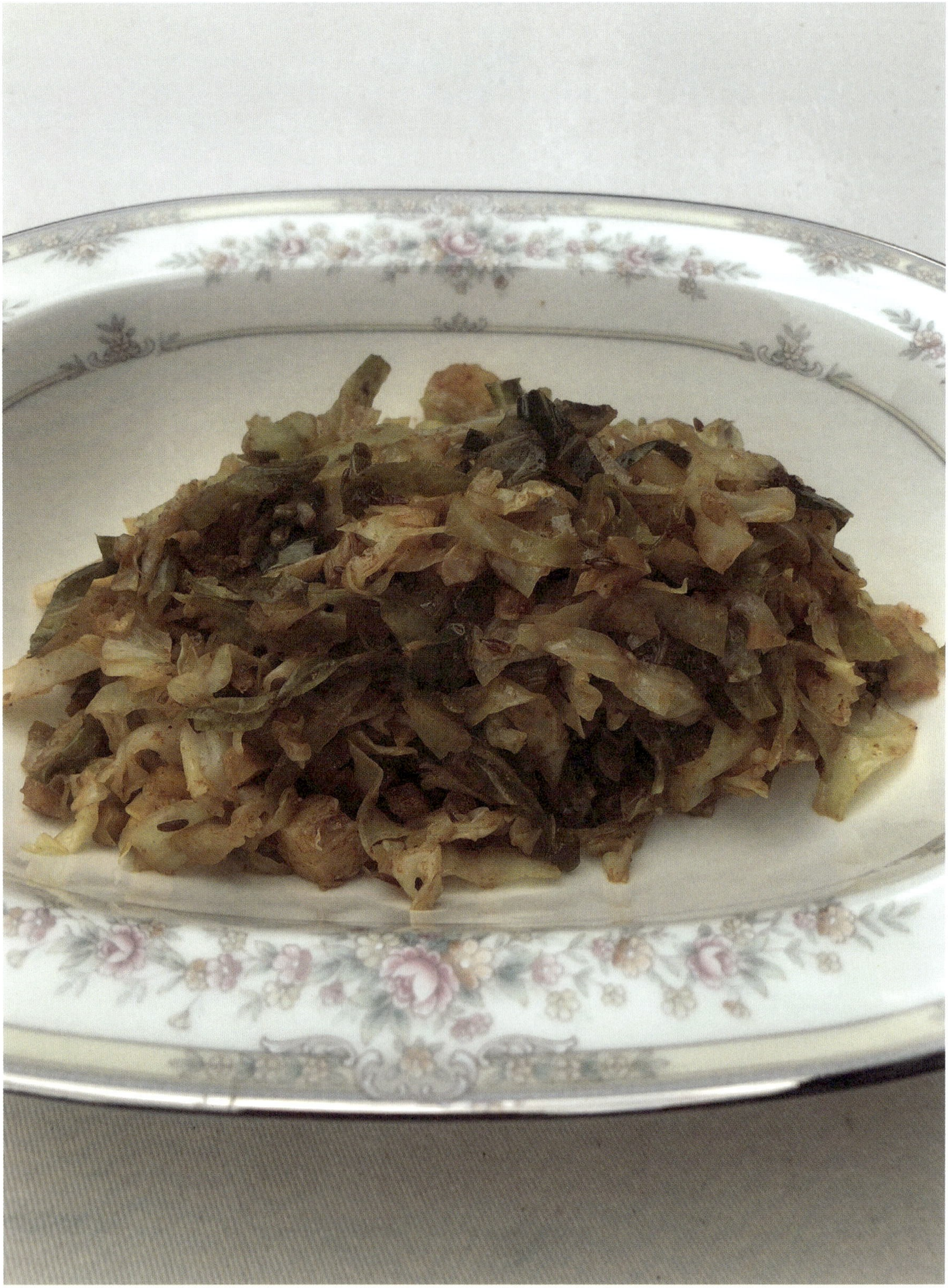

DRY VEGGIE DISHES

Cabbage

READY IN 20 MINS

SERVES 3-4

Indian Nanny's recipe. Any cabbage can be used for this dish, although I haven't tried it with a red cabbage… yet!

INGREDIENTS

1 sweetheart or any other cabbage, washed and chopped

2 tablespoons light olive oil

2 teaspoons sugar (optional)

SPICES

1 teaspoon jeera

1 teaspoon coriander powder

1 teaspoon salt

½ teaspoon paprika

¼ teaspoon chilli powder

½ teaspoon garam masala

METHOD

1. Add the jeera and coriander powder to the oil in a wok on a medium to high heat.

2. Once these spices are warm, add the cabbage, the salt, paprika and chilli powder.

3. Give it a quick stir, then cover and cook over a medium heat.

4. The vegetable will cook in its own water, this will take about 10 minutes.

5. Once the water has dried, take the lid off, add the garam masala & 2 teaspoons sugar, give it a quick stir and then the dish is ready.

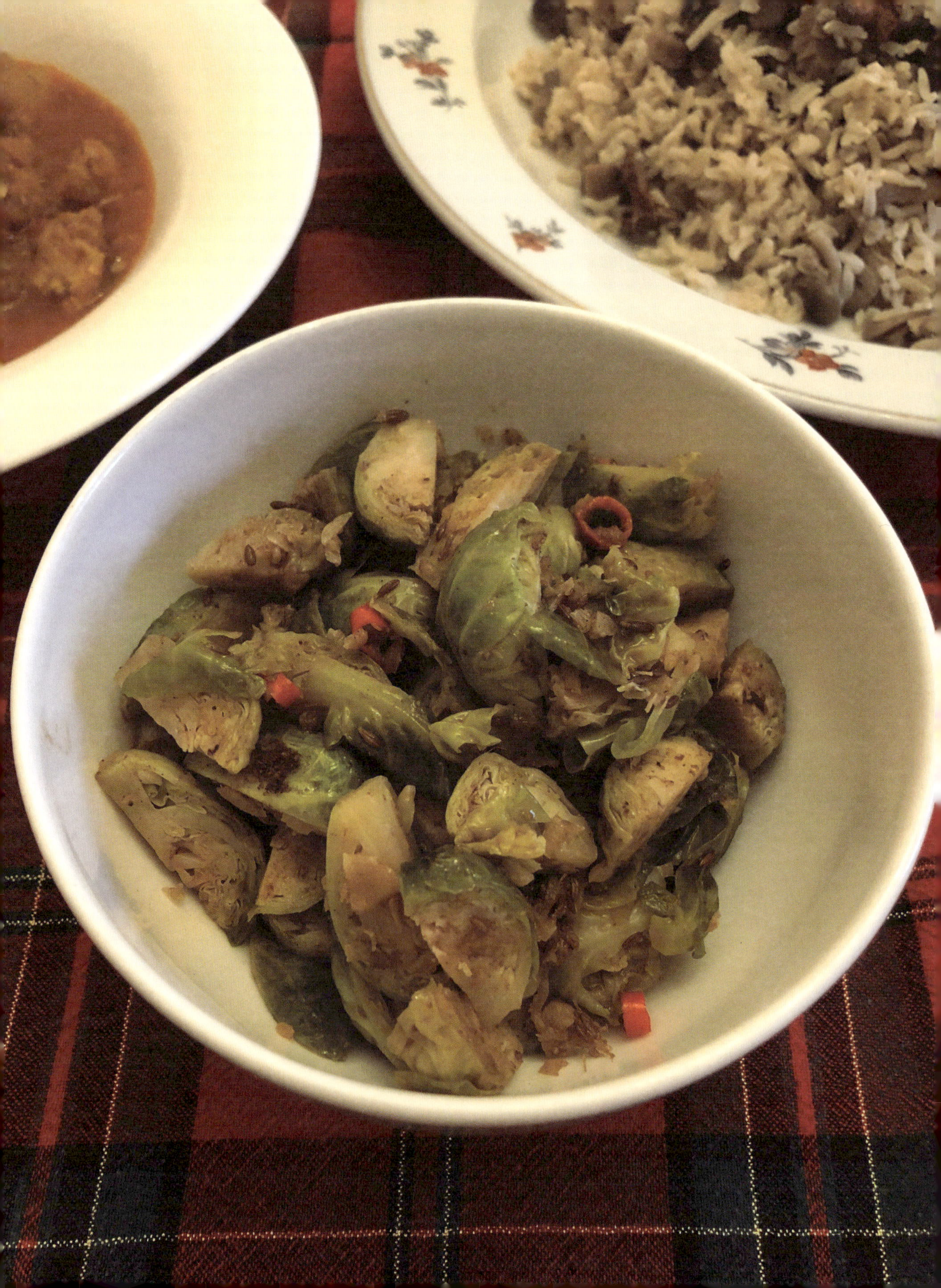

DRY VEGGIE DISHES

Sprouts Indian Style!

READY IN 20 MINS

SERVES 3-4

INGREDIENTS

1 packet sprouts (approx. 500g)

2 tablespoons light olive oil

1 inch ginger, remove the skin, finely chop and wash

½ red chilli, deseeded and chopped into slices (optional)

SPICES

1 teaspoon jeera

1 teaspoon coriander powder

1 teaspoon salt

½ teaspoon paprika

¼ teaspoon chilli powder

½ teaspoon garam masala

This is a great dry veg dish to accompany the turkey curry. You will never look at these little green fellas as the underrated Christmas veg again!

If you cook your sprouts "al dente" and have them left over from Christmas, they can also be used in this dish as an alternative to fresh sprouts. I have also been known to add any left-over Christmas veg (cabbage, carrots, cauliflower). Carrots especially work well as they are slightly sweet and add great colour.

METHOD

1. Take the outer layers of the sprouts off if necessary and chop a little off the stalk end. Wash and chop them into quarters, half or shredded – however you prefer your sprouts! Leave to drain.

2. Add the jeera and coriander powder to the oil in a wok on a medium to high heat.

3. Once these spices are warm, add the ginger and give a quick stir.

4. Then add the sprouts, fresh chilli, salt, paprika and chilli powder.

5. Give it a quick stir, then cover with a lid and cook over a medium heat.

6. The vegetable will cook in its own water, this will take about 10 minutes.

7. Once the water has dried, take the lid off, add ½ teaspoon garam masala, give it a quick stir and then the dish is ready.

DRY VEGGIE DISHES

Peppers & Potatoes

READY IN 40 MINS   **SERVES** 3-4

Indian Nanny's recipe. This is a great vegetable that goes well with English and Indian cooking. Quick to prepare and cook.

INGREDIENTS

2 tablespoons light olive oil

½ onion, peeled and finely sliced

2 peppers – any colour (red, yellow or orange works well as green can be a little bitter)

6 small potatoes

Large handful of chopped fresh coriander (optional)

SPICES

1 ½ teaspoons salt

½ teaspoon jeera

½ teaspoon coriander powder

½ teaspoon paprika

½ teaspoon haldi

½ heaped teaspoon garam masala

½ heaped teaspoon mango powder

METHOD

1. Add 2 tablespoons of oil to a wok, put on a medium heat. Add the finely sliced onion and cook on a medium heat.

2. While this is cooking, peel and cut your potatoes into 2cm cubes, wash and drain.

3. Wash and deseed the peppers, cut into 3cm pieces.

4. Once the onion is cooked (not too brown) add 1 ½ teaspoons salt, the potatoes and the peppers.

5. Give it a quick stir.

6. Then add ½ teaspoon jeera, ½ teaspoon coriander powder, ½ teaspoon paprika and ½ teaspoon haldi.

7. Cook on a low heat with the lid on.

8. Simmer and stir very occasionally until the potatoes are cooked, approximately 20-25 minutes.

9. Once cooked, add ½ heaped teaspoon garam masala, ½ heaped teaspoon mango powder.

10. Gently stir.

11. Serve with a large handful of fresh coriander on top.

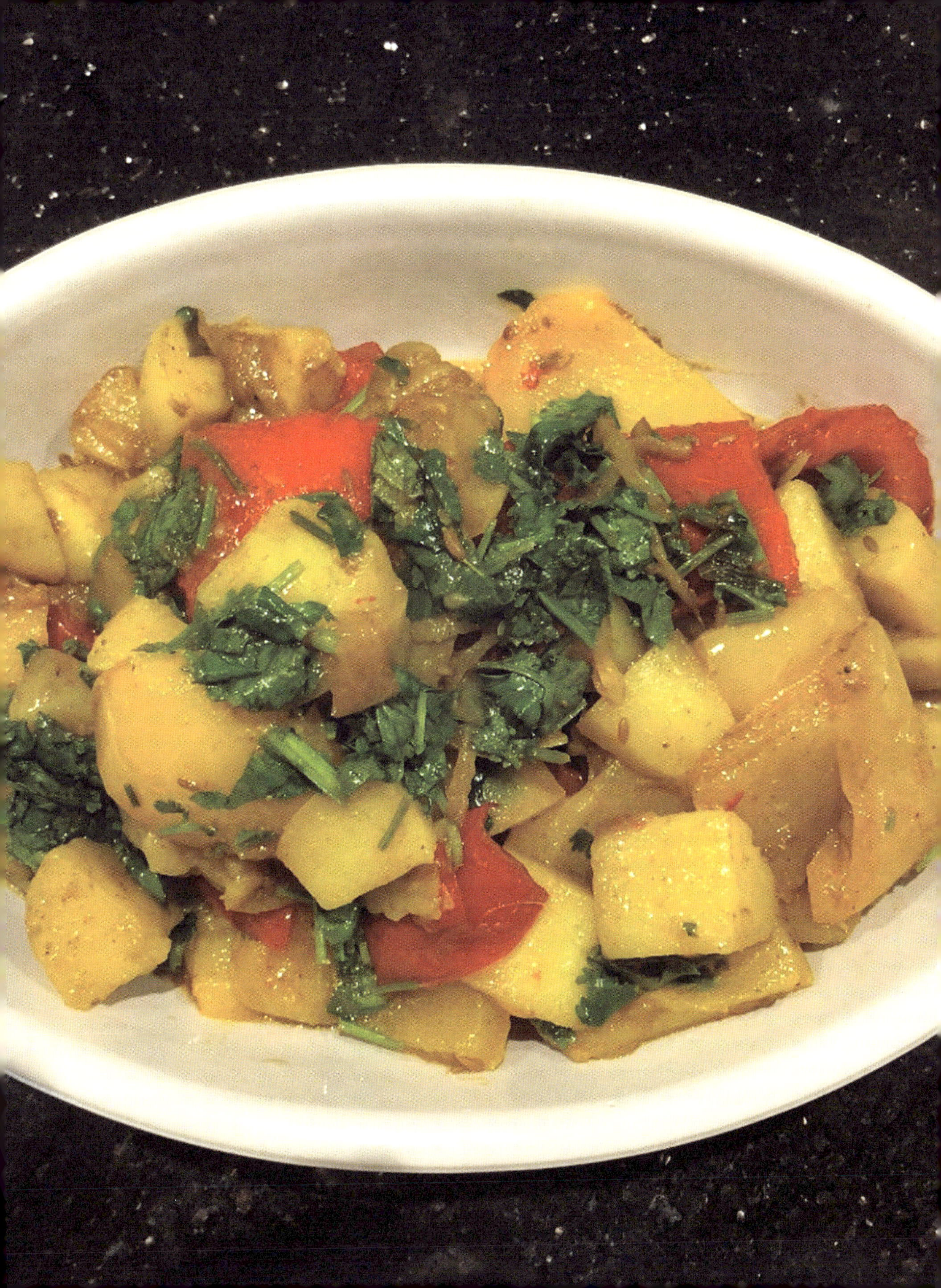

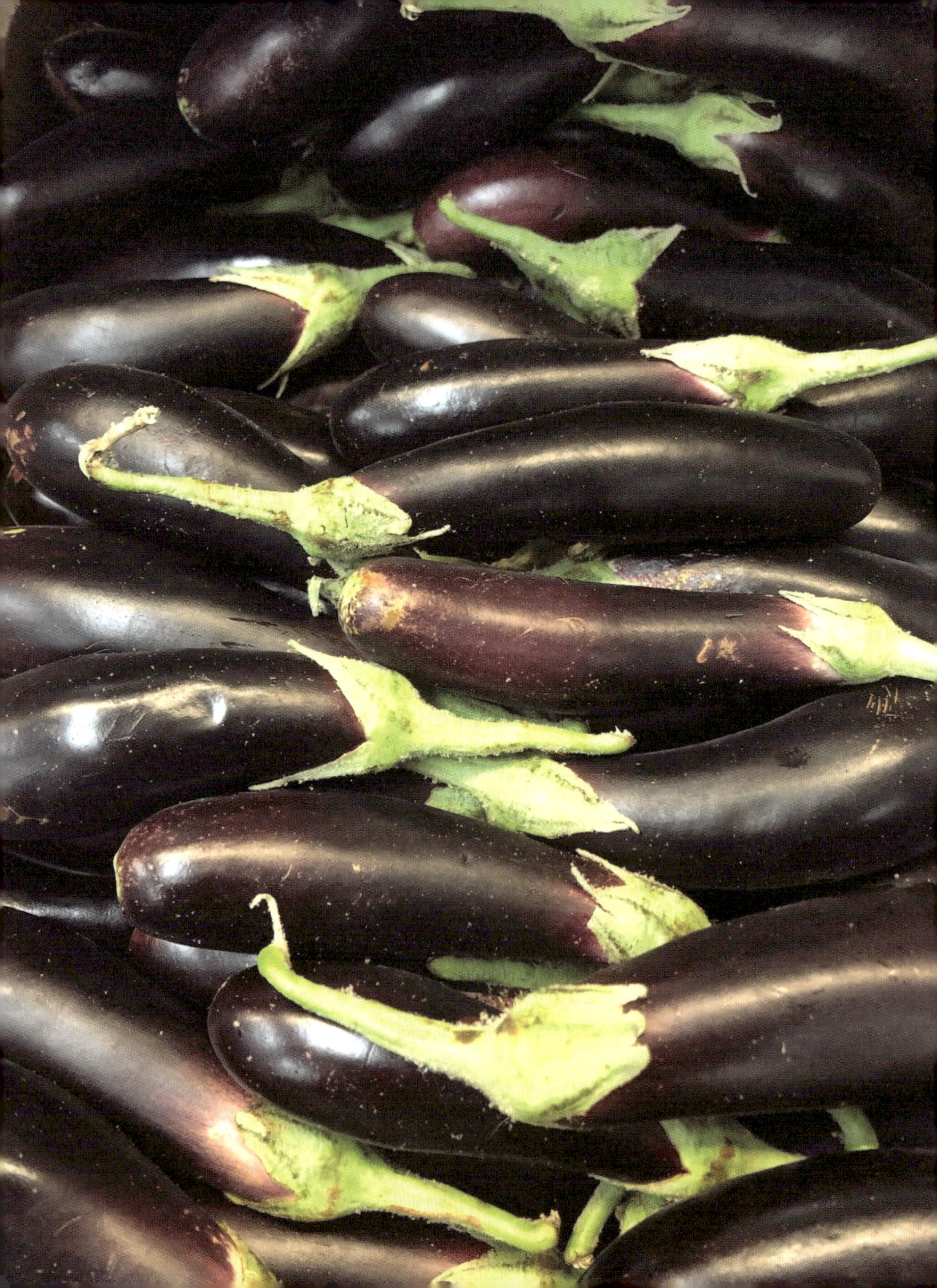

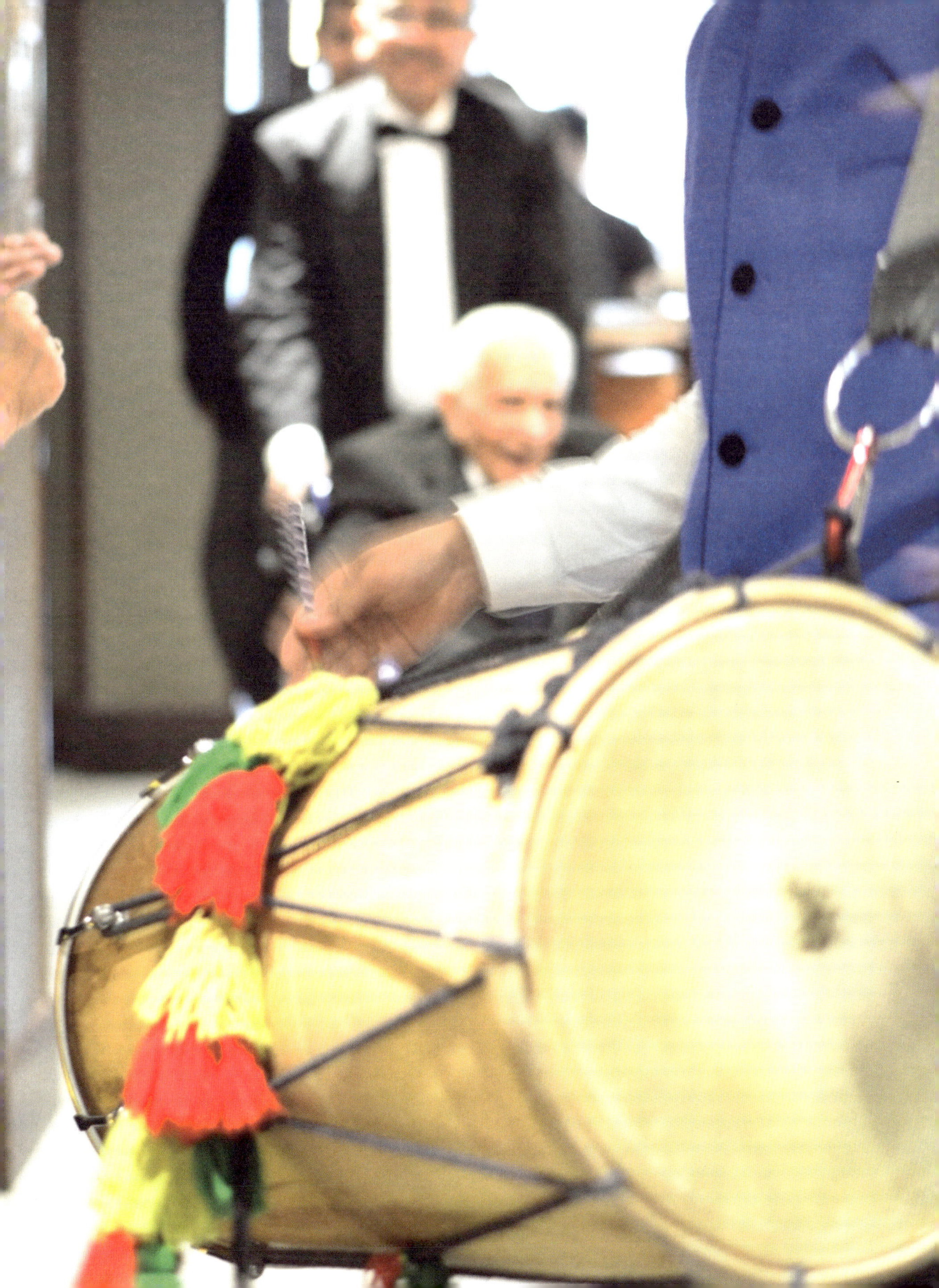

DRY VEGGIE DISHES

Aubergine & Potatoes

READY IN 40 MINS

SERVES 3-4

My dad loves aubergines however they are cooked! This dish uses potatoes, it is a popular dish and easy to make. Indian Nanny's recipe.

INGREDIENTS

4 tablespoons light olive oil

1 large aubergine

2 medium onions, peeled and thinly sliced

1 tomato, cut into 8 segments

1 inch ginger, peeled and finely chopped (optional)

2 or 3 medium potatoes

Fresh, chopped coriander for decoration (optional)

SPICES

1 teaspoon jeera

2 teaspoons salt

½ teaspoon haldi

1 teaspoon paprika

¼ teaspoon chilli powder

½ teaspoon garam masala

METHOD

1. Add the oil to a wok, add the onion and cook on a high / medium heat for about 10 minutes. The onions don't need to go very brown. Check and stir regularly.

2. Whilst the onion is cooking, peel the potatoes and chop into 2cm cubes, wash and leave on the side to drain.

3. Wash the aubergine, slice into approx. 2cm slices, then into cubes.

4. Once the onions are cooked, add the jeera, give it a quick stir. Fry for a minute, then add the tomato segments and ginger (if using), cook over a low heat for a few minutes.

5. Now add the chopped aubergine and potatoes to the wok.

6. Then add the salt, haldi, paprika and chilli, give it a good stir and simmer on a medium to low heat for 15 – 20 minutes with the lid on. Check regularly to make sure there is still water in the bottom, stir gently 2 or 3 times during cooking.

7. Check the potatoes are soft by stabbing them with a knife. Once the potatoes are cooked, add the garam masala and give it a gentle stir.

8. Add fresh, chopped coriander for decoration (optional).

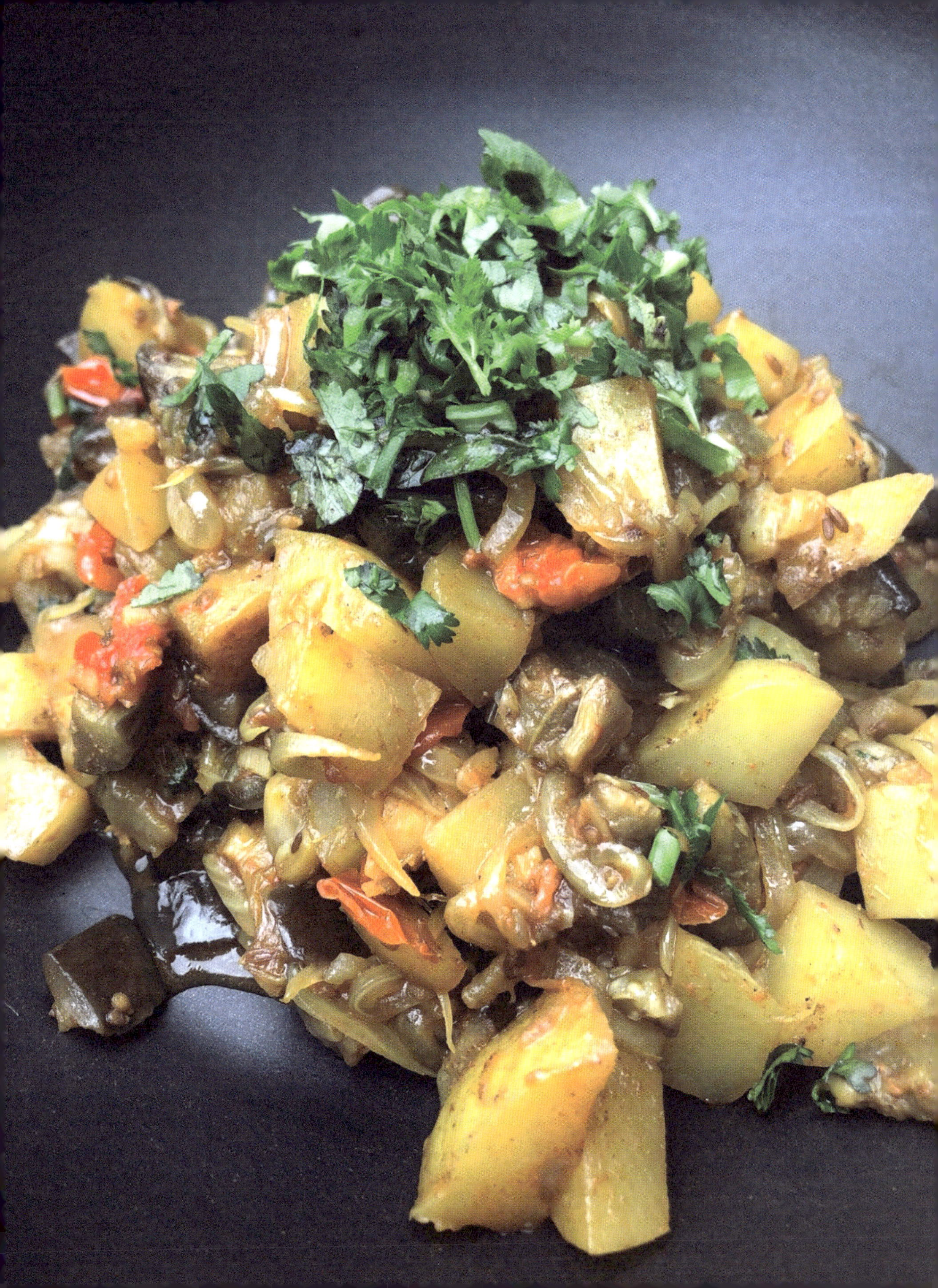

DRY VEGGIE DISHES

Aubergine Partha

READY IN
1 HOUR

SERVES
3-4

Now, as I said aubergine is my dad's favourite vegetable, and cooked this way is his absolute favourite way of cooking aubergine. This is Indian Nanny's recipe.

Nanny taught me the trick with aubergines is to buy ones that feel light when you pick them up as they will not have any seeds in them.

INGREDIENTS

2 aubergines

3 tablespoons light olive oil

1 large onion peeled and thickly sliced

2 fresh tomatoes cut into 8 segments, or 1 large tomato thickly sliced

1 large cup peas or petit pois, washed

Fresh chopped coriander for decoration (optional)

SPICES

1 teaspoon jeera

1 ½ teaspoons salt

½ teaspoon paprika

¼ teaspoon chilli powder

1 teaspoon garam masala

METHOD

1. Wash and prick the aubergines all over, then place under a hot grill on foil. Turn every 10 minutes for 30 – 40 minutes, until they look burnt and the skin is shrivelled with some of the juice coming out onto the foil.

2. Remove from under the grill still on the foil and put them in the sink to cool for 15 minutes. If you are in a rush, put them in a bowl of cold water to cool down.

3. Then run the cold water tap over the aubergines and peel the skin off with your hands; cut off the stalk end. If some of the flesh is left on the skin, peel this off too.

4. Put the aubergine into a large bowl and then mash with a masher or fork. (This can be frozen and used at a later time for cooking, NB you must defrost before cooking, by leaving out for 2-3 hours before using.)

5. Now add the oil to a wok, fry the onion and tomatoes on a medium heat, add the jeera and continue to cook until soft and the onions are pink.

6. Add the peas, cook for 5 minutes with the lid on.

7. Then add the aubergine, salt, paprika and chilli. Cook for 5 to 10 minutes with the lid on.

8. Once done, add the garam masala and stir through.

9. Add fresh coriander for decoration if you like.

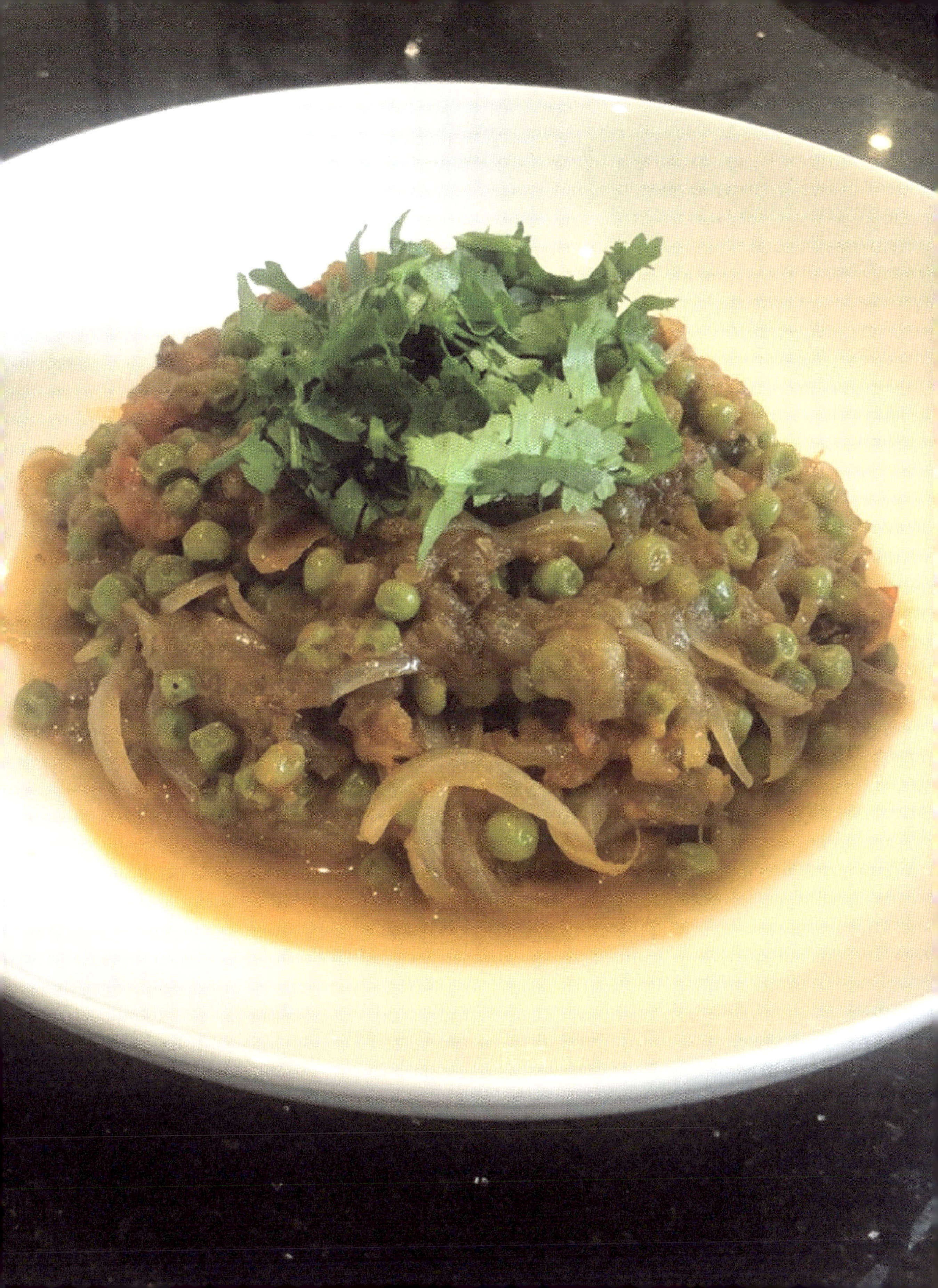

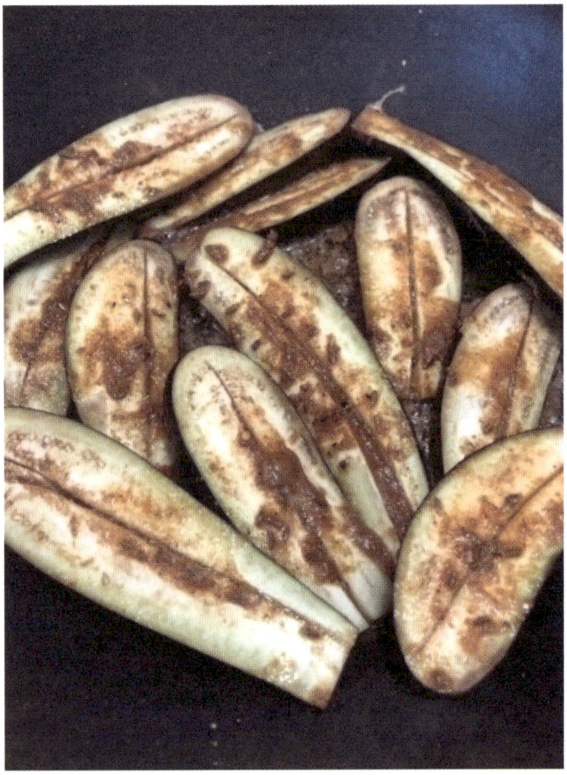
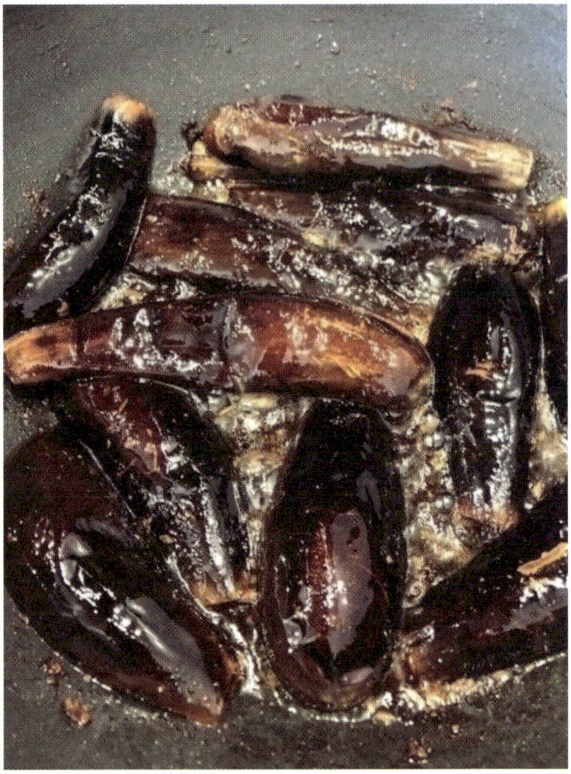
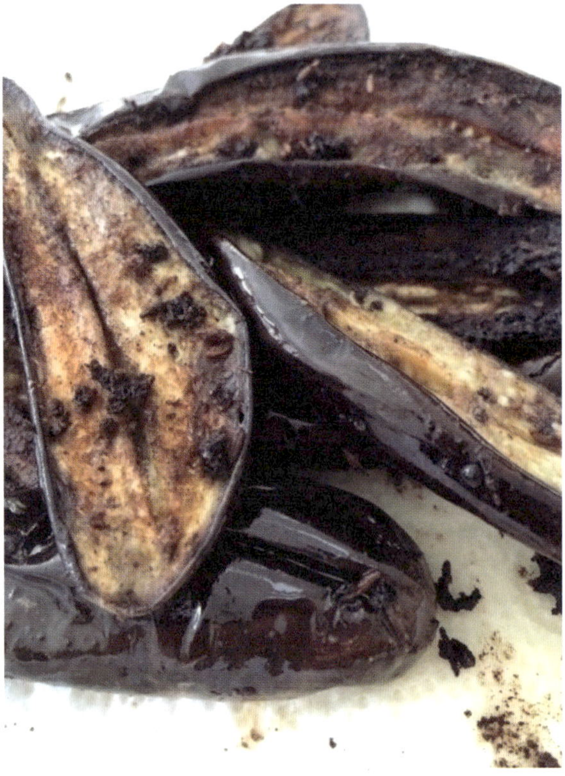
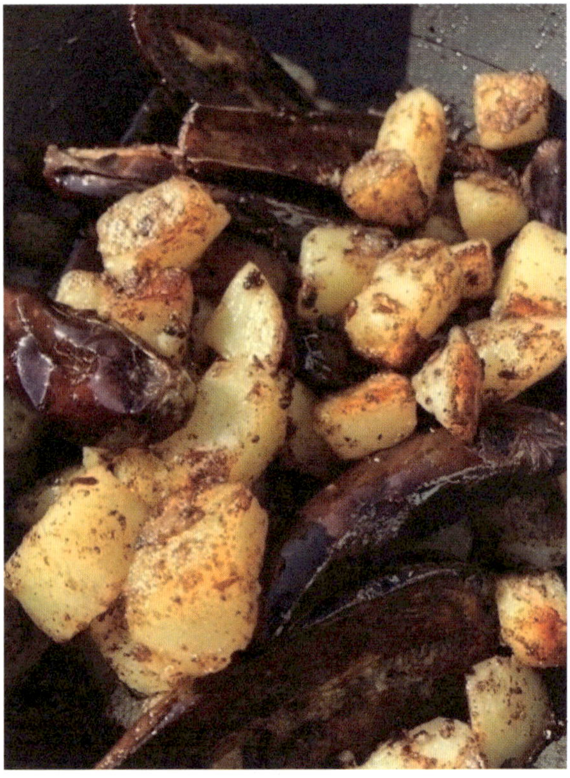

DRY VEGGIE DISHES

Mini Aubergines & Potatoes

READY IN 45 MINS

SERVES 3-4

Indian Nanny taught me to cook this. I have to go to the Indian shop to buy mini aubergines but it's well worth the visit.

INGREDIENTS

6 mini aubergines (soft ones)

4 tablespoons light olive oil for frying

3 medium potatoes

Few teaspoons water

SPICES

1 teaspoon jeera

1 ½ teaspoons salt

½ teaspoon chilli powder

1 teaspoon garam masala

2 teaspoons mango powder

METHOD

1. Put all the spices into a bowl and add a few teaspoons of water at a time to make a masala paste (note "masala" means "spice").

2. Wash the aubergines, chop off the green stem and cut them in half lengthways. Make a cut in the middle of each half and stuff with the masala paste.

3. Add approximately 4 tablespoons of oil to a frying pan or wok and shallow fry the aubergines.

4. Cook for about 10 minutes on a medium heat with the lid on, then turn over and cook for another 10 minutes with the lid on.

5. While the aubergines are cooking, peel, wash and chop the potatoes into 2.5cm chunks, put them in a saucepan of water and bring to the boil for approximately 10 minutes.

6. Once the aubergines are soft take then out of the oil and leave them on the side, on a plate covered with some kitchen towel – this will mop up the excess oil.

7. Then drain the potatoes and add them to the oil and spices, which is already in the wok or frying pan from frying the aubergines earlier.

8. Fry the potatoes for about 10 minutes on a medium heat with the lid on.

9. Once the potatoes are cooked, add the aubergines and mix them in gently.

136

DRY VEGGIE DISHES

Punjabi Bhain

READY IN
45 MINS

SERVES
3-4

I was once given a gift of a lotus root, the Hindu name of this vegetable is Kamal Kakdi, resembling a very large baked potato. I made some enquiries with the Aunties as to how to cook this Asian beauty. Veena was delighted as she said that she used to cook this vegetable a lot with Nanny. She recalls coming to England and eventually finding this vegetable in tins!

INGREDIENTS

1 lotus root

1 onion

2 tablespoons light olive oil

1 inch ginger, peeled and finely chopped

1 tomato, chopped

½ cup water

SPICES

1 teaspoon jeera

1 heaped teaspoon salt

½ teaspoon paprika

¼ teaspoon haldi

½ teaspoon coriander powder

¼ teaspoon chilli powder

½ garam masala

1 teaspoon mango powder

METHOD

1. Peel the lotus root, then cut it into really thin round circles (2mm). The vegetable can be a bit slimy so wash it in a colander.

2. Thinly slice the onion, put it into the wok and add 2 tablespoons of oil and the jeera, put on a medium / high heat for 10 minutes (no need to go very brown).

3. Add the ginger and tomato, give it a stir and cook for a few minutes.

4. Then add the lotus root, give it another stir and cook for a few minutes.

5. Add salt, paprika, haldi, coriander powder, chilli powder, stir and cover. Simmer on a low heat.

6. After 5 minutes give the vegetables a gentle stir. You may need to add a little water (1/2 cup).

7. After 20-25 minutes, check the vegetable is cooked.

8. Finally, add garam masala and mango powder.

DRY VEGGIE DISHES

Turnips

READY IN 45 MINS

SERVES 3-4

INGREDIENTS

3 tablespoons light olive oil

1 large tomato, chopped

Turnips (approx. 700g), peeled and chopped into 2cm chunks, wash and drain

4 teaspoons sugar

SPICES

1 teaspoon jeera

2 teaspoons salt

½ teaspoon haldi

½ heaped teaspoon coriander powder

½ heaped teaspoon paprika

¼ teaspoon chilli powder

½ heaped teaspoon garam masala

2 teaspoons mango powder

I remember my Nan cooking this in the pressure cooker. If you want to do this, the turnips become really soft, like mash and it is delicious. One steam and turn the heat down, simmer for 5 minutes. I prefer to cook in the wok, so in this recipe the turnips are cooked through but not as soft.

METHOD

1. Heat the oil in a wok over a medium heat with 1 teaspoon of jeera, add the tomato, quick stir then add the turnips.

2. Add the salt, haldi, coriander powder, paprika and chilli powder. Give it a stir and cook on a low heat with a lid on.

3. Cook for about 25 mins until the vegetables are cooked and soft.

4. Add the sugar, garam masala and mango powder. Give it a very gentle stir. Turn the heat off and cook for a few more minutes with the lid on.

Note – Cook the veg until really nice and soft; if all the water has been absorbed and the veg is still a little hard, add a couple of tablespoons of water, low heat and put the lid on for about another 5 minutes until the veg is soft.

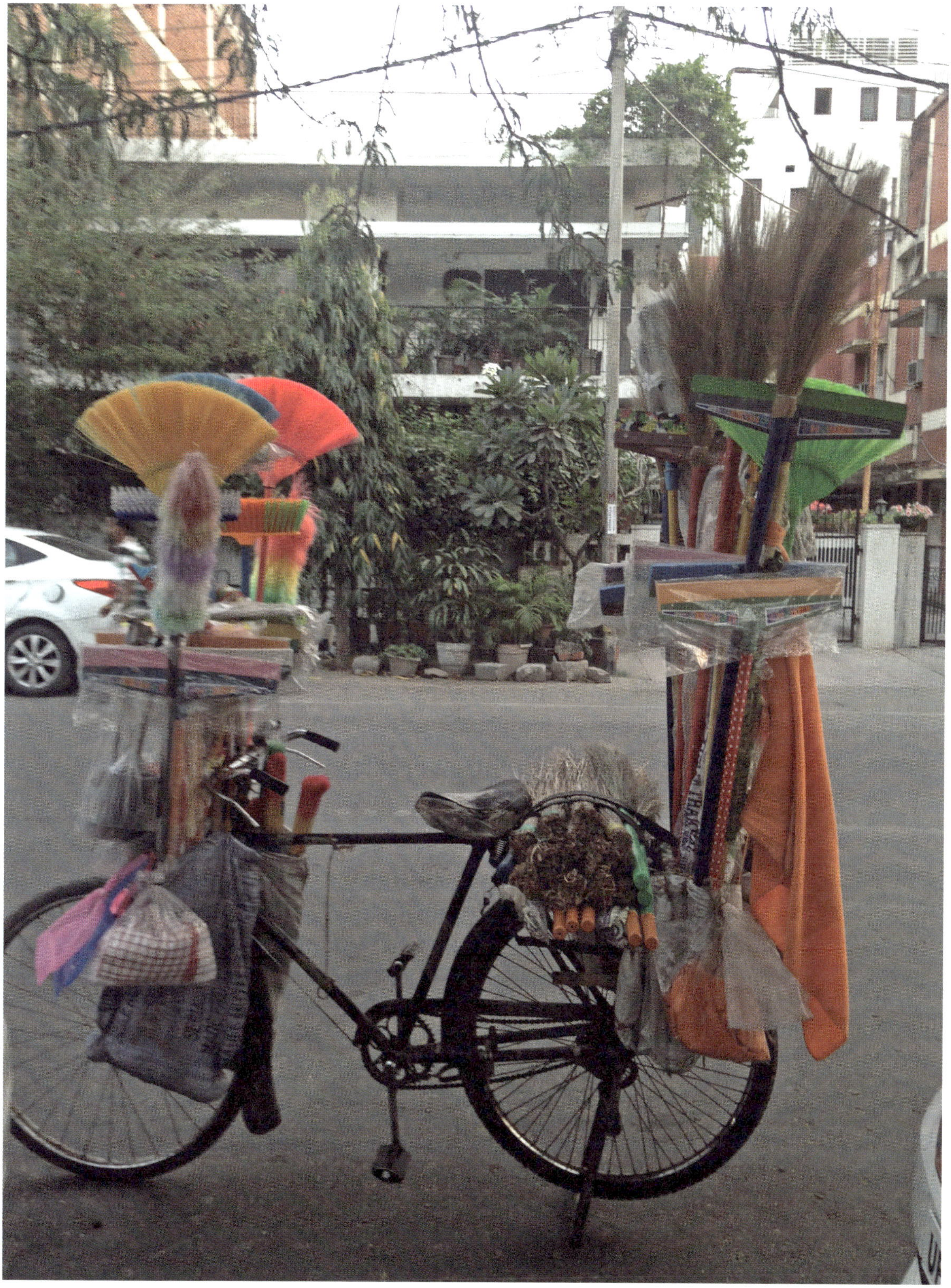

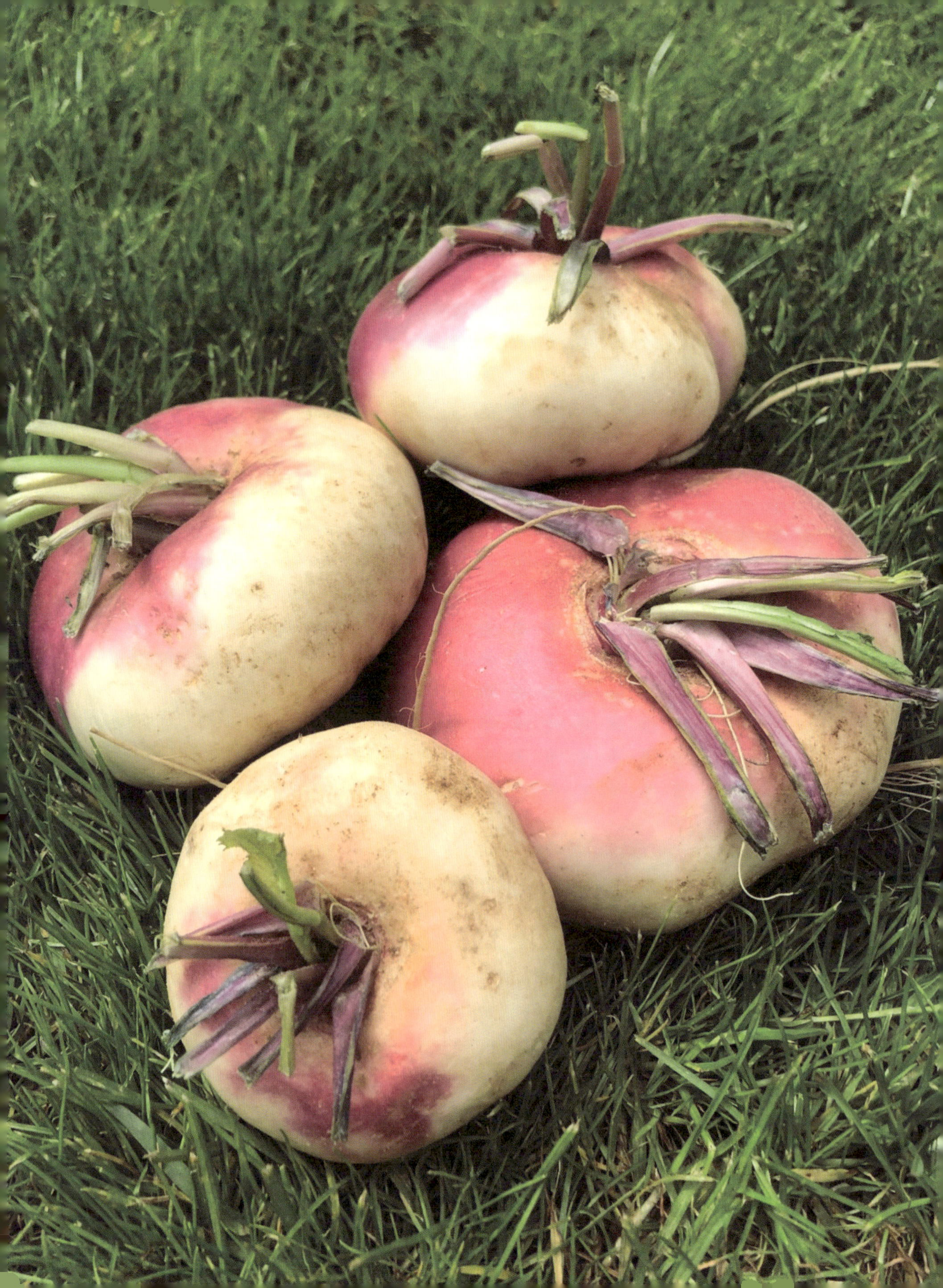

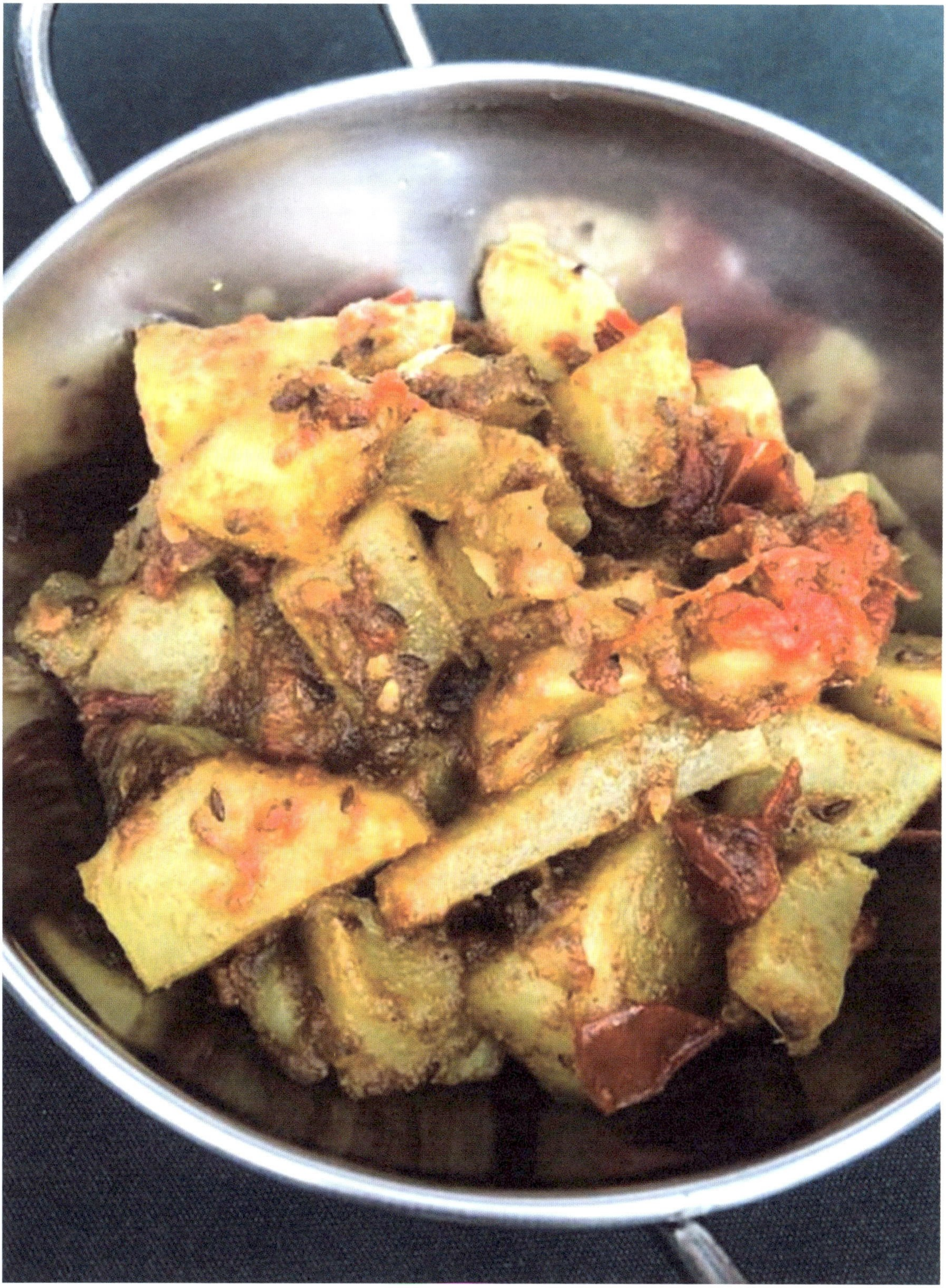

DRY VEGGIE DISHES

Punjabi Potatoes

READY IN
25 MINS

SERVES
3-4

Indian Nanny's recipe. When you only have new potatoes left for dinner! These little fellas are easy and quick to cook up with a bit of spice. Will go nicely with an Indian meal or English barbecue meat, fish or tofu.

As the dish uses boiled potatoes, you can also use leftover boiled potatoes.

The flavour of this dish is delicious, I would recommend frying the potatoes and serving them straight away.

INGREDIENTS

Small bag of new potatoes (500g)

2 tablespoons light olive oil

SPICES

½ teaspoon jeera

1 teaspoon salt

1 teaspoon mango powder

Pinch chilli powder

½ teaspoon garam masala

METHOD

1. Put the potatoes (skin on) in a medium pan, cover with water and boil on a high heat.

2. Turn down to simmer and cook until the potatoes are cooked (check with a knife), approximately 10-15 minutes.

3. Drain in a colander and wait until they have cooled.

4. Remove the skin with your fingers or the edge of a teaspoon and cut them into quarters. If you are in a hurry or prefer skin on, that works well too.

5. Add the oil to a wok on a medium to high heat. Add the jeera, once it's warm (sizzling) then add the potatoes. Add the salt, mango powder, chilli powder and garam masala.

6. Fry for approximately 5 minutes — once the potatoes are nicely coated in the spice they are done.

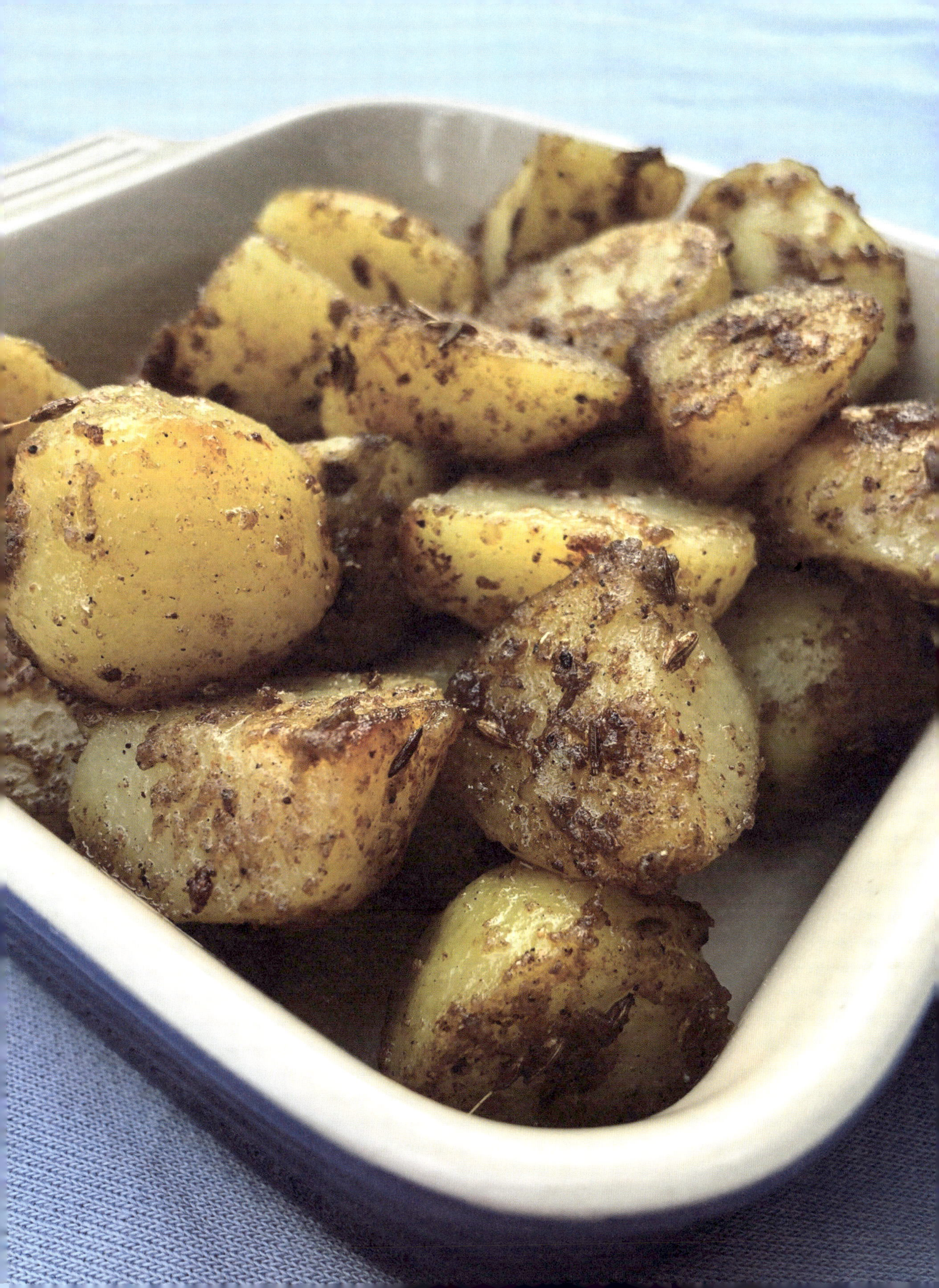

If there is light in the soul,
there will be beauty in the person.
If there is beauty in the person,
there will be harmony in the home.
If there is harmony in the home,
there will be order in the nation.
If there is order in the nation,
there will be peace in the world.

- Chinese Proverb

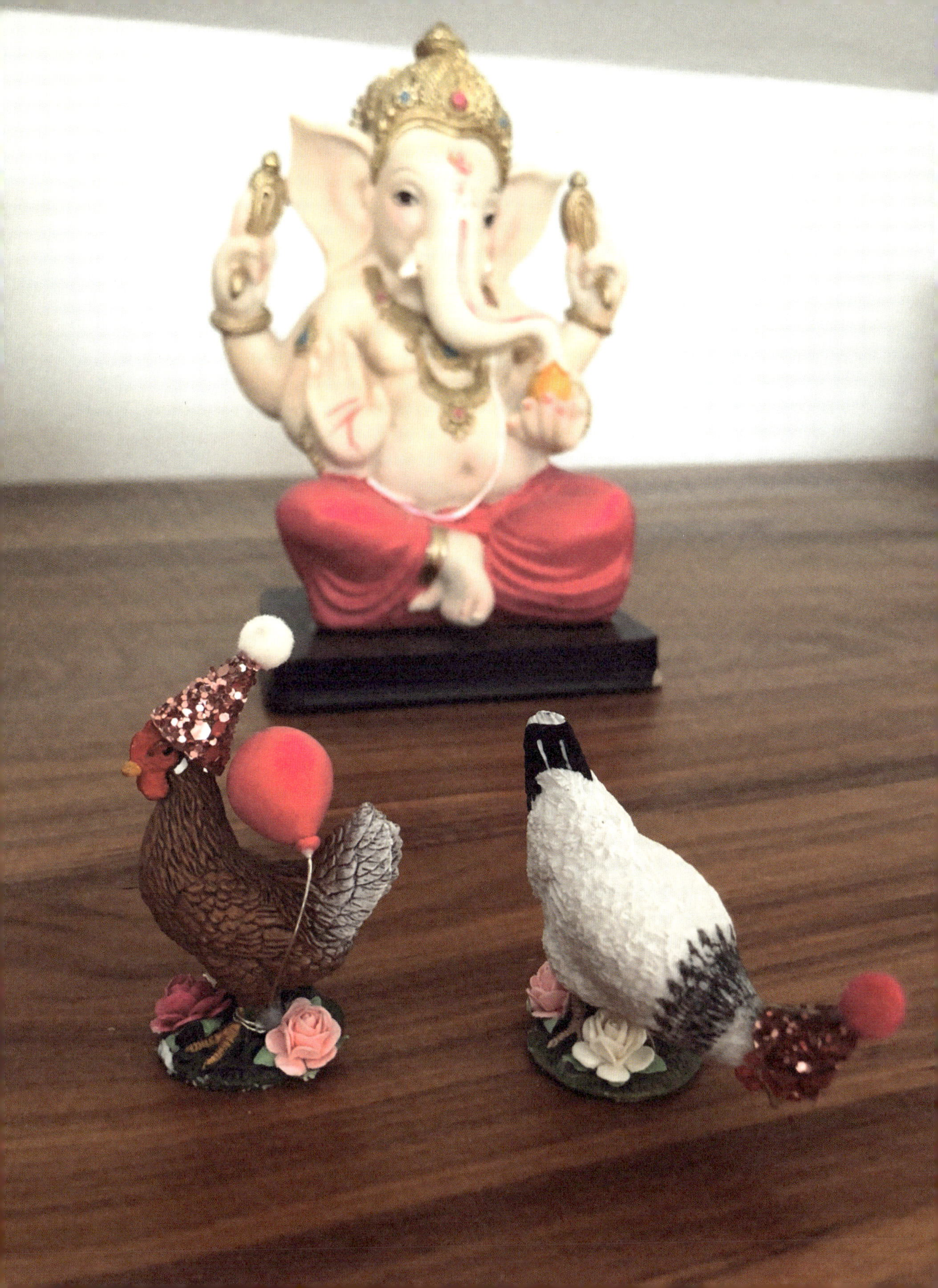

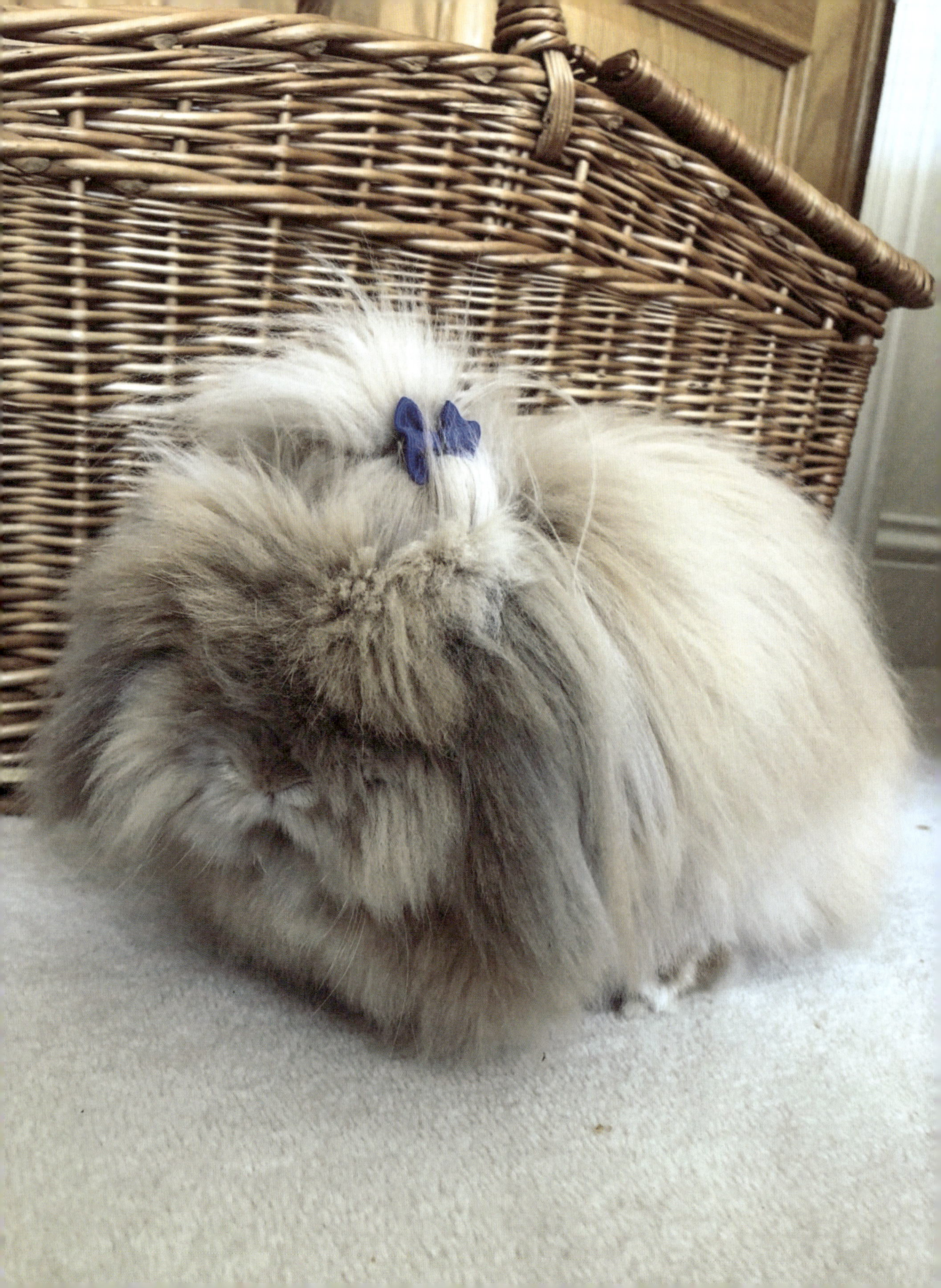

VEGGIE CURRIES

VEGGIE CURRIES

Puri Aloo

READY IN 30 MINS
SERVES 3-4

This is a really tasty potato dish taught to me by Indian Nanny. Traditionally served with puris, I remember my grandad frying the puris as nanny was rolling them. We would eat puris and puri aloo until we literally popped! Madhu and Eshan's favourite.

INGREDIENTS

8 small/medium white potatoes (new)

2 tablespoons light olive oil

½ tin chopped tomatoes

2 teaspoons mango pickle

4 tablespoon plain, natural set yoghurt – (Onken is our favourite and found in supermarkets) or you can use oat yogurt as a vegan alternative

1 cup water

Fresh coriander (optional)

SPICES

1 teaspoon jeera

1 teaspoon salt

½ teaspoon haldi

1 teaspoon paprika

½ teaspoon coriander powder

¼ teaspoon chilli powder

1 teaspoon garam masala

METHOD

1. Boil the new potatoes in water until soft but leave them a little hard (al dente). A wok is best to use with a little water in the bottom. Let the potatoes cool in a colander and then peel with your fingers / back of a knife.

2. Using a wok, heat 2 large tablespoons of oil and 1 teaspoon jeera. Once sizzling (30 secs), add the chopped tomatoes, give it a little stir, cook for a few minutes and let the tomatoes go soft. Then add 1 teaspoon mango pickle and 1 teaspoon of sauce from the bottom of the mango pickle jar. Beat the yogurt with a fork and add to the wok.

3. Once cooked, approximately 5 minutes, add the salt, haldi, paprika, coriander powder and chilli powder.

4. Add the potatoes; any larger ones can be chopped in half or quarters, really small ones can be left whole. Gently coat them in the sauce, then add a cup of water. High heat, then simmer on medium heat for 10 minutes with the lid on.

5. After heating, add a teaspoon of garam masala and a handful of fresh coriander if you wish.

Note – If you do not have any mango pickle, add a tablespoon of extra yogurt.

149

VEGGIE CURRIES

Courgette Curry

READY IN 30 MINS

SERVES 3-4

This is a great dish taught to me by Indian Nanny. If you can find yellow courgettes – fantastic! They are slightly sweeter than their green cousins.

INGREDIENTS

6 tablespoons light olive oil

2 medium onions, peeled, washed and thinly sliced

1 tomato, washed and cut into 8 wedges, or 8 cherry tomatoes

2 large courgettes, thinly sliced (approx. 1-2mm)

1 large tin sweetcorn (340g)

2 tablespoons water

1 tablespoon beaten natural set yogurt (optional)

fresh/frozen coriander for decoration (optional)

SPICES

1 teaspoon jeera

2 teaspoons salt

½ teaspoon haldi

1 teaspoon paprika

1 heaped teaspoon coriander powder

¼ teaspoon chilli powder

1 teaspoon garam masala

METHOD

1. Add the oil to a normal saucepan or wok and heat over a medium to high heat.

2. Add the onions and fry them until pink, add the jeera and tomato wedges and stir, heat for a few minutes.

3. Drain the sweetcorn through a colander and give it a quick rinse under cold water, set to one side with the sliced courgettes.

4. To the pan add 2 teaspoons salt, ½ teaspoon haldi, 1 teaspoon paprika, 1 heaped teaspoon coriander powder, ¼ teaspoon chilli powder.

5. Stir and mash up the tomatoes, then add the courgettes and sweetcorn.

6. Cook on a medium to high heat, add 2 tablespoons of water and give it a quick stir for a few minutes until the liquid starts to bubble.

7. Then turn down the heat, put lid on and simmer for about 10 minutes until the courgettes are cooked.

8. Add the spoon of beaten yogurt (optional) & 1 teaspoon garam masala, give a gentle stir then turn off. A sprinkle of fresh/frozen coriander for decoration.

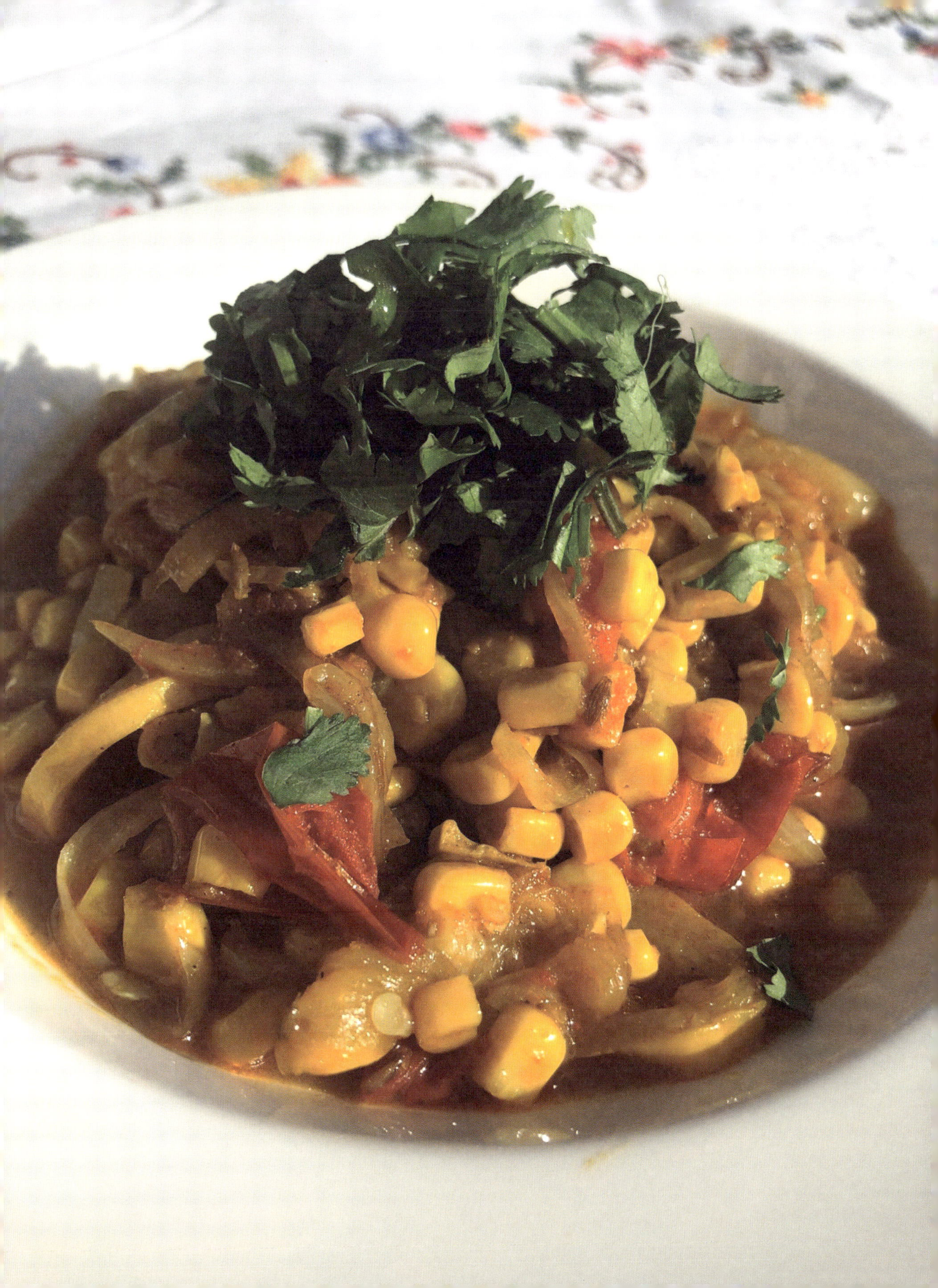

VEGGIE CURRIES

Squash or Pumpkin Curry

READY IN 30 MINS **SERVES 3-4**

This is a really tasty dish, Indian Nanny's recipe. Although peeling and cutting the squash can be quite hard work, it's well worth it for the flavour this dish brings.

If you have a very large squash or pumpkin, I would suggest doubling up on the spices and cooking for slightly longer until the vegetable is cooked so it melts in your mouth…

INGREDIENTS

3 tablespoons light olive oil

1 tomato, chopped (optional)

1 squash or pumpkin (approx. 750g), peeled and chopped into 2cm chunks, washed and drained

4 teaspoons sugar

SPICES

1 teaspoon jeera

2 teaspoons salt

½ teaspoon haldi

½ heaped teaspoon coriander powder

½ heaped teaspoon paprika

¼ teaspoon chilli powder

½ heaped teaspoon garam masala

2 teaspoons mango powder

METHOD

1. Heat the oil in a wok over a medium heat with 1 teaspoon of jeera, add the tomato, quick stir then add the squash/pumpkin.

2. Add the salt, haldi, coriander powder, paprika and chilli powder. Give it a stir and cook on a low heat with a lid on.

3. Cook for about 15 mins until vegetables are cooked and soft.

4. Add the sugar, garam masala and mango powder. Give it a very gentle stir. Turn the heat off and cook for a few more minutes with the lid on.

Note – Cook the veg until really nice and soft; if all the water has been absorbed and the veg is still a little hard, add a couple of tablespoons of water, low heat and put the lid on for about another 5 minutes until the veg is almost mushy.

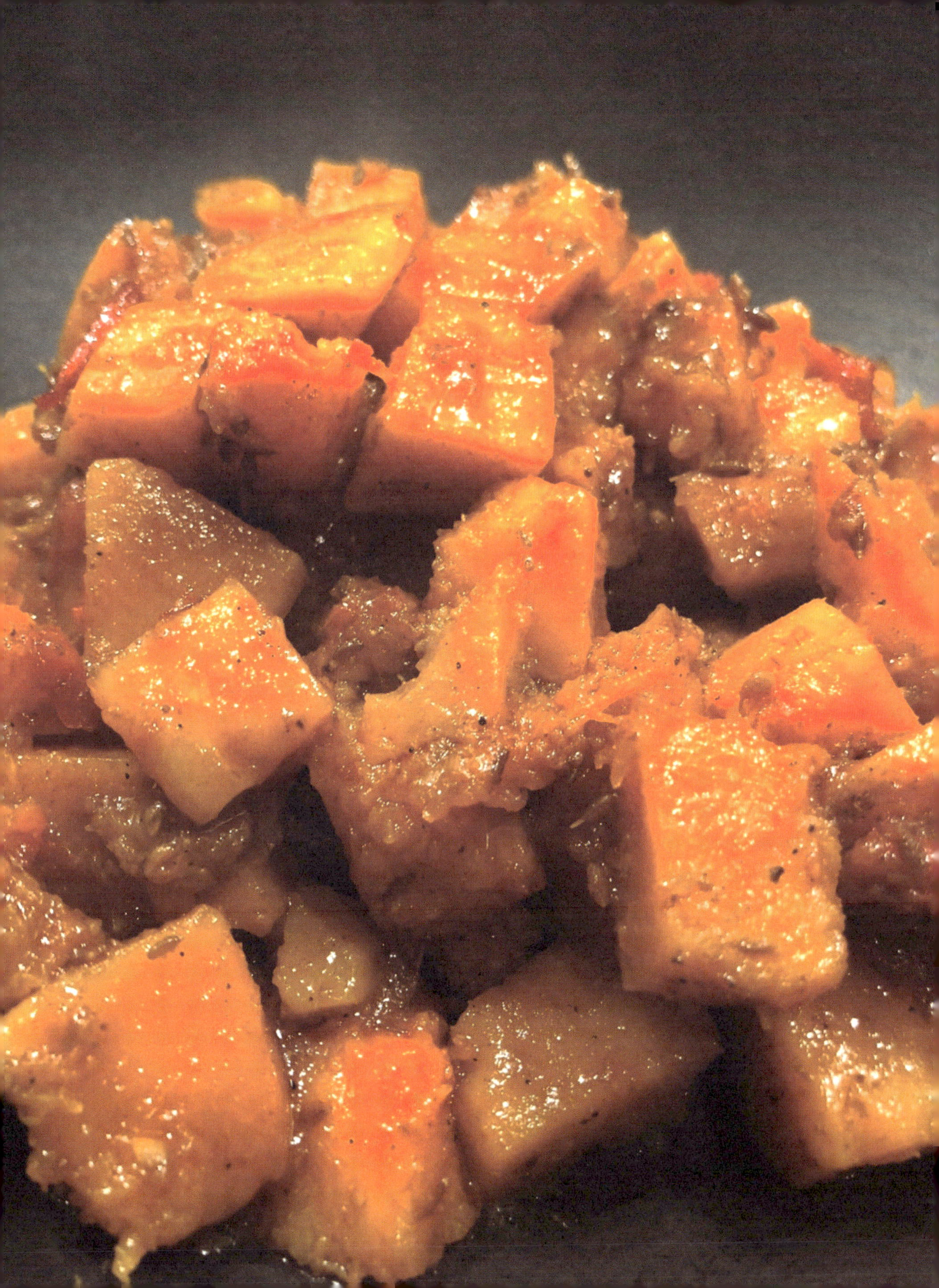

VEGGIE CURRIES

Baked Tofu & Potato Curry

READY IN 45 MINS **SERVES** 3-4

This recipe got my family eating tofu; it comes from Nanny's chicken curry recipe. A simple, delicious plant-based curry that goes really well on a bed of rice.

INGREDIENTS

2 tablespoons light olive oil and a bit more to drizzle

1 large onion

4 cloves garlic

600g (2 packets) tofu

½ tin tomatoes, chopped or plum

3 medium potatoes, peeled and chopped into 1 inch cubes

1 tablespoon natural oat yogurt

500ml water

Handful of chopped coriander (optional)

SPICES

½ teaspoon jeera

2 teaspoons salt

½ teaspoon haldi

¼ teaspoon chilli powder

½ teaspoon paprika

1 teaspoon garam masala

METHOD

1. Preheat the oven to 220°C.

2. Drain the tofu and tear into chunks and put onto a foil lined tray with a drizzle of olive oil (so the tofu doesn't stick). Bake in the oven for about 15 - 20 minutes.

3. While the tofu is baking, finely chop the onions and garlic, preferably using a mini chopper or food processor.

4. Using a medium heavy pan or a wok, add 2 tablespoons of oil on a medium heat, add the chopped onion and fry in the oil until pink, then add the garlic and fry for a bit longer.

5. Add ½ tin of tomatoes, jeera, salt, haldi, chilli and paprika. Stir and cook for a few minutes, until the juice from the tomatoes has gone. Add the potatoes with 500ml of water and 1 tablespoon oat yogurt to the pan. Then add the tofu chunks to the curry, give it a quick stir.

6. Put the lid on and turn the heat up until it boils, then down to simmer. Cook until the potatoes are done, approximately 25 minutes.

7. Add 1 teaspoon garam masala and turn the heat off.

8. It is ready to serve with a handful of chopped coriander (optional).

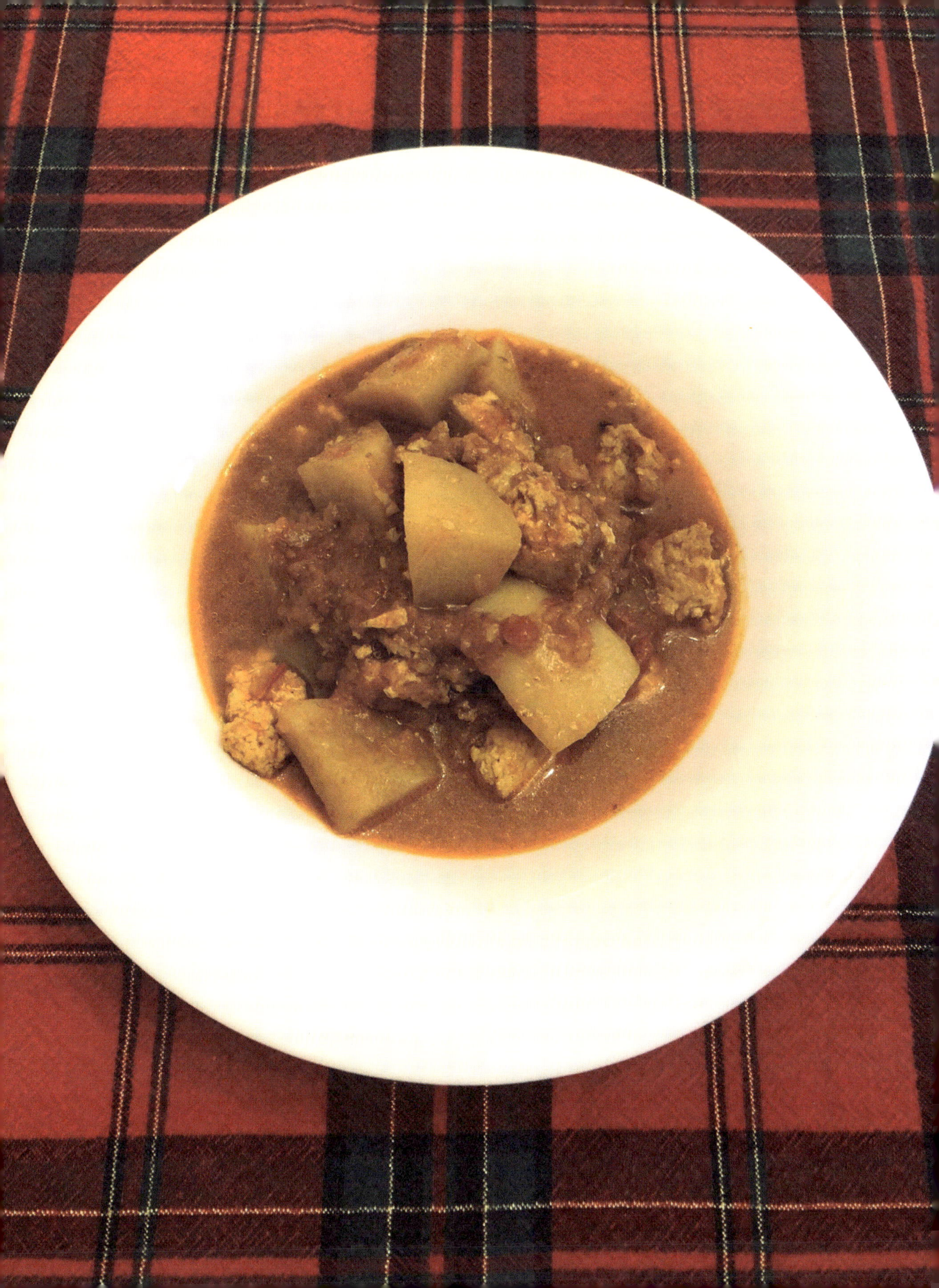

VEGGIE CURRIES

Veggie Mince

READY IN 45 MINS

SERVES 3-4

I used to love a bit of veggie mince as a vegetarian. I know quite a few meat eaters who now eat veggie mince rather than minced meat. The Indian flavours are an awesome complement to veggie mince. This dish is packed with your basic spices and very easy to make. Indian Nanny taught me this recipe.

INGREDIENTS

1 ½ large onions

2 inches ginger, peeled

2 cloves garlic, peeled

3 tablespoons light olive oil

500g Quorn mince or vegan mince (I like Sainsbury's frozen Plant Pioneers)

1 fresh tomato, chopped

½ tin chopped tomatoes

1 cup petit pois or peas

1 cup water

SPICES

1 teaspoon jeera

2 teaspoons salt

½ teaspoon haldi

1 teaspoon paprika

¼ teaspoon chilli powder

1 teaspoon coriander powder

1 teaspoon garam masala

METHOD

1. Finely chop the onion, garlic and ginger in a food processor.

2. In a medium heavy pan or wok, put the oil and jeera, once warm (30 seconds) add the onion, ginger and garlic mixture, fry on a medium heat, until it is a little darker than pink.

3. Add the mince and fry for 5 minutes, stir regularly.

4. Add the tomato and tinned chopped tomatoes, stir regularly. Continue to cook for about 5 minutes until the juice has evaporated.

5. Add the salt, ½ teaspoon haldi, 1 teaspoon paprika and ¼ teaspoon chilli powder, 1 teaspoon coriander powder, stir and lower the heat.

6. Fry for a couple of minutes then add the peas and 1 cup of water.

7. Simmer on a low heat with the lid on for 20-25 minutes, then add 1 teaspoon garam masala, quick stir and turn off the heat.

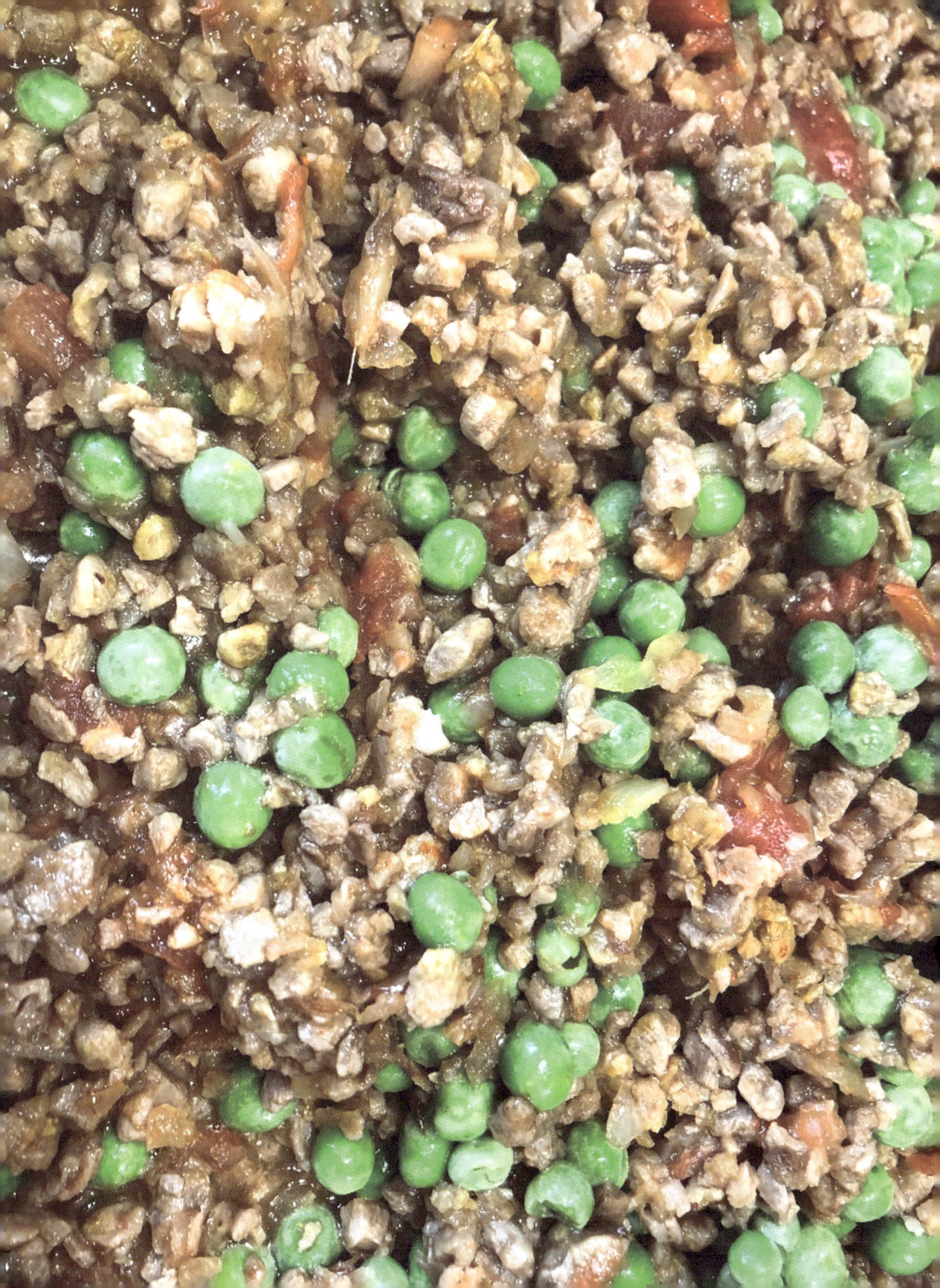

158

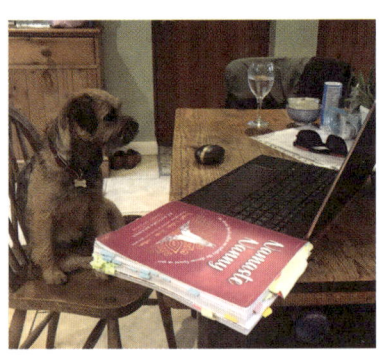

159

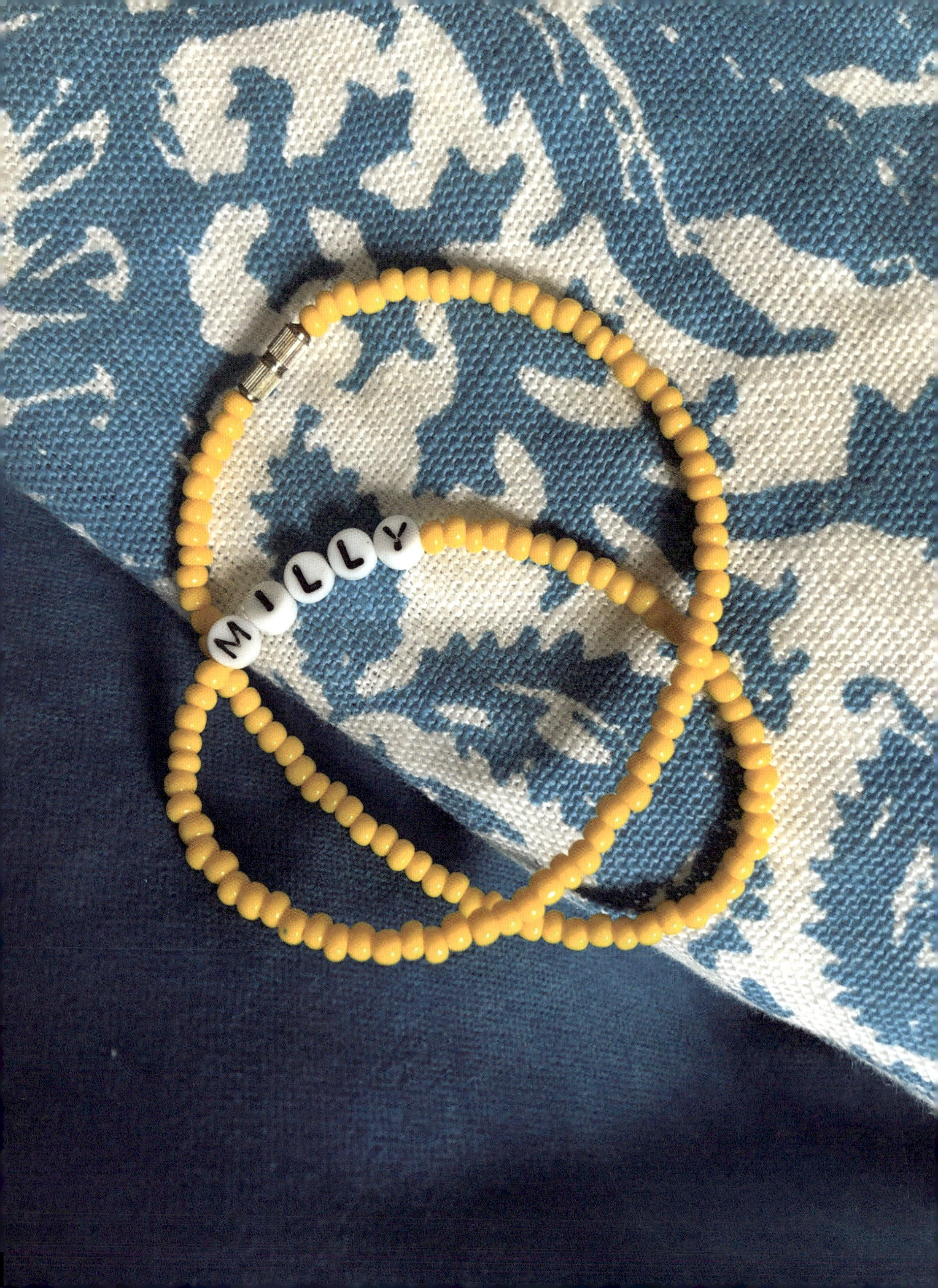
MILLY

PANEER

Paneer

Paneer is Indian cheese. Traditionally, my Nan taught me to make it from scratch with whole milk and a cheese cloth (see homemade paneer recipe). In some dishes you then fry it to make a really delicious Indian dish. Nowadays, it's readily available to purchase from most supermarkets in the cheese section, so this reduces the preparation and cooking time considerably.

Vegan Paneer

Tofu is a great alternative to paneer for a vegan. Its texture is similar, and it will soak up the gravy to give you a great flavoured dish. In most instances it needs a little more spice and salt than paneer. Tofu can be bought commonly in blocks of about 300g in most supermarkets. The other benefit is it usually has a long use by date so can be stored unopened for a few weeks in the fridge.

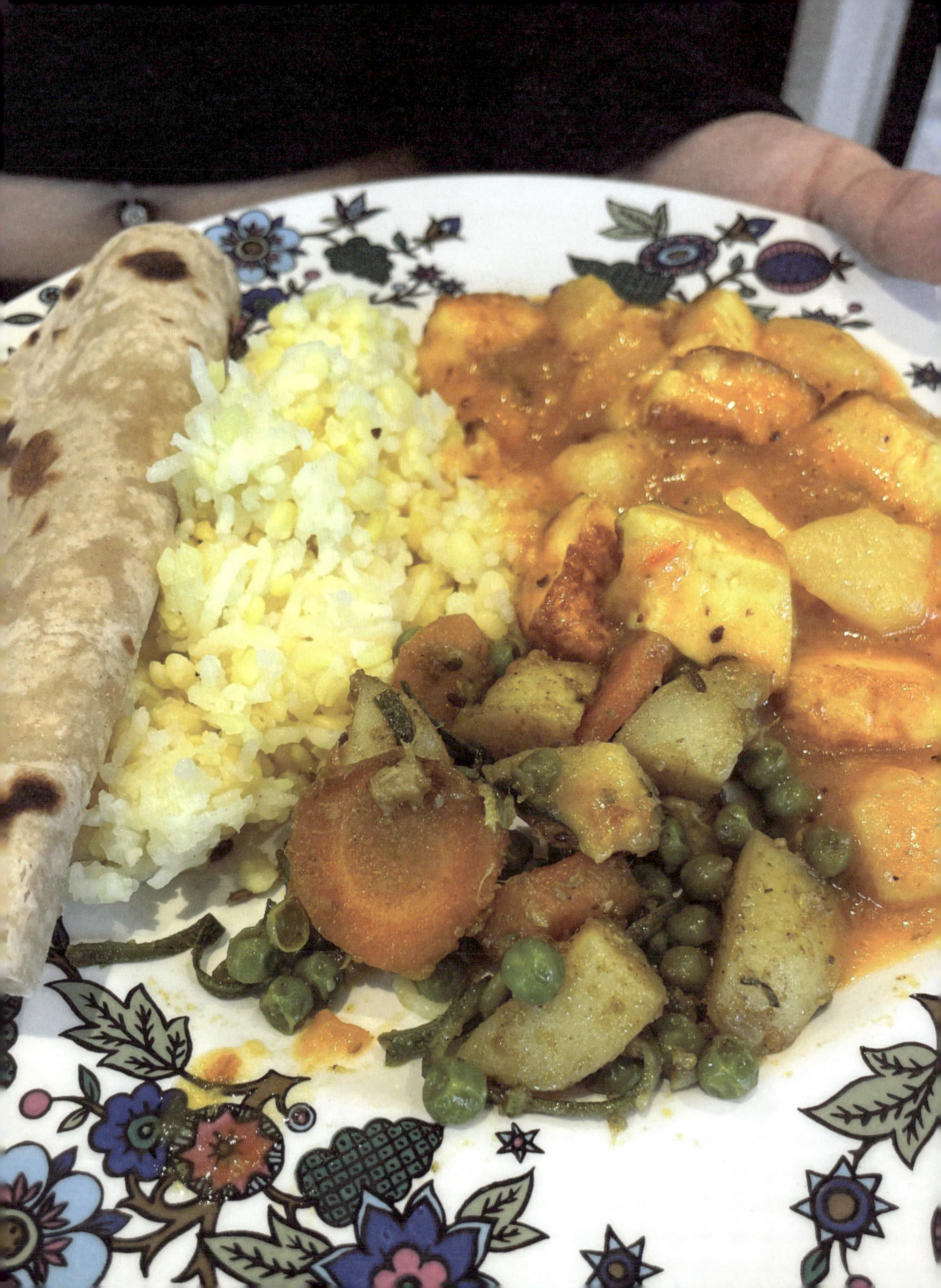

PANEER

Make your own
Homemade Paneer

Pre-made Paneer can now be commonly found in most supermarkets. This makes cooking paneer dishes less time consuming, although the children's favourite is always homemade. Both homemade and shop bought paneer can be frozen. If quick fried before freezing, it only needs to come out of the freezer 30 minutes before to defrost. If still in a block, then allow 3 hours.

You will need a paneer cloth to strain the cheese. This can be bought online; search butter or cheese cloth / muslin, they are reasonably cheap to purchase. This is Indian Nanny's recipe.

INGREDIENTS

2½ pints whole milk

2 or 3 tablespoons white vinegar

200g natural low fat set yogurt

Sunflower oil for frying

METHOD

1. Using a wok/pan wash with water and leave it damp so the milk doesn't stick to the pan. Put the milk into the pan and bring to the boil (medium to full heat).

2. When the milk is nearly boiling, put the yogurt in with a few tablespoons of white vinegar, stir but do not touch the bottom of the pan.

3. The milk will then separate. Turn off the heat.

4. Put a paneer cloth over a strainer in the sink and pour the mix in. Strain the paneer through the cloth, then put on one side and fold the cloth around it.

5. Fill a large pot /pan with cold water to use as a weight. Push it down onto the paneer and leave for 10 minutes. Once cool, uncover paneer and chop into cubes.

6. Frying the paneer definitely creates extra taste. It will have a much higher fat content so it is really optional. If you choose to fry the paneer, heat a pan of sunflower oil (approx. 2 to 3 inches deep). Check the temperature of the oil by popping a small bit of paneer into the oil – once it sizzles the oil is hot enough. Add the paneer cubes, between 7 and 10 at a time. Turn them gently and fry for 5 minutes until light brown. Use a slotted spoon to remove the paneer cubes from the oil. Put them on a plate with kitchen towel to blot up the excess oil.

   Note: This paneer can then be used for a variety of dishes or frozen until you wish to use it.

PANEER

Paneer – Indian Nanny's Special Recipe

READY IN 45 MINS **SERVES** 3-4

This is the classic paneer dish. Cooked in a tomato gravy with peas & potatoes is a family favourite. It's delicious, Amir and Sameer love it!

INGREDIENTS

4 tablespoons light olive oil

2 packets paneer (approx. 250g each, available from most supermarkets) or homemade if you prefer, see recipe on page 163

½ large onion

1 inch ginger, peeled

2 cloves garlic, peeled

½ tin chopped tomatoes

3-4 medium sized potatoes

2 cups frozen peas or petit pois

400ml water

1 heaped tablespoon set natural yogurt

Fresh Coriander to decorate (optional)

SPICES

1 teaspoon jeera

½ teaspoon paprika

½ teaspoon haldi

¼ teaspoon chilli powder

1 teaspoon coriander powder

1 ½ teaspoons salt

1 teaspoon garam masala

METHOD

1. Peel and finely chop the onion, garlic and ginger, preferably in a food processor.

2. Put this mixture into a large pan with 4 tablespoons of olive oil on a medium heat. Stir regularly to ensure it doesn't stick or burn.

3. Whilst this is cooking, peel and chop the potatoes into 2cm cubes, rinse them under cold water in a colander and set to one side.

4. Chop the paneer into cubes.

5. Once the onion mix has turned light brown, add 1 teaspoon of jeera and the chopped tomatoes. Quick stir, then add ½ teaspoon paprika, ½ teaspoon haldi, ¼ teaspoon chilli powder and 1 teaspoon coriander powder. Fry this mixture for 5 minutes.

6. Add the potatoes and 1 ½ teaspoons of salt. Fry for a further 5 minutes.

7. Add the paneer and water (I usually fill up the empty tomato tin with water!). Then add the peas. Put a lid on and leave simmering until potatoes are cooked, approximately 20 – 25 minutes. Then add 1 tablespoon yogurt (it's best to beat this in a cup with a fork before adding) and 1 teaspoon garam masala; stir and cook for a few more minutes.

8. Garnish with fresh chopped coriander leaves.

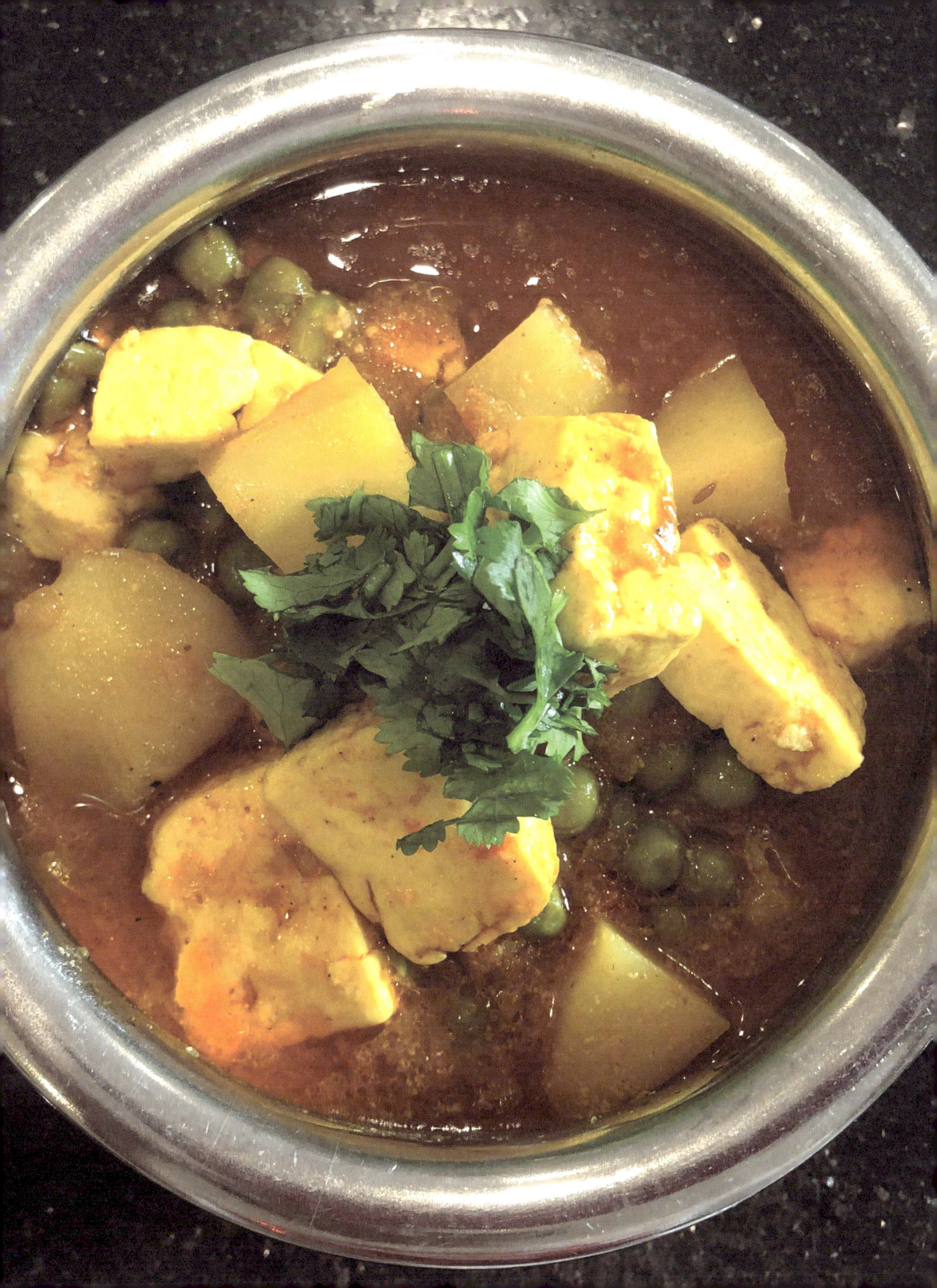

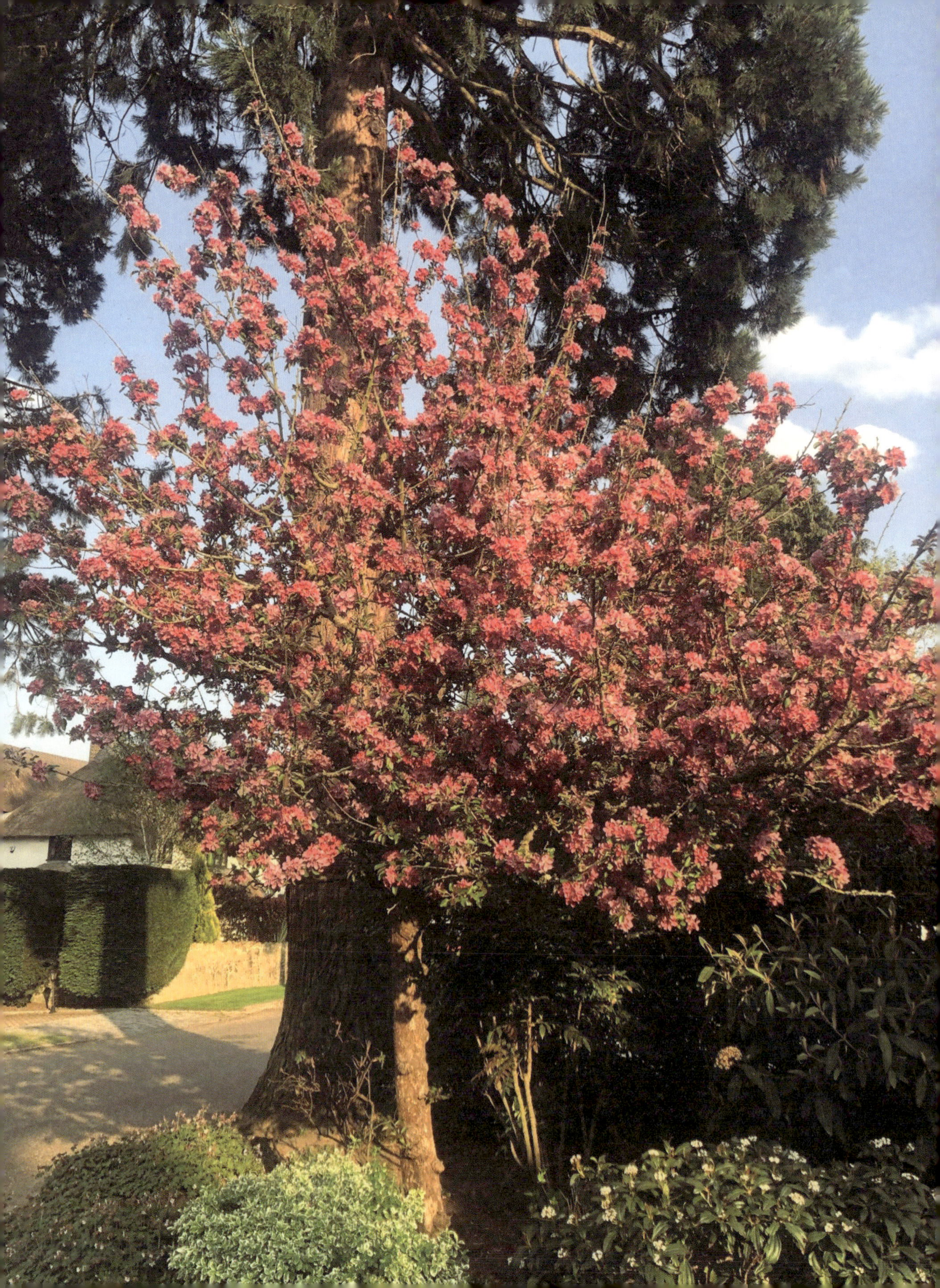

PANEER

Tofu – Indian Nanny's Special Recipe

READY IN 45 MINS

SERVES 3-4

This is our family's favourite paneer recipe and I've adapted it to be vegan using tofu as an alternative to paneer.

INGREDIENTS

4 tablespoons light olive oil

1 packet tofu (300g)

½ large onion

1 inch ginger, peeled

2 cloves garlic, peeled

½ tin chopped tomatoes

3-4 medium sized potatoes

2 cups frozen peas or petit pois

400ml water

1 heaped tablespoon unsweetened plant-based yogurt (optional)

Fresh coriander to decorate (optional)

SPICES

1 heaped teaspoon jeera

1 teaspoon paprika

½ teaspoon haldi

½ teaspoon chilli powder

1 heaped teaspoon coriander powder

2 teaspoons salt

1 teaspoon garam masala

METHOD

1. Peel and finely chop the onion, garlic and ginger, preferably in a food processor.

2. Put this mixture into a large pan with 4 tablespoons of olive oil on a medium heat. Stir regularly to ensure it doesn't stick or burn.

3. Whilst this is cooking, peel and chop the potatoes into 2cm cubes, rinse them under cold water in a colander and set to one side.

4. Chop the tofu into cubes.

5. Once the onion mix has turned light brown, add 1 heaped teaspoon of jeera and the chopped tomatoes. Quick stir, then add 1 teaspoon paprika, ½ teaspoon haldi, ½ teaspoon chilli powder, 1 heaped teaspoon coriander powder. Fry this mixture for 5 minutes.

6. Add the potatoes and 2 teaspoons of salt. Fry for a further 5 minutes.

7. Add the tofu and 400ml water (I usually fill up the empty tinned tomatoes tin with water!). Then the peas. Put a lid on and leave simmering until potatoes are cooked for approximately 20 minutes. If using yogurt, add 1 heaped tablespoon (it's best to beat this in a cup with a fork before adding) and 1 teaspoon garam masala, stir and cook for a few more minutes.

8. Garnish with fresh chopped coriander leaves.

PANEER

Scrambled Paneer or Tofu

READY IN 30 MINS   **SERVES** 3-4

This is a great way of serving paneer or tofu, quite quick to make and tastes great. It's one of my Auntie Veena's signature dishes so she taught me this one.

INGREDIENTS

4 pints of milk and follow homemade paneer recipe or 1 block of paneer or a block of plain tofu

1 large onion

2 to 3 tablespoons light olive oil

2 teaspoons tomato puree

½ tin chopped tomatoes (can use plum tomatoes instead and liquidise in the mini chopper)

1 cup peas or petit pois

Fresh coriander chopped for decoration (optional)

SPICES

1 teaspoon jeera

1 teaspoon salt

1 teaspoon haldi

½ teaspoon chilli powder

1 teaspoon coriander powder

1 teaspoon garam masala

METHOD

1. Make your paneer using 4 pints of milk or use shop bought paneer / tofu if you prefer.

2. Thinly slice a large onion.

3. Add 2 to 3 tablespoons of olive oil and 1 teaspoon of jeera to a large pan. Once the jeera starts to "pop", add the onion and fry until soft and pinkish, light brown.

4. Add ½ tin chopped tomatoes and give it a quick stir. Add 1 teaspoon of salt, 1 teaspoon haldi, ½ teaspoon chilli powder, 1 teaspoon coriander powder and 2 teaspoons tomato puree. Give it a stir then add a cup of peas. Cook and stir for a little while.

5. After 5 minutes add the paneer / tofu. If you are using a block, you can thickly grate it straight into the pan or if you are using fresh paneer, it will crumble straight in. With tofu, you mash it up once in the pan.

6. Cook for 10-15 minutes on a low heat.

7. Add 1 teaspoon garam masala.

8. Fresh coriander chopped on top.

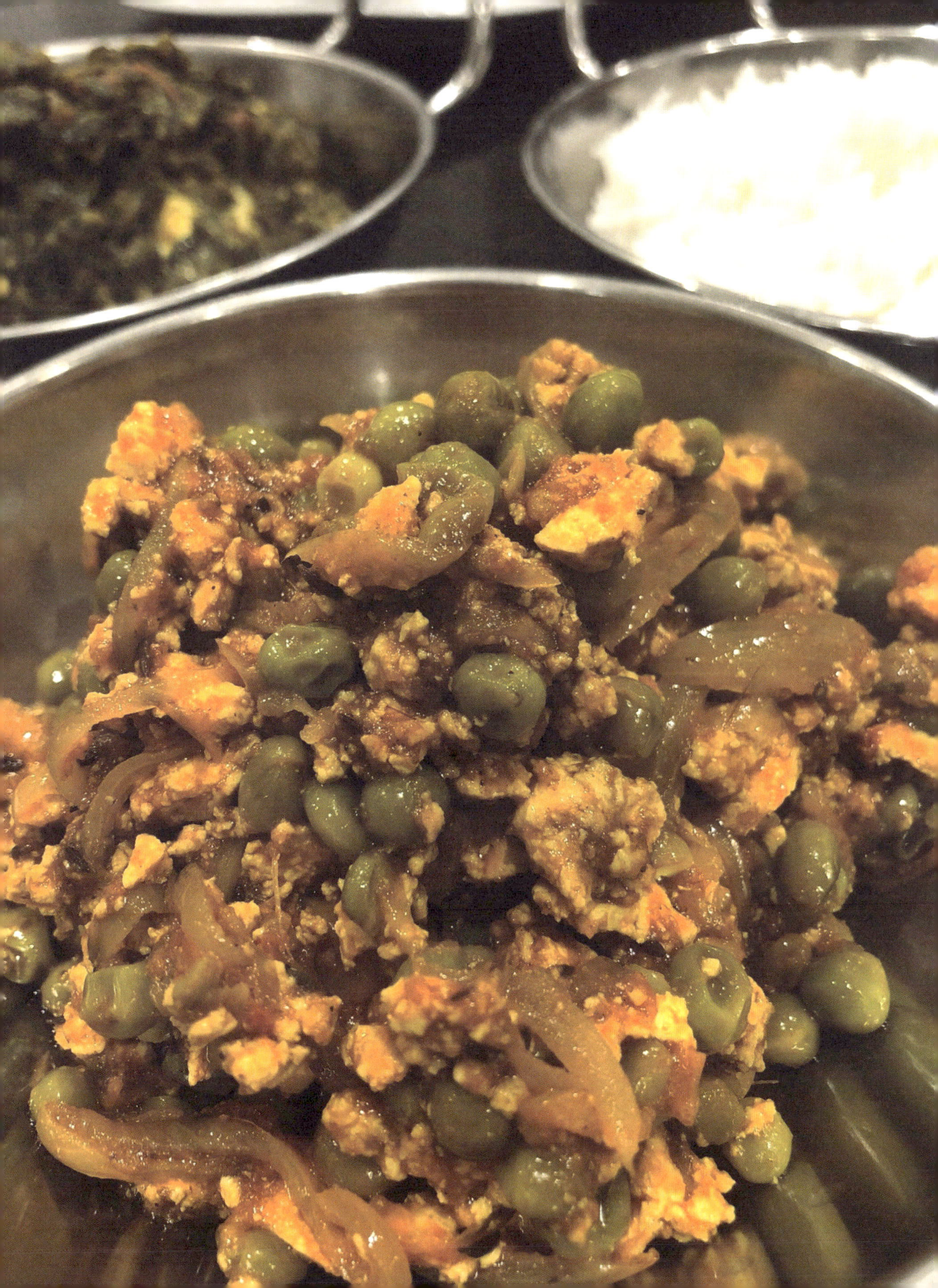

PANEER

Shahi Paneer

READY IN 30 MINS   **SERVES** 3-4

Milly's favourite, this recipe makes a lovely paneer. Easy to make, even a teenager can cook it! My Auntie Veena taught me this recipe; she uses cinnamon powder to give it a really warming flavour. Rita makes a similar version without the cinnamon powder, so this is an optional spice.

INGREDIENTS

500g paneer (2 packets) cut into cubes

2 medium onions

4-6 tablespoons light olive oil

1 tin chopped tomatoes

1 cup water

150g single cream or crème fraiche

Chopped fresh coriander (optional)

SPICES

1 teaspoon jeera

1 teaspoon salt

1 teaspoon paprika

½ teaspoon chilli powder

1 teaspoon haldi

½ teaspoon cinnamon powder (optional)

1 teaspoon garam masala

METHOD

1. In the food processor, finely chop 2 medium onions.

2. Into a large pan or wok, put the olive oil on a medium to high heat. Add 1 teaspoon of jeera, heat until the oil and jeera mixture is warm – the jeera will "pop", usually about 30 seconds.

3. Add the onion and cook on a medium heat until the onions are light brown in colour.

4. Add the tin of chopped tomatoes and give a quick stir.

5. Then add the spices, 1 teaspoon salt, 1 teaspoon paprika, ½ teaspoon chilli powder, 1 teaspoon haldi, ½ teaspoon of cinnamon powder (optional). Give it a good stir then turn the heat off.

6. Put this mixture into the food processor and liquidise using the rotational blade, blitz for a minute, then add a cup of water. Then blitz again for a few minutes until the mixture is the consistency of a liquid.

7. Put it back into the saucepan on a medium heat. Add the paneer cubes and simmer on a low to medium heat for approximately 15 minutes with the lid on. Stir occasionally.

8. Once the paneer is cooked, it will be soft as it has absorbed some of the liquid. Add the single cream or crème fraiche, 1 teaspoon of garam masala and chopped fresh coriander.

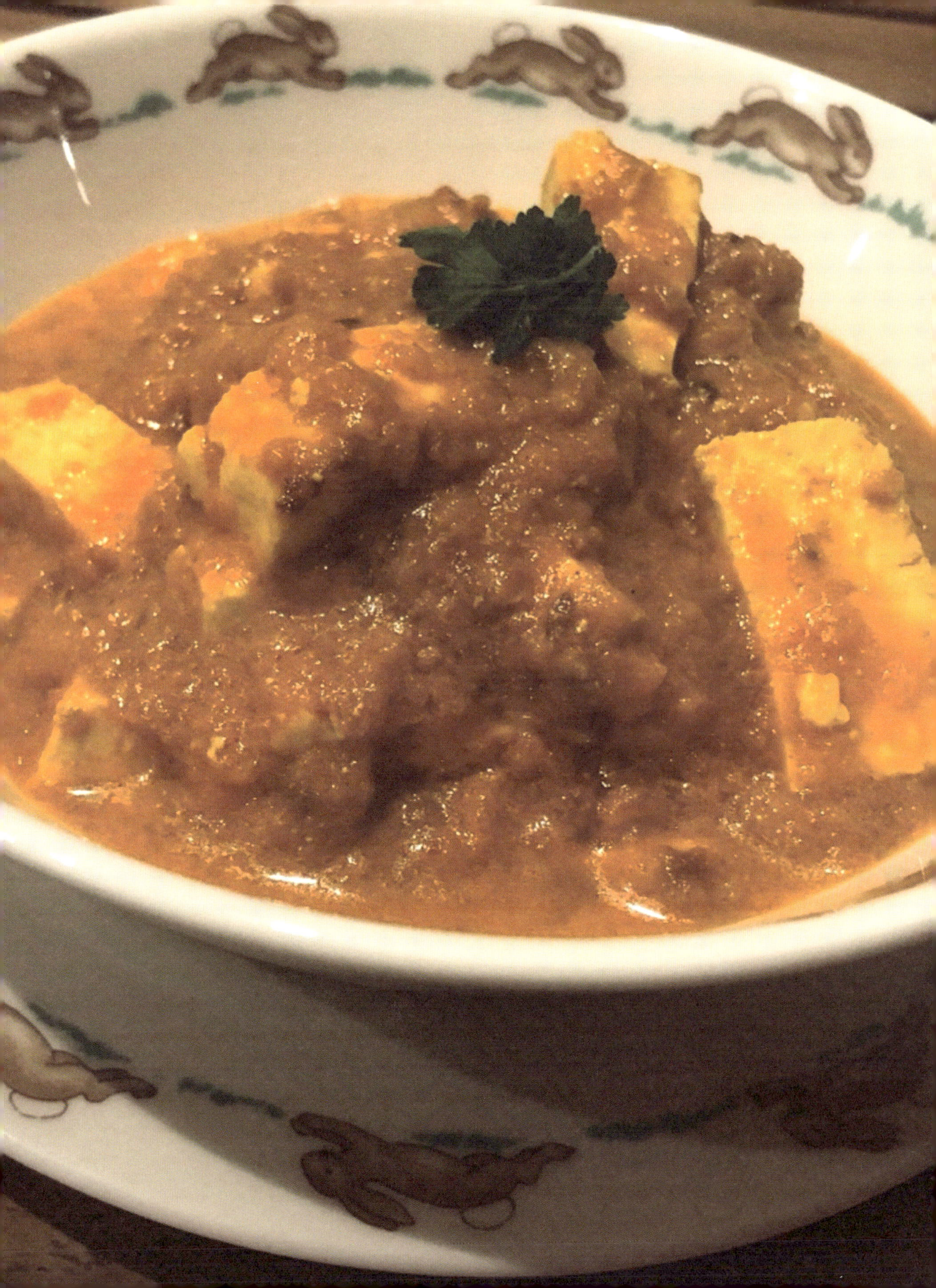

PANEER

Shahi Tofu

⏳ READY IN **30 MINS** 🍽 SERVES **3-4**

When Milly decided to give a plant-based diet a go, we modified her favourite recipe. This was a big hit; the sauce is amazing and the taste is fantastic with tofu.

INGREDIENTS

300g tofu (1 packet) cut into cubes

2 medium onions

4-6 tablespoons light olive oil

1 tin chopped tomatoes

1 ½ cups water

150g oat single cream

Chopped fresh coriander (optional)

SPICES

1 teaspoon jeera

2 teaspoons salt

1 teaspoon paprika

½ teaspoon chilli powder

1 teaspoon haldi

½ teaspoon cinnamon powder (optional)

1 teaspoon garam masala

METHOD

1. In the food processor, finely chop 2 medium onions.

2. Into a large pan or wok, put the olive oil on a medium to high heat. Add 1 teaspoon of jeera, heat until the oil and jeera mixture is warm – the jeera will "pop", usually about 30 seconds.

3. Add the onion and cook on a medium heat until the onions are light brown in colour.

4. Add the tin of chopped tomatoes and give a quick stir.

5. Then add the spices, 2 teaspoons salt, 1 teaspoon paprika, ½ teaspoon chilli powder, 1 teaspoon haldi and ½ teaspoon of cinnamon powder (optional). Give it a good stir then turn the heat off.

6. Put this mixture into the food processor and liquidise using the rotational blade, blitz for a minute, then add a cup of water. Then blitz again for a few minutes until the mixture is the consistency of a liquid.

7. Put it back into the saucepan on a medium heat. Add the tofu cubes and simmer on a low to medium heat for approximately 15 minutes with the lid on. Stir occasionally.

8. Once the tofu is cooked, it will be soft as it has absorbed some of the liquid. Add the oat single cream, 1 teaspoon of garam masala and chopped fresh coriander (optional).

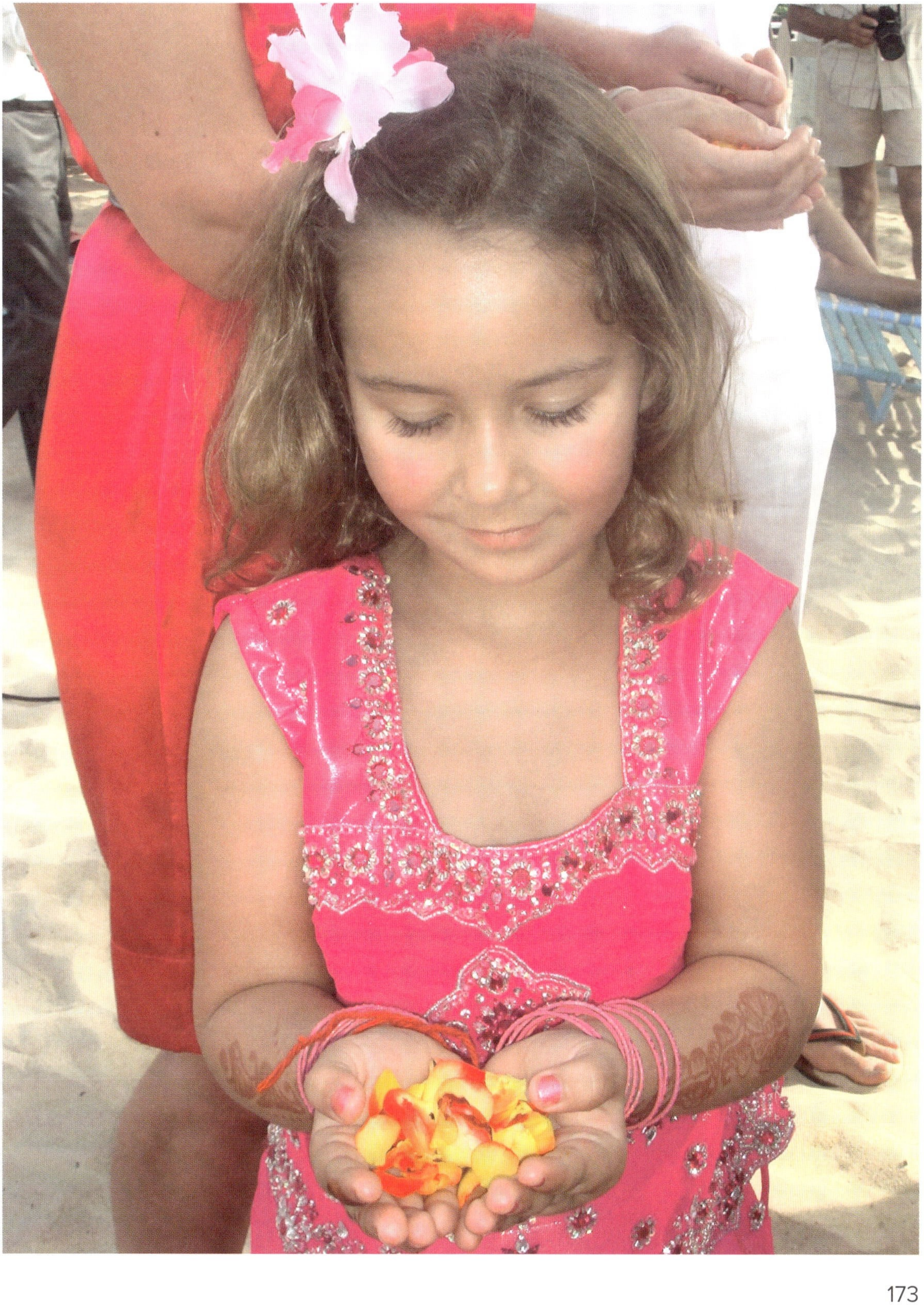

PANEER

Paneer with Cashews, Peppers & Sweetcorn

READY IN 30 MINS **SERVES** 3-4

This is one of our favourite paneer dishes; my Auntie Veena taught me this recipe. You can also mash up the paneer rather than cook it in cubes if you prefer. Our favourite way is with fried paneer cubes as it is so tasty! Make it vegan – fried tofu chunks, natural tofu chunks or mash up the tofu. Heap the spices and salt quantities – awesome!

INGREDIENTS

4 medium onions

6 tablespoons light olive oil or sunflower oil

1 tin chopped tomatoes

450g paneer, this is 2 x 225g shop bought or approximately 50 cubes of paneer, either freshly made or de-frosted*.

500g button mushrooms

1 or 2 handfuls unsalted cashew nuts

1 green pepper

1 red pepper

1 cup frozen sweetcorn

Fresh coriander for decoration

SPICES

2 teaspoons jeera

2 teaspoons salt

1 teaspoon haldi

1 teaspoon paprika

¼ teaspoon chilli powder (more if desired)

1 teaspoon coriander powder

1 teaspoon garam masala

Veena's tip: to defrost the paneer, take the cubes out of the freezer and soak in a bowl of boiling water.

METHOD

1. Peel the onions, cut into quarters and then coarsely slice. Put them in a large heavy pan or wok. Add 6 tablespoons of olive oil or sunflower oil, 2 teaspoons jeera, put on a medium heat. Stir occasionally until the onions go pink. While this is frying, wash the mushrooms, cut any larger ones in quarters, put to one side.

2. Add the tinned chopped tomatoes to the pan. Cook this for 5 minutes, then add 2 teaspoons salt, 1 teaspoon haldi, 1 teaspoon paprika, ¼ teaspoon chilli powder (more if desired), 1 teaspoon coriander powder.

3. Stir and add a handful or two of unsalted cashew nuts. Add the mushrooms to the pan. Turn the heat right down, add 1 cup of sweetcorn. Give it a quick stir.

4. Cut the peppers into quarters, then chop into 1 inch by ½ inch pieces, discard the white flesh and the seeds. Add to the pan.

5. Strain the water from the paneer if you defrosted it, then add the paneer cubes. Give it a good stir then put the lid on and cook on a low heat until everything is cooked, approximately 15 minutes. Cooking this dish with the lid on means very quickly the juice from the sweetcorn and the mushrooms help to cook all of the food, giving it good flavour. When cooked the dish should still be moist.

6. Add 1 teaspoon of garam masala and some fresh coriander for decoration if required.

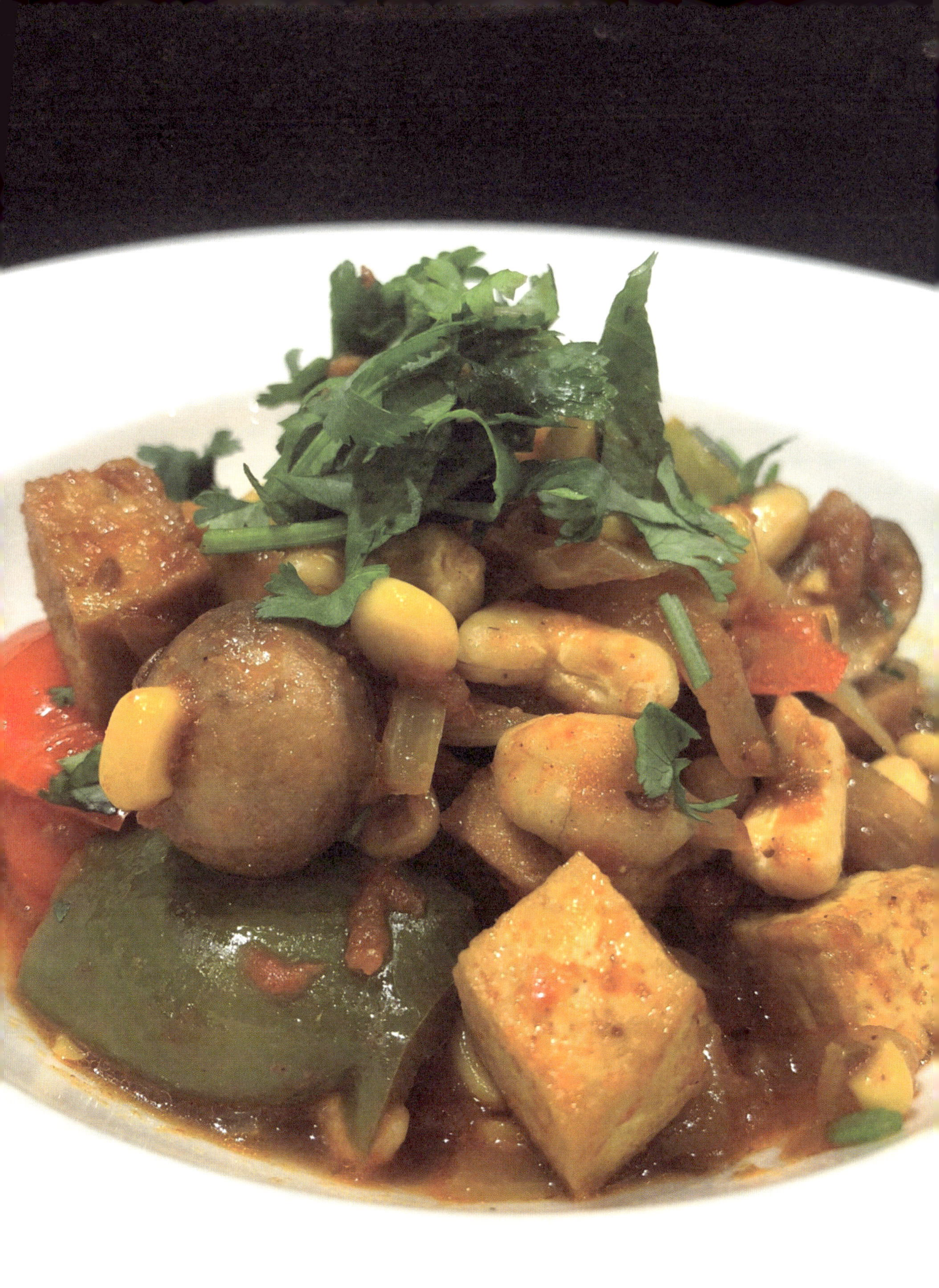

PANEER

Paneer with Peas

READY IN 30 MINS

SERVES 3-4

This is one of Auntie Rita's famous paneer recipes.

INGREDIENTS

2 tablespoons light olive oil

1 medium onion, peeled and finely chopped

Ginger & green chilli chopped finely (to taste) – I would probably use an inch of ginger & one fresh chilli

250g paneer

1 cup frozen peas or petit pois

2 tomatoes, finely chopped

¼ cup tinned tomatoes

½ cup water

Fresh coriander (optional)

SPICES

1 teaspoon jeera

1 ½ teaspoons salt

1 teaspoon paprika

1 teaspoon coriander powder

1 teaspoon garam masala

METHOD

1. Heat the oil in a wok and add the jeera. When the jeera starts to pop / sizzle 30-60 seconds, add the onions. If using, add the ginger and green chillies. Stirring occasionally, on a medium heat.

2. When the onions are light brown, add the fresh tomatoes, cover and let them soften for a few minutes.

3. Now add the peas, tinned tomatoes and all of the other core spices. Add the water and stir, then cover and allow to simmer until the peas are cooked. This should take about 15 minutes.

4. Once cooked, uncover and crumble or dice the paneer into the wok. Mix then cover and simmer for about 3 – 4 minutes.

5. Uncover and gently dry up any liquid by continuing to cook on a low heat. Turn the heat off and sprinkle with chopped coriander if you wish.

We need to be the change we wish to see in the world - Gandhi

PANEER

Tofu with Peas

READY IN 30 MINS   **SERVES** 3-4

Auntie Rita's famous paneer recipe, I modified to a vegan recipe using tofu. It mashes up the same as paneer, however needs a bit more spice and less water.

INGREDIENTS

3 tablespoons light olive oil

1 medium onion, peeled and finely chopped

Ginger & green chilli finely chopped (to taste) – I would probably use an inch of ginger & one fresh chilli

300g plain tofu

1 cup frozen peas or petit pois

2 tomatoes, finely chopped

¼ cup tinned tomatoes

¼ cup water

Fresh coriander (optional)

SPICES

1 heaped teaspoon jeera

2 teaspoons salt

1 heaped teaspoon paprika

1 heaped teaspoon coriander powder

1 heaped teaspoon garam masala

METHOD

1. Heat the oil in a wok and add the jeera. When they pop / sizzle (30-60 seconds), add the onions. If using, add the ginger and green chillies, stirring occasionally, on a medium heat.

2. When the onions are light brown, add the fresh tomatoes, cover and let them soften for a few minutes.

3. Now add the peas, tinned tomatoes and all of the other core spices. Add the water, stir, then cover and allow to simmer for 5 minutes until the peas are cooked.

4. Now uncover and crumble or dice the tofu into the wok. Mix then cover and simmer for about 10 minutes. The tofu will soften nicely; mash up any larger chunks with a fork if you wish.

5. Uncover and gently dry up any liquid by continuing to cook on a low heat. Turn the heat off and sprinkle with chopped fresh coriander (optional).

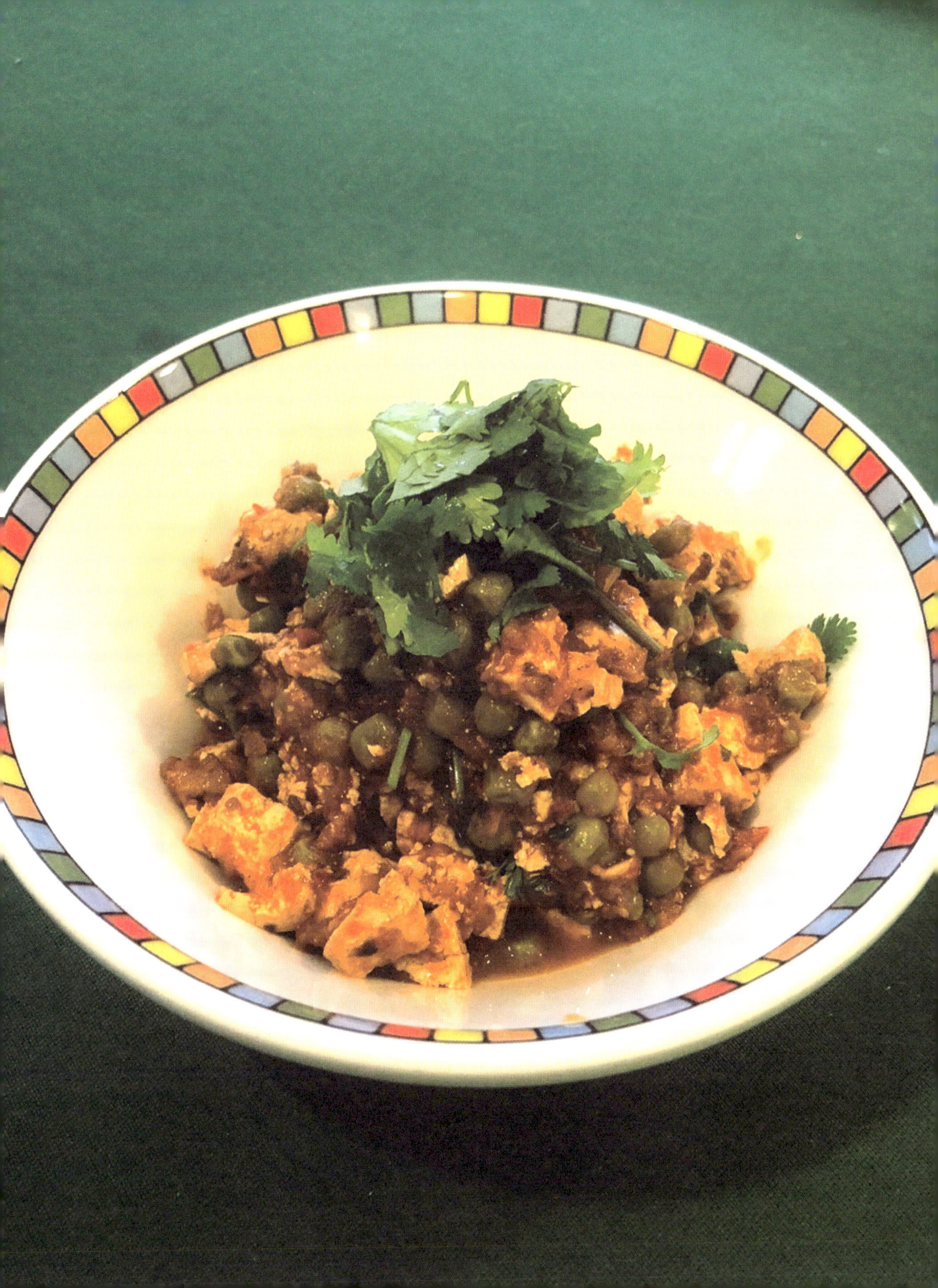

PANEER

Spinach Tofu

READY IN 30 MINS **SERVES** 3-4

This is another one of Auntie Rita's famous recipes – she cooks it with paneer or chicken, which is Sanj and Robin's favourite. I modified it slightly to a vegan recipe using tofu. The flavour is incredible. Even friends who shy away from tofu like this one!

INGREDIENTS

750g fresh or frozen spinach

2 medium onions, peeled

4 cloves garlic, peeled

1 inch ginger, peeled

2 green chillies

3 tablespoons light olive oil

2 tomatoes, finely chopped

½ tin chopped tomatoes

300g plain tofu, chopped into cubes

SPICES

1 heaped teaspoon jeera

2 teaspoons salt

1 teaspoon haldi

1 heaped teaspoon paprika

1 heaped teaspoon coriander powder

½ teaspoon garam masala

METHOD

1. If you are using fresh spinach, wash and put in a wok with ½ cup water on a low to medium heat with the lid on. Once wilted remove and blitz in a food processor. If you are using frozen spinach, just defrost in the microwave for a few minutes, then set to one side.

2. Using the food processor finely chop the onions, garlic, ginger and green chillies.

3. Heat the oil in a wok and add the jeera. When they pop / sizzle (30-60 seconds), add the onions, ginger, garlic and green chillies. Stirring occasionally on a medium heat.

4. When the onions are light brown, add the fresh tomatoes, cover and let them soften for a few minutes.

5. Now add the tinned tomatoes, spinach, salt and all of the other spices, except the garam masala. Cook for 5 minutes on a medium heat with the lid on.

6. Add the tofu and stir it in nicely to the spinach, cover and allow to simmer for 15 minutes with the lid on.

7. If there is too much water take off the lid and cook for a few minutes. Then add the garam masala and turn off the heat.

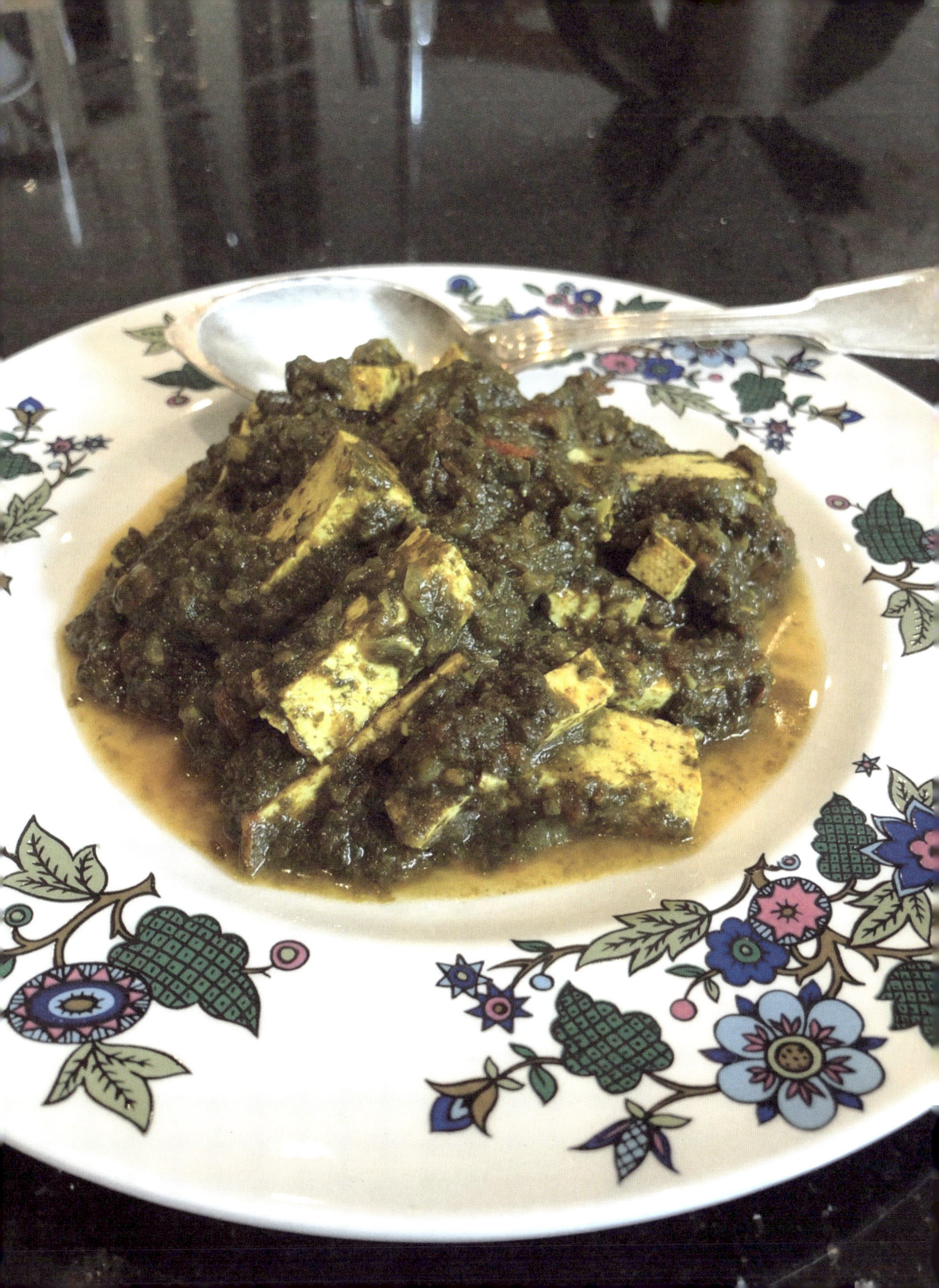

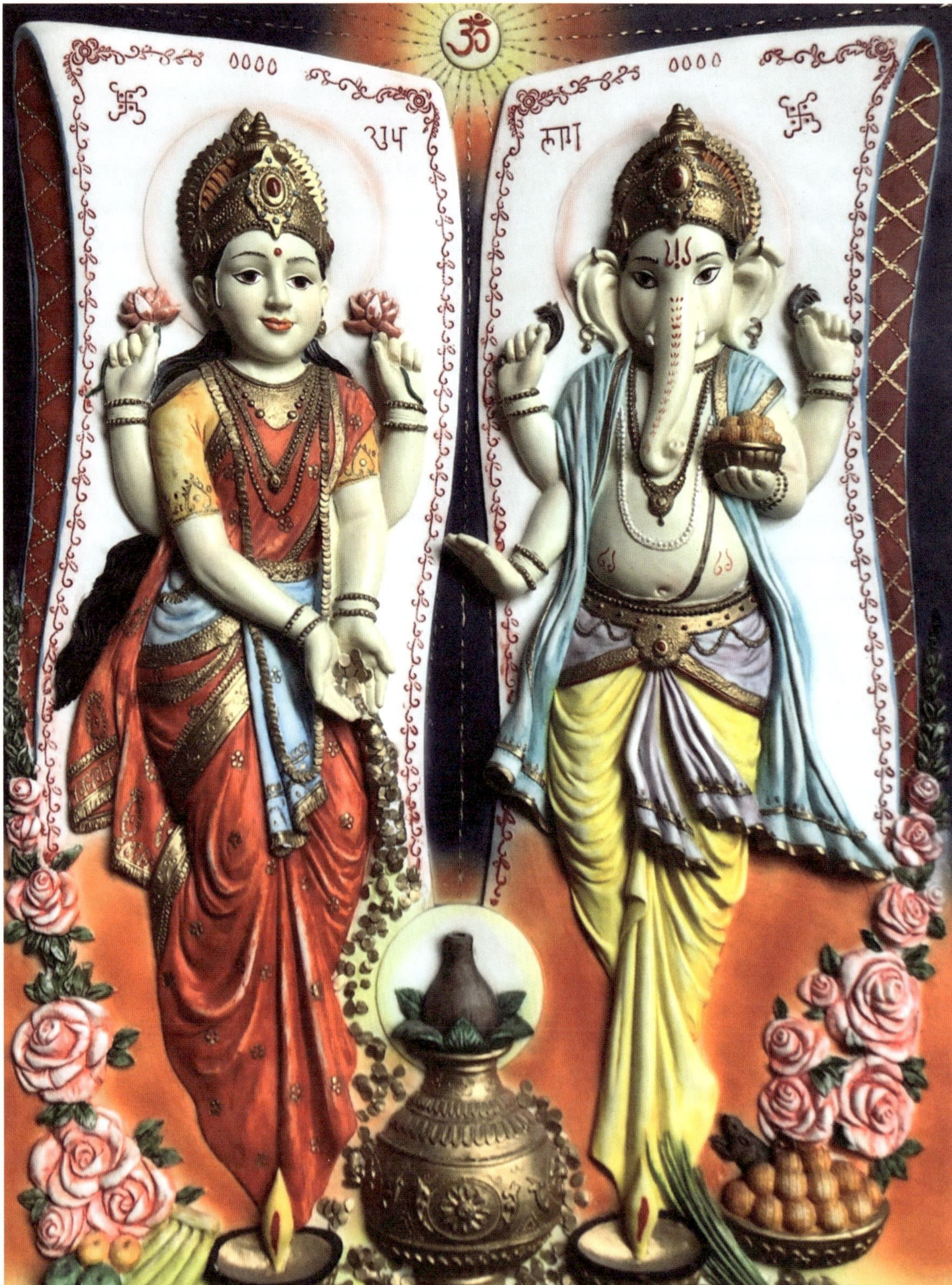
ॐ

DAHL

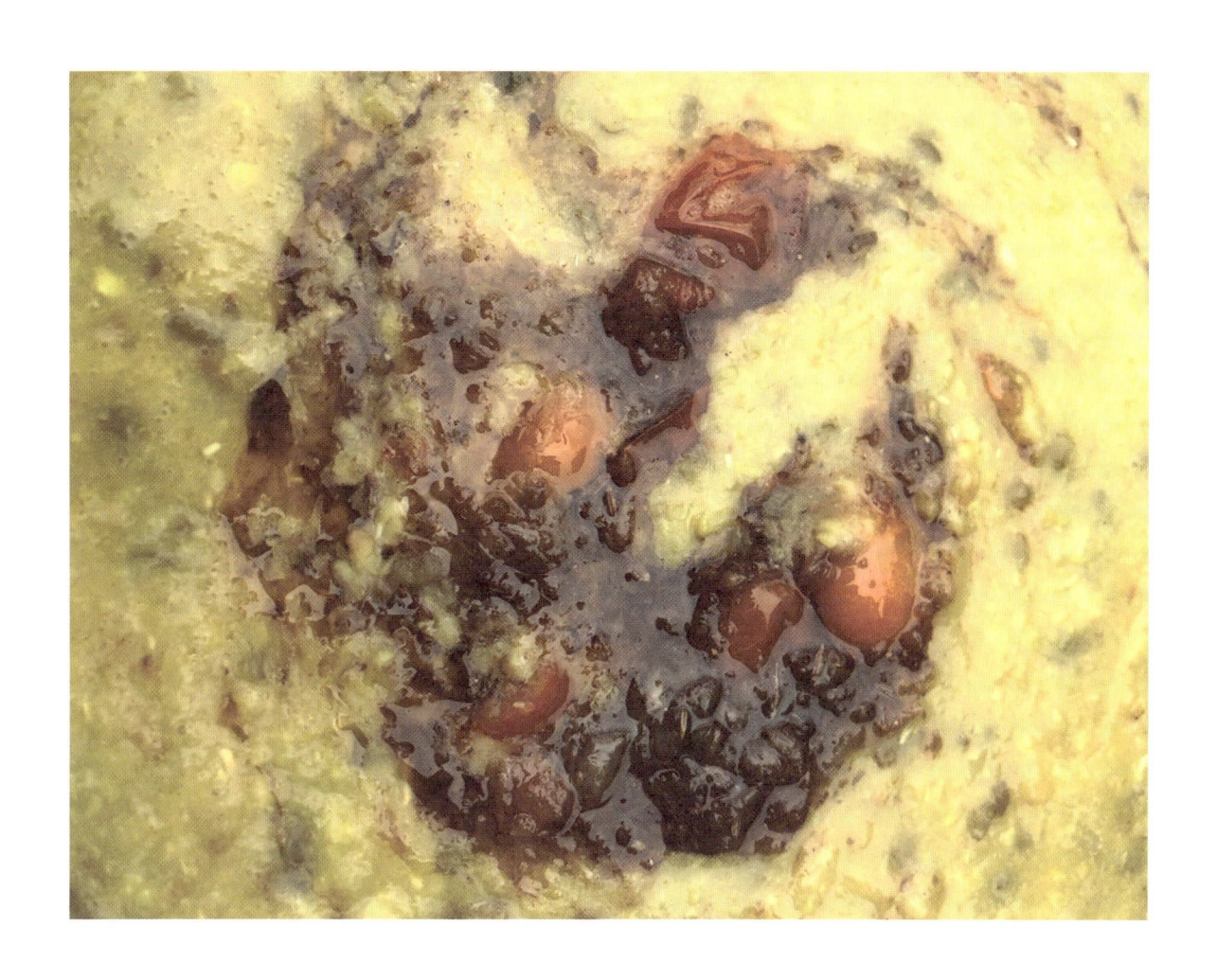

Different Dahls (Lentils) & Beans

As children, my dad and aunties recall that the evening meal would be a dahl, a vegetable side dish and a few chapatis or bowl of rice. This was a satisfying and healthy meal. Packed with vitamins and flavour. A good balance of protein, carbohydrates and fat. Meat was eaten once a week.

Dahls are a very traditional Indian dish. They are rich in nutrients and are packed with many health benefits. Excellent protein source for vegetarians and vegans, all are gluten free. They are great as you can cook them in the morning and leave on the stove until you want to reheat in the evening. They will also keep for a good few days in the fridge. You may need to add an extra cup of water when reheating as they do tend to thicken when left. A staple Indian dish loaded with goodness and flavour. They are also very cheap to buy and superior in quality. Below is a summary of some of the different dahls, and our family recipes can be found in this section of the book.

The majority of dahls and beans can be purchased dried or tinned in main supermarkets; however, there is a wider selection generally available in Indian supermarkets. Just a few pounds will get you a 500g bag, and trust me, this goes a long way!

Nowadays we generally do the same and serve these dishes alongside a rice of your choice, maybe a veggies dish and usually mop up the sauce with a chapati or naan bread. For a simple meal, a bowl of rice and dahl is filling and nutritious. For a lavish spread you will always cook and serve a dahl alongside many other Indian dishes.

Yellow mung dahl – this is a split lentil known to me as the baby grain. It is the quickest to cook. Just needs a good wash, no need to soak it or if you want to, just for 10 minutes. In a pressure cooker, one steam pressure and switch it off very quickly. Or simmer for 20 - 30 minutes in a pan. Simply add haldi and salt.

Chana dahl – slightly larger lentil, soaking is recommended but not required. If using a pressure cooker, soak for between 15 minutes and an hour, as this does speed up the cooking time. In a pressure cooker, one steam pressure and cook for 10 - 15 minutes. If you are not going to use a pressure cooker, soak for 4-5 hours and simmer for 30 minutes or so, until the grain is slightly soft to mash.

Chana – The Indian name for chickpeas. Probably one of the best known lentils in the western world. These can be purchased in a tin too. Chana & mushroom is an excellent dish for beginners wanting to cook chana but nervous about soaking / using a pressure cooker. Once you develop your dahl cooking skills, give Nanny's chana recipe a go, it really is a very tasty chana dish which is well known and delicious. Dried chana must be soaked overnight or for a minimum of 9 hours prior to cooking.

Whole Urad dahl / black lentils – My Auntie Rita told me this is called "the mother of all dahls", this is a whole dahl with the skin on. The recipe we use to cook this was taught by my Nan to her daughters. They later taught it to my dad so see the recipe "Vipi Uncles brown dahl". Urad dahl is one of the richest sources of protein and vitamin B. This simple lentil is full of iron, folic acid, calcium, magnesium and potassium, which makes this dahl beneficial for pregnant women. Urad dahl is light and known to please most people's taste.

Urid dahl / white lentils – This is made from hulled and split urad beans. It requires no pre-soaking. This lentil is an important ingredient in Indian cooking and is used for a variety of well-known products. Ground urid dahl is used to make poppadoms, dosas and fried dumplings as well as a special yogurt with dahl dumplings. It has a creamy and slightly nutty texture when cooked as a dahl, but quite bland, so if cooking this dahl, we would suggest mixing it 50/50 with chana dahl and cooking as per that recipe. Or with split mung dahl and masoor dahl.

Masoor dahl / brown dahl – this is a whole dahl, it has a brown skin and the dahl inside is orange. You may have come across this type of lentil with the skin off and called red or orange lentils. Light, versatile, healthy, filling and delicious like all other dahls. Also packed with nutrients and easy to cook. Soak for an hour and cooks in 20 minutes.

Split Mung dahl – this is a split dahl. It needs soaking for an hour prior to cooking.

Mung beans – this is a whole dahl and needs soaking for an hour before cooking.

Red kidney beans – the kidney bean is a variety of the common bean. Don't try this at home, but one of the Sobte sisters actually tried to put one up their nose as a toddler! Red kidney beans are packed full of nutrients and can be purchased in tins; however, Indian cooking usually refers to dried red kidney beans. They can cause food poisoning if not prepared and cooked correctly so must be soaked overnight and boiled on a high heat for 20 minutes during their initial cooking. Also do not cook them in the water they have been soaked in, but drain and then rinse them well before putting into fresh water. The soaking water absorbs much of the ingredient / toxin that upsets the gut. Don't let this scare you! They are amazing, soft and packed with flavour when cooked using the simple to follow recipe.

Black eye beans – these are rich in fibre, protein, vitamins and minerals. Low in fat, sodium and cholesterol. If you buy dried black eye beans they must be soaked for 6 to 8 hours and then cooked in a pressure cooker. Tinned can be cooked without soaking, but should be drained and given a good rinse.

Tarka

This is the "gold" to the dahl. We finish most dahl dishes with a blend of spices, onion, tomato and oil. You can follow this at the end of each dahl recipe and add to give the dahl an amazing flavour. They vary in colour from golden yellow to deep red, depending on what you put in them; it's the secret to a really beautiful dahl.

DAHL

Yellow Mung Dahl

READY IN
20 MINS
+SOAKING

SERVES
3-4

This is Indian Nanny's recipe, when I eat it, it reminds me of Big Dada. She taught me to cook yellow dahl, it is the quickest dahl to cook. Just a good wash, if you really want to cook quickly there is no need to soak it. In a pressure cooker, one steam pressure and switch it off. Or simmer for 20 - 30 minutes in a heavy pan. Simply add haldi and salt to make a delicious dahl. Ria's favourite!

DAHL INGREDIENTS

¾ cup yellow mung dahl

2 cups water

2 small spoons ghee / butter / or vegan butter (optional)

DAHL SPICES

1 teaspoon salt

½ teaspoon haldi

¼ teaspoon chilli powder

TARKA INGREDIENTS

2 tablespoons light olive oil

½ onion, finely chopped

1 small tomato, chopped

TARKA SPICES

½ teaspoon garam masala

½ teaspoon jeera

Alternative to pressure cooker?
If you really do not like a pressure cooker, or you do not have one, you can cook this dish in a saucepan with a tight-fitting lid. I would only suggest this cooking method with this particular dahl as it does not need soaking overnight. Soak for 10 minutes as above, then cook using a heavy pan with a lid and simmer for about 20 - 30 minutes.

METHOD

1. Soak dahl in warm water for 10 minutes. Wash / rinse as you would rice then put in a pressure cooker with the water, salt, haldi & chilli powder.

2. Put the steamer on top of the pressure cooker lid (if yours has one of these).

3. Put the lid on the pressure cooker, high heat for approximately 5 minutes until you get 1 steam pressure. Then switch it off until the pressure drops (approximately 15 minutes).

4. Meanwhile, make your tarka by adding 2 tablespoons of oil to a small saucepan on a medium heat.

5. Add the chopped onion, chopped tomato, ½ teaspoon garam masala, ½ teaspoon jeera and fry for a little bit until the tomato and onion changes colour, approximately 5 minutes. Remove it from the heat.

6. Once the pressure has dropped in your pressure cooker, open the lid and cook for 5 minutes with a normal lid on (or the pressure cooker lid but not closed) on a low heat.

7. You then add the tarka to the dahl and give it a little stir. If you would like to make the dish extra delicious, add the ghee / butter / vegan spread as it will make it really creamy.

8. Turn off the heat and it is ready to serve.

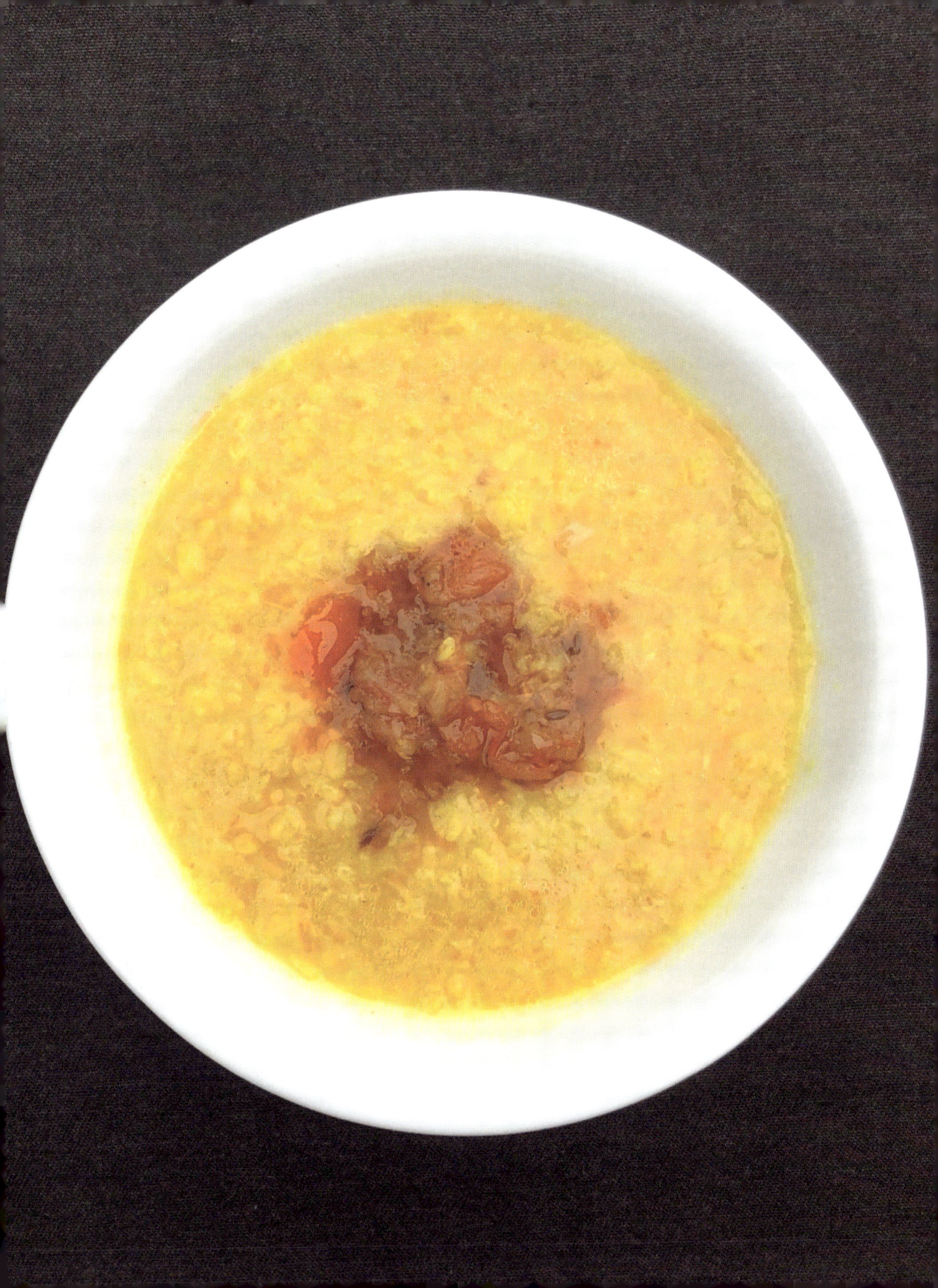

DAHL

Dahl with Spinach

READY IN 45 MINS   **SERVES** 3-4

I love this dahl! Auntie Rita taught me to cook this, the leaves of the spinach break up the rich taste of the dahl. Easy to make and full of vitamins, nutrients and iron.

DAHL INGREDIENTS

¾ cup dahl yellow mung & orange dahl mixed

2 cups water

DAHL SPICES

1 teaspoon salt

½ teaspoon haldi

¼ teaspoon chilli powder

TARKA INGREDIENTS

2 tablespoons light olive oil

1 medium onion, peeled & finely chopped

1 inch ginger, peeled & finely chopped

1 tomato, skin off, finely chopped

100g spinach leaves, washed & chopped

TARKA SPICES

½ teaspoon jeera

½ teaspoon paprika

½ teaspoon coriander powder

½ teaspoon garam masala

METHOD

1. Wash the dahl a few times in warm water then rinse and drain through a colander. Put the dahl in a pressure cooker with the water, salt, haldi & chilli powder. Tightly close the lid.

2. Cook it on a high heat for approximately 5 minutes until you get 1 steam pressure. Then switch it off until the pressure drops (approximately 15 minutes).

3. While this is cooking make your tarka. Add 2 tablespoons of oil to a small saucepan on a medium heat with the ½ teaspoon of jeera. When it pops (30 seconds) add the finely chopped onion. Cook this for 5 minutes on a high / medium heat, checking and stirring often. Do not let the onion go too brown.

4. Then add the chopped tomato, ½ teaspoon paprika, ½ teaspoon coriander powder, ½ teaspoon garam masala and fry for a few minutes until the tomato changes colour. Add the chopped spinach and cook until wilted. Turn off the heat.

5. You then add this tarka to the dahl and give it a little stir. Cook the dahl for 5 minutes on a low heat. The dahl should be soft but you can still see the grains.

6. Once cooked it is ready to eat.

Note – you can make this with yellow mung dahl and not mix with orange dahl if you prefer / do not have it.

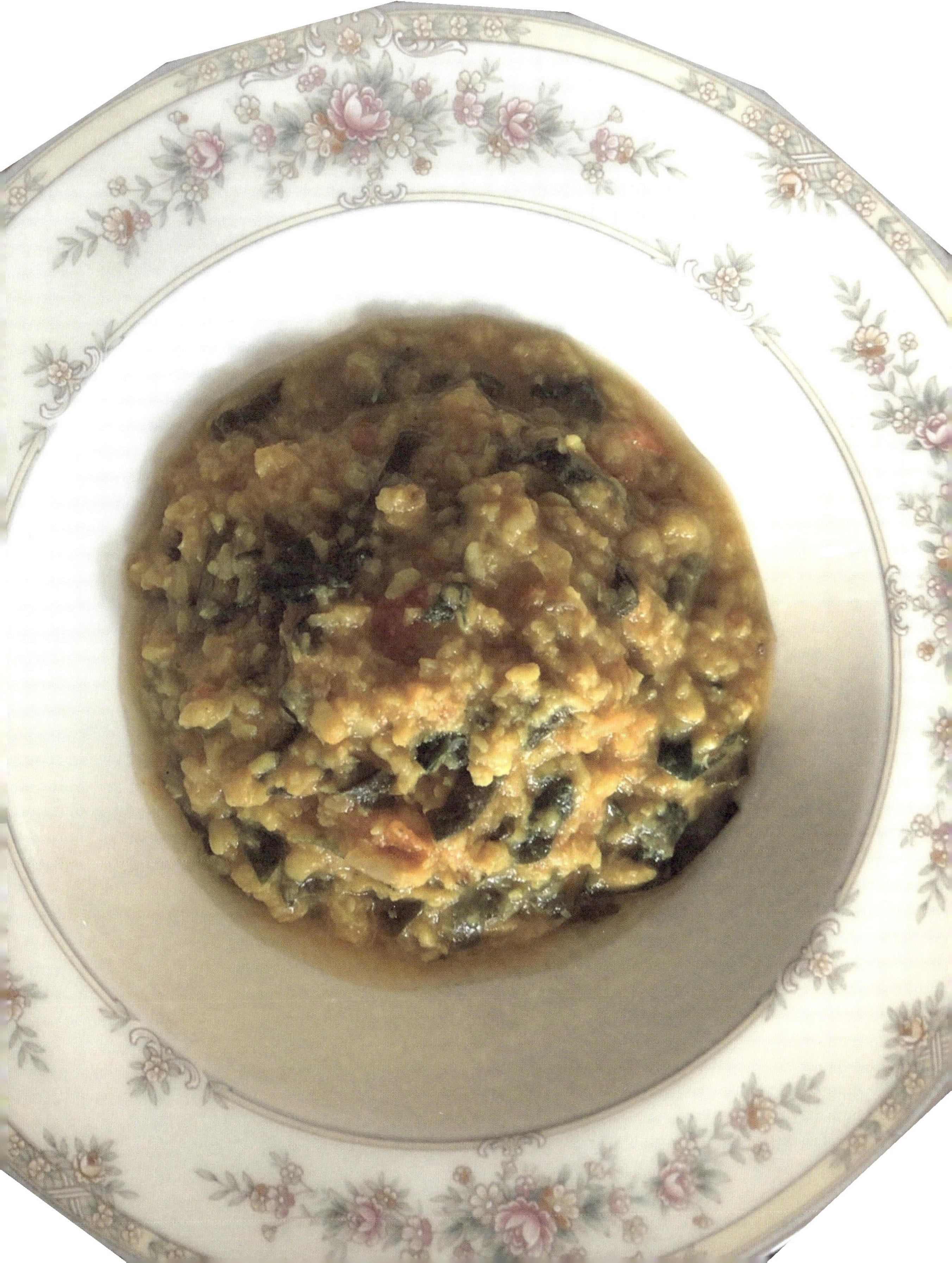

DAHL

Chana Dahl

READY IN
45 MINS
+SOAKING

SERVES
3-4

The grain of this dahl is slightly larger. It can be quite a substantial meal with a bowl of fluffy rice. It's Indian Nanny's recipe.

DAHL INGREDIENTS

2 cups chana dahl

4 cups water

1 inch ginger, peeled & finely chopped

4 cloves garlic, peeled

DAHL SPICES

1 heaped teaspoon salt

½ teaspoon haldi

¼ teaspoon paprika

¼ teaspoon chilli powder

TARKA INGREDIENTS

2-3 tablespoons light olive oil

1 medium onion, finely chopped

1 tomato, skin off, finely chopped

TARKA SPICES

1 heaped teaspoon jeera

1 teaspoon garam masala

METHOD

1. Take the 2 cups of dahl, wash it a few times in a bowl of cold water then if you are using a pressure cooker, soak for about 1 hour. *If you are not going to use a pressure cooker soak for 4 to 5 hours.*

2. In a pressure cooker or pan with a tightly fitting lid, chop 4 cloves of garlic into small bits and add with the ginger, salt, haldi, paprika & chilli powder.

3. Wash and drain the dahl, add this to the pan and 4 cups of water. Put the lid on, high heat, once you get one steam pressure, turn it onto a low heat and simmer for 10 minutes. After this time turn off the heat and wait until the pressure drops before opening the lid (15 - 20 minutes). *If you are not using a pressure cooker, simmer with the lid on for 30 minutes or so.*

4. While this is cooking make your tarka. In a small saucepan, add the finely chopped onion and cover this with oil (2 or 3 tablespoons). Heat this for 5 minutes on a high / medium heat, checking and stirring often. Do not let the onion go too red, add the tomato and fry on a medium heat until you see the tomato change colour and the red colour comes out of the tomato.

5. Now mash up the tomato and cook for 5 minutes more on a low heat. Once the onion is fried, add the heaped teaspoon of jeera and 1 teaspoon of garam masala. Give it a stir and turn off the heat.

6. Now open the lid of the dahl, give it a stir and make sure it's cooked; the grain should be slightly soft to mash, yellow and a bit runny. If not, turn the heat back on, leave the lid ajar. In my experience if you are not using a pressure cooker, the dahl usually needs an extra 20-30 minutes on the heat.

7. Once cooked, add the tarka to the dahl and it is ready to eat.

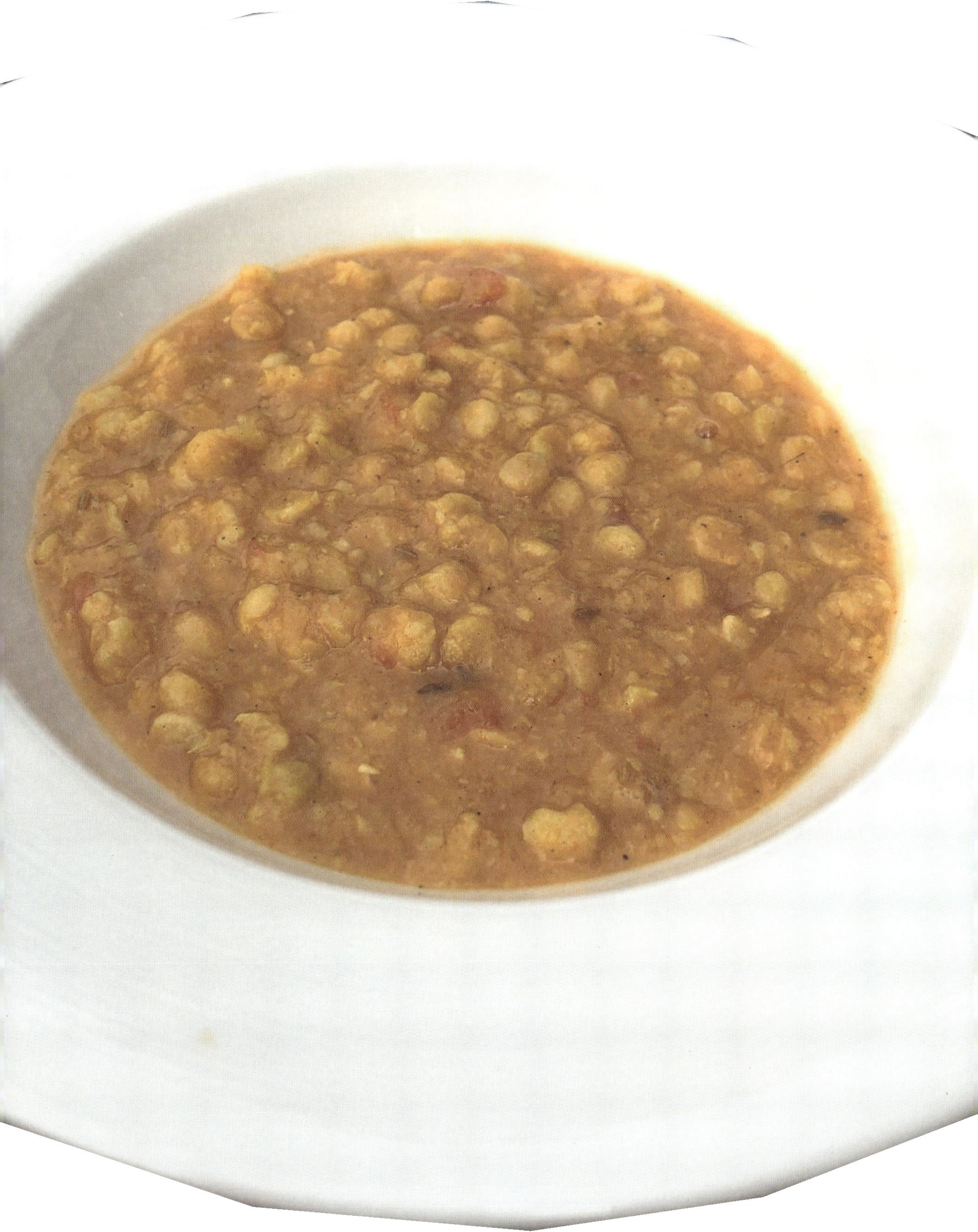

DAHL

Chana Dahl & Indian Marrow

READY IN 45 MINS +SOAKING

SERVES 3-4

Most of the ingredients in this book can be picked up in a supermarket. However, you will probably need to go to an Indian shop or market to find an Indian Marrow. It's worth the visit. Not only will you probably come out with a few cheap bunches of coriander, some other veg and bags of dried lentils, for those of you that have not had the experience of visiting India, an Indian shop is a fun place to go!

Nanny taught me to cook this recipe, it has mild spices and less salt which lets the beautiful flavour of the marrow and dahl be tasted. Baby Lauren loves this and it's also great if you prefer to follow a low salt diet. If you prefer to increase the potency, I would suggest doubling the salt and spice.

DAHL INGREDIENTS

2 cups chana dahl

1 Indian marrow

4 cups water

1 inch ginger, peeled and finely chopped

4 cloves garlic, peeled

Handful of chopped coriander (optional for decoration)

DAHL SPICES

1 heaped teaspoon salt

½ teaspoon haldi

¼ teaspoon paprika

¼ teaspoon chilli powder

TARKA INGREDIENTS

2 to 3 tablespoons light olive oil

1 medium onion, peeled and finely chopped

1 tomato, skin off, finely chopped

TARKA SPICES

1 heaped teaspoon jeera

1 teaspoon garam masala

METHOD

1. Take the 2 cups of dahl, wash it a few times in a bowl of cold water then soak for 15 minutes in a bowl of warm water. Peel an Indian marrow (like you would with a cucumber) and cut into large chunks. Wash it through a colander and let it drain on the side.

2. In a pressure cooker, chop 4 cloves of garlic into small bits. Add 1 inch of ginger and all the spices. Add the marrow. Wash and drain the dahl, add this plus 4 cups of water to the pressure cooker. Put the lid on, high heat and wait for one steam pressure, then turn onto a low heat and cook for 5 minutes. After this time turn off the heat and wait for the pressure to drop (15 - 20 minutes) before opening the lid.

3. While this is cooking make your tarka. In a small saucepan, add the finely chopped onion and cover this with oil (2 or 3 tablespoons). Heat this for 5 minutes on a high / medium heat, checking and stirring often. Do not let the onion go too red, add the chopped tomato and fry on a medium heat until you see the tomato change colour and the red colour comes out of the tomato. Now mash up the tomato and cook for 5 minutes more on a low heat. Once the onion is fried, add 1 heaped teaspoon of jeera and 1 teaspoon of garam masala. Give it a stir and turn off the heat.

4. Now open the lid of the dahl, give it a stir and make sure it's cooked (it will be yellow and runny), turn the heat back on, leave the lid off, add the tarka to the dahl and cook for 5 minutes, stirring often. It is ready to eat, add chopped coriander for decoration when you serve, if you wish.

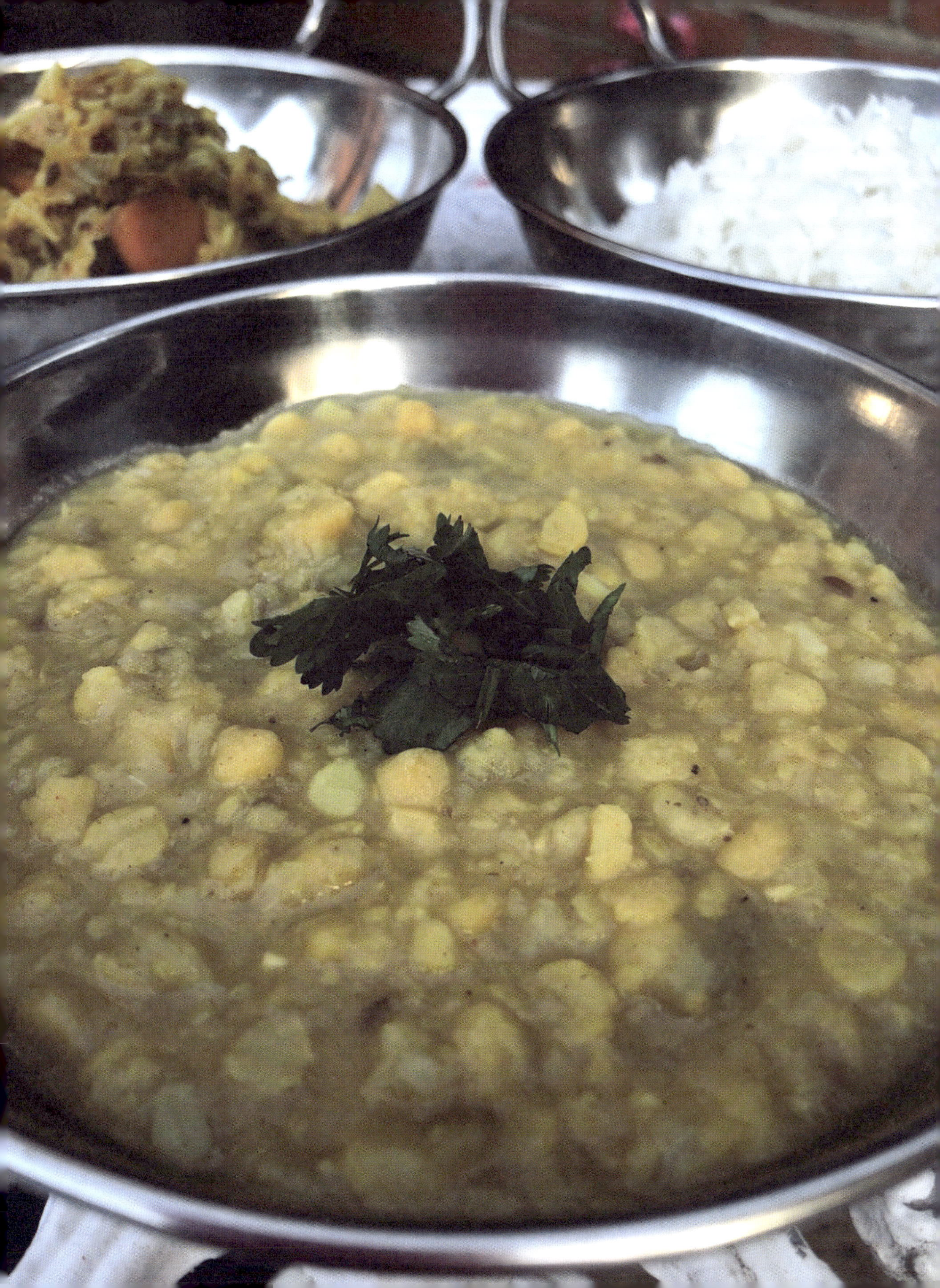

DAHL

Nanny's Chana

READY IN
70 MINS
+SOAKING

SERVES
3-4

INGREDIENTS

500g chickpeas

1 teaspoon bicarbonate of soda

4 tablespoons light olive oil

1 medium green chilli, deseeded and chopped

2 inches ginger, peeled, washed & finely chopped

½ tin chopped tomatoes or ¼ tin & 1 fresh tomato, chopped

Coriander for decoration if you wish

SPICES

3 teaspoons salt

2 teaspoons jeera

1 teaspoon paprika

2 teaspoons coriander powder

2 - 4 teaspoons garam masala

2 - 4 teaspoons mango powder

¼ teaspoon chilli powder

Note: To cook using tinned chickpeas and no pressure cooker omit the bicarbonate of soda and maybe cook for a little longer. The dish tastes great but the chickpeas are not as soft.

This is the best way of cooking chana, Indian Nanny's recipe. The smell of this cooking reminds me of her house! If you are scared of using a pressure cooker or would prefer to use tinned chickpeas, that is possible; however, if you follow the recipe below it really is simple and you will create the tastiest chana you have ever tried.

Nanny taught me to cook this on two occasions, once she put in 2 spoons of garam masala and mango powder, on the other it was 4 spoons of each! It really does depend on how strong you like your flavours.

METHOD

1. Soak the dried chickpeas in a large bowl of water overnight, for a minimum of 8 hours (you do not do this if using tinned cooked chickpeas).

2. Drain most of the water away, pick out any off colour or small chickpeas. Wash and drain through a colander.

3. Put the chickpeas in a pressure cooker. Cover with 1 inch of water. Add 3 teaspoons salt and 1 level teaspoon of bicarbonate of soda. Put the lid on and bring to the boil. One steam pressure, then turn down the heat and simmer for 20 minutes.

4. Into a wok add 4 tablespoons of olive oil, on a high heat. Add 2 level teaspoons jeera, 1 teaspoon paprika, 2 teaspoons coriander powder, add the chopped green chilli and ginger. Lightly fry this for a few minutes. Lower the heat to medium / low. Add the tomatoes, squash them and stir occasionally. When the mixture becomes juicy (approx. 5 minutes) add the garam masala, mango powder and ¼ teaspoon of chilli powder. This will make a dark-coloured paste, simmer it for a couple more minutes, checking and stirring often, then turn off the heat.

5. Go back to the chickpeas, they need turning off after 20 minutes of cooking. Do not overcook as it will make them soggy. Leave it to stand for 30 minutes until the pressure drops.

6. Open the pressure cooker after this time; if there is a little skin on top then remove this with a spoon. Add the paste from the wok and bring to the boil (lid off). Simmer for 5-10 minutes to thicken the gravy, stir a few times and it is ready!

7. Add coriander for decoration if you wish.

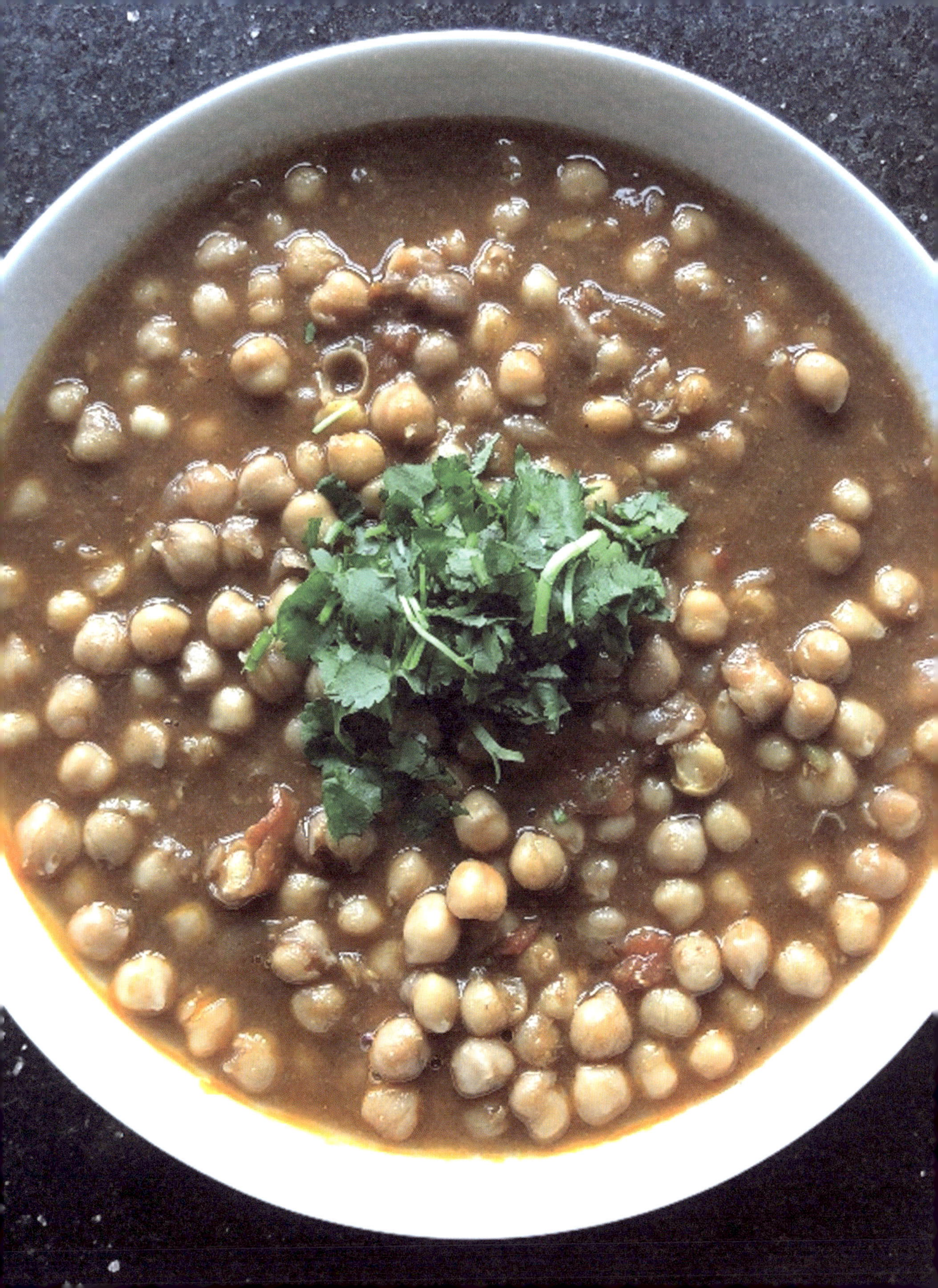

DAHL

Mushroom & Chana

READY IN 35 MINS   **SERVES** 3-4

My friends love cooking this one! It's Indian Nanny's recipe. I think that it can be quickly put together using a couple of tins of chickpeas, the gravy is delicious and the mushrooms make it a complete meal with some nice fluffy white rice.

INGREDIENTS

- 2 tins chickpeas, rinsed & drained (800g)
- ½ tin plum tomatoes (200g)
- 250g fresh mushrooms, cut into quarters (bigger is better)
- 1 large onion, peeled & finely chopped (in the food processor is probably best)
- 1 inch ginger, peeled & finely chopped (in the food processor is probably best)
- 6 tablespoons light olive oil
- Fresh/frozen coriander for decoration (optional)

SPICES

- 1 teaspoon jeera
- 4 teaspoons salt
- ½ teaspoon haldi
- 1 teaspoon paprika
- 1 heaped teaspoon coriander powder
- ¼ teaspoon chilli powder
- 1 teaspoon garam masala

METHOD

1. Add the oil to a large saucepan and heat over a medium to high heat.

2. Add the onion and fry them until pink, add the jeera and ½ tin of tomatoes and stir.

3. Add the ginger and stir, heat for 5 minutes.

4. Add 4 teaspoons salt, ½ teaspoon haldi, 1 teaspoon paprika, 1 heaped teaspoon coriander powder, ¼ teaspoon chilli powder.

5. Stir and mash up tomatoes, add the chana and mushrooms, on a high heat add 2 to 3 cups of water so the chana and mushrooms are covered.

6. Turn up the heat to full until it boils. Then turn down the heat, put the lid on and simmer for 15 minutes.

7. Turn off the heat, add 1 teaspoon garam masala and fresh/frozen coriander for decoration.

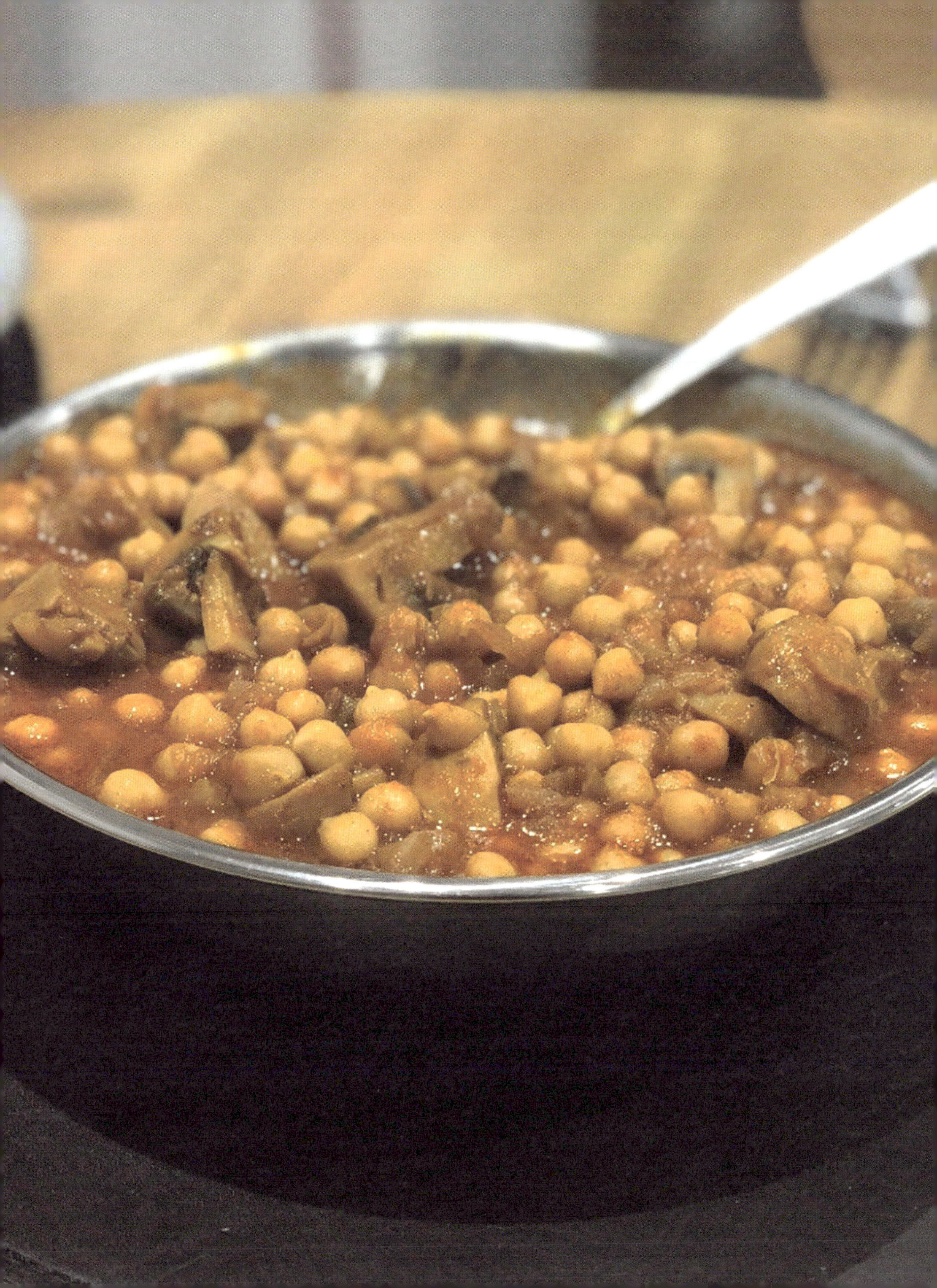

DAHL

Black Chana

READY IN 20 MINS **SERVES 3-4**

Indian Nanny's recipe. Quick to prepare and tasty too. Uses tinned chickpeas so you do not need to soak them or use a pressure cooker.

INGREDIENTS

1 medium onion, peeled and thinly sliced

1 inch ginger, peeled & chopped

2 tablespoons light olive oil

1 tin chickpeas (400g)

1 teabag

SPICES

1 teaspoon jeera

1 ½ teaspoons salt

½ teaspoon paprika

1 heaped teaspoon garam masala

1 heaped teaspoon coriander powder

¼ teaspoon chilli powder

1 very heaped teaspoon mango powder

METHOD

1. Add 2 tablespoons of olive oil to the wok, add the sliced onion and chopped ginger, fry for 5 – 7 minutes over a medium to high heat.

2. Drain the tin of chickpeas in a colander and rinse in cold water, then add to the wok.

3. Add the spices: 1 teaspoon of jeera, 1 ½ teaspoons of salt, ½ teaspoon paprika, 1 heaped teaspoon garam masala, 1 heaped teaspoon coriander powder, ¼ chilli powder, 1 very heaped teaspoon mango powder.

4. Soak the teabag in ½ cup of boiling water, add this water to the wok (not the teabag). Simmer over a low heat, with the lid on. Once the water has evaporated and wok is dry, the dish is ready.

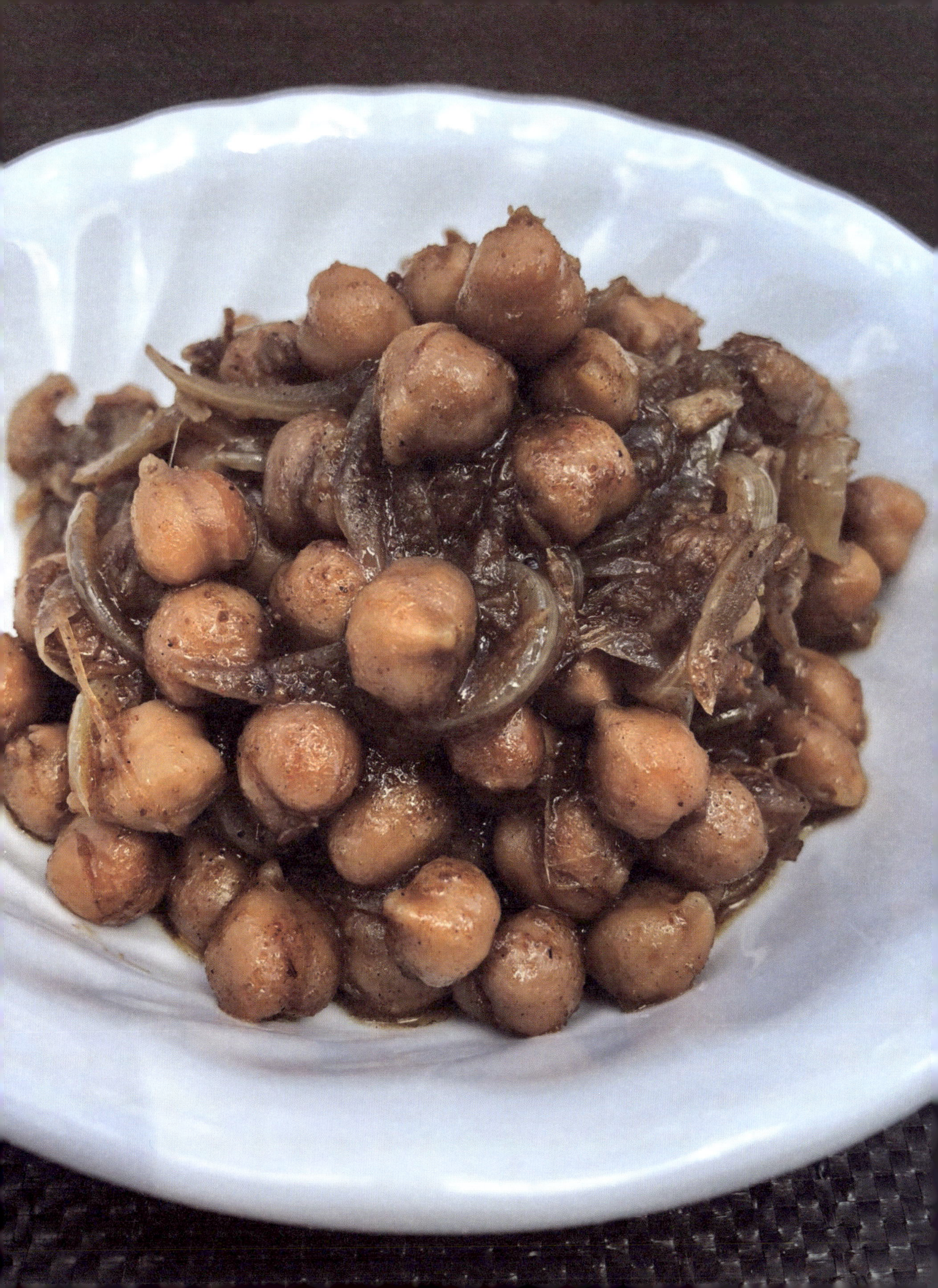

DAHL

Punjabi Kitcher Chana

READY IN 30 MINS

SERVES 4-6

On our visit to India in 2016, Uncle Gigi took us to Amritsar to see the Golden Temple and visit some family. Uncle took us to eat in the most amazing street café. The wires from the fan went straight into the socket with no plug (do not do this); they served chole which was mouth-watering. This is Indian Nanny's recipe from Rita. She told me that Punjabi kitcher chana translates as muddy chana!

INGREDIENTS

1 tablespoon light olive oil

750g boiled chickpeas, this can either be tinned (3 tins) or cook your own in the pressure cooker

2 tomatoes, chopped

1 inch ginger, peeled and finely chopped

½ tin chopped tomatoes

2 green chillies, whole

1 cup of water

½ red onion, finely sliced

Chopped coriander (optional)

SPICES

1 teaspoon jeera

1 ½ teaspoons salt

1 teaspoon coriander powder

1 teaspoon paprika

3 teaspoons mango powder

3 teaspoons garam masala

METHOD

1. In a pan heat up the oil (high heat), add the jeera, and when the seeds start to pop (30 seconds), add the fresh tomatoes, ginger and green chillies. Cover, turn down to a medium heat and allow the tomatoes to soften for about 5 minutes.

2. Now add the tinned tomatoes and all the other spices. Mix well and add the chickpeas. Add a cup of water if the mixture is a little dry.

3. Cover and allow to simmer for about 15 minutes, stirring occasionally.

4. Serve garnished with thinly sliced red onions and coriander if desired.

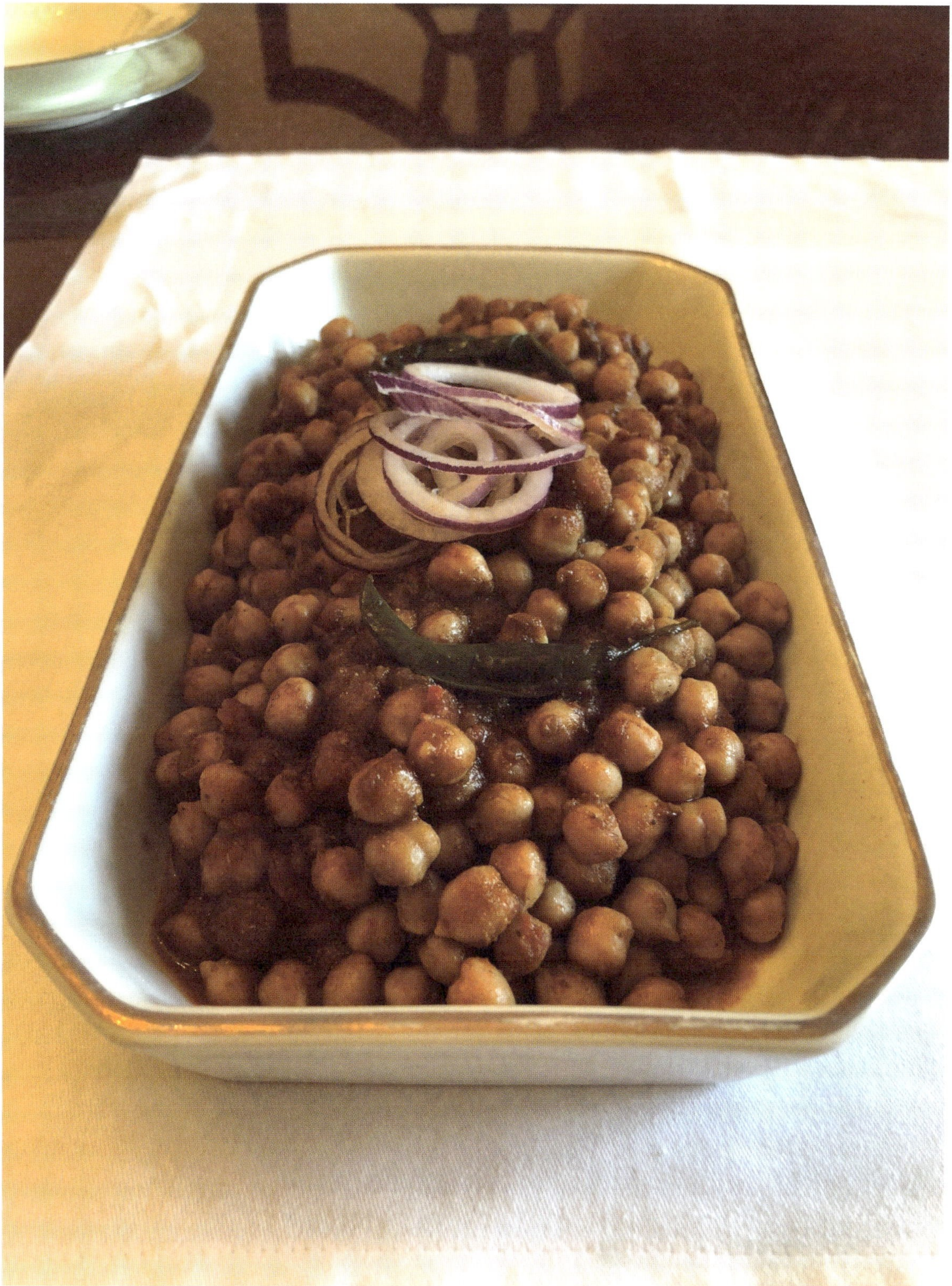

DAHL

Urad Dahl

READY IN 50 MINS

SERVES 3-4

Known as the mother of dahls, this is a split dahl without skin. It is really popular in Northern India, where my Grandad and Nanny were originally from. In English it is known as split black gram. Urad dahl is very nutritious. There are many health benefits of split black gram including its ability to aid digestion, boost energy and improve the skin health.

Requires no pre-soaking. Easy to cook and digest, Urad dahl is very easy to prepare and can also be eaten as a side dish.

DAHL INGREDIENTS

¾ cup urad dahl

2 cups water

2 tablespoons set natural yogurt

2 small spoons of ghee / butter / or vegan butter (optional)

DAHL SPICES

1 teaspoon salt

½ teaspoon paprika

½ teaspoon coriander powder

¼ teaspoon chilli powder

TARKA INGREDIENTS

2 tablespoons light olive oil

½ onion, thinly sliced

1 small tomato, chopped, or ½ tin chopped tomatoes

TARKA SPICES

½ teaspoon garam masala

½ teaspoon jeera

Alternative to pressure cooker?
If you really do not like a pressure cooker, or you do not have one, you can cook this dish in a heavy saucepan with a tight-fitting lid, simmering for about 20 minutes. I would only suggest this cooking method with this particular dahl as it does not need soaking overnight. Soak it for 2 hours instead and follow the recipe as above.

METHOD

1. Wash the dahl as you would rice, then put in a pressure cooker with the water and spices.

2. Put the lid on the pressure cooker, high heat for approximately 5 minutes until you get one steam pressure. Then simmer for 15 minutes on a low heat. Switch off the pressure cooker and leave it for 15 minutes or until the pressure has dropped.

3. Meanwhile, make your tarka. Add 2 tablespoons of oil to a small saucepan on a medium heat.

4. Add the chopped onion, chopped tomato, ½ teaspoon garam masala, ½ teaspoon jeera and fry for a little bit until the tomato and onion changes colour, approximately 5 minutes. Check and stir often.

5. Remove it from the heat.

6. Once the pressure has dropped, open the lid of the pressure cooker and cook for 5 minutes with a normal lid on (or the pressure cooker lid but not closed).

7. You then add the tarka to the dahl and give it a little stir. Then add 2 tablespoons of beaten yogurt.

8. If you would like to make the dish extra delicious, add the ghee / butter / vegan spread as it will make it really creamy.

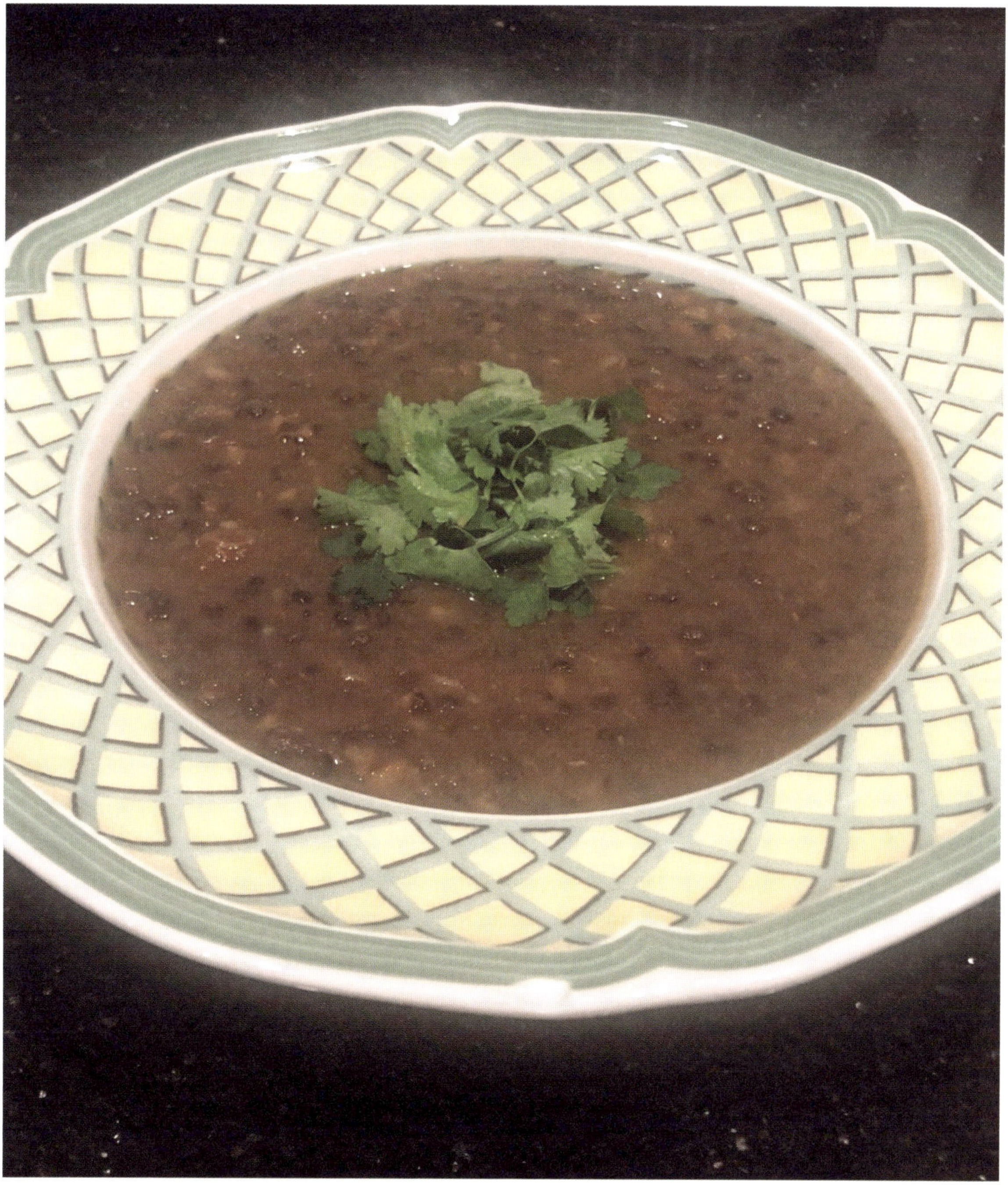

DAHL

Vipi Uncle's Brown Dahl

READY IN 80 MINS
SERVES 3-4

The Aunties all make a wicked brown dahl, it's Milly's favourite so they often make it for her. During the 2020 1st Coronavirus lockdown, my dad quizzed Rita and Veena about how to make this type of dahl as he remembered his grandmother (Biji) making it for him in Amritsar. He then perfected it using the family recipe and adding a few of his own ideas. We ate a lot of this during lockdown!

The tarka holds the flavours to this dish and the dahl has a really nice texture.

INGREDIENTS

1 cup urad dahl

3 cups water

1 tin red kidney beans (400g)

1 large onion

2 cloves garlic

1 inch ginger

2 tablespoons light olive oil

1 tin chopped tomatoes (400g)

Chopped fresh coriander

Optional add a couple of tablespoons single cream

SPICES

1 heaped teaspoon salt

1 teaspoon jeera

½ heaped teaspoon paprika

½ heaped teaspoon haldi

1 heaped teaspoon coriander powder

¼ teaspoon chilli powder or a whole green chilli

1 teaspoon garam masala

METHOD

1. Put the dahl in a bowl of cold water and wash it well under the cold tap. Put it in a pressure cooker, cover with 3 cups of cold water (approximately 2 inches above the top of the dahl). Rinse and drain the tin of red beans, add these too.

2. Add the salt, put the lid on tightly and cook on a high heat. One steam pressure, then turn the heat down and simmer for 40 minutes. The dahl is now cooked. Turn off and leave to one side. Do not open the pressure cooker.

3. To make the tarka, peel and finely chop the onion, garlic and ginger in a mini chopper / food processor.

4. In a saucepan add this with 2 tablespoons of olive oil and a spoon of jeera. Cook until the onions are soft / pink. Check and stir often.

5. The pressure cooker will be fine to open after the pressure has dropped, about 30 minutes.

6. Then add this mix to the dahl in the pressure cooker, with the chopped tomatoes, paprika, haldi, coriander powder, chilli powder or a whole green chilli. Put on a high heat then simmer for 20 - 30 minutes.

7. Add 1 teaspoon garam masala and some chopped fresh coriander. Turn off the heat.

Note – If you would like to add a couple of tablespoons of single cream, this can also be done at the end and it would be how my Auntie Veena would cook it!

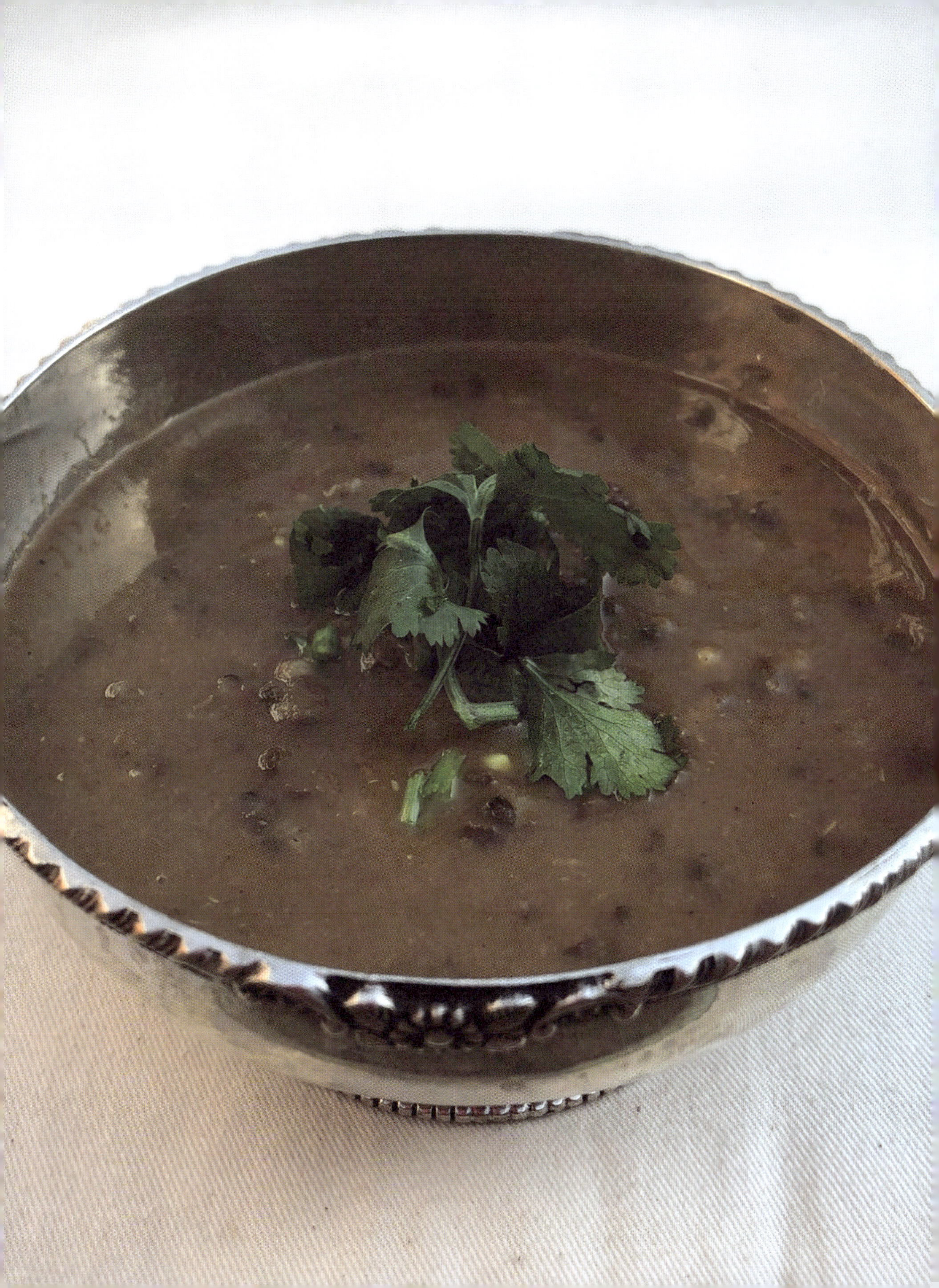

DAHL

Split Mung Dahl

READY IN
45 MINS
+SOAKING

SERVES
3-4

DAHL INGREDIENTS

¾ cup split mung dahl

3 - 4 cups water

1 inch peeled and finely chopped ginger

DAHL SPICES

1 teaspoon salt

TARKA INGREDIENTS

3 tablespoons light olive oil

1 medium onion, finely chopped

1 tomato, finely chopped

1 green chilli, finely chopped

TARKA SPICES

1 teaspoon jeera

¼ teaspoon haldi

¼ teaspoon salt

½ heaped teaspoon paprika

½ teaspoon coriander powder

½ teaspoon garam masala

Auntie Veena taught me this dahl dish, it's Nisha's favourite. She enjoys it for lunch with bread and butter for dipping!

METHOD

1. Take ¾ cup of dahl, rinse under a cold tap in a colander then soak in a bowl of cold water for about 1 hour.

2. Drain the dahl through a colander and again rinse under a cold tap. Add the dahl into a pressure cooker with 2 cups of water. Add the ginger and a teaspoon of salt. Put the lid on, high heat, one steam and turn onto a low heat and cook for 5 minutes.

3. While the dahl is cooking, you can make your tarka.

4. In a small saucepan, add the oil and the jeera on a high heat, once this sizzles (30 seconds) add the chopped onion. Give it a stir and once it starts to fry, turn down to a medium heat. Fry for 5 minutes until the onions are soft.

5. Add the tomato, chilli and all the other spices for your tarka. Checking and stirring often, mashing up the tomatoes. Fry on a medium heat for about another 5 minutes until you see the tomatoes are soft and have changed colour slightly. Then turn it off.

6. Once your dahl is cooked, turn it off and wait for the pressure to drop 15 - 20 minutes before opening the lid. Give it a stir and add 1 cup of water. Put back on a high to medium heat, then simmer on a low heat for 5 minutes with the lid ajar. When it is cooked, the dahl should be slightly soft.

7. If not, you may need to add some more water and turn the heat back on low with the lid ajar for another 5 to 10 minutes.

8. Once cooked, stir the tarka into the dahl and it is ready to eat.

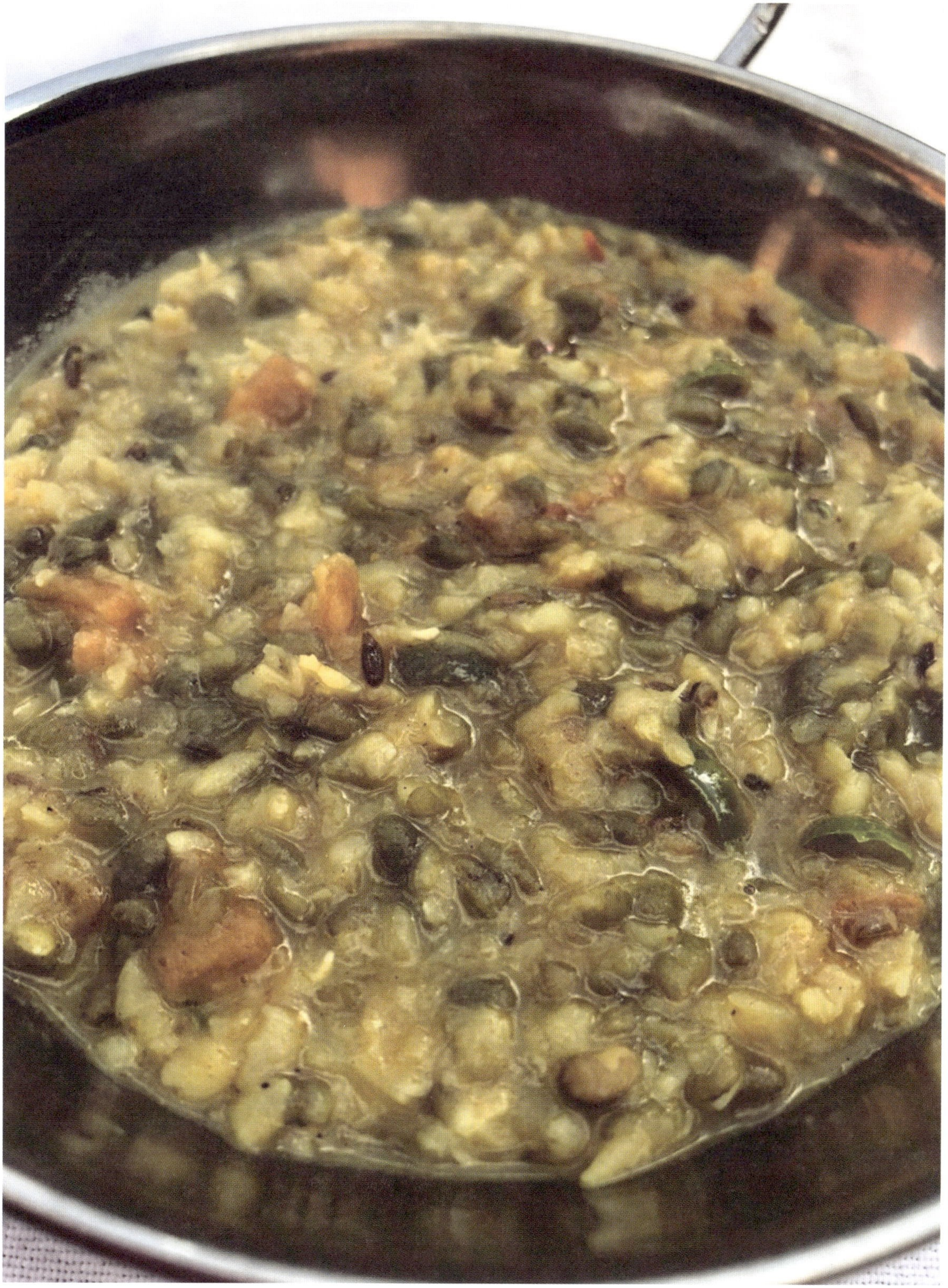

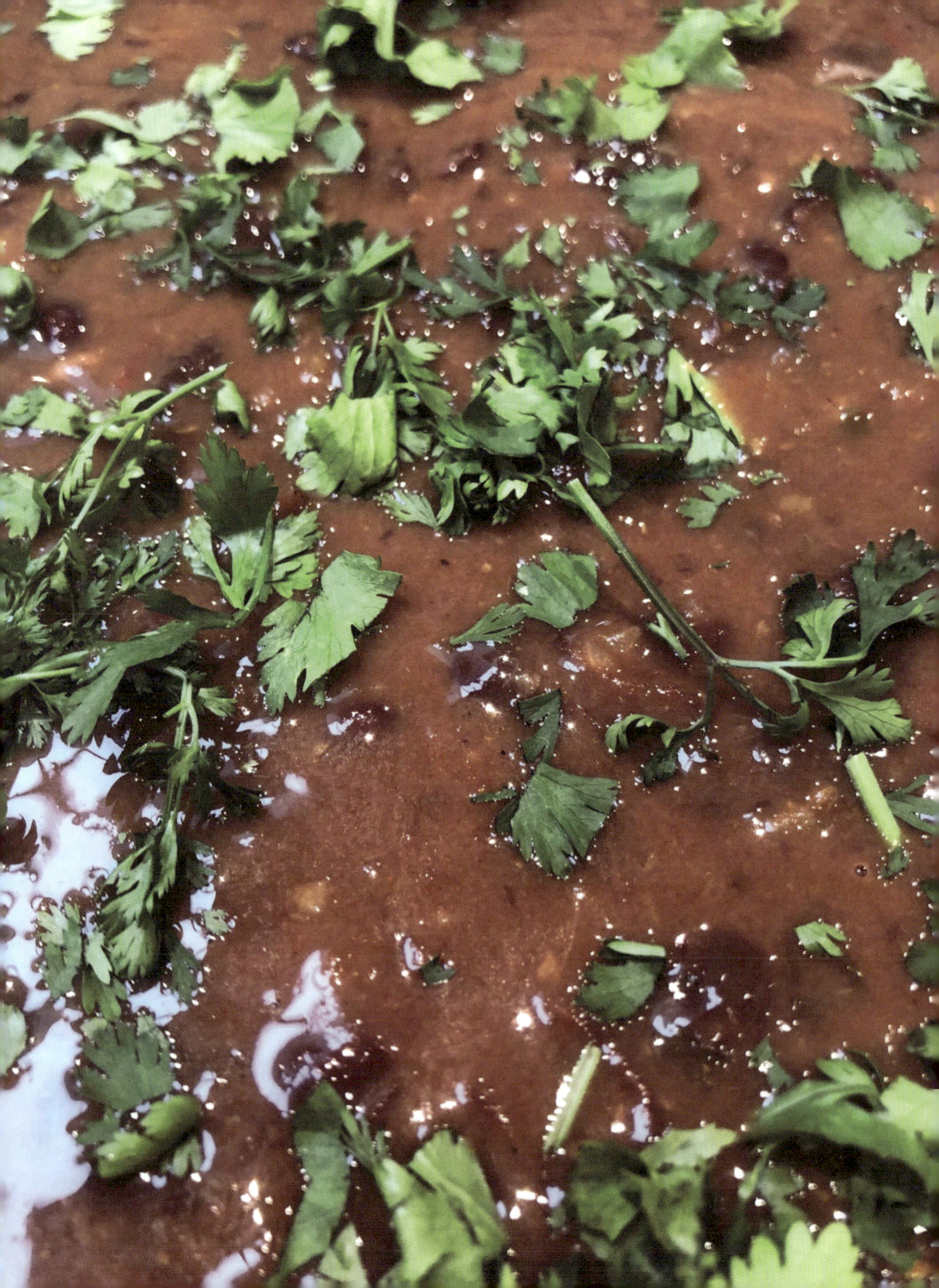

DAHL

Indian Nanny's Red Beans

READY IN
90 MINS
+SOAKING

SERVES
4-6

There is a story to these. Every time Indian Nanny and I attempted to cook this dish, my grandad fell ill, so we stopped trying. It's a firm family favourite. The kids love it too, so I was desperate to learn, so Indian Nanny told me the recipe and later Rita taught me to cook it as well.

INGREDIENTS

500g dried red beans (Nanny likes them best from Sainsbury's, I don't know why!)

1 medium onion

4 cloves garlic

1 ½ inch ginger

4 tablespoons light olive oil

⅔ tin chopped tomatoes (270g)

Fresh chopped coriander for decoration

SPICES

2 heaped teaspoons salt

1 heaped teaspoon jeera

1 heaped teaspoon coriander powder

1 heaped teaspoon paprika

¼ teaspoon haldi

¼ teaspoon chilli powder

1 heaped teaspoon garam masala

METHOD

1. Rinse the red beans in cold water, then soak in a large bowl of water (fill the water to the top of the bowl to allow them to swell), put a plate on top of the bowl and leave it on the side overnight / 8-12 hours.

2. After this period, rinse the red beans in cold water through a colander. Put the beans and some water in a pressure cooker; the water must cover the beans by about 1-2 inches to allow them to swell.

3. Add 2 heaped teaspoons of salt and put it on a high heat with the lid on. Bring to the boil, when the steam pressure releases twice, turn the heat down and simmer for 20 minutes.

4. Turn it off and wait until the pressure drops before opening the lid of the pressure cooker, this would usually be about 15 minutes. Then put it in a bowl on one side.

5. Peel and wash the onion, garlic and ginger, then using a food processor finely chop them. Put this mixture into the pressure cooker with 4 tablespoons of olive oil. Cook on a high / medium heat until the mixture is brown and the oil separates from the mixture (approximately 10 minutes).

6. Add ⅔ tin of chopped tomatoes into the pan, stir and put on a high heat until all of the water has evaporated, leaving a dry mix (approximately 10 minutes).

7. Add 1 heaped teaspoon jeera, 1 heaped teaspoon coriander powder, 1 heaped teaspoon paprika, ¼ teaspoon haldi, ¼ teaspoon chilli powder. Add the red beans and enough water to cover the beans, put the lid on with a high heat. When the water is boiling / steam comes out, turn it onto a low heat for 15 minutes. Then turn it off and leave for 15 minutes until the pressure has gone.

8. Add 1 heaped teaspoon garam masala and coriander if using. If the liquid is a bit runny, turn the heat back on until the sauce has thickened.

DAHL

Rita's Rajma

READY IN 75 MINS +SOAKING

SERVES 4-6

Rita calls red beans "Rajma". Nanny and Rita cook very similarly. I think Rita's way is slightly quicker, and she taught me to cook this way.

INGREDIENTS

500g dried red kidney beans

1 large onion, peeled

2 cloves garlic, peeled

1 ½ inch ginger, peeled

2 green chillies

4 tablespoons light olive oil

2 fresh tomatoes, finely chopped

½ tin chopped tomatoes (200g)

1 litre water

Fresh chopped coriander for decoration

SPICES

1 teaspoon jeera

2 teaspoons salt

1 teaspoon coriander powder

1 teaspoon garam masala

1 heaped teaspoon paprika

½ teaspoon haldi

METHOD

1. Rinse the red beans in cold water, then soak in a large bowl of hot water (you can use either boiling water or the hot tap), put a plate on top of the bowl and leave it on the side *overnight*.

2. In the morning, rinse the red beans well through a colander and again fill up the bowl with hot water with the beans.

3. In a food processor finely chop the onion, garlic, ginger and green chillies.

4. Put the oil in a good size pressure cooker and heat, add the jeera. When they start to pop (30 seconds) add the onion, garlic, green chilli and ginger mix.

5. Fry this on a medium heat until it's medium brown, stir regularly. Add the fresh tomato and the tinned tomatoes, cook on a low heat until they are soft. Again, stir regularly. Once this sauce is ready, it will become paste-like, put on a low heat.

6. Drain the kidney beans. Add the beans to the paste and let them fry for a few minutes.

7. Add all the spices, salt and mix together, cook for a few more minutes.

8. Add 700ml water and stir. Cover with the pressure cooker lid and leave on a high heat until the pressure releases, then simmer for 45 minutes.

9. Turn off and leave until the pressure cooker is ready to be opened (30 minutes).

10. Add approximately 300ml water and simmer for another 5 minutes.

11. Once cooked add chopped coriander for decoration (optional).

DAHL

Red Beans – Natasha's quick way!

READY IN 35 MINS

SERVES 4-6

Rita and Nanny's red beans taste wicked, but I needed a speedy way to cook this dish. So, this is Natasha's quick way...

INGREDIENTS

2 tins (400g each) red kidney beans, drained & rinsed

1 medium onion

2 cloves garlic

1 inch ginger

4 tablespoons light olive oil

½ tin chopped tomatoes (200g)

450ml water

A handful of fresh chopped coriander for decoration (optional)

SPICES

1 teaspoon jeera

1 teaspoon salt

1 teaspoon coriander powder

1 teaspoon paprika

½ teaspoon haldi

¼ teaspoon chilli powder

1 teaspoon garam masala

METHOD

1. Peel, wash and finely chop using a food processor the onion, garlic and ginger. Put this mixture into a large saucepan with 4 tablespoons of olive oil.

2. Cook on a medium heat until the mixture is brown and the oil separates from the mixture (approximately 8 - 10 minutes). Stir regularly to avoid it sticking to the bottom of the pan.

3. Add ½ tin of chopped tomatoes into the pan, stir and put on a medium heat until all of the juice has evaporated, leaving a fairly dry mix (approximately 8 - 10 minutes). Stir regularly.

4. Add 1 teaspoon jeera, 1 teaspoon salt, 1 teaspoon coriander powder, 1 teaspoon paprika, ½ teaspoon haldi and ¼ teaspoon chilli powder.

5. Add the red beans and enough water to cover the red beans, put the lid on with a high heat. Once boiling, turn onto a low heat and simmer for 8-10 minutes.

6. Then turn it off and leave for 5 minutes; the sauce will naturally thicken slightly in this time.

7. Add 1 teaspoon garam masala and the coriander (if using).

DAHL

Black Eye Beans

READY IN
45 MINS
+SOAKING

SERVES
4-6

This is Rishi and my brother Kevin's favourite! Nanny always made this with them in mind; it is Indian Nanny's recipe.

INGREDIENTS

1 cup (225g) black eye beans soaked overnight in a large bowl of water, or 2 x tins (400g each) cooked black eye beans (drained & rinsed) if you prefer

½ tin plum tomatoes (200g)

1 large onion – peeled & chopped (in the food processor is probably best)

1 inch ginger, peeled & chopped (in the food processor is probably best)

6 tablespoons light olive oil

2 tablespoons beaten natural set yogurt (for vegan either oat yogurt or omit)

Fresh/frozen coriander for decoration (optional)

750g water / 2 ½ cups (2 cups if using tinned black eye beans)

SPICES

1 teaspoon jeera

3 teaspoons salt (2 if using tinned black eye beans)

½ teaspoon haldi

1 teaspoon paprika

1 heaped teaspoon coriander powder

¼ teaspoon chilli powder

1 teaspoon garam masala

METHOD

1. Add the oil to a pressure cooker and heat over a medium to high heat.

2. Add the onions and fry them until pink (about 10 minutes), add the jeera, ½ tin of tomatoes and stir.

3. Add the ginger and stir regularly, heat for 5 minutes on a medium heat.

4. Add salt, haldi, paprika, coriander powder, chilli powder. Stir and mash up tomatoes.

5. Drain the black eye beans through a colander, rinse well. Then add them to the pressure cooker with 2 ½ cups of water; this will fill approximately ¾ pan. Put the lid on.

6. Turn up the heat to high. Once the steam is released, turn down the heat, simmer on a very low heat for 15 - 20 minutes. Turn it off and leave for 10 - 15 minutes until the pressure drops. Remove the lid, the beans should look soft.

7. Add 2 tablespoons of beaten natural set yogurt and 1 teaspoon garam masala, give it a good stir and heat again if necessary.

8. Add the fresh/frozen coriander for decoration on top when serving.

Note – If you prefer to use cooked tinned black eye beans this recipe works very well. Just cook in a large pan, follow the recipe and simmer for 15 - 20 minutes.

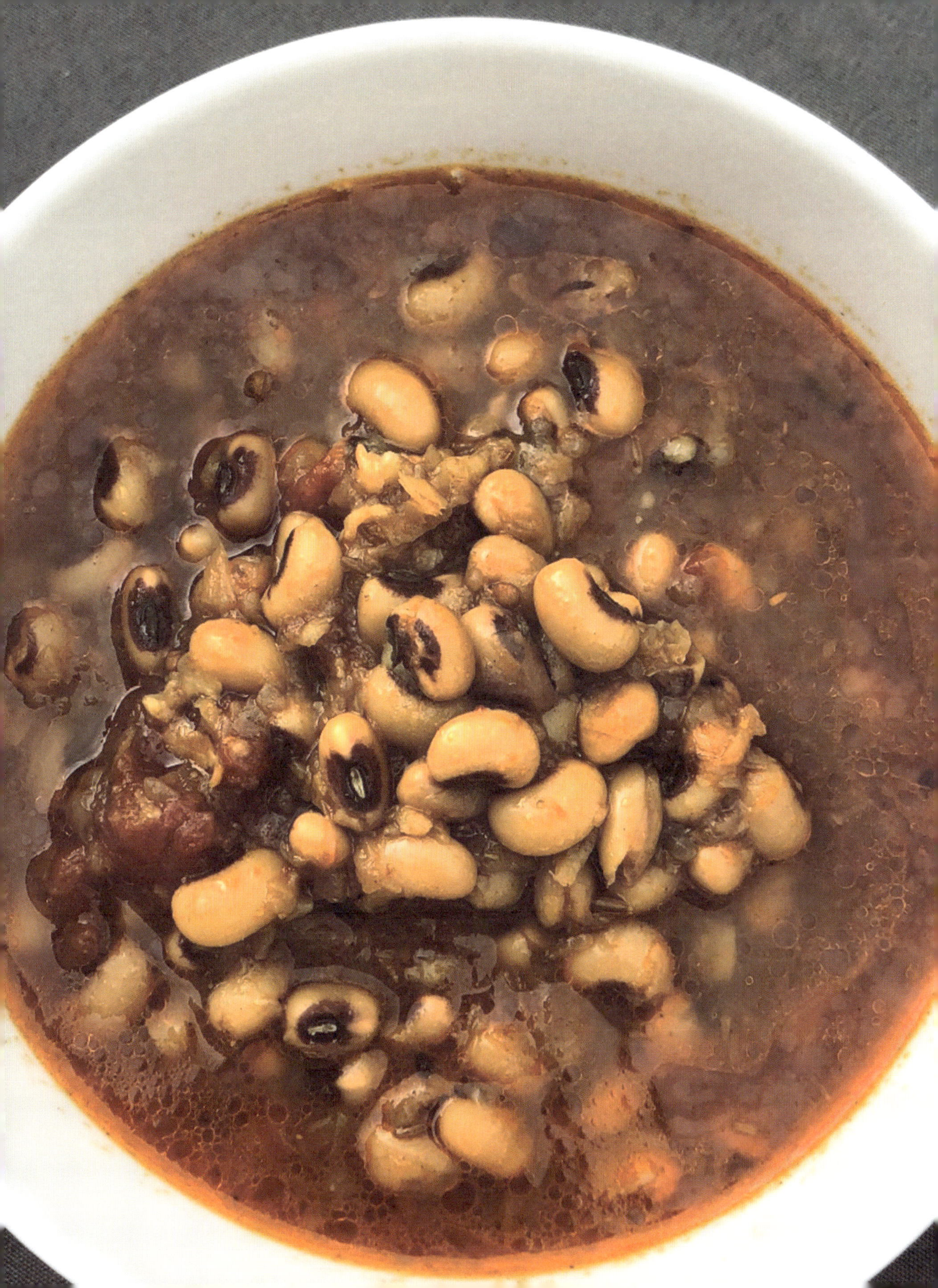

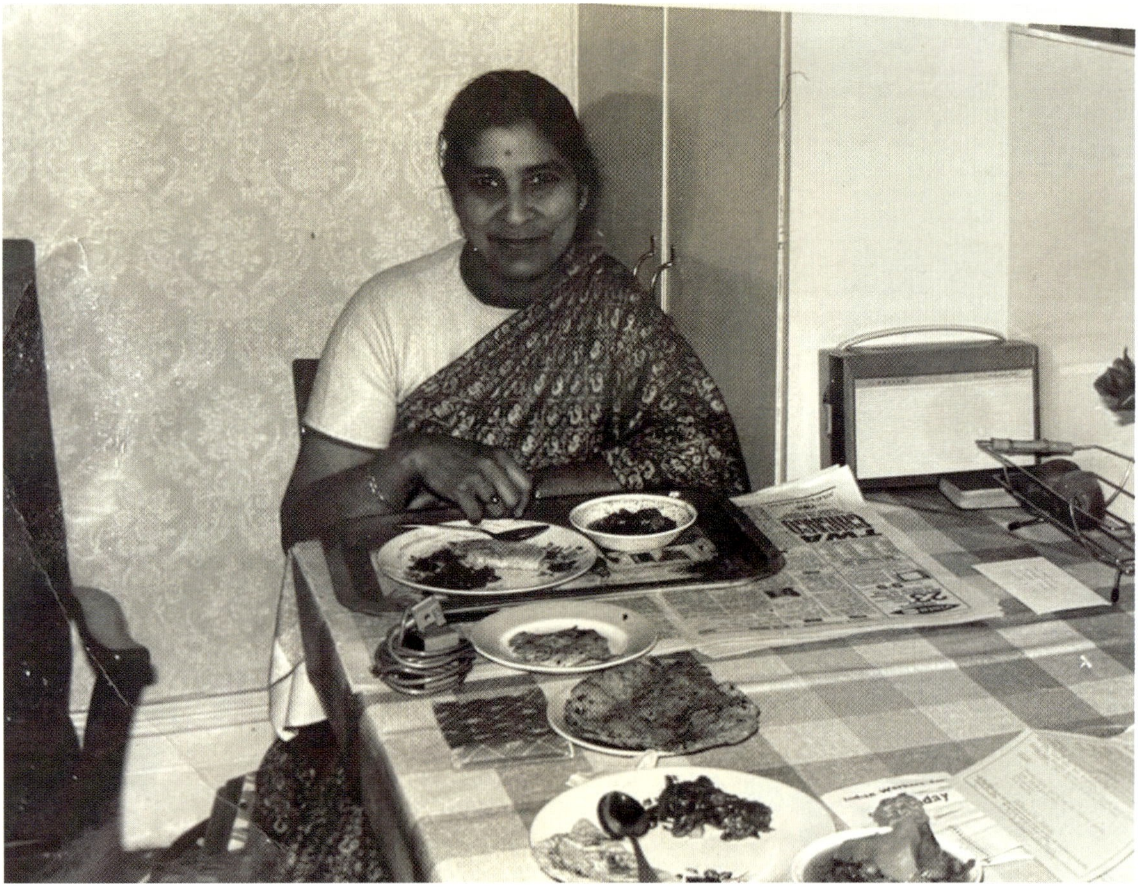

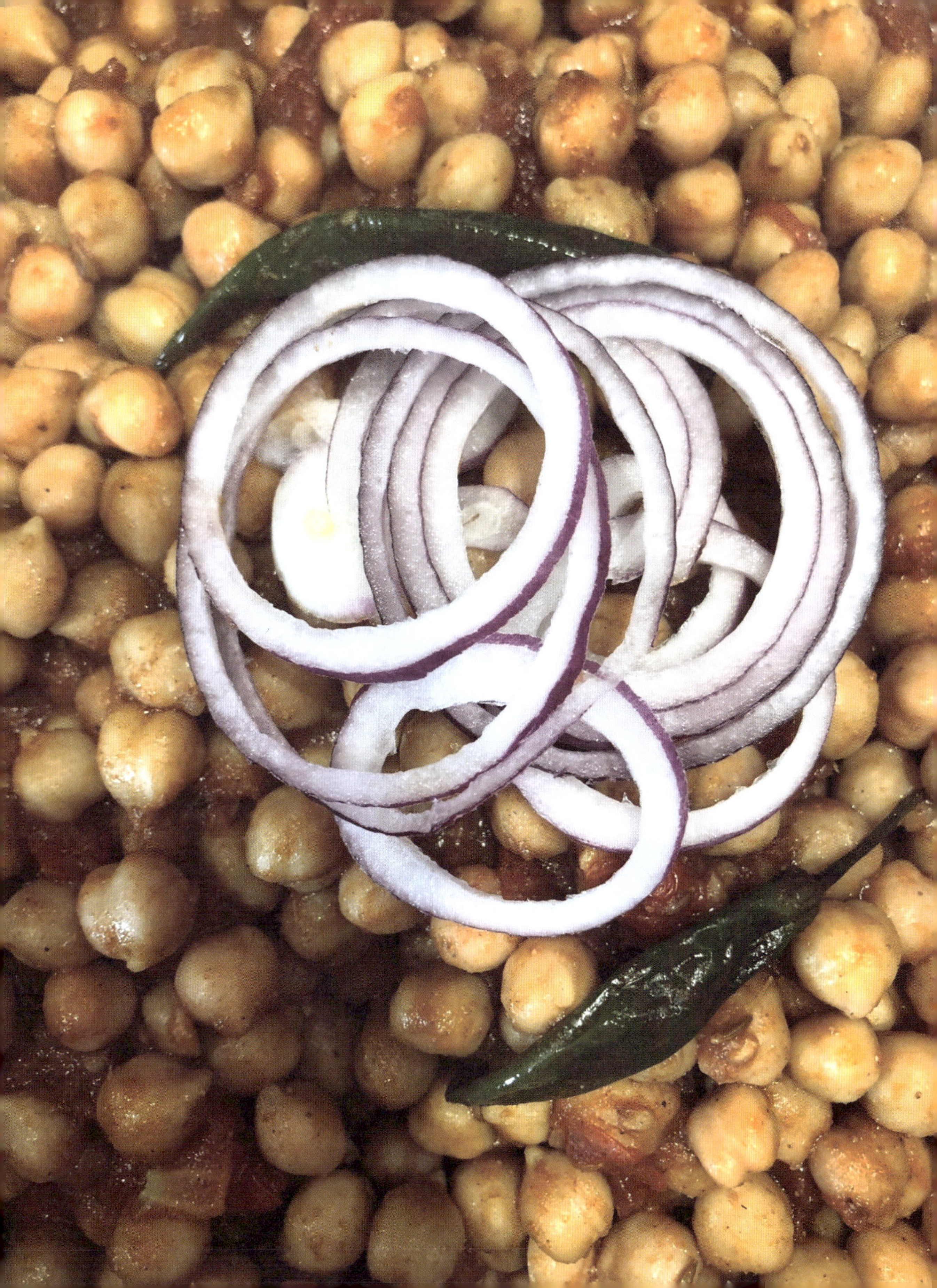

THANKS TO YOU

CELEBRATING 50 YEARS

Tilda

PURE ORIGINAL BASMATI

Our signature rice grains loved for their magical aroma and tantalising taste.

GLUTEN FREE

2kg

RICE & BREAD

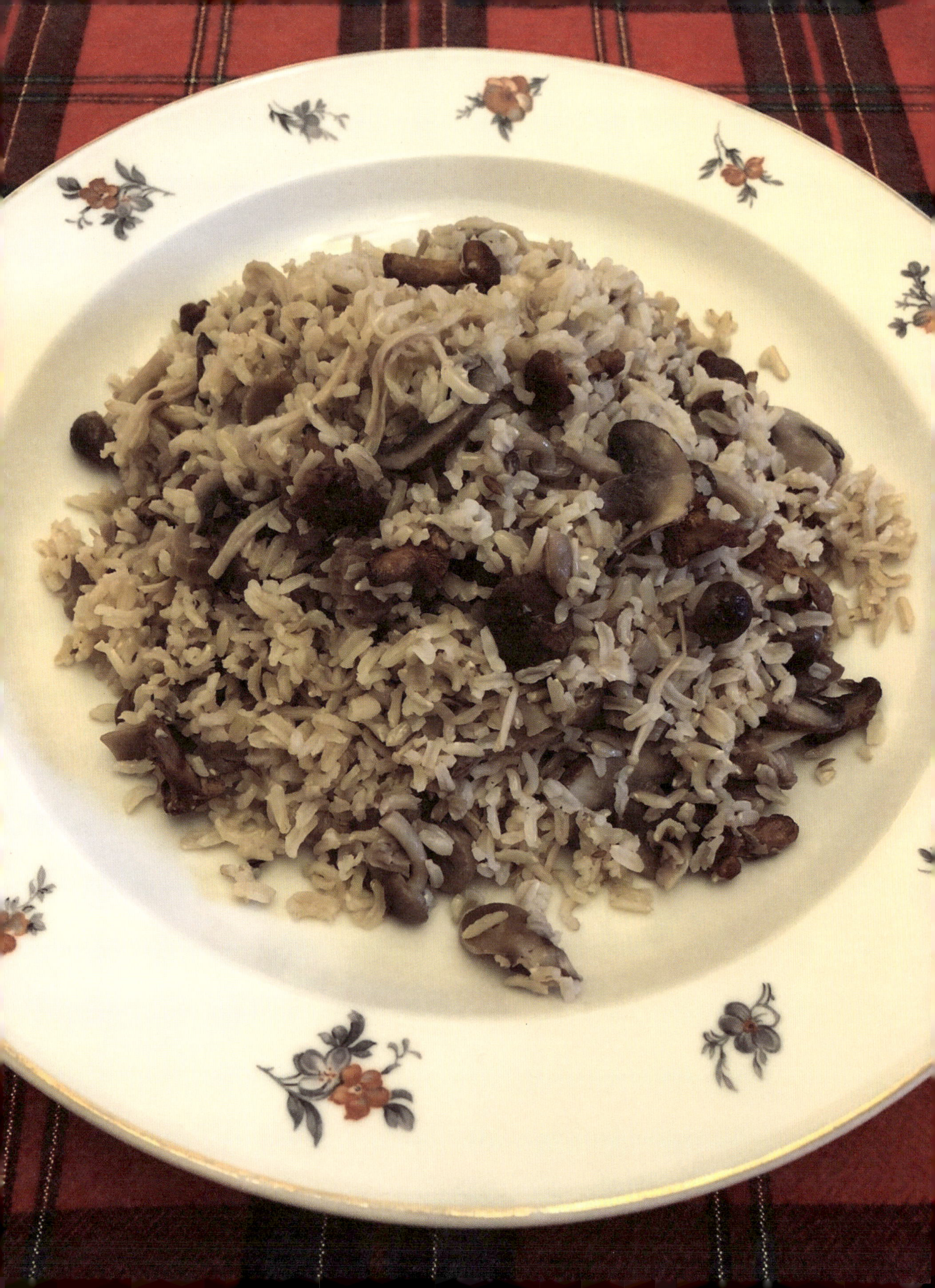

Rice

A note about rice: perfect rice cooking is actually really simple as long as you follow a few basic rules;

- Never use a spoon in the rice as this breaks up the grains and it may become mushy. When you think the rice is done, put a fork in the side of the pan and pull the rice to one side – there should be little, or no water left. Turn the heat off.

- Always take the rice off the hob, even once you have turned the heat off as it will continue to cook if the hob is still warm and you risk overcooking the rice.

- If you are in a real hurry (I know this from when my children were young and hunger comes on instantly!), while you soak the rice, add the water to the pan and boil. You can then add the rice to the boiling water as opposed to waiting, then cooking the rice with cold water. Whilst this may only shave off a few minutes, we all know time is precious!

- If you need to cook for a larger party of guests, it's very simple – just remember it's twice the amount of water to rice and increase the salt and oil by the same amounts. See below for some examples:

Rice	Water	Salt	Oil
1 cup	2 cups	1 teaspoon	1 tablespoon
2 cups	4 cups	2 teaspoons	2 tablespoons
3 cups	6 cups	3 teaspoons	3 tablespoons
4 cups	8 cups	4 teaspoons	4 tablespoons

During the Covid-19 lockdown in April 2020, Mum decided to cook, once a week, 100 meals for the NHS at our local hospital. That was a lot of rice!

RICE & BREAD

Fluffy White Rice

READY IN
15 MINS

SERVES
3-4

Nanny taught me to cook fluffy white rice; it is a perfect accompaniment to most Indian dishes. Really easy to cook – this will change the way you cook rice forever!

INGREDIENTS

1 cup basmati rice

2 cups water

1 tablespoon light olive oil

SPICES

½ teaspoon jeera (optional, the children do not seem to like it!)

1 teaspoon salt

METHOD

1. Put a cup of rice in a bowl of cold water, leave for 2 minutes, drain through a metal sieve or colander with small holes, put under the tap and rinse – this is to wash it thoroughly. Let it drain for a couple of minutes.

2. Put the oil, jeera and salt into a pan and heat for a few seconds on a low to medium heat. Do not let the jeera burn. Add the rice and 2 cups of cold water, lid on the pan. Bring to the boil then low heat/simmer. Once the water has evaporated/soaked up, rice is ready, approximately 12 minutes.

Note – Never use a spoon in the rice as this breaks up the grains and it may become mushy. When you think the rice is done, put a fork in the side of the pan and pull the rice to one side, there should be little, or no water left. Turn the heat off.

Always take the rice off the hob, even once you have turned the heat off as it will continue to cook if the hob is still warm and you risk over cooking the rice.

If you are in a real hurry (I know this from when my children were young and hunger comes on instantly!). While you soak the rice, add the water to the pan and boil. You can then add the rice to the water as it warms as oppose to waiting, then cooking the rice from cold water. Whilst this may only shave off a few minutes, we all know time is precious!

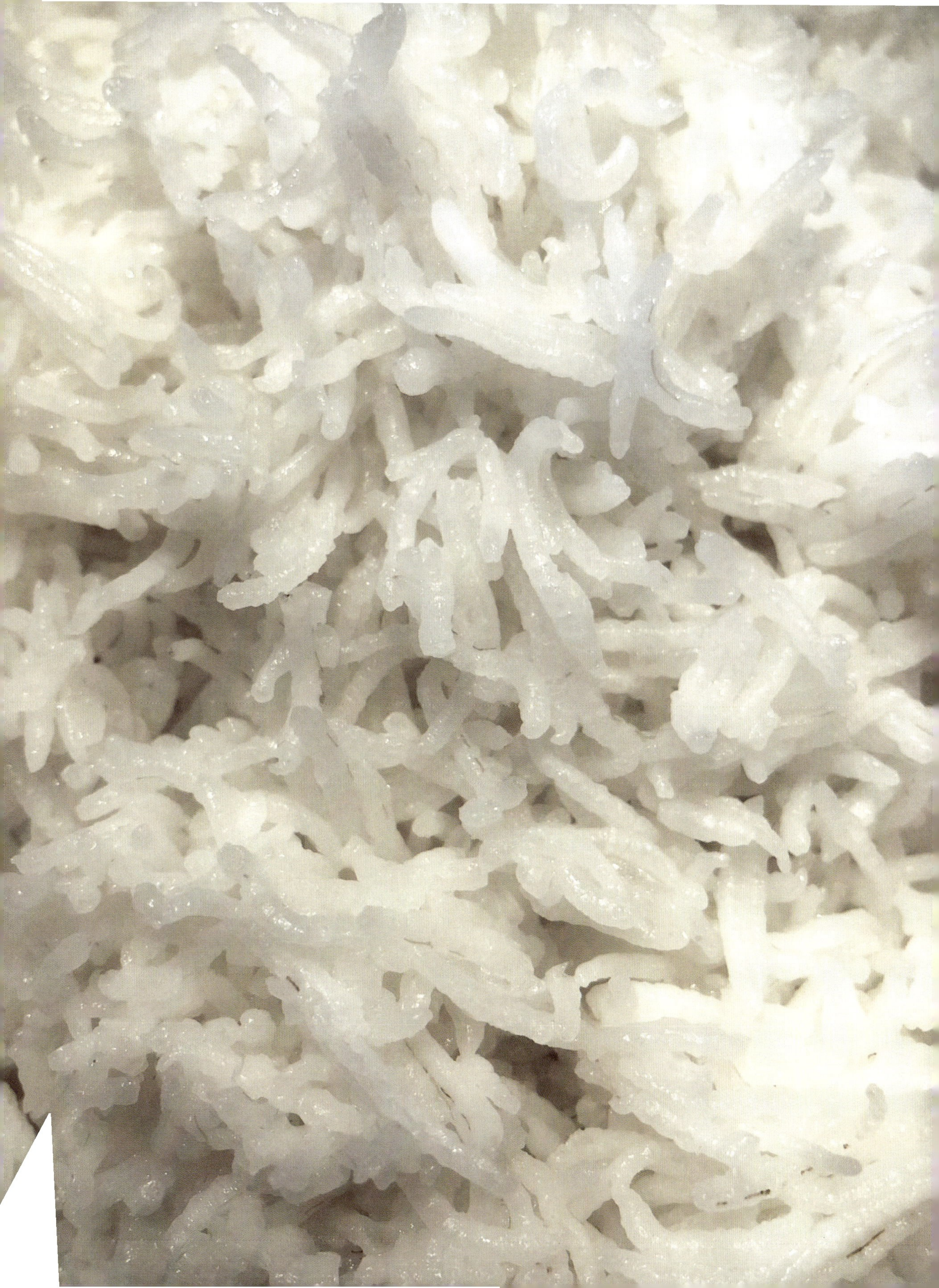

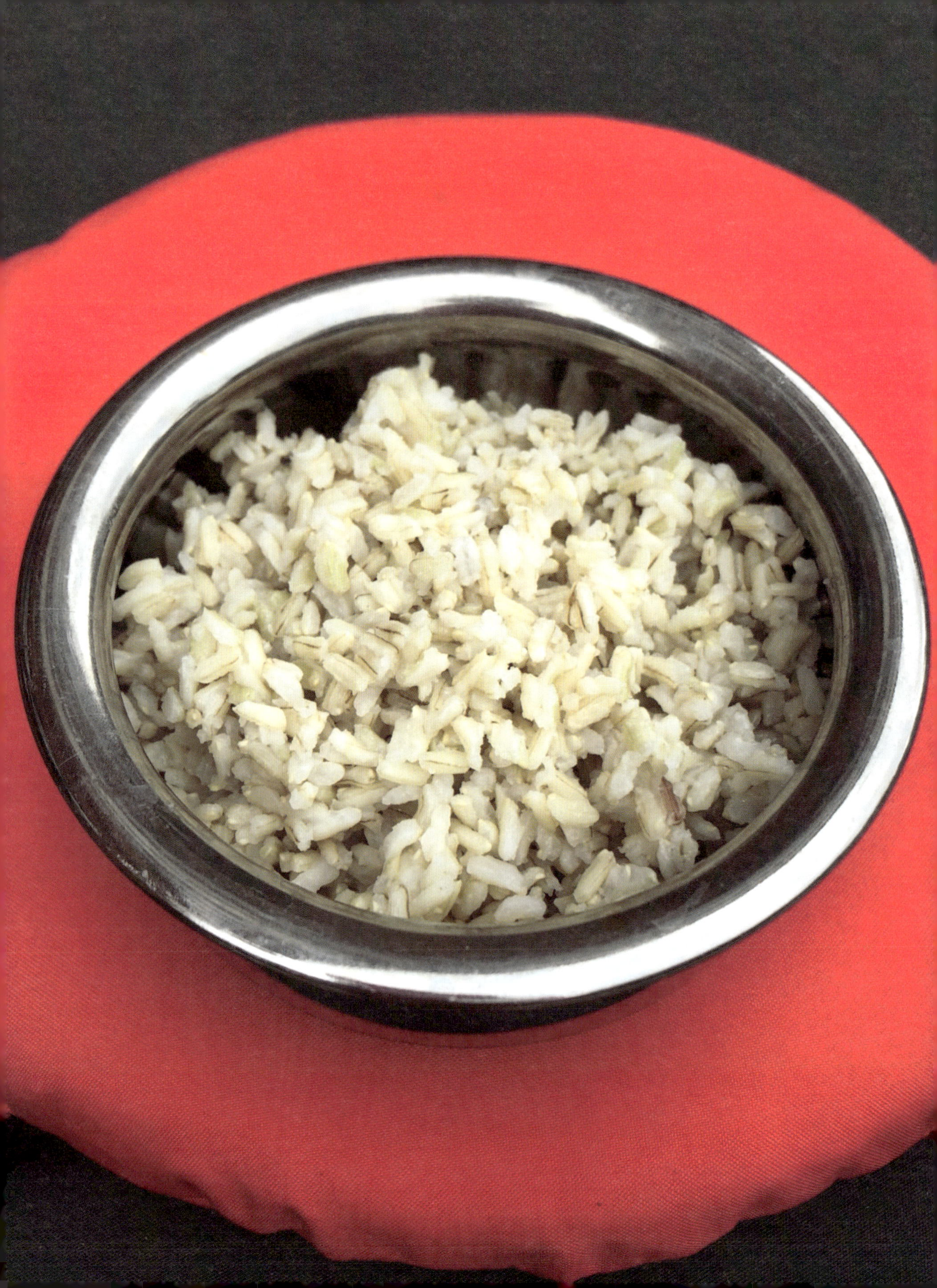

RICE & BREAD

Brown Rice

READY IN 35 MINS **SERVES** 3-4

I love brown rice; I prefer its nutty flavour so you can substitute brown rice for white rice in any of the dishes. Brown rice does take a lot longer to cook though.

This is a really simple brown rice recipe.

INGREDIENTS

1 cup brown rice (preferably basmati)

2 cups water

1 tablespoon light olive oil

SPICES

½ teaspoon jeera (optional)

1 teaspoon salt

METHOD

1. Put a cup of rice in a bowl of cold water, leave for 2 minutes, drain through a metal sieve or colander with small holes, put under the tap and rinse, this is to wash it thoroughly.

2. Let it drain for a couple of minutes while you start the cooking process.

3. Put the oil, jeera and salt into a pan and heat for a few seconds on a low to medium heat. Do not let the jeera burn.

4. Add the rice and 2 cups of cold water, lid on the pan. Bring to the boil then low heat/simmer.

5. Once the water has evaporated/soaked up, rice is ready, approximately 30 minutes.

Note - Never use a spoon in the rice as this breaks up the grains and it may become mushy. When you think the rice is done, put a fork in the side of the pan and pull the rice to one side, there should be little, or no water left. Turn the heat off.

Always take the rice off the hob, even once you have turned the heat off as it will continue to cook if the hob is still warm and you risk over cooking the rice.

If the rice is still a little hard add a bit more water (a tablespoon or two) and cook until done.

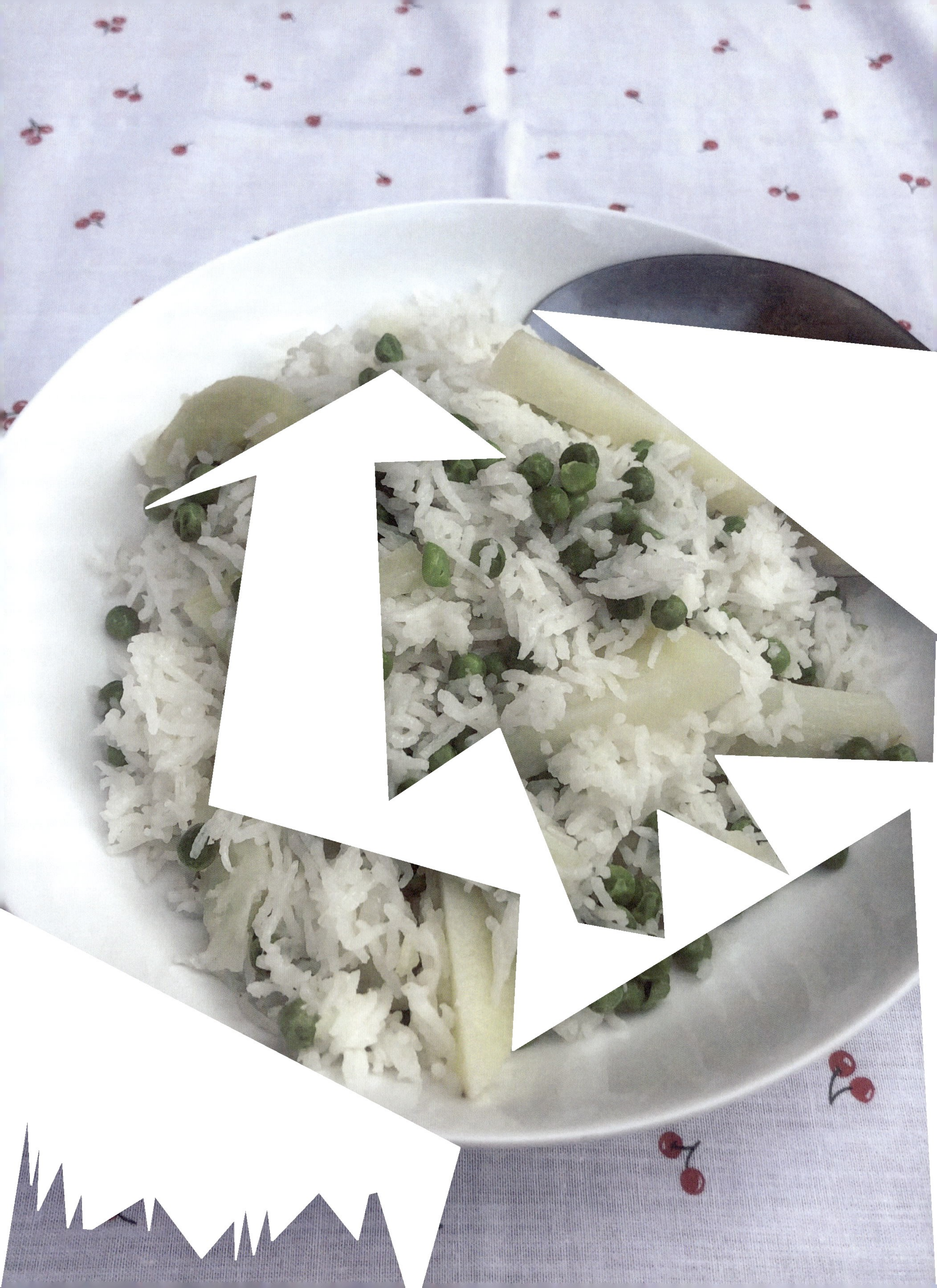

RICE & BREAD

Peas & Potato Rice

READY IN 25 MINS | **SERVES** 3-4

This dish was a favourite of Indian Nanny's for the youngest great-grandchildren, my children were fed this from a very young age (practically weaned on it!) and it was one of the first Indian dishes they ate.

As adults we also enjoy this simple but tasty rice dish. A healthy spoon of set yogurt on the side, makes a delicious lunch or light dinner.

INGREDIENTS

1 cup basmati rice

2 cups water

1 tablespoon light olive oil

1 small onion, peeled & thinly sliced

3 medium size potatoes, peeled and sliced into fingers

1 cup petit pois or peas

SPICES

½ teaspoon jeera (optional, the children do not seem to like it!)

1 teaspoon salt

METHOD

1. Put a cup of rice in a bowl of cold water, leave for 2 minutes, drain through a metal sieve or colander with small holes, put under the tap and rinse – this is to wash it thoroughly. Let it drain for a couple of minutes while you start the cooking process.

2. Put 1 tablespoon of oil in a pan on a medium heat, add the onions. Cook until the onions are pink, stirring occasionally, then add the jeera and salt, heat for a few seconds on a low to medium heat. Do not let the jeera burn.

3. Wash the potatoes and the peas through a colander under a cold tap, add them to the pan and give a quick stir.

4. Add the rice and 2 cups of cold water, put the lid on the pan. Bring to the boil then low heat/simmer. Once the water has evaporated/soaked up, rice is ready, approximately 12 minutes.

Note - Never use a spoon in the rice as this breaks up the grains and it may become mushy. When you think the rice is done, put a fork in the side of the pan and pull the rice to one side, there should be little, or no water left. Turn the heat off.

Always take the rice off the hob, even once you have turned the heat off as it will continue to cook if the hob is still warm and you risk over cooking the rice.

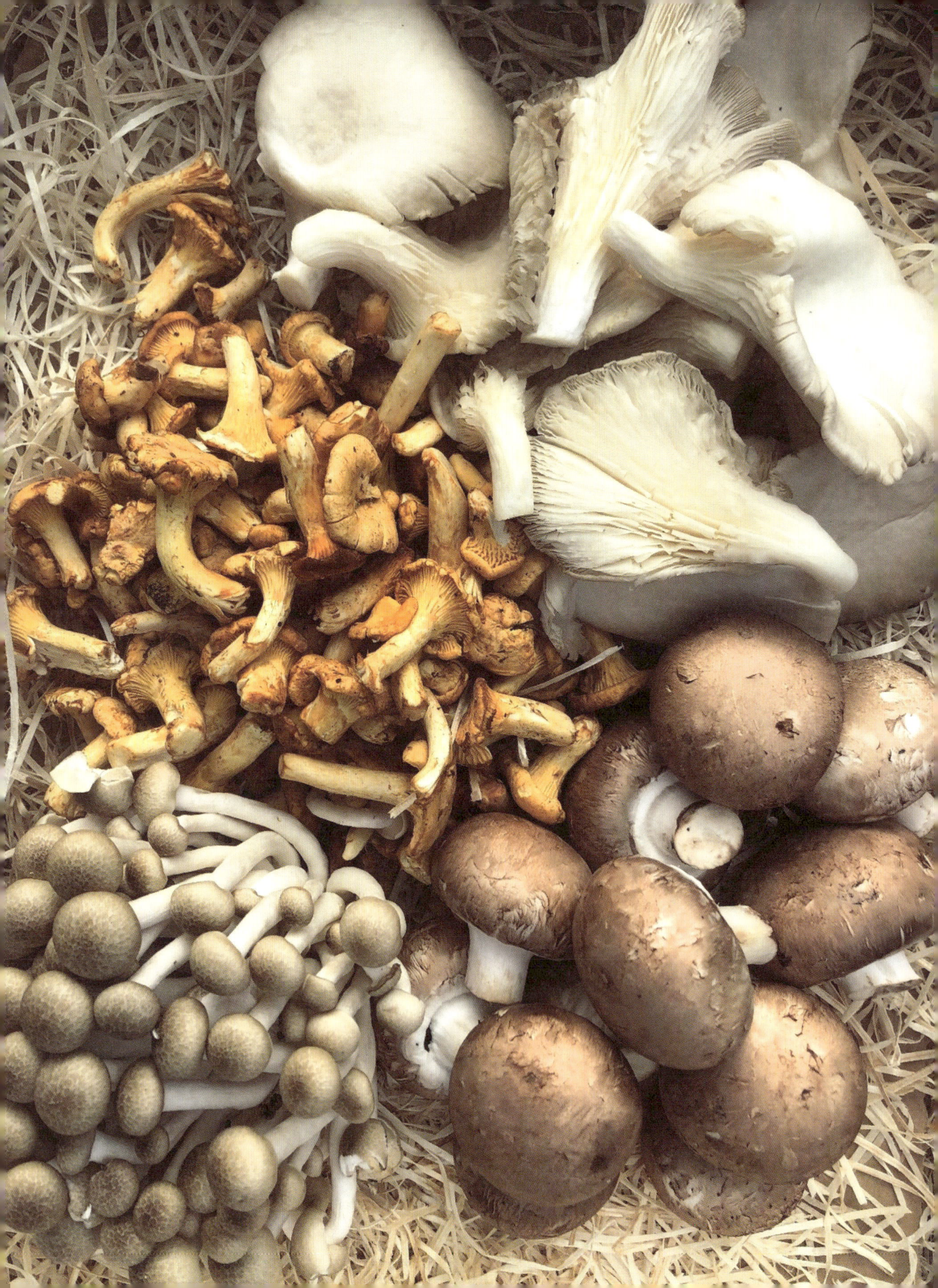

Gucchi Mushrooms – Indian Vegetable

When we were cooking mushroom rice, my Nan told me about a speciality mushroom that is sold fresh in Kashmir and dried from where she came from. It is excellent cooked in a mushroom rice. Best bought in Amritsar or a market in Delhi. I have since done a bit of research and found out that Gucchi mushrooms are a "morel" mushroom, it is a speciality vegetable that grows like a mushroom and cannot be cultivated commercially. Instead, they grow wild only in some regions like the Kangara Valley, Jammu and Kashmir, Manali and other parts of Himachal Pradesh after the snowfall period. Now, this once local and market vegetable is a super expensive luxury food. You can purchase them dried and soak them overnight then add to rice.

Recently, I have been lucky enough to be introduced to a whole variety of different mushrooms – for a vegetarian, they are probably the most expensive vegetable we will eat!

Here are a few different varieties to try if you like mushrooms and fancy trying them, they will cook perfectly in the mushroom rice recipe:

- Cep
- Girole
- Chanterelle
- Trompettes
- Oyster
- Pied de mouton

RICE & BREAD

Mushroom Rice

READY IN 45 MINS

SERVES 3-4

I prefer this recipe with brown rice and brown mushrooms, they complement each other with a nutty flavour. If you prefer white rice or only have white in your store cupboard, follow the recipe; however, reduce the cooking time to approximately 12 minutes once the rice has soaked up the water during cooking.

INGREDIENTS

1 cup brown rice (preferably basmati)

2 cups water

1 tablespoon light olive oil

1 small onion, peeled & thinly sliced

8 medium size mushrooms, brown or white, thinly sliced

SPICES

½ teaspoon jeera (optional)

1 teaspoon salt

METHOD

1. Put a cup of rice in a bowl of cold water, leave for 2 minutes, drain through a metal sieve or colander with small holes, put under the tap and rinse – this is to wash it thoroughly.

2. Let it drain for a couple of minutes while you start the cooking process.

3. Put 1 tablespoon of oil in a pan on a medium heat, add the onions. Heat for a minute or two until the onions are starting to cook (they are slightly transparent).

4. Add the sliced mushrooms, jeera and salt. Cook, stirring occasionally, until the onions are pink and the mushrooms are cooked; the water should have evaporated. Do not let the jeera burn.

5. Add the rice and 2 cups of cold water, put the lid on the pan. Bring to the boil then low heat/simmer.

6. Once the water has evaporated/soaked up, rice is ready, approximately 30 minutes.

Note - Never use a spoon in the rice as this breaks up the grains and it may become mushy. When you think the rice is done, put a fork in the side of the pan and pull the rice to one side, there should be little, or no water left. Turn the heat off.

Always take the rice off the hob, even once you have turned the heat off as it will continue to cook if the hob is still warm and you risk over cooking the rice.

If the rice is still a little hard add a bit more water (a tablespoon or two) and cook until done.

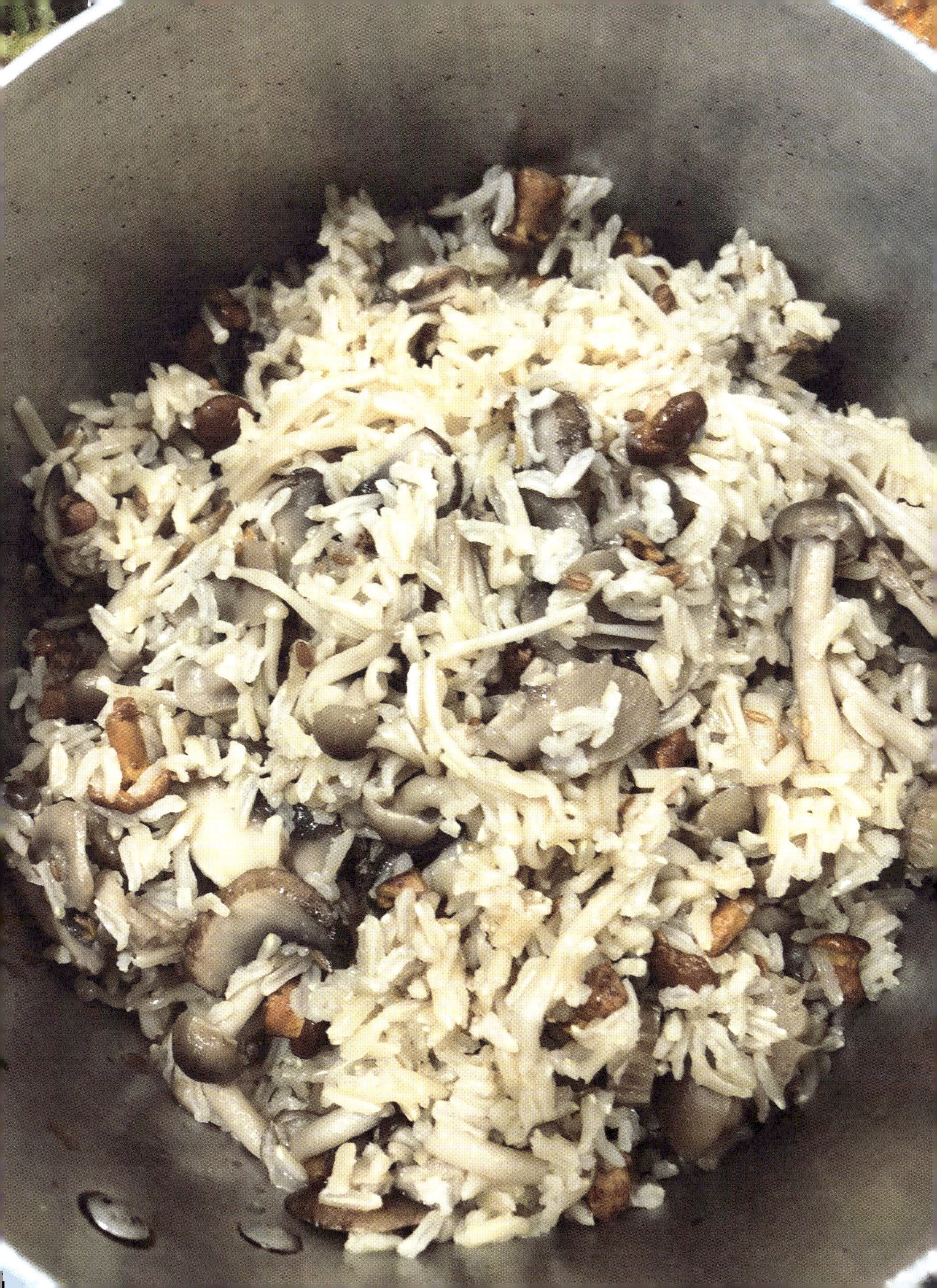

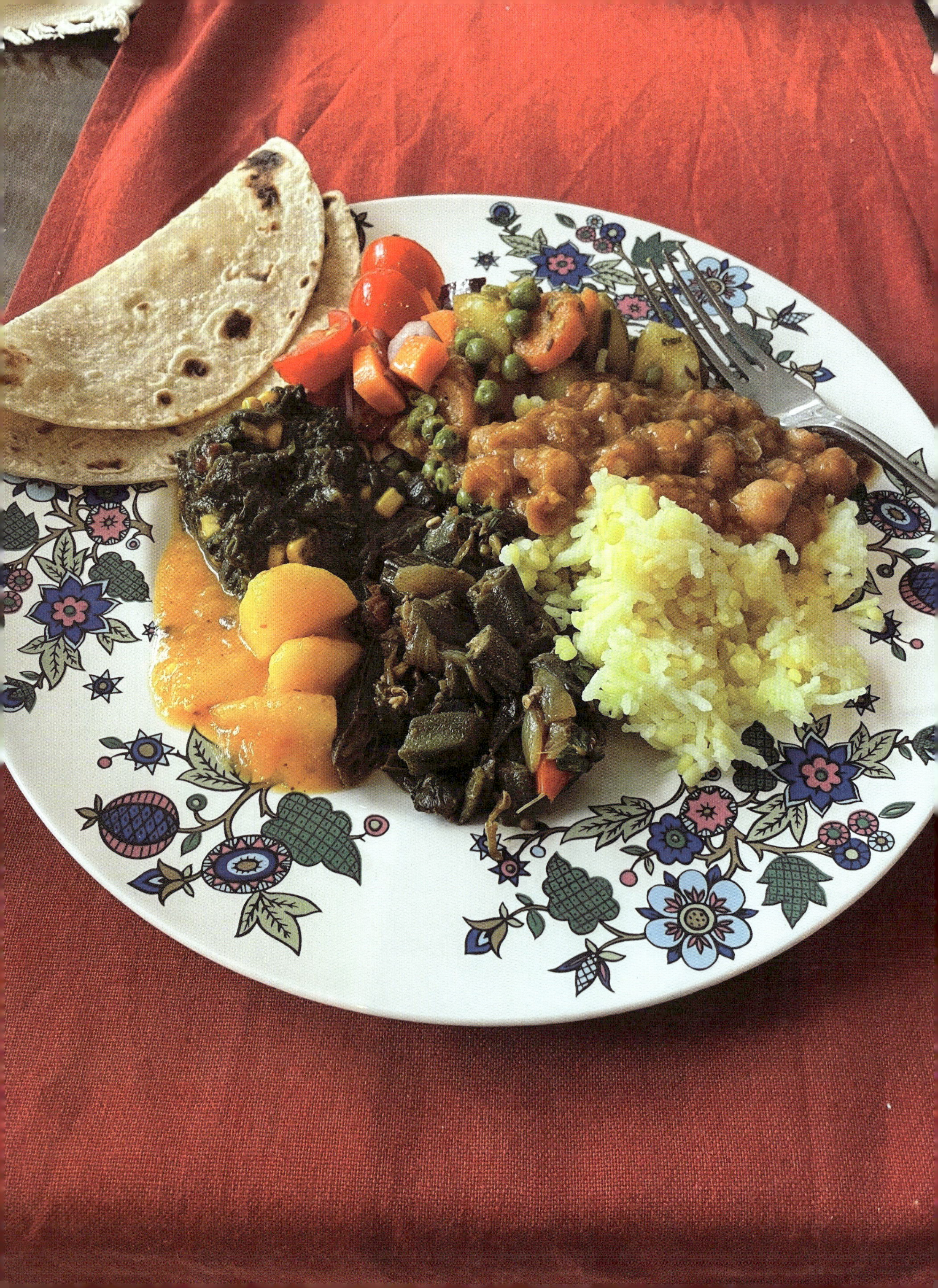

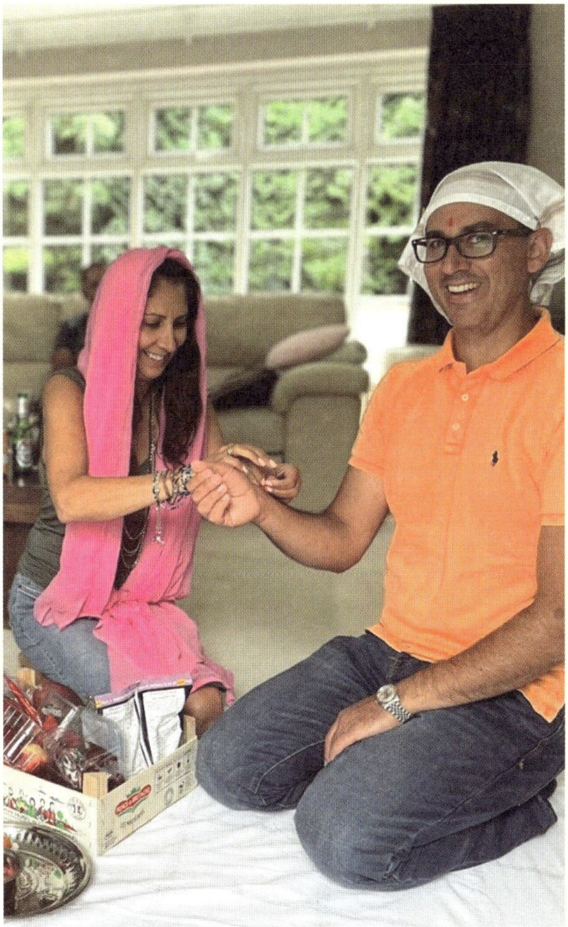

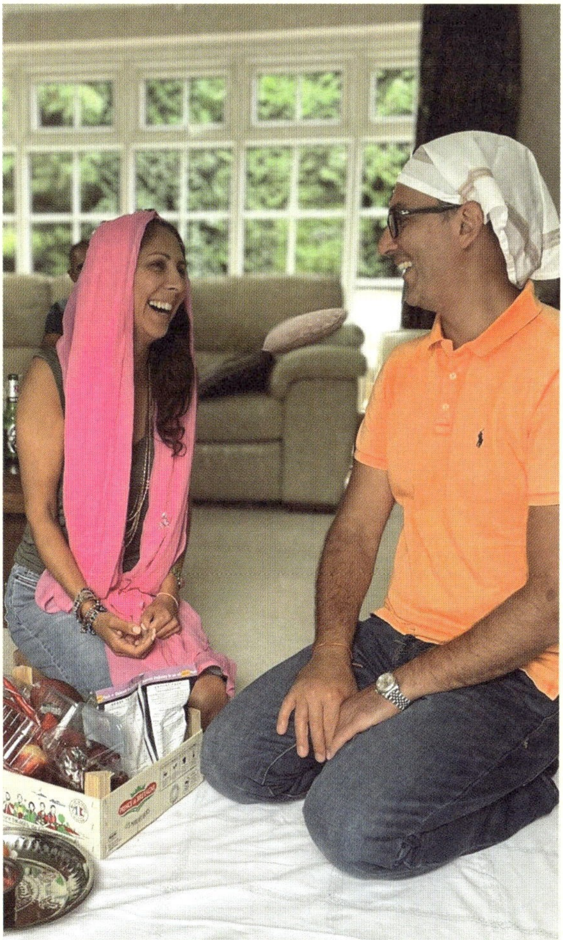

RICE & BREAD

Kitchari – Rice with Yellow Dahl

READY IN 40 MINS   **SERVES** 4-6

"We will always stick together like rice and dahl!"
Indian Nanny taught me to cook this rice. It is traditionally eaten in our family at a special celebration called Raksha Bandhan, known as ruckerery to us kids!

This is a special celebration of brother / sister love. We understand it as the brother always looks after the sister (he gives her money during the ceremony) and the sister will feed and clothe him (she gives him a basket of fruit and an item of clothing). We like this family tradition!

This traditional dish is also served when people are unwell or recovering. Full of protein and easy to digest.

INGREDIENTS

- 1 cup rice
- 1 cup yellow dahl (mung dahl)
- 4 cups water
- 3 tablespoons light olive oil

SPICES

- 1 teaspoon jeera
- 4 teaspoons salt (reduce if you wish)

METHOD

1. Soak the dahl for 15 minutes in a bowl of warm water.

2. While the dahl is soaking, wash the rice. To do this put the rice in a bowl of cold water, leave for 2 minutes, drain through a metal sieve or colander with small holes, put under the tap and rinse – this is to wash it thoroughly.

3. Then drain the dahl, wash it through a colander in the same way as you did the rice.

4. Let it drain for a couple of minutes while you start cooking.

5. Into a pan add 3 tablespoons oil, 1 teaspoon jeera, once warm (sizzles), add the rice and dahl with 4 teaspoons salt and 4 cups of water.

6. Bring to the boil then simmer with the lid on over a medium to low heat for approximately 20 minutes until it is done/ all the water is soaked up.

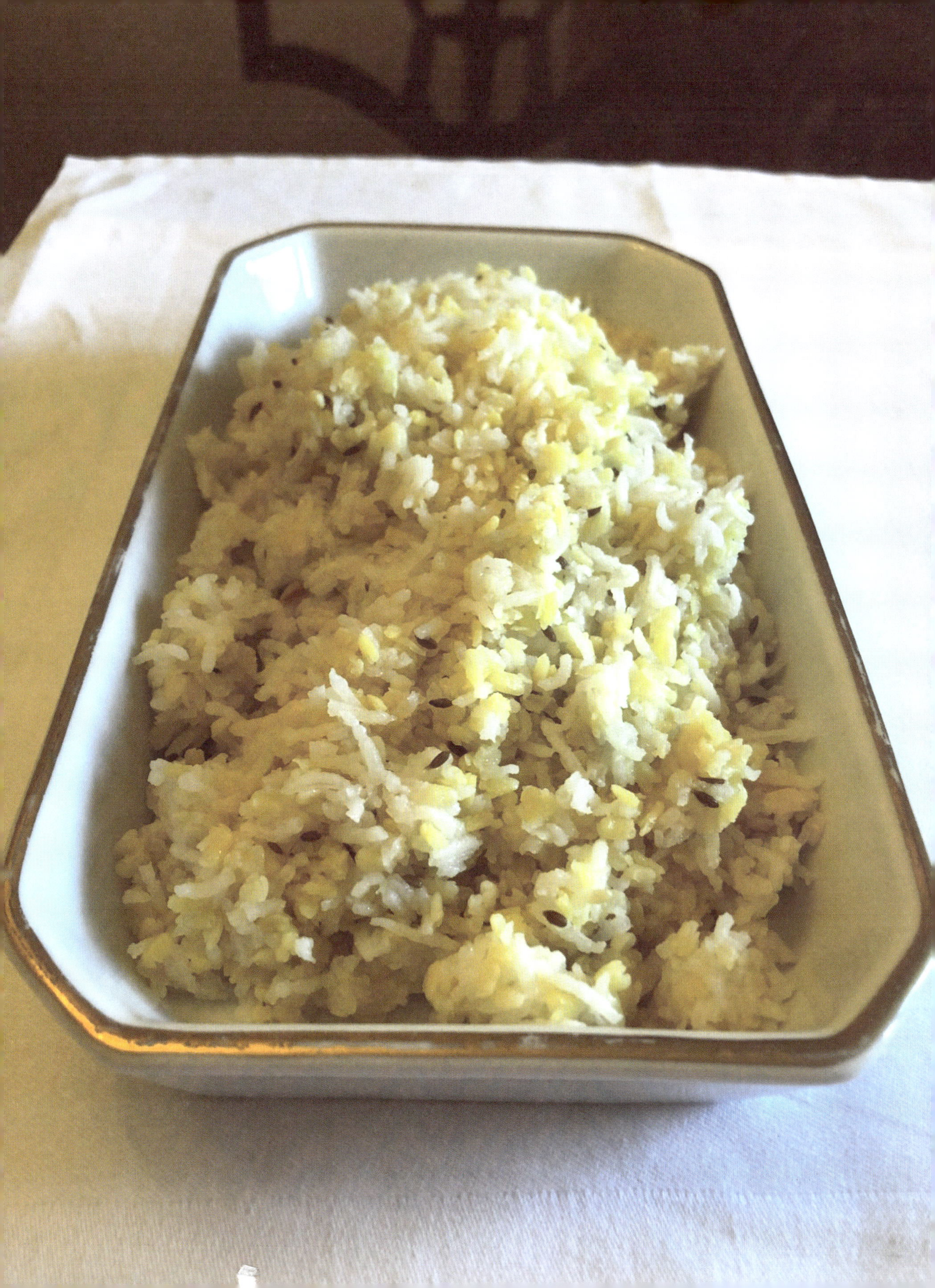

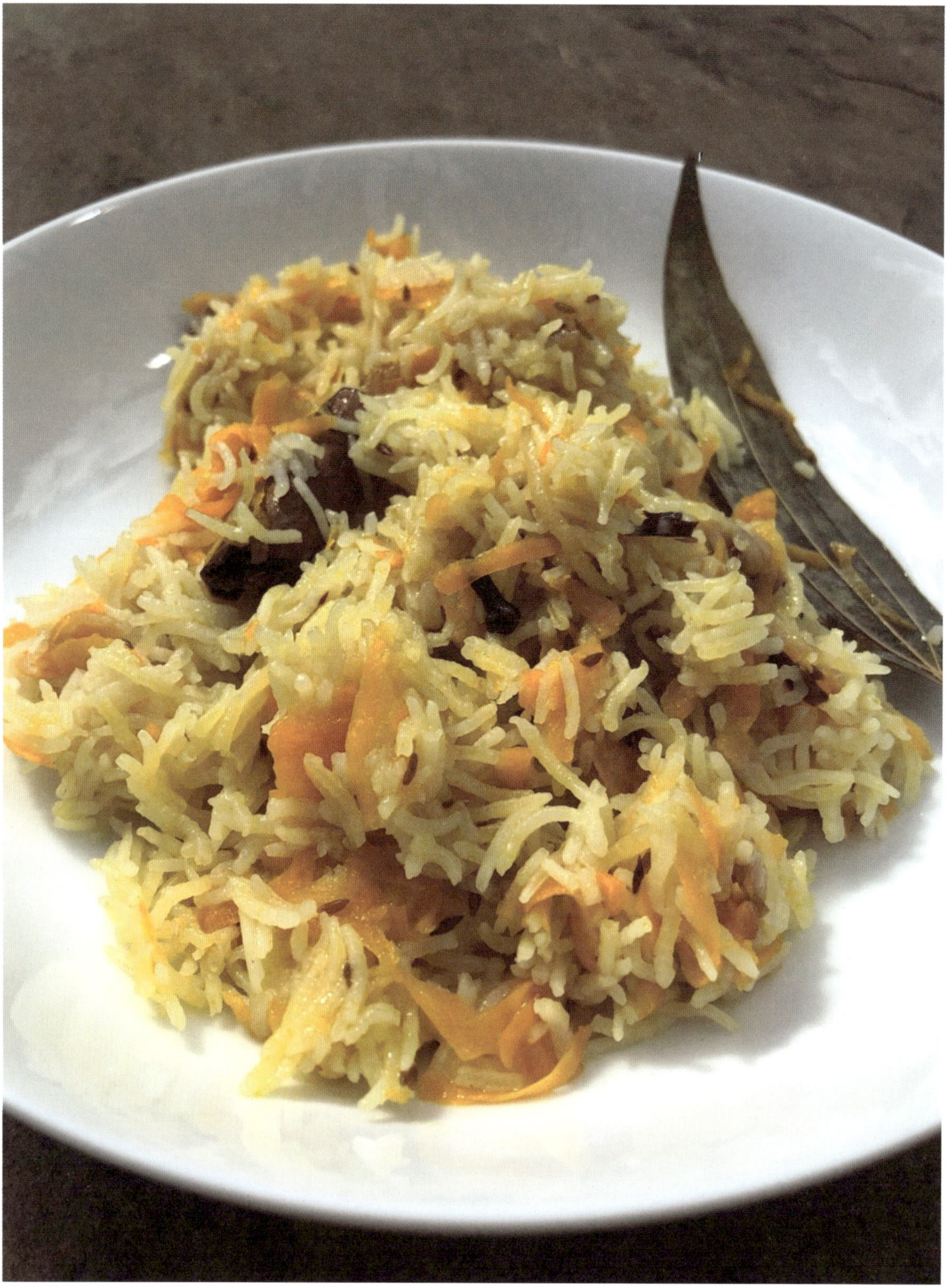

RICE & BREAD

Vegetarian Rice – Veena Style

READY IN 30 MINS
SERVES 4-6

The grated carrot in this rice gives it an amazing colour. It works really well just using jeera and salt if you do not have the other spices.

INGREDIENTS

2 medium onions

4 tablespoons light olive oil

4 grated carrots

1 cup basmati rice, soaked for 10 minutes in a bowl of water then rinsed under a cold water tap through a colander

2 ¼ cups water

SPICES

2 teaspoons jeera

3 bay leaves

4 cloves

2-inch cinnamon stick

2 green cardamon pods

1 teaspoon salt

METHOD

1. Using a medium size pan (with a tight-fitting lid), peel and finely slice lengthways the onions into the pan.

2. Add 4 tablespoons of oil and put it on a high heat.

3. Add the jeera and fry the onions, keep stirring until they are light brown and a bit crispy.

4. Then add ¼ cup of water, it will sizzle a bit!

5. Add 3 bay leaves, 4 cloves, 2-inch cinnamon stick and 2 green cardamon pods.

6. Add the grated carrots, stir and reduce to a medium heat. Cook for 5 minutes until the water has been absorbed and add 1 teaspoon of salt.

7. Put on a low heat. Add the rice and twice the amount of water (one cup rice, 2 cups of water).

8. Cover with a lid and turn the heat up until it boils. Turn the heat down to a simmer and cook until the water has been absorbed by the rice, approximately 12 minutes. Turn the heat off. The rice will be nice and fluffy.

Notes – Remember the rice rule! Do not stir. Fluff up with a fork at the end.

If you soak the rice for too long, then cook with slightly less water or it will go soggy. You can always start with a little less water and add a bit if it still needs cooking.

Seema always asks her mum to remove the "wood" spices before serving to avoid them being eaten!

RICE & BREAD

Vegetable Biriyani – Nanny Style!

READY IN 20 MINS

SERVES 4-6

A colourful rice dish, that can form part of a meal or can be great eaten on its own, when you are looking for a quick filling bowl of your favourite rice and veggies.

INGREDIENTS

4 tablespoons light olive oil

1 large onion, peeled & thinly sliced

1 cup rice

2 cups water

1 carrot, peeled and diced or grated

6 medium mushrooms, cut into quarters or 6 pieces if large

1 cup peas

Add any vegetable ingredients you like or a cup of frozen mixed vegetables

SPICES

½ teaspoon jeera

3 teaspoons salt

7 bay leaves

3 cinnamon sticks

6 cloves

6 whole cardamon

METHOD

1. Add the oil to a wok over a medium heat, add the onion and fry until crispy brown.

2. Then add ½ teaspoon jeera, 3 teaspoons salt, all the vegetables and cook over a low heat for approximately 5 minutes.

3. The mushrooms should start to change colour and the juice comes out of them.

4. Then add the bay leaves, cinnamon sticks, cloves and cardamon, stir and cook for a few minutes.

5. While the veggies are cooking, put a cup of rice in a bowl of cold water, leave for 2 minutes, drain through a metal sieve or colander with small holes, put under the tap and rinse – this is to wash it thoroughly. Let it drain for a couple of minutes.

6. Add the one cup of rinsed rice, 2 cups of cold water into the pan with the veg, on a high heat with the lid on until boiling, then simmer (as per the fluffy rice recipe). Once the water has been absorbed, the dish is ready, approximately 12 minutes.

Note - Remember the rice rule! Do not stir and remove from the heat immediately once cooked.

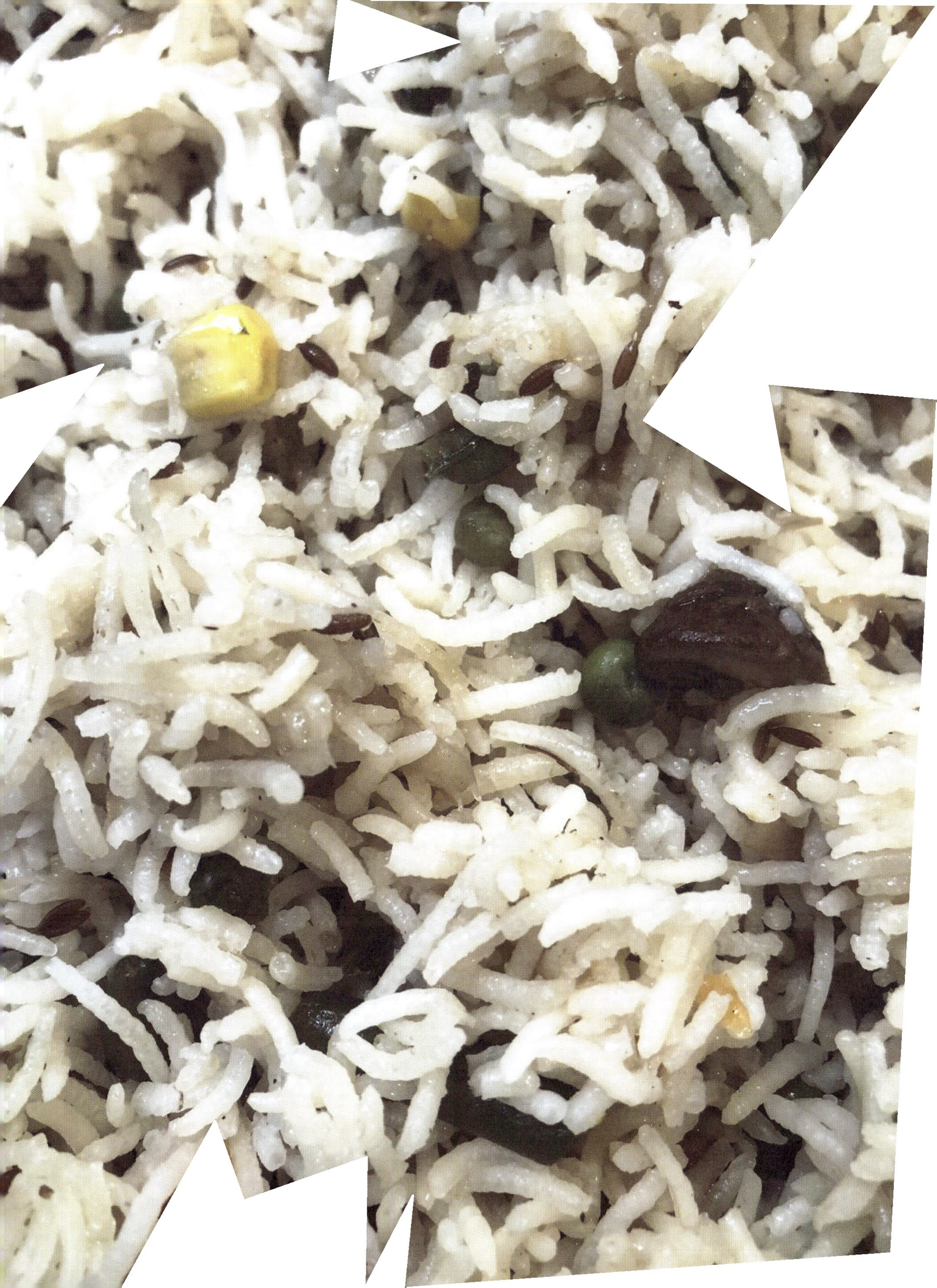

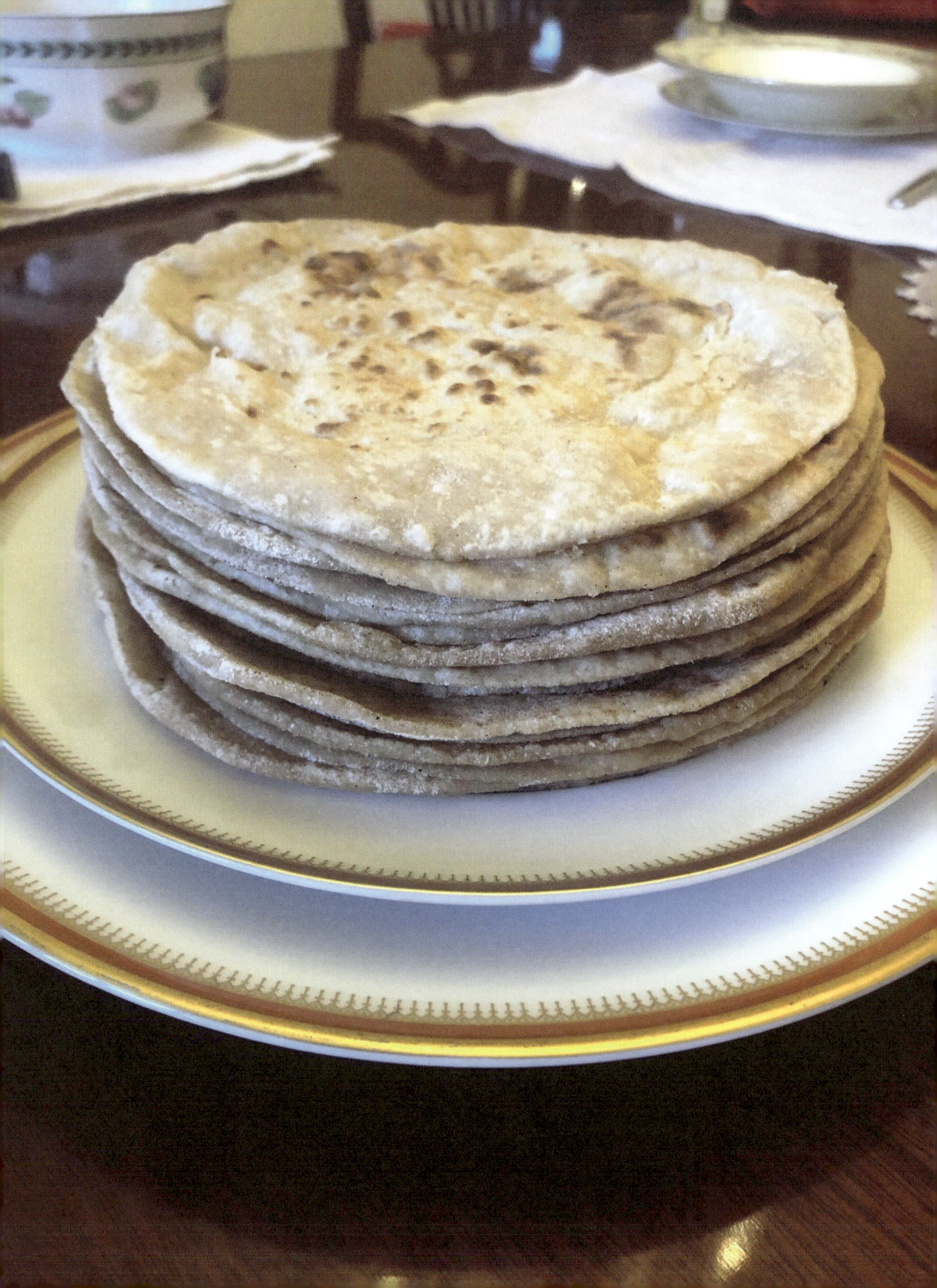

Indian Bread

We love Indian bread to mop up the delicious curry sauces. Nothing goes to waste! There are a variety of Indian breads. Traditionally, we make these to accompany a meal. Now there are some shop-bought alternatives that are actually quite good.

Tawa

What to cook your chapatis in? Traditionally this is done on a "tawa". The story goes that whoever takes the tawa out (usually stored in the oven) must put it back or there will be quarrelling between them! A flat pan is also absolutely fine to cook them on.

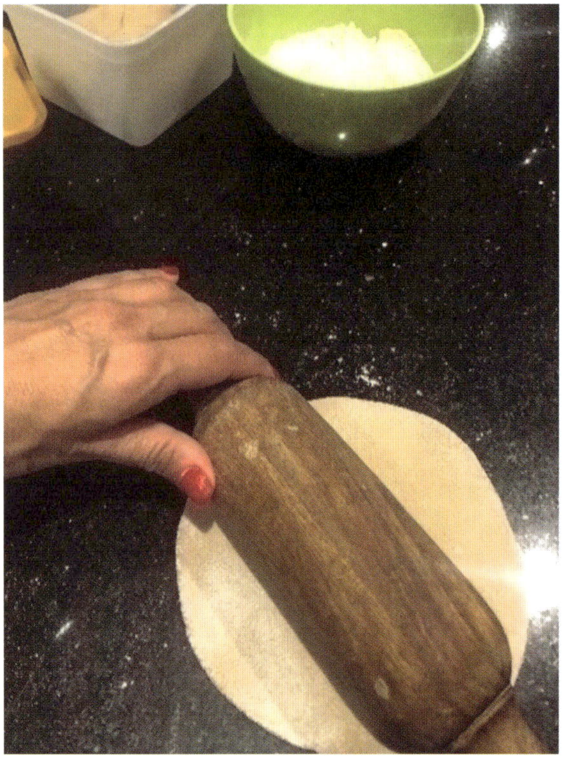
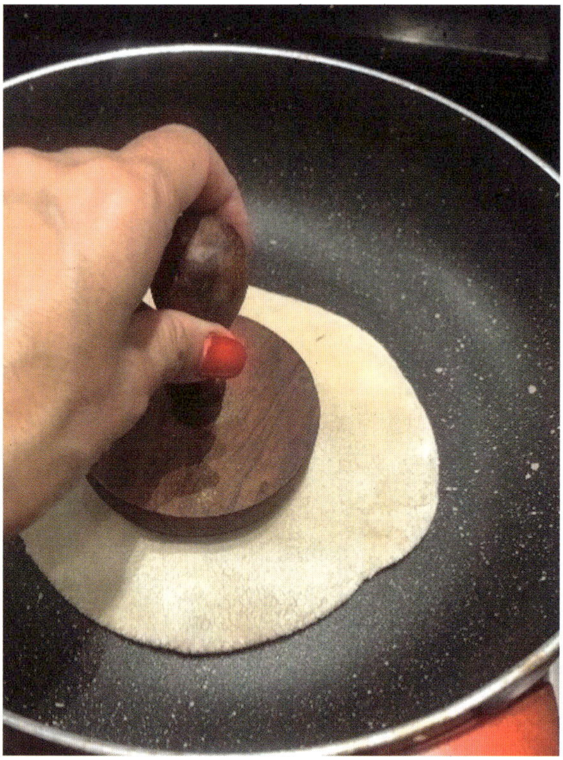
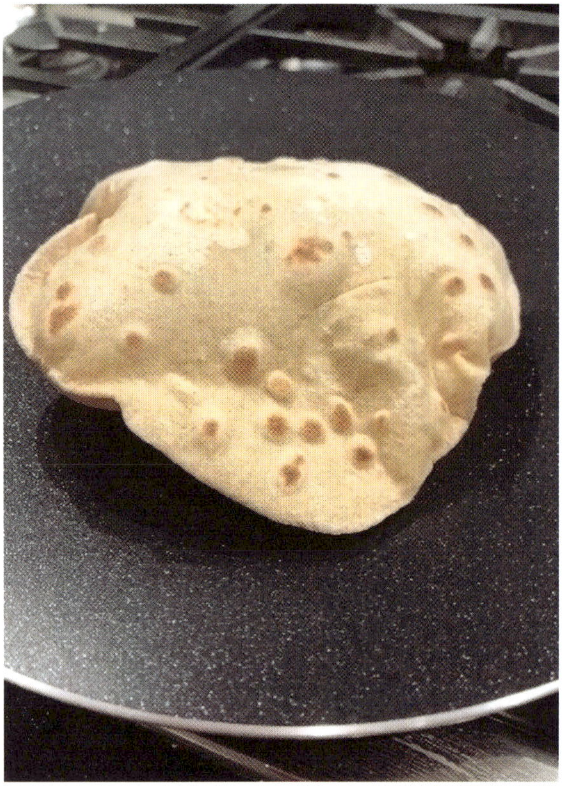
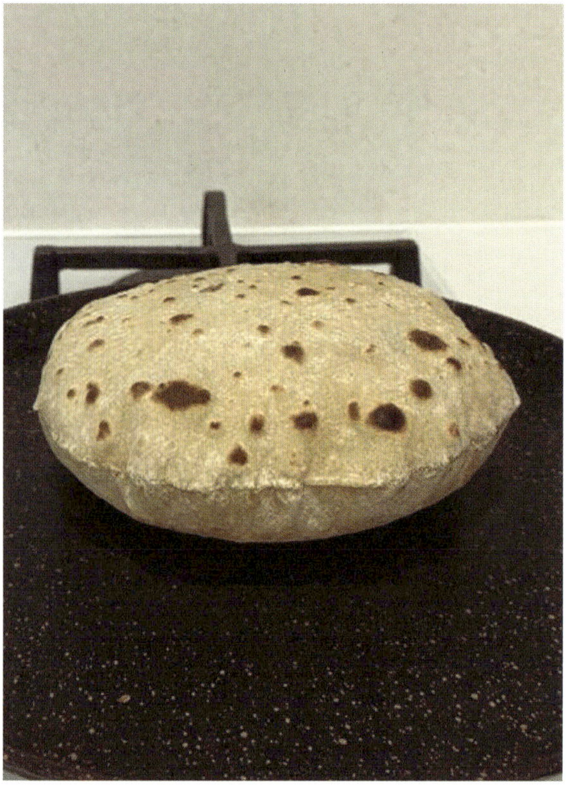

RICE & BREAD

Rita's Chapatis

READY IN 45 MINS

SERVES 3-4

Chapatis are Indian bread, easy to make and great with paneer or any Indian dishes where you can mop up the tasty gravy! Indian Nanny and the Aunties make wicked chapatis. It makes my mouth water thinking about their warm, fresh chapatis, with a thin spread of butter on. My cousins Tina and Nisha are chapati ninjas! They have been known to make a good 50 or so for a family get-together. They are always perfectly round and beautifully thin.

When I was cooking with Nanny, she told me I wasn't ready to make chapatis. So, Rita taught me. My chapatis are not beautifully round – in the beginning they sometimes resembled country shapes, so I asked the children to guess what countries and we have a little fun with it. Honestly, to get chapati making right, it does take a bit of practice. Well worth the effort because once mastered, you will be chuffed.

INGREDIENTS

200g chapati flour

200ml water

Note: Makes 8 chapatis

METHOD

1. In a bowl, make the atta (dough) by adding half the water to the flour first, give it a little mix then add the rest slowly. Knead the dough really well. You can knead it in the bowl or on a surface. Add a little flour or water if necessary to get the right consistency. You will feel the texture of the dough change and become elastic; if you press your thumb into the dough, it should not stick and the hole rise again slowly.

2. Once the dough is made, leave in an airtight container for a minimum of 15 minutes. This is for the gluten to work. If you are going to leave it for a few hours or overnight, you can put it in the fridge. The dough should be at room temperature when you are ready to roll, so remove from the fridge at least 15 minutes before you would like to use it.

3. Take the dough and divide into 8 balls.

4. Take one of the balls, dip it in a little flour both sides then roll out the dough using a rolling pin on a surface. To get them round, rotate them ¼ turn at a time. Also flip them over and roll on each side. Add a sprinkle of flour if necessary. Each chapati should be about 13cm in diameter.

5. Heat a large flat pan and cook each chapati for 1 minute or so on each side, turning over until cooked and brown spots appear. If you press them with chapati press, a tea towel or cloth, you will see them swell into a ball.

6. Enjoy plain or with a spread of butter.

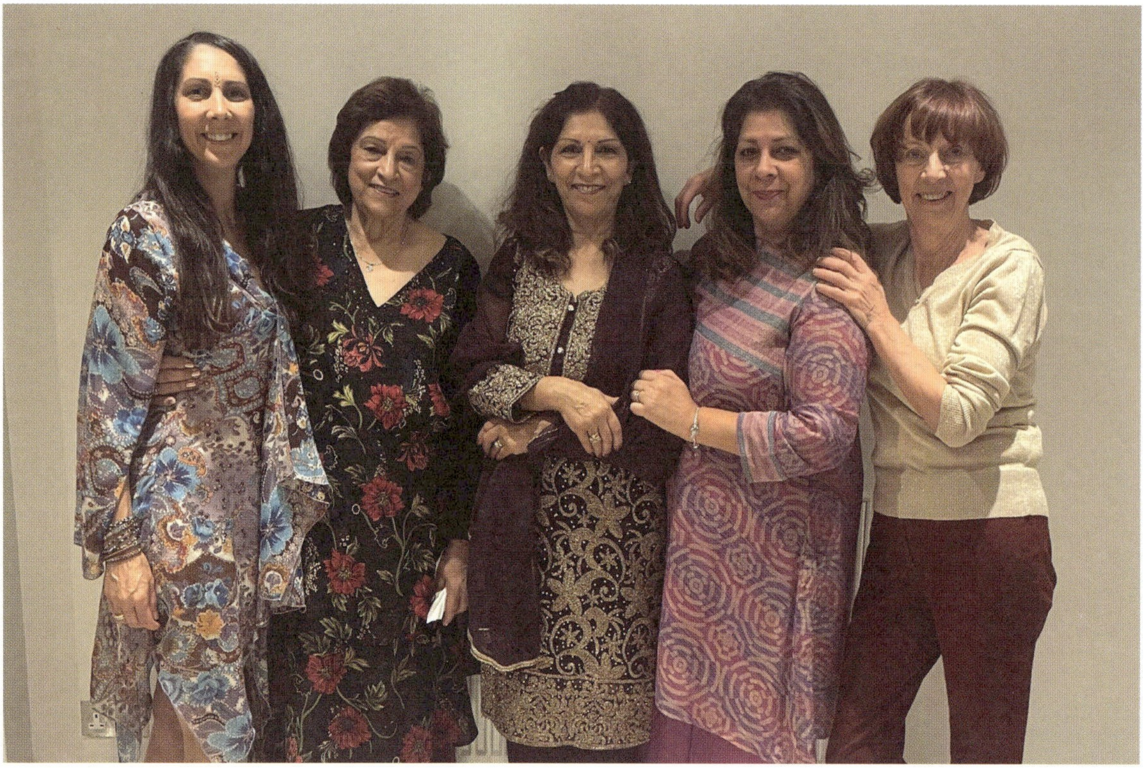

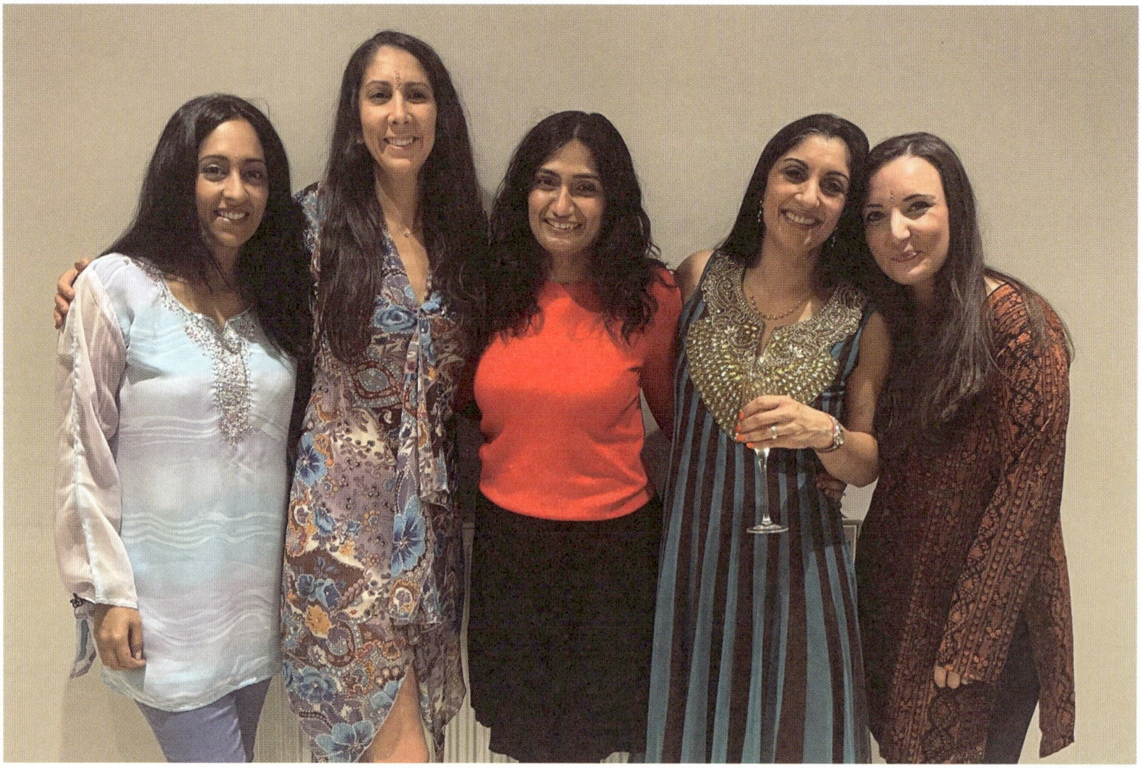

Perfecting your chapatis

Ok, so I spoke with Tina and Nisha (chapati ninjas) about perfecting your chapatis. Our family recipes are from the Punjab state of India and traditionally our chapatis are not as thin as Tina's – her family originate from the Gujrat state. I guess it's a bit like bread, we have different varieties based on where it comes from.

Veena, Madhu and Rita's chapatis

The Aunties were taught to make chapatis by Nanny so follow Rita's recipe.

Veena likes to rub a little rapeseed oil on her hands before handling the atta and rolling it.

Madhu likes to leave atta in the bowl and cover with a wet tea towel to prove before rolling hers.

RICE & BREAD

Tina's Chapatis

READY IN
45 MINS

SERVES
3-4

INGREDIENTS

200g Chapati flour (Pillsbury is her favourite)

Water

Oil (sunflower or vegetable)

Note: *Makes 8 chapatis*

METHOD

1. Put the flour in a bowl, then add a drizzle of oil – the more oil you use the softer / easier they will be to make thin. Half boil the kettle and use the water from here so it is slightly hotter than warm.

2. Knead for a good 5 minutes. Leave it on the side to settle for 15-20 minutes, 30 minutes maximum. It does not need to go in the fridge.

3. Knead the atta again for 5 minutes, have a small bowl of chapati flour on the side.

4. Make the atta into little round balls. Take a round ball and dip in the flour. Start to roll using a rolling pin.

5. Once it is about 4cm, dip it back in the flour and roll again.

6. The skill to making them round is to let them roll themselves, it's about the lightness of your hand, it should be as easy as possible.

7. Turn the heat on the hob and warm the tawa / flat pan. Add the chapati, cook for 1 minute or so on each side, if you want them to rise, it needs to be of a certain heat. Careful, don't burn them. Remove and serve with a little oil or butter.

RICE & BREAD

Nisha's Chapatis

READY IN 45 MINS

SERVES 3-4

METHOD

1. No real measurements, add the flour to a bowl, then add some water, less to start off with then add more as necessary. Go easy with the water, sometimes you may just need to wet your hand under the tap.

2. Knead until it is the consistency of dough. The more you knead it, the better the chapati will roll. It should not stick to your hands when you pick it up, roll it round the bowl and if it is the correct consistency, it will leave a "clean bowl". It should have a little elasticity, stiffness and should be soft.

3. You can use it straight away or make it in the morning and keep it in the fridge.

4. Divide into 8. Take one and make a small ball, flatten it, roll with the rolling pin then keep turning it over. If it sticks to the surface add a little more flour. Repeat for the other 7.

5. Warm a tawa, Nisha likes to use a crepe pan but a flat-bottomed frying pan is also good. Add the chapati, warm for 1 minute and turn, when you see brown spots and starts to puff up, press with the chapati press or tea towel to make it rise, flip until cooked. Add a little oil or butter and serve.

INGREDIENTS

200g Chapati flour (Chakki atta is her favourite)

Water

Note: *Makes 8 chapatis*

246

RICE & BREAD

Puris

⏳ **READY IN**
45 MINS
+ PROVING

🍴 **SERVES**
3-4

Traditionally this bread is served with puri aloo. Teamwork is great for this as one person can be rolling the puris out and the other frying. I remember my Nan and Grandad doing this as well as Rita and Gigi. Puris are an Indian fried bread which is so tasty. A classic Indian brunch would be chana, puri aloo, lassi and puris.

INGREDIENTS

250g chapati flour

250ml warm water

Sunflower oil for frying

Notes: *This recipe makes 12 puris*

Try to roll each puri an even thickness, similar to a pancake

When you have the puris in the oil, gently pat them going clockwise

After cooking a few puris lower the heat

METHOD

1. Put the flour in a large bowl and pour in the warm water. With your hand bring the flour and water together. Knead to make a dough, continue to do this until the flour and water is totally combined and the bowl is clean.

2. Put the dough ball on a large clean surface and knead for a good few minutes to release the gluten. The more you knead and throw the dough around, the better the dough will be. In India, they say "give it a good moti" which I think would be similar to use your elbow grease! You will be able to make a dent with your fingers that then slowly rises out when it is done. Then put the dough into an airtight container and allow it to rest at room temperature for about 1 hour.

3. Into a deep fat frying pan or karahi, heat 2 inches of sunflower oil on a high heat. Add a pinch of dough; once this rises in the oil, the oil is the correct temperature for frying your puris.

4. Have a small bowl with sunflower oil and a small bowl with chapati flour for dipping. Divide the dough into 12 equal balls.

5. You have the choice of sealing it with oil or flour.
Oil – Take a dough ball and slightly flatten it, tap the edges of the dough ball on the oil plate, then put on the surface and using a rolling pin roll it into a round circle.
Flour – Take a dough ball and slightly flatten it, put each side in the plate of flour, then put on the surface and using a rolling pin roll it into a round circle.

6. Gently lift it off the surface and add to the pan of oil. The top of the puri will start to rise; using a skimmer spoon, tap the puri, this will encourage the puri to swell. Press the edges of the puri, submerging the edges periodically. Turn it over and fry for a few minutes on each side.

7. Have a plate with a few sheets of kitchen paper on the side. Once a golden colour, remove the puri from the oil with the skimmer spoon, resting the puri on the side of the pan so the oil drains from the puri. Then put on the papered plate. Repeat with the other dough balls.

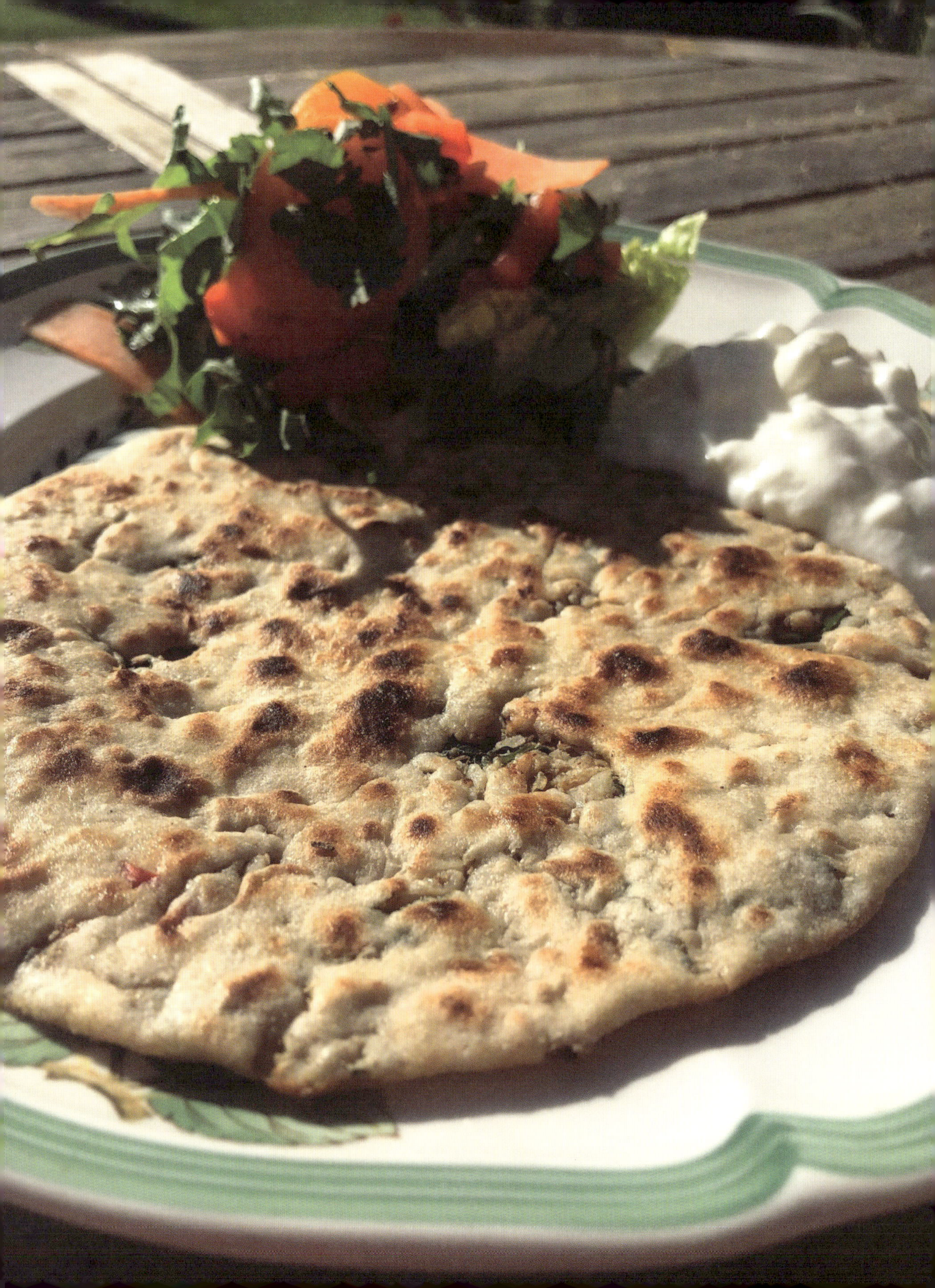

Stuffed Chapatis
(prontis, paratha or rotis)

Prontis as my Nanny used to call them are the same as rotis, it's basically a stuffed chapati. Great as a brunch, she would serve them at the weekend when we would go over. She would have the utta (dough) made and the mixture in the fridge so when we arrived, she would warm up the tawa and start cooking them. She wouldn't stop until we popped!

Great with a dollop of natural yogurt on the side to dip in.

You can serve them as a starter if you cut them up to share.

I like them for lunch with some salad.

I guess they are like an "Indian sandwich", so easy to pop in a lunchbox too!

Aloo prontis, **paneer** prontis and **gobi** roti's recipes in this section from the Aunties. Here are a few more which are known favourites in the Khanna family:

Mooli – peel and grate a mooli, add the salt (same as the gobi roti recipe). Cover with a tea towel and leave on the side for a good few hours. This will allow the water to come out of the mooli. Drain using the cheese cloth / spatula or squeeze it in your hand, then follow the recipe.

Mince – cook as per mince recipe. Drain the mince in the colander to remove any excess water, roll the chapati and add a tablespoon of mince then encase, roll and heat as per pronti recipe. Anjali, Emma and Reeyan's favourite!

Dahl – best to use a yellow dahl that has been cooked and left in the fridge overnight; this will naturally thicken so ideal for prontis.

Sugar – I remember Indian Nanny making sugar prontis for us as children, Natalie & Ajay's favourite! Roll the chapati, add a teaspoon of sugar, encase, roll and heat as per pronti recipe.

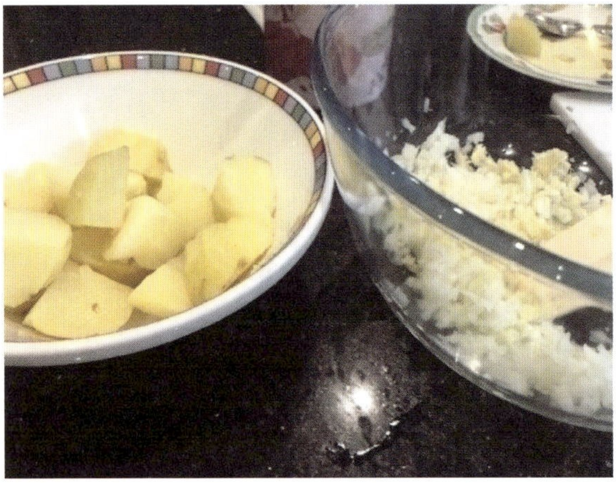
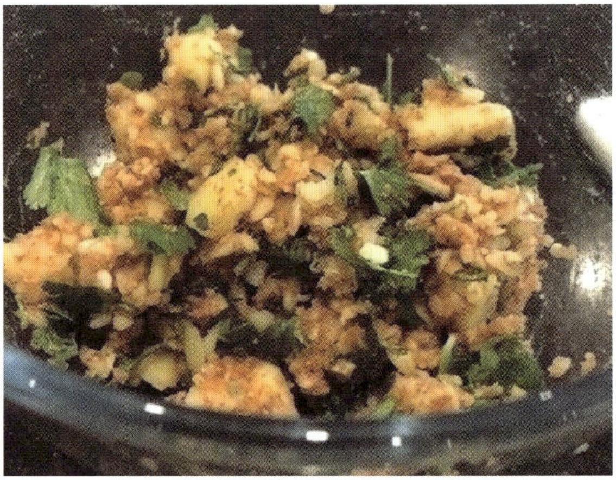
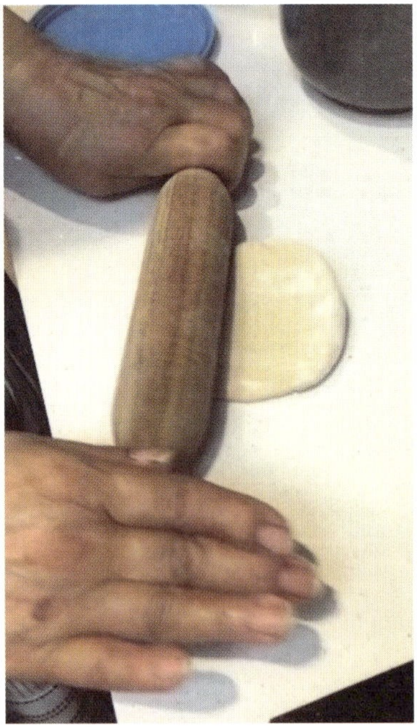
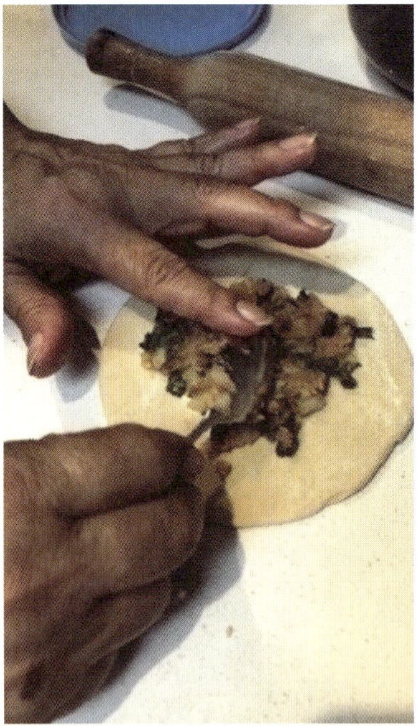
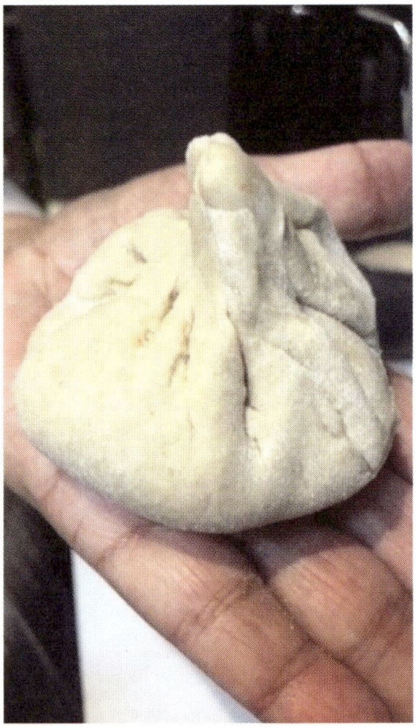
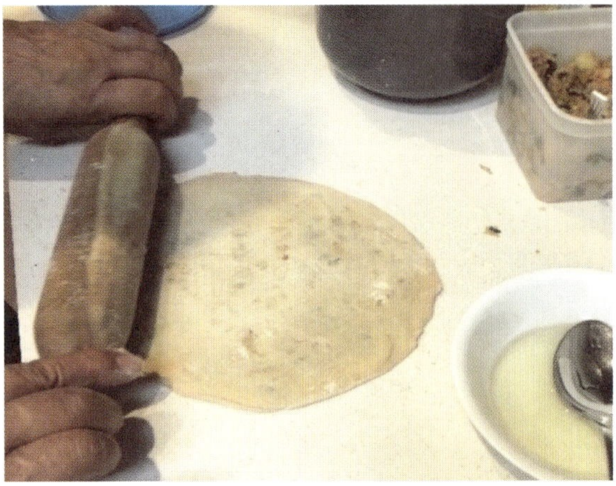
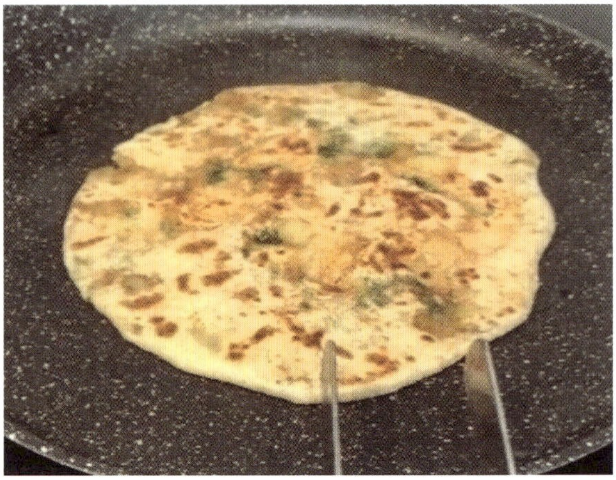

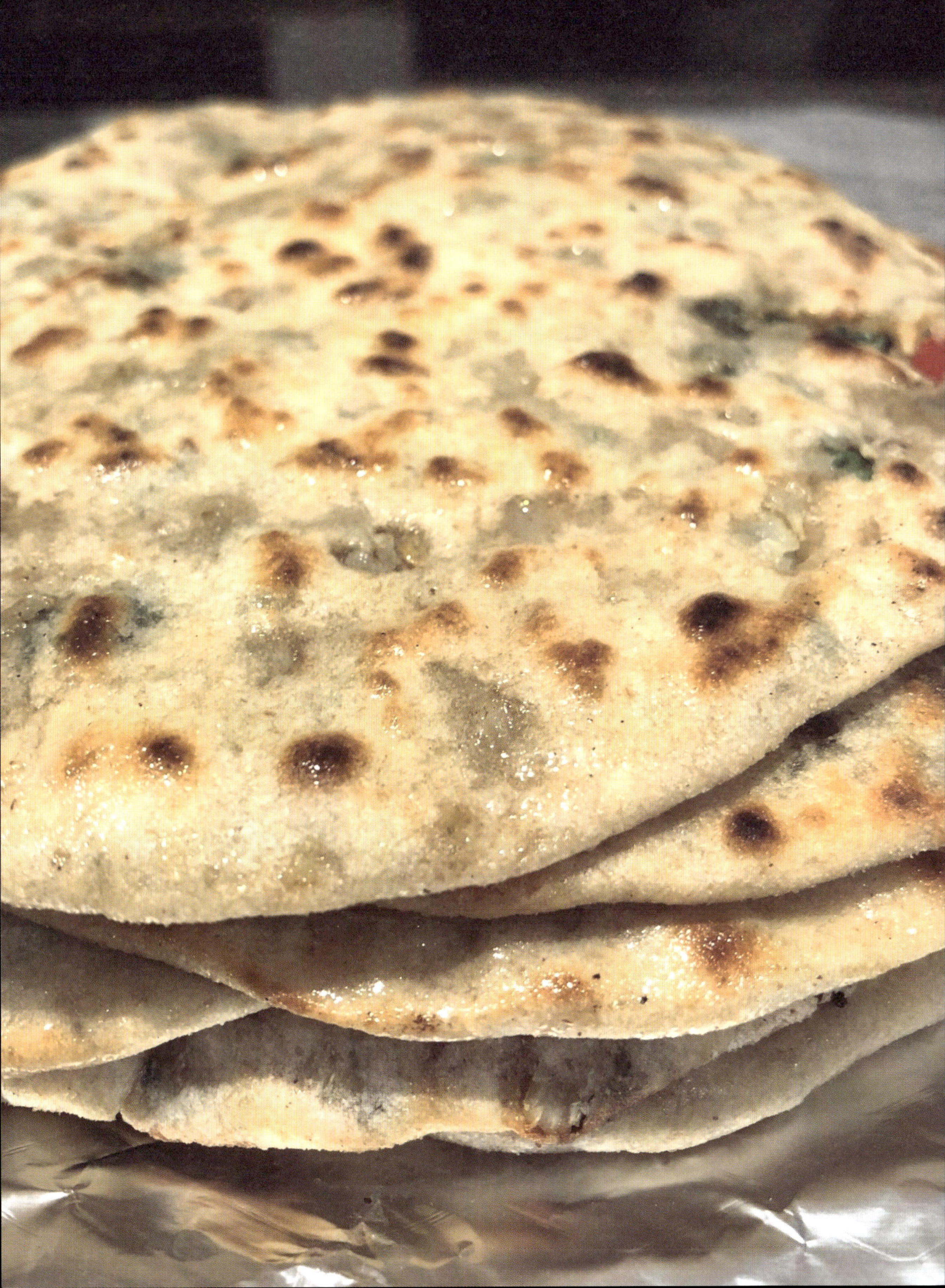

RICE & BREAD

Aloo Prontis

READY IN
1 HOUR
+ PROVING

SERVES
3-4

These are delightful and the filling is easy to make. Auntie Veena and I cooked these with Jude as a starter one day at a family get-together, we cut each pronti into 8 like a pizza. They were a hit! Veena prefers to use new potatoes as they are easier to roll and do not make the utta sticky.

INGREDIENTS

250g chapati flour

250ml water

Drizzle olive oil / rapeseed oil

3 to 4 medium potatoes

½ small onion

1 green chilli

Small piece of ginger, peeled & finely chopped (optional)

Handful fresh coriander

SPICES

2 teaspoons salt

1 teaspoon coriander powder

1 teaspoon paprika

1 teaspoon garam masala

METHOD

1. Put the flour in a large mixing bowl and add half the water. Knead. Continue to knead, adding the water slowly as necessary to make a nice dough.

2. In the final knead add a drizzle of olive oil (optional) and mix well into the dough. Put it in a covered container and leave in the fridge for a few hours. Remove an hour before using.

3. Boil the new potatoes, drain and cool. Peel them with your fingers or the back of a teaspoon, then mash them together with your hands or a fork into a large bowl.

4. Finely chop the onion and green chilli in a mini chopper or food processor. Add to the potato and then add the spices, ginger and mix well.

5. Finely chop the coriander and mix that in too.

6. Rub a little oil in your hands. Take approximately half a fist of dough and make into a ball.

7. Flour a clean surface and roll out a small circle from the dough using a rolling pin. Add a large, heaped dessert spoon of the potato mixture to the middle and fold all the ends over, encasing the mixture.

8. Roll out again, dusting with dry flour, into a circle that's about the size of a dessert plate.

9. Cook both sides on a flat griddle or tawa, flipping regularly after a minute or so until golden. On the final flip spread a teaspoon of olive oil or rapeseed oil onto either side, with the back of a spoon, when just about cooked to give a final browning.

10. Remove and serve with some plain yogurt.

RICE & BREAD

Paneer Prontis

READY IN
45 MINS
+ PROVING

SERVES
3-4

These are mouth wateringly good, Auntie Rita's recipe.

INGREDIENTS

250g chapati flour

250ml water

Drizzle olive oil

1 block paneer (250g)

½ small onion, chopped

1 green chilli

Small piece ginger, peeled & finely chopped (optional)

Handful fresh coriander

SPICES

1 teaspoon salt

1 teaspoon coriander powder

1 teaspoon paprika

1 teaspoon garam masala

METHOD

1. Put the flour in a large mixing bowl and add half the water. Knead. Continue to knead, adding the water slowly as necessary to make a nice dough. In the final knead add a drizzle of olive oil and mix well into the dough. Put it in a covered container and leave in the fridge for a few hours. Remove the dough an hour before using.

2. Drain the paneer and mash it up with a fork. Finely chop the onion and green chilli in the food processor or mini chopper. Add to the paneer and then add the spices, ginger and mix well.

3. Finely chop the coriander and mix that in.

4. Take approximately half a fist of dough and make into a ball.

5. Flour a clean surface and roll out a small circle from the dough using a rolling pin. Add a large, heaped dessert spoon of the paneer mixture to the middle and fold all the ends over, encasing the mixture.

6. Roll out again, dusting with dry flour into a circle that's about the size of a dessert plate.

7. Cook both sides on a flat griddle or tawa. Spread about a teaspoon of olive oil onto either side, with the back of a spoon, when just about cooked to give a final browning.

8. Remove and serve with some plain yogurt.

RICE & BREAD

Gobi Rotis

READY IN
45 MINS
+ PROVING

SERVES
3-4

Auntie Madhu calls them "rotis", this is her recipe. My mum's favourite.

Once cooked, serve with a little spread of butter if you like.

Great served with a large spoon of unsweetened natural yogurt to dip them in.

INGREDIENTS

1 medium cauliflower, separate the florets with your hands, wash and drain them in a colander

2-inch cube of ginger, peeled

Green chilli (more if you like it hot!)

250g chapatis flour

Water – 250ml

Little olive oil

SPICES

1 heaped teaspoon salt

2 teaspoons garam masala

½ teaspoon chilli flakes or chilli powder

2 teaspoons coriander powder

METHOD

1. First make your atta (dough) by adding the flour to a bowl, add half the water to the flour then add the rest slowly. Knead the dough for 5 minutes. Once the dough is made, leave on the side in an airtight container for a minimum of 15 minutes; if you are going to leave it overnight put in the fridge and remove an hour before using.

2. Grate the cauliflower in the food processor, using the coarse grater attachment. Put the mix into a bowl. Add the salt, cover this with a tea towel and leave on the side for 30 minutes.

3. Squeeze the water out of the cauliflower using your hand, a thin net, a tea towel or spatula. Transfer the mix back into the bowl. At this stage the secret is to make sure there is as little or no water left in the cauliflower.

4. In the mini chopper finely chop the ginger and green chilli. Add this to the cauliflower, add all the spices. Give it a quick stir.

5. Make the atta into small balls of dough. Dip the small ball of dough in the flour on either side and roll it until 3 to 4 inches round. Then put a large tablespoon of your cauliflower mix in the middle of the chapati. Pick up the 4 ends of the chapati and add to the middle, squeeze ends together like you have made a parcel. Flatten the chapati and start rolling again. If the atta is a bit sticky, then add a little bit of extra flour.

6. The rolling will take a little bit of practice. However, once you have mastered this tasty dish, friends and family will eat them until they literally pop!

7. Warm a flat pan on a medium to low heat. Then add the roti to a warm pan, one side of the chapati without the oil and then turn it, rub ¼ teaspoon olive oil using the back of the spoon on the roti. Never put olive oil on the cold side of the chapati. Use as little oil as possible.

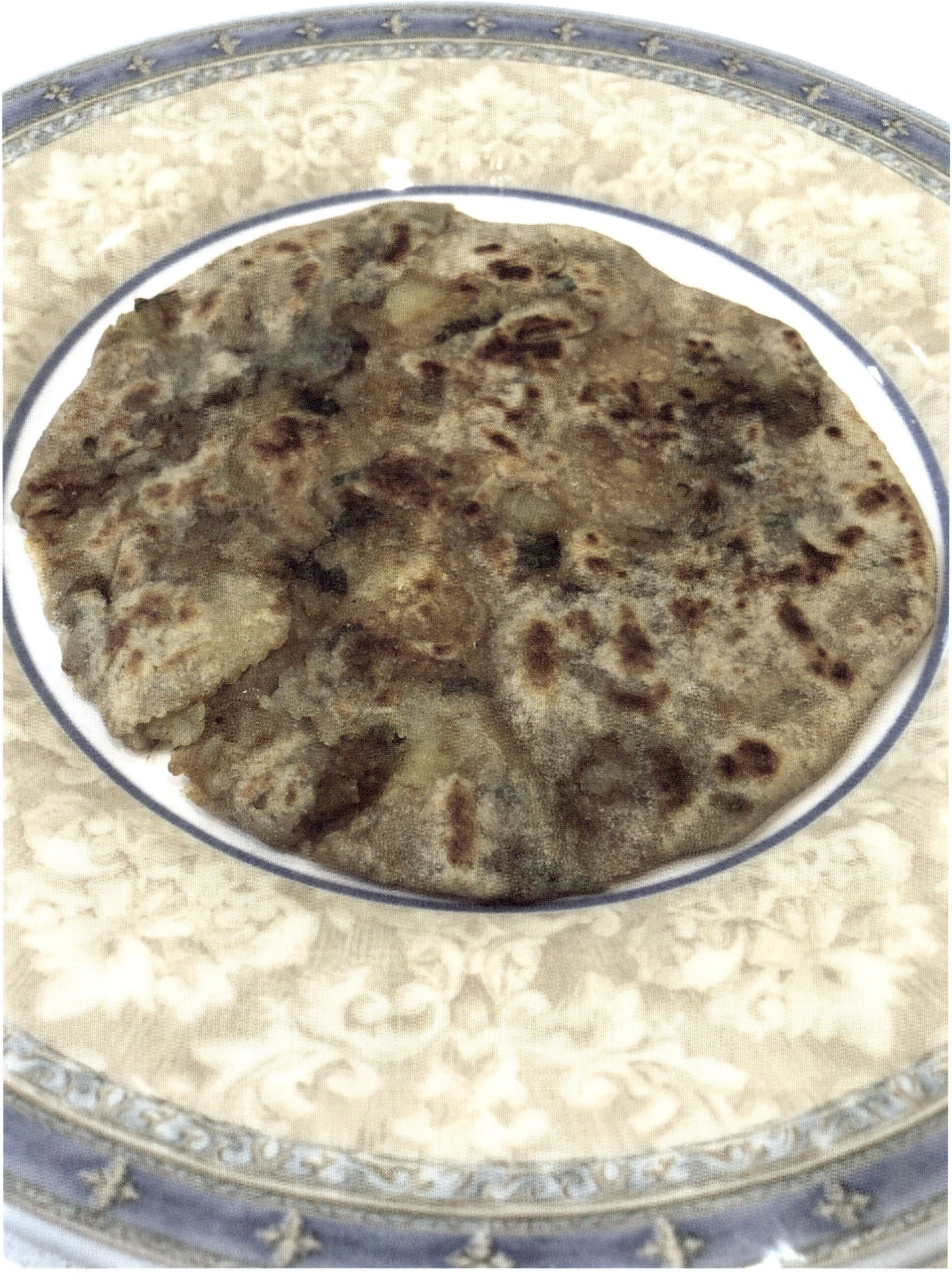

Gayatri Mantra - A Universal Hindu Prayer

The Gayatri is a life-enhancing prayer which was written around 3000 years ago. Reciting the Gayatri Mantra is one of the most common practices to achieve spiritual benefits.

Om bhur bhuvaha svaha
Tat savitur varenyam
Bhargo devasya dhimahi
Dhiyo yonah prachodayat

Meaning:
We meditate upon the Divine Light of that adorable Sun of Spiritual Consciousness, which stimulates our power of spiritual perception; May It open our hearts and enlighten our intellect.

OM SHANTI OM
(Peace in body, peace in mind)

Auntie Veena

In between writing and publishing this cookbook, our lovely Auntie Veena was called to blow out Nanny's birthday candles on 10th January 2023. I am so grateful to her for the wonderful recipes and the help that she contributed towards this book. We will remember our lovely Auntie Veena fondly when cooking her delicious recipes.

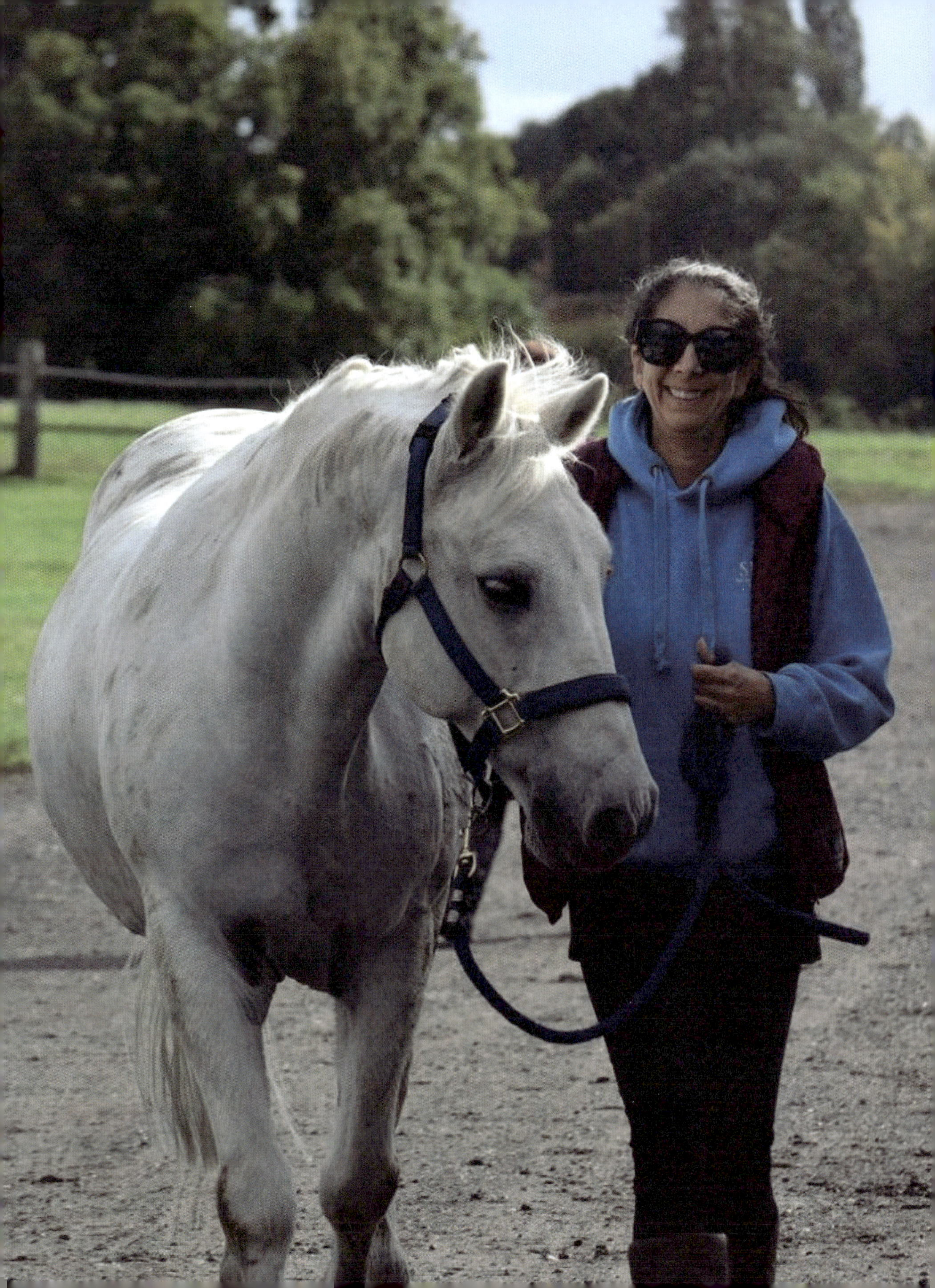

NON-VEGETARIAN

A note about meat.

I am an animal lover. I have strong ethical values and beliefs about animals. In fact, I have requested that when I am old, please do not put me in an old person's home. Leave me with my animals, plenty of them to keep me company and busy caring for them.

If I think about it for too long, I do find it odd that people choose to eat meat; they also decide the animals that are their friends. Hindus do not eat beef as cows are sacred. Muslims do not eat pig as they are regarded as unclean. The French are known to eat ponies, snails and frogs. Rabbits and birds commonly eaten in some countries and are children's beloved pets in others. Some Asian countries choose to eat dog, whilst other countries regard "man's best friend" as the loyal dog.

I weaned my children to be vegetarian, until they were old enough to make their own choices about meat. For Milly it was bacon rolls on the Duke of Edinburgh weekend and for Jude it was chicken pie! A few years later, during Milly's PE A-Level course she watched "Game Changers" and decided to go the whole hog and follow a plant-based diet. This makes me proud.

However, I am a realist and whilst I have chosen not to consume animal products, I understand that this is a personal decision. Yes, if it was down to me, I would love everyone to leave the animals to roam free and we have a kind relationship with all animals. I know that in my lifetime that's probably not going to happen.

That said, I do see a shift and people are more aware of the other meal choices other than "meat and two veg". Awareness around climate change and ethical farming, along with the efforts of some top celebrity chefs that have done some incredible work encouraging the nation to eat less meat. I also see this change reflected in my friends. When I became vegetarian, I honestly did not know another vegetarian at school; however, now it is regarded as a healthy and popular diet choice. It's great to see some of my friends turning vegetarian or even vegan after years of eating meat, as well as vegetarian / vegan menus and even restaurants.

Anyway, so as I was saying, I am a realist and appreciate that we live in a free country where we all choose what we eat (I do think that if people had to physically kill the animals themselves or witness it happening, they would definitely think carefully about eating meat and would probably eat a lot less). You probably will have friends and family that eat meat, and if you do not mind preparing it, then the following pages have some of our family recipes to try which have become firm favourites among meat eaters.

If you are responsible for the purchasing of meat and animal products in your home, please do seriously consider organic, free range and outdoor reared produce to ensure the highest standard of animal welfare. Note, outdoor bred means it is bred outside then intensively farmed inside.

Also, take a careful look at the packaging. There are various quality assurance schemes that have a set of animal welfare regulations that producers have to adhere to in order to display their logo and retain membership. The Soil Association is one of the better organisations in terms of welfare standards across multiple species (for more information, see the Soil Association website). One thing to be cautious of when looking at labels is marketing tips and tricks. Often, dairy and meat products will come in packaging of a certain colour (e.g. green). It will have phrases such as 'farm fresh' printed on it and may be accompanied by pictures or illustrations of animals grazing on pasture. Whilst these features may imply that the animals are reared on or have access to the outdoors, unless it is explicitly stated on the packaging or required by the certification body, the product will come from intensively reared animals. I would encourage you to take a look at the standards producers have to meet in order to be compliant with different certification bodies and to familiarise yourself with their logos. A cheap chicken is not good for the chicken or the farmer, and definitely not the consumer. Prices are driven down by competition and large supermarkets; however, this type of cost cutting has a serious impact on all.

I personally choose not to prepare or cook meat, therefore these family recipes have been "rubber stamped" by my mum, dad, friends and family who chose to be non-vegetarian at the time of writing this book. Most can be easily modified to suit a vegetarian or vegan diet using a meat substitute.

Thank you for reading.

Anyone say chicken?

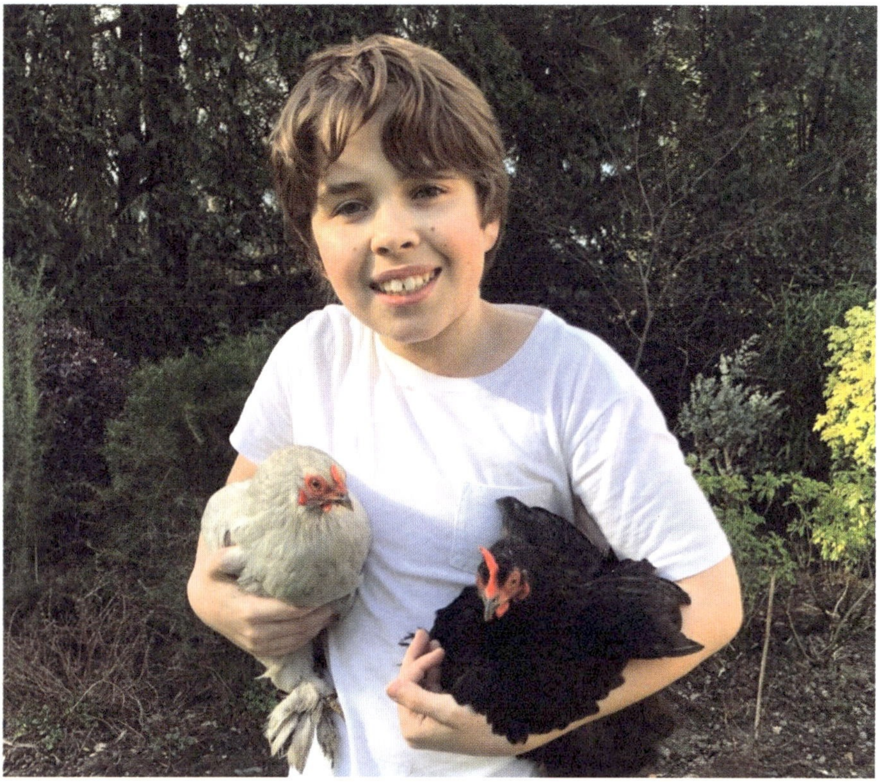

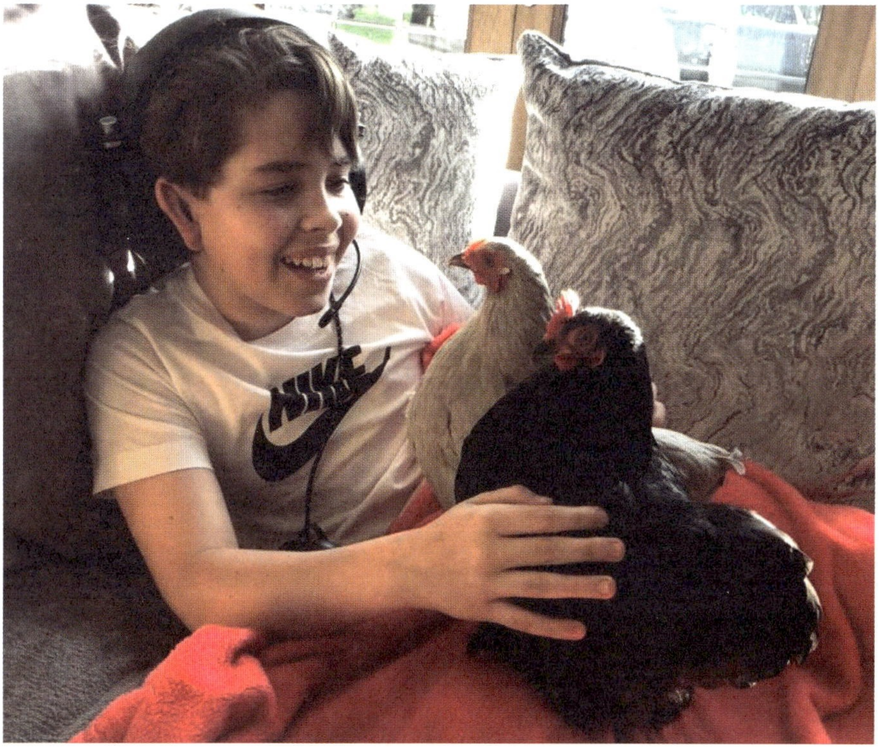

264

STARTERS & SNACKS

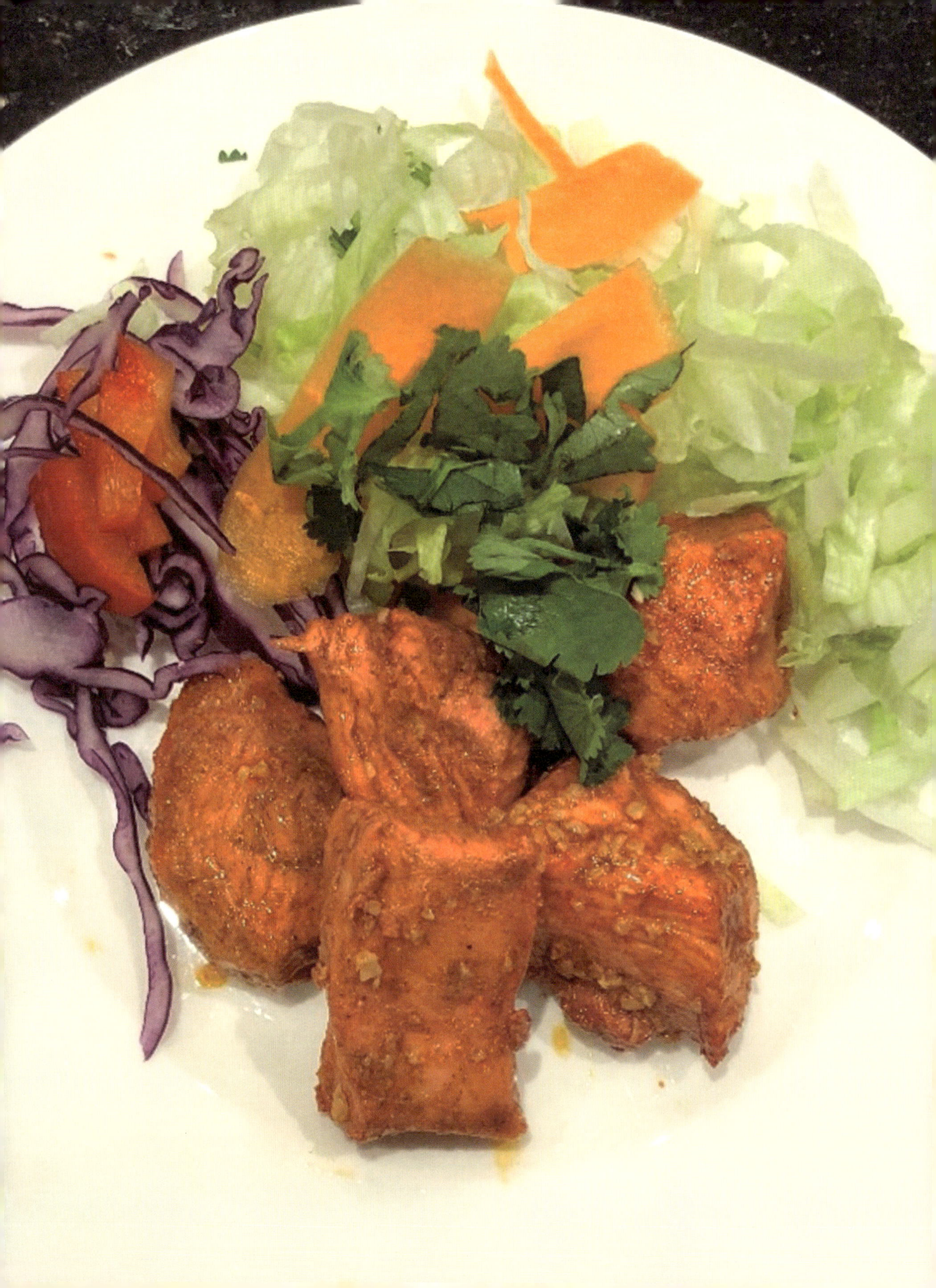

STARTERS & SNACKS

Dad's Best Chicken Tikka

READY IN
25 MINS
+ MARINATING

SERVES
3-4

My dad likes to experiment, rather than follow Nanny's recipes. Most of the time he is very lucky and the dishes come out really well! The Aunties tell him the food tastes amazing; this is one of those times.

Tikka is great as a starter, snack or as a main dish.

Very simple recipe and tastes delicious!

INGREDIENTS

2 tablespoons light olive oil

1 pack chicken breast (4 fillets approx. 500g)

1 inch ginger (peeled)

2 cloves garlic (peeled)

Small handful fresh coriander (optional)

SPICES

1 teaspoon salt

1 teaspoon tandoori masala (available from Indian supermarkets)

Pinch food colouring powder (optional, the more you add the brighter the colour)

¼ teaspoon chilli powder

1 teaspoon garam masala

METHOD

1. In the mini chopper put the ginger, garlic and small handful of coriander. Blitz until finely chopped and put in a large bowl.

2. Cut each chicken fillet into 6 pieces. Add this to the bowl with 1 teaspoon of salt and 2 tablespoons of olive oil, give it a good stir.

3. Then add to the bowl 1 teaspoon of tandoori masala, pinch of food colouring powder (if using), ¼ teaspoon chilli powder, 1 teaspoon of garam masala and mix thoroughly. Cover the bowl with cling film and marinate in the fridge for a minimum of 1 hour or so; you can leave it overnight if you prefer. The longer you leave it the better.

4. Once marinated, the chicken is ready to cook.

5. Preheat the oven to 180°C, put the chicken on a foiled baking tray and once the oven is hot, put the chicken in for 12 minutes. Check it is cooked to perfection. You do not need to turn it over.

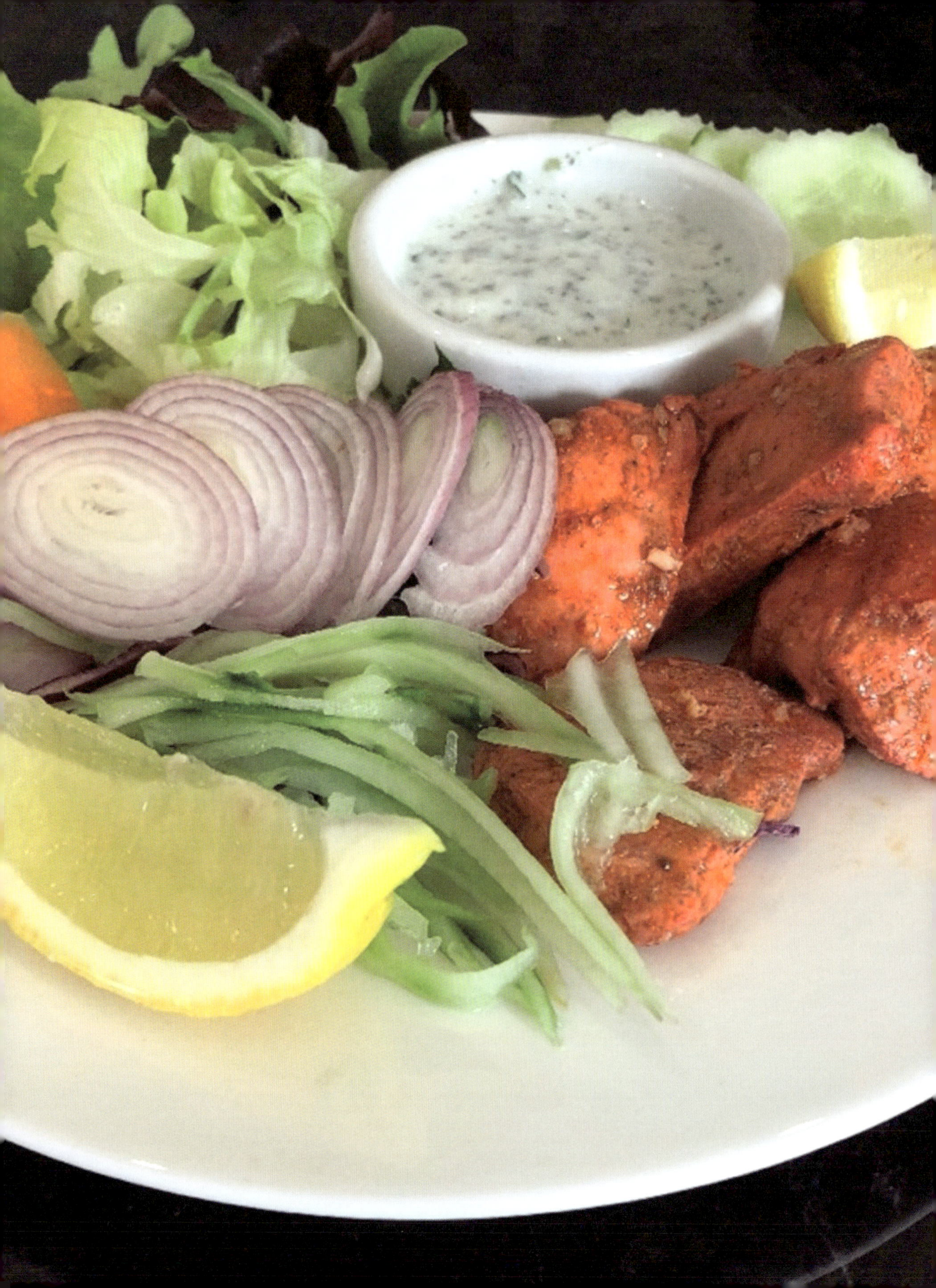

STARTERS & SNACKS

Maharani's Wicked Chicken Tikka Salad

READY IN
8 MINS

SERVES
3-4

Mum makes a wicked chicken tikka salad. Use the recipe for chicken tikka, add mint yogurt and some salad for a beautiful starter or main meal.

INGREDIENTS

4 or 5 chicken tikka pieces cooked as per recipe

Handful salad leaves

½ tomato, cut into wedges

¼ cucumber, sliced or grated

½ carrot, grated

½ red onion, peeled and thinly sliced

2 lemon wedges

Handful chopped coriander (optional)

Mint yogurt as per recipe

METHOD

1. Wash and chop the salad leaves, add the tomato, cucumber, carrot and onion to a plate.

2. Add the chicken tikka and a serving of mint yogurt.

3. Chopped coriander to decorate.

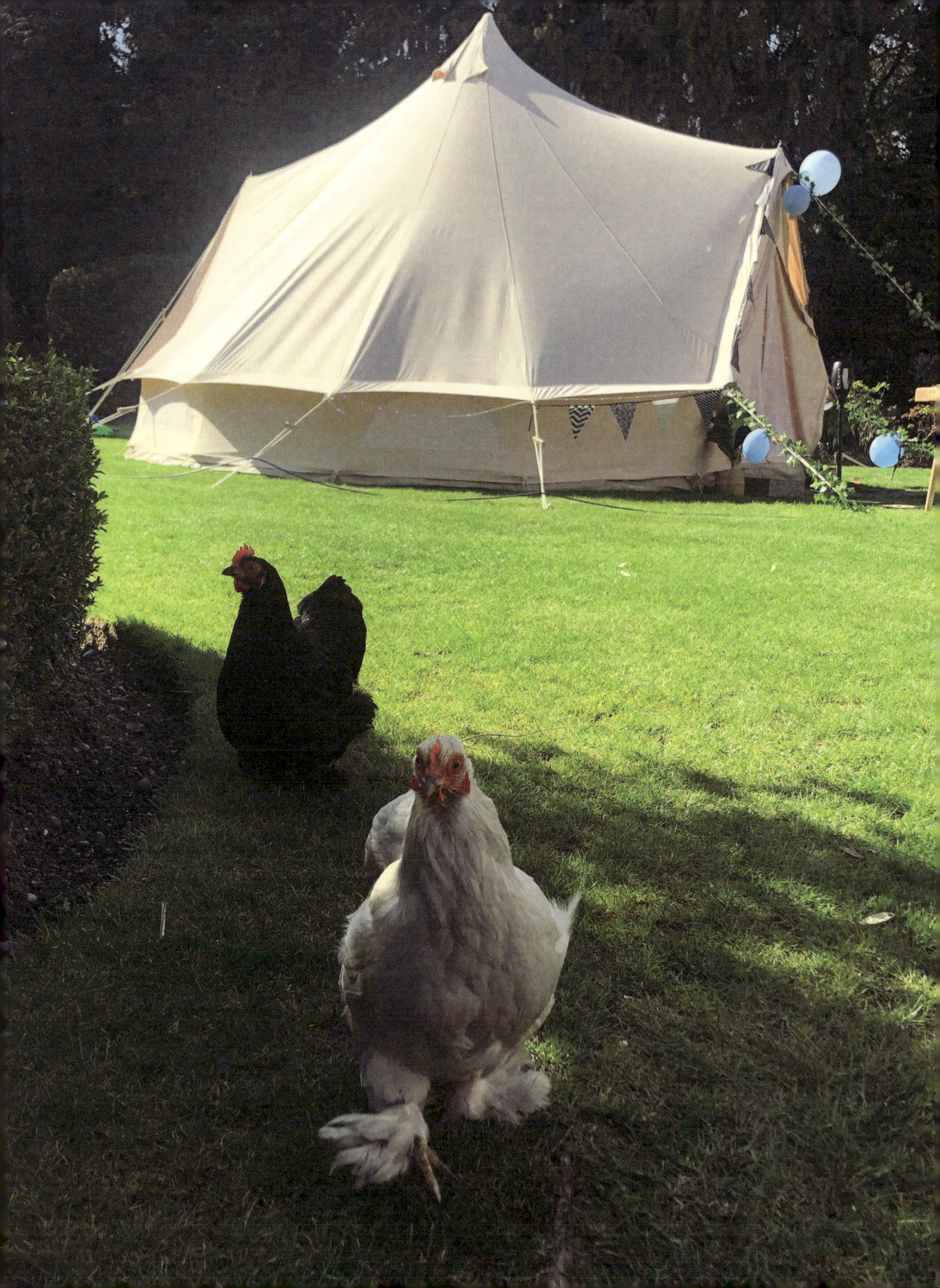

STARTERS & SNACKS

Dad's Plain Chicken Tikka

READY IN
25 MINS
+ MARINATING

SERVES
3-4

The kids like it plain. So just like Nanny used to, Dad loves cooking for the children and see their smiling faces when he's told them he has cooked chicken tikka, especially for them. Plain.

INGREDIENTS

2 tablespoons light olive oil

1 pack chicken breast (4 fillets approx. 500g)

SPICES

1 teaspoon salt

1 teaspoon tandoori masala (available from Indian supermarkets)

Pinch of food colouring powder (optional, the more you add the brighter the colour)

1 teaspoon garam masala

1 teaspoon jeera powder (cumin)

METHOD

1. Cut each chicken fillet into 6 pieces. Add this all to a bowl with 1 teaspoon of salt and 2 tablespoons of olive oil, give it a good stir.

2. Add to the bowl 1 teaspoon of tandoori masala, pinch of food colouring powder (if using), 1 teaspoon of garam masala and 1 teaspoon jeera powder. Mix thoroughly. Cover the bowl with cling film and marinate in the fridge for a minimum of 1 hour or so; you can leave it overnight if you prefer. The longer you leave it the better.

3. Once marinated, the chicken is ready to cook.

4. Preheat the oven to 180°C. Put the chicken on a foiled baking tray and once the oven is hot, put the chicken in for 12 minutes. Check it is cooked to perfection. You do not need to turn it over.

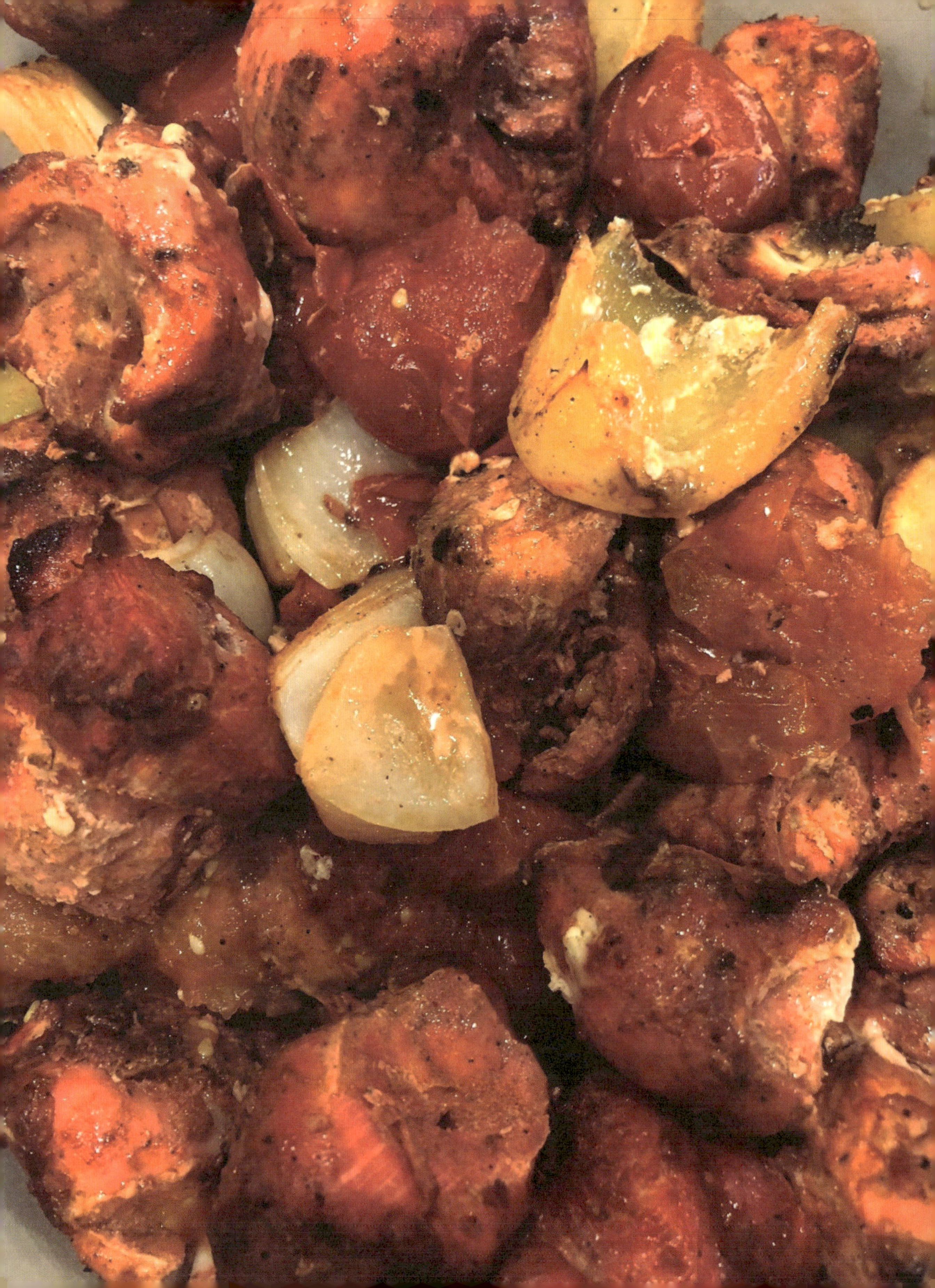

STARTERS & SNACKS

Dad's Chicken Shaslik

READY IN
35 MINS
+ MARINATING

SERVES
3-4

This is really easy to cook! The recipe is the same as chicken tikka but with some vegetables too.

INGREDIENTS

2 tablespoons light olive oil

1 pack chicken breast (4 fillets approx. 500g)

1 inch ginger, peeled

2 cloves garlic, peeled

Small handful fresh coriander (optional)

One pepper (red, green or yellow) deseeded and cut into pieces

2 tomatoes, cut in halves

2 medium onions, cut in quarters

SPICES

1 teaspoon salt

1 teaspoon tandoori masala (available from Indian supermarkets)

Pinch of food colouring powder if you like (optional)

¼ teaspoon chilli powder

1 heaped teaspoon garam masala

METHOD

1. In the mini chopper put the ginger, garlic and small handful of coriander. Blitz until finely chopped and put in a large bowl.

2. Cut each chicken fillet into 6 pieces. Add this to the bowl with 1 teaspoon of salt and 2 tablespoons of olive oil, give it a good stir.

3. Then add to the bowl 1 teaspoon of tandoori masala, pinch of food colouring powder (if using), ¼ teaspoon of chilli powder and 1 heaped teaspoon of garam masala. Cover the bowl with cling film and marinate in the fridge for a minimum of 1 hour or so; you can leave it overnight if you prefer. The longer you leave it the better.

4. Once marinated, the chicken is ready to cook.

5. Preheat the oven to 180°C. Remove the chicken from the fridge and add the peppers, tomatoes and onions, give it a good stir.

6. Then put this on a foiled baking tray and once the oven is hot, put it in for 12 minutes. Check it is cooked to perfection. You do not need to turn it over.

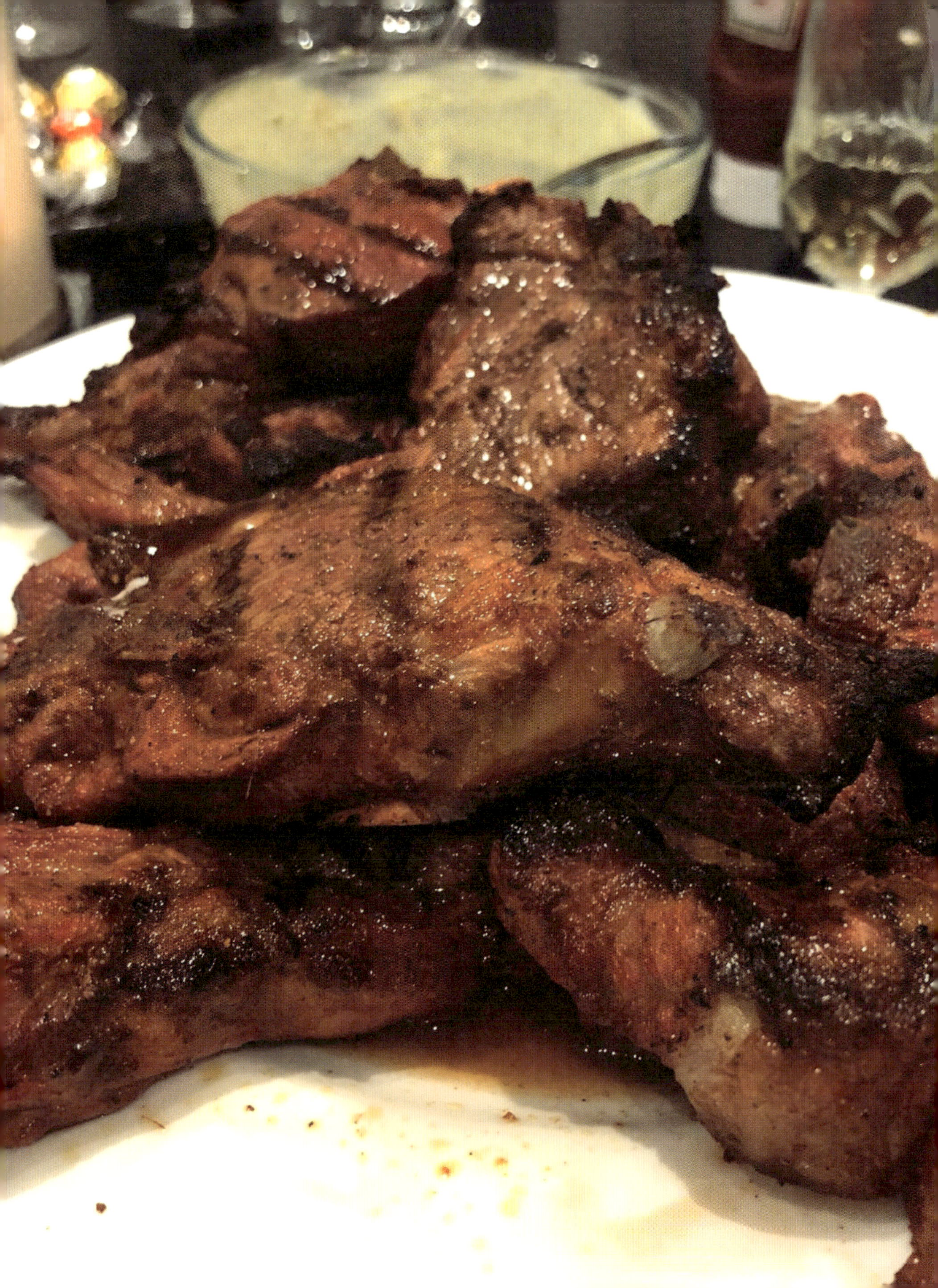

STARTERS & SNACKS

Lamb Chops

READY IN
30 MINS
+ MARINATING

SERVES
3-4

INGREDIENTS

12 lamb chops (preferably 2 x rack of lamb)

4 cloves garlic

4 tablespoons light olive oil

2 teaspoons mint sauce

SPICES

2 teaspoons tandoori masala

1 teaspoon jeera (cumin) powder

½ teaspoon coriander powder

1 teaspoon salt

½ teaspoon garam masala

¼ teaspoon red food colouring (optional)

Uncle Gigi and my dad cook wicked lamb chops, they are famous in our family! Awesome on the barbecue, they also cook just as well in the oven.

This is Vipi Uncle's special 75th Birthday lamb chops recipe, I am told they are finger licking good.

French trimmed rack of lamb, sliced into chops are his favourite meat for cooking this, or chops with little fat are recommended.

METHOD

1. Take your 2 racks of lamb and trim them into chops.

2. Finely chop 4 cloves of garlic using a food processor, put this into a large mixing bowl with the olive oil, mint sauce and all the spices. Give this a good stir then add the chops. Mix this really well and cover with cling film. Marinate overnight in the fridge.

3. When you are ready to cook the chops, remove from the fridge and cook on a hot barbecue. They need 2 - 3 minutes each side.

4. You can also cook in the oven or grill on foil.

5. Serve with mint yogurt.

Note – This dish needs marinating overnight prior to cooking

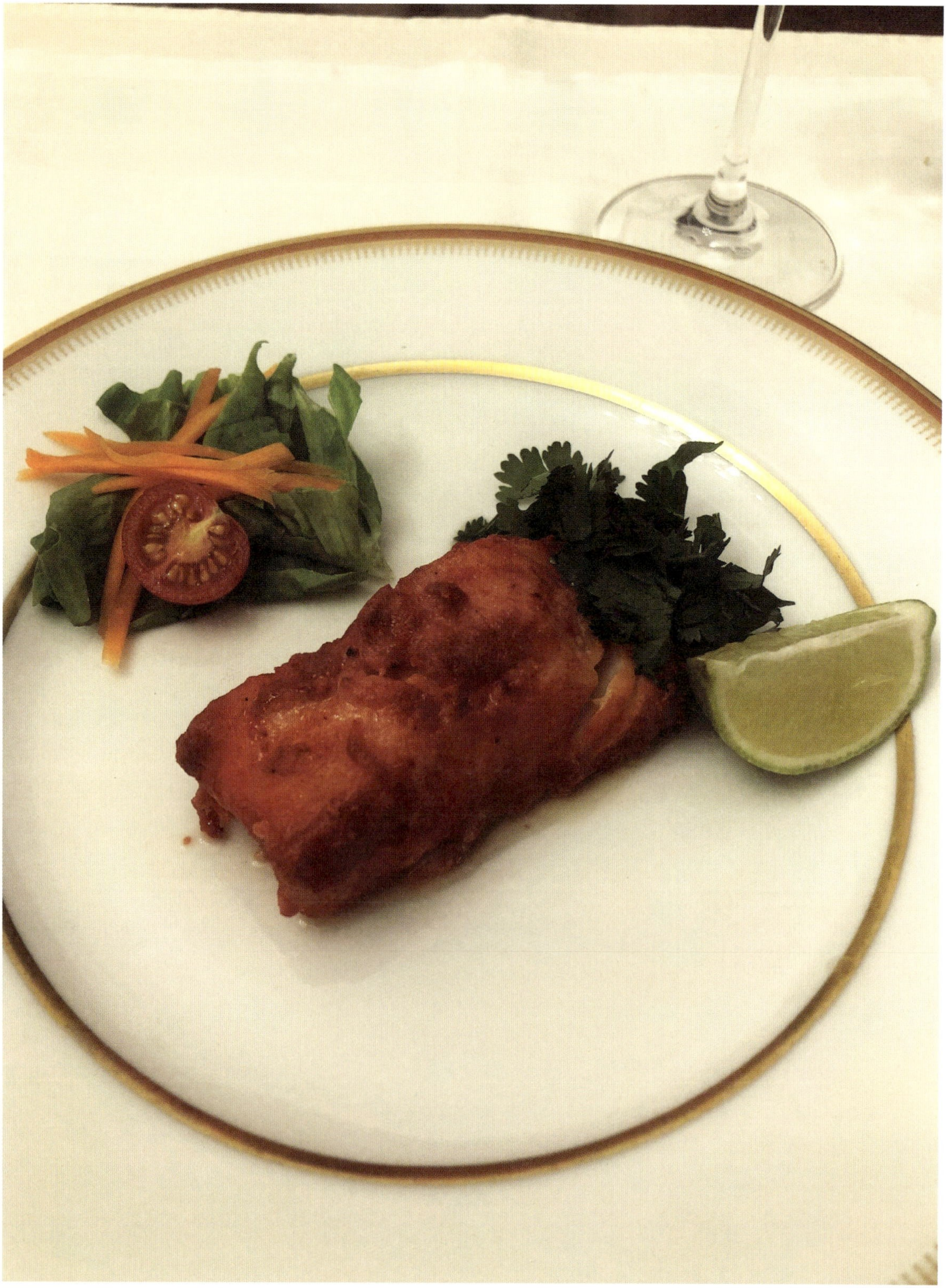

STARTERS & SNACKS

Amritsari Fish

READY IN
30 MINS
+ MARINATING

SERVES
3-4

Nanny taught me, generally, the rule is that you eat what you can locally source and what is in season. Amritsar is in northern India, miles from the coast, so they would use a fresh water fish known as Singhara or Sole. It is a thick and chunky white, boneless fish. In Amritsar, this continues to be a very popular street food dish. My Nan cooked this really well. She would use cod, sole or whatever freshwater fish she could get locally.

Beautiful as a starter or part of a main meal. This will make 10 pieces.

INGREDIENTS

1kg skinless and boneless cod fillets

3 to 4 heaped tablespoons gram flour

7 tablespoons water

1 clove garlic, peeled and finely chopped

1 inch ginger, washed, peeled and finely chopped

½ green chilli, chopped

Sunflower oil for frying

tamarind sauce and / or mint sauce for serving

1 lemon or lime

SPICES

2 teaspoons salt

2 teaspoons paprika

2 teaspoons coriander powder

½ teaspoon chilli flakes

1 heaped teaspoon garam masala

½ teaspoon red colouring powder

Note – You can oven bake this fish on foil instead of frying, the result is the batter is less crispy but still tasty

METHOD

1. Wash the fish and cut into approximate 3-inch squares, pat dry with kitchen paper.

2. Add the gram flour to a large mixing bowl and slowly add the water until it is a thick but runny consistency. Beat it with a fork. Add all the spices, garlic, ginger and chilli; you may need to add a little more water. Put in the fish and gently mix it with your hands so the pieces are evenly coated (you may want to put gloves on).

3. Cover the bowl with cling film and leave the fish to marinate in the fridge for a minimum of one hour or overnight.

4. Into a shallow frying pan add approximately ½ inch of oil on a high heat. There needs to be enough oil so that when you do add the fish, the fillets are half covered with oil. Once the oil is warm, turn down to a medium heat and add a few fish fillets at a time. Fry for approximately 2 minutes on each side, turning over using a skimmer or slotted spoon once crispy and brown. Only turn once or twice during frying as it is a soft fish that can break up if you are not careful. Check the fish is cooked by putting a fork into the middle.

5. Remove the fillets from the oil using the skimmer or slotted spoon to drain the oil, put them onto a plate with kitchen paper to further remove excess oil.

6. Repeat until you have cooked all the fillets.

7. Serve with a wedge of lemon or lime plus tamarind sauce or mint sauce or both.

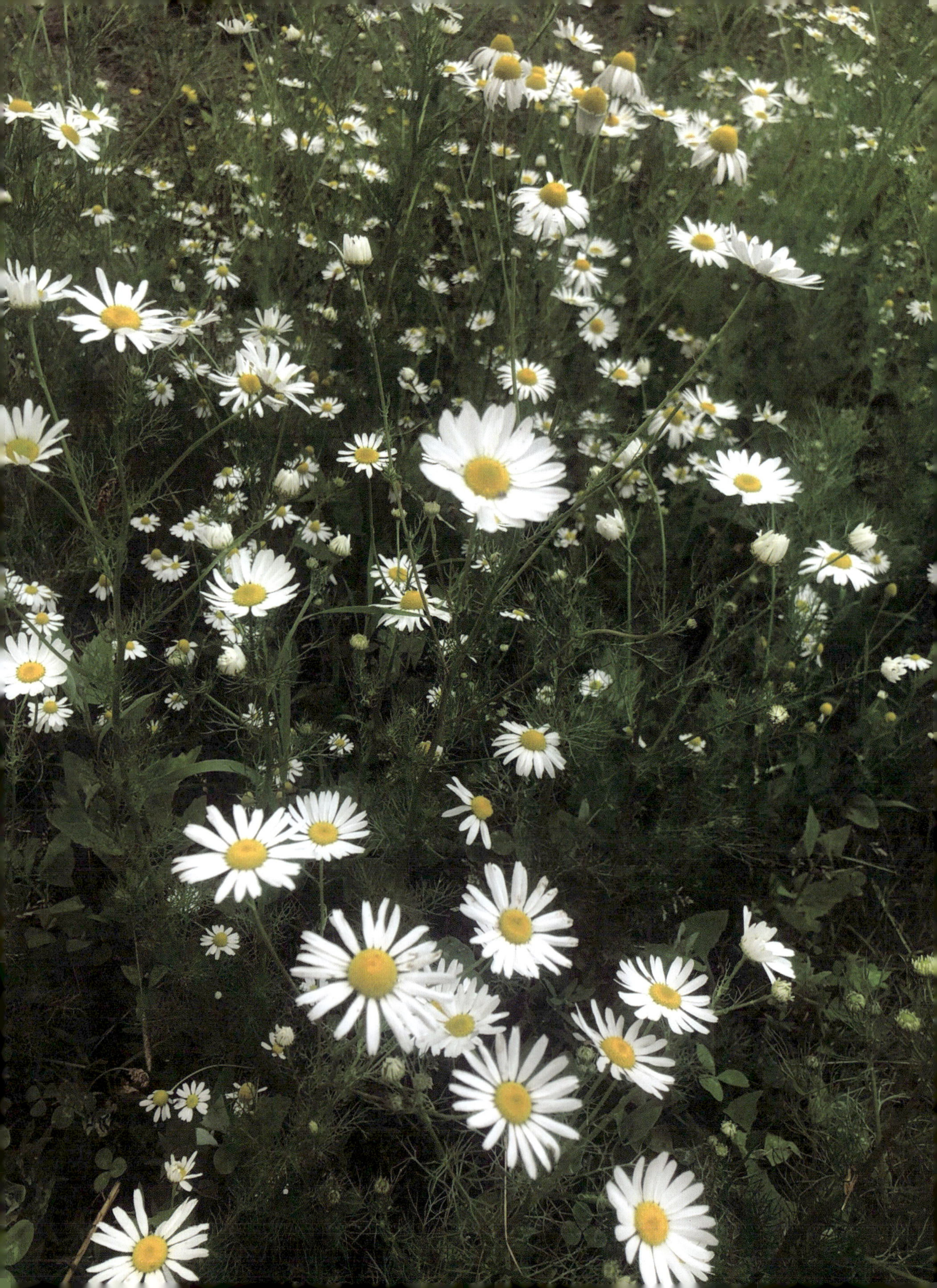

NON-VEG CURRIES

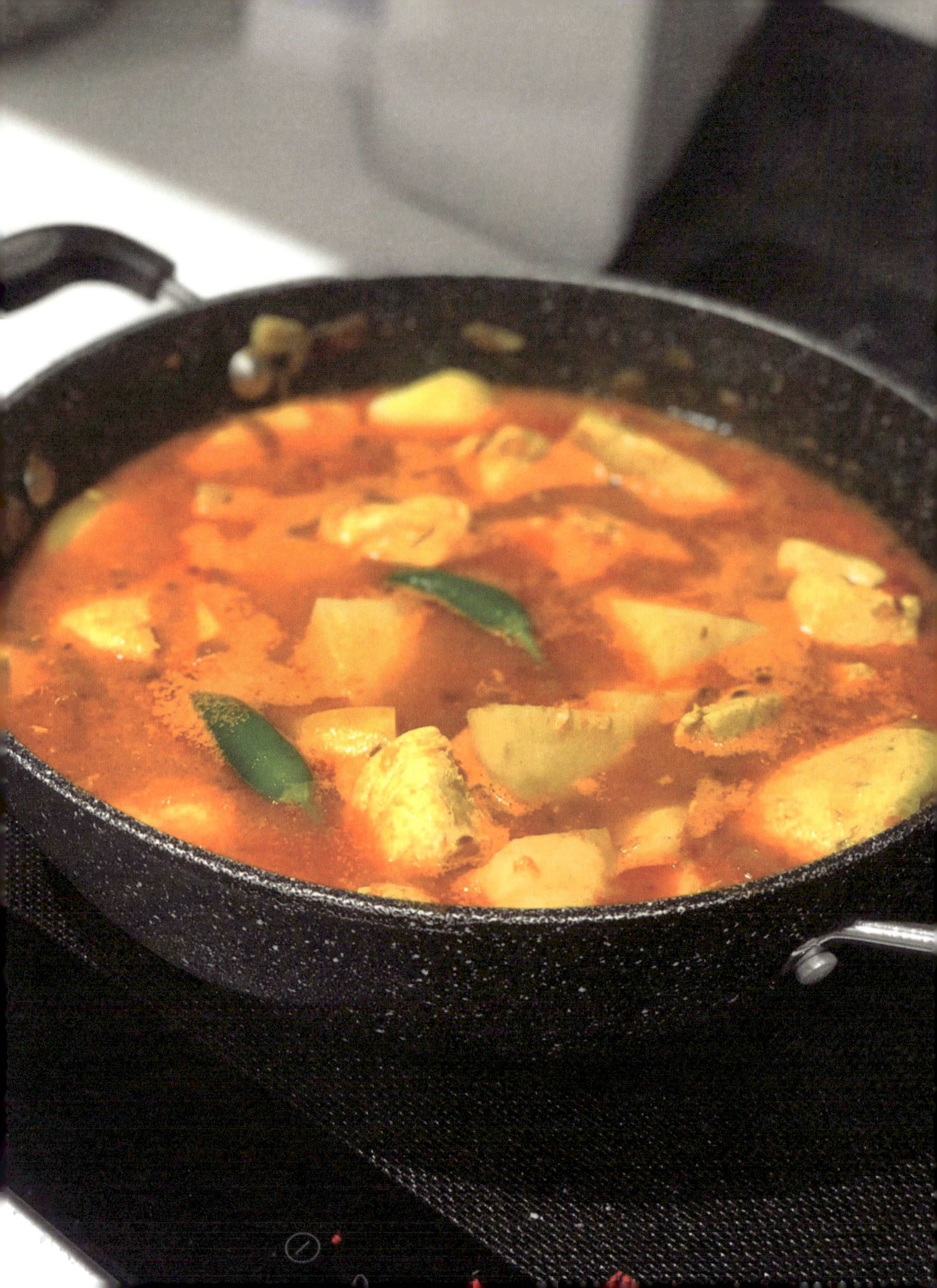

NON-VEG CURRIES

Chicken Curry

READY IN
45 MINS

SERVES
3-4

Easy to cook (apparently) and tasty (apparently too!). An instant hit with my friends. Indian Nanny taught me this recipe, but I have never cooked it. My family cook it and the children love it, especially Lewis and Elliot. My friends have confirmed that Indian Nanny's recipe is easy to cook and really tasty.

INGREDIENTS

2 tablespoons light olive oil

1 large onion, finely chopped (in the food processor)

4 – 5 cloves garlic, finely chopped (in the food processor)

4 – 5 chicken thighs

½ tin of tomatoes (200g)

2 medium potatoes, peeled and chopped into 1-inch chunks

2 tablespoons beaten natural set yogurt

1 cup water

2 or 3 small green chillies (optional)

SPICES

½ teaspoon jeera

1 teaspoon salt

½ teaspoon haldi

½ teaspoon paprika

1 teaspoon garam masala

METHOD

1. Using a medium heavy pan, add the oil on a medium heat, add the finely chopped onion and fry in the oil until pink, add the garlic, fry for a bit longer.

2. Then add the chicken thighs and fry for about 10 minutes, turning, so they are evenly browned.

3. Add the ½ tin of tomatoes, jeera, salt, haldi and paprika and cook until the tomato water has gone.

4. Add the potatoes with 1 cup of water, beat 2 tablespoons of yogurt in a cup with a fork then add this to the curry. Add the green chillies (whole) if you are using.

5. Put the lid on and turn the heat up until it boils, then down to simmer. Cook until the potatoes are done.

6. Add 1 teaspoon garam masala.

7. It is now ready to serve.

Note – You can also cook the chicken curry in a pressure cooker, the benefit of this is the meat will be very succulent. If you prefer to do this, follow the method as above; however, add only ½ cup of water and one steam of pressure.

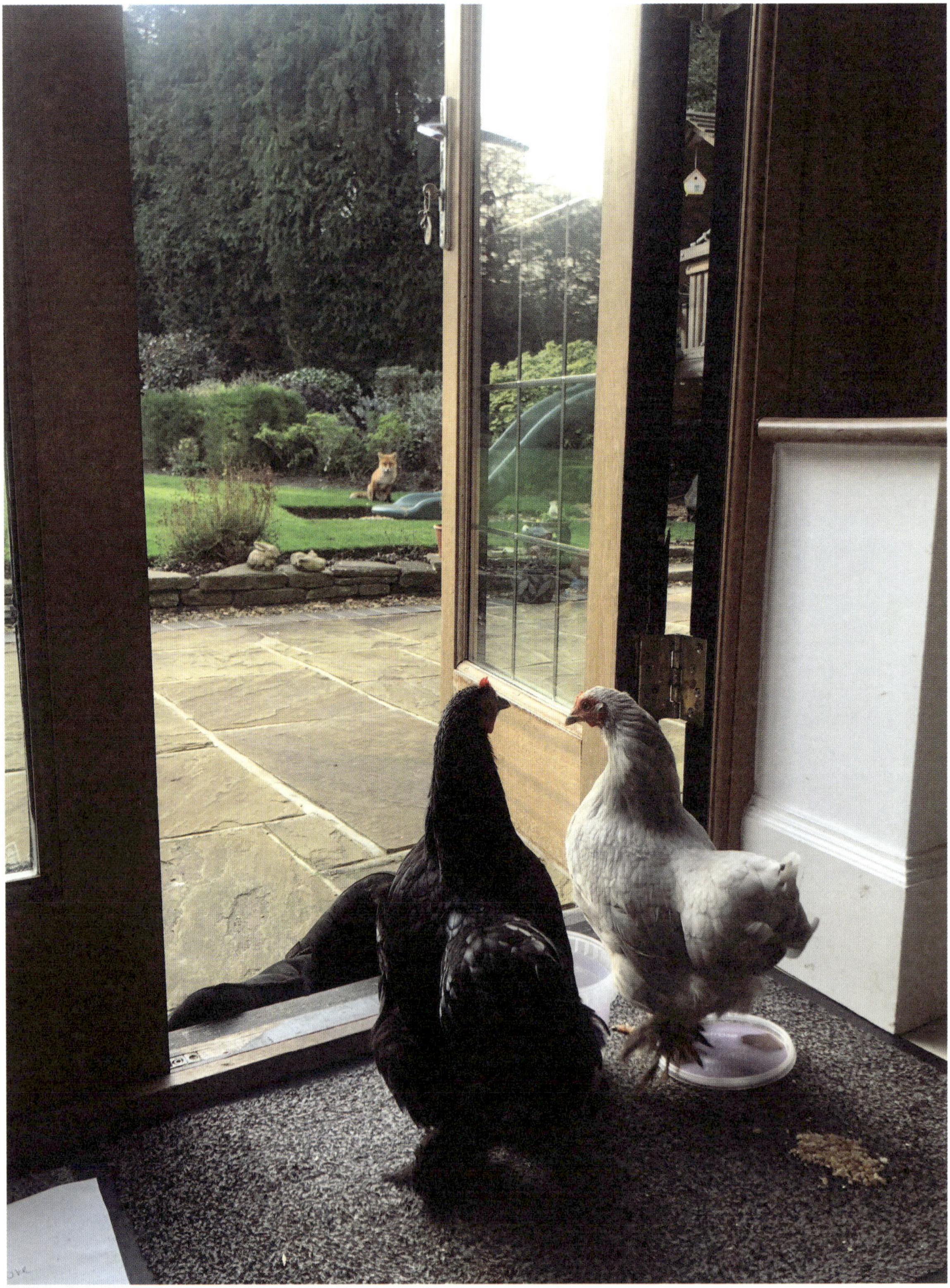

NON-VEG CURRIES

Shahi Chicken

READY IN 1 HOUR   **SERVES** 3-4

This is not one of Indian Nanny's recipes! I was asked for a milder chicken curry recipe by my friend, so Rita helped me with this. It's the Shahi paneer recipe, except with chicken. The kids love it.

If you want to spice it up, then add a couple of green chillies to turn up the heat.

INGREDIENTS

- 2 medium onions
- 4 tablespoons light olive oil
- 1 tin chopped tomatoes (400g)
- 1 cup water
- 1kg chicken breast, diced
- 150g single cream or crème fraiche (or dairy free equivalent)
- Chopped fresh coriander (optional)
- 2 green chillies (optional)

SPICES

- 1 teaspoon jeera
- 1 teaspoon salt
- 1 teaspoon paprika
- ½ teaspoon chilli powder
- 1 teaspoon haldi
- ½ teaspoon cinnamon powder (optional)
- 1 teaspoon of garam masala

METHOD

1. In the food processor, finely chop 2 medium onions.
2. Into a wok, put 4 tablespoons of olive oil on a medium to high heat. Add 1 teaspoon of jeera, heat until the oil and jeera mixture is warm – the jeera will "pop", usually about 30 seconds.
3. Add the onion and cook on a medium heat until the onions are light brown in colour.
4. Add the tin of chopped tomatoes and give a quick stir.
5. Then add the spices, 1 teaspoon salt, 1 teaspoon paprika, ½ teaspoon chilli powder, 1 teaspoon haldi, ½ teaspoon of cinnamon powder (optional). Give it a good stir then turn the heat off.
6. Put this mixture into the food processor and liquidise using the rotational blade, blitz for a minute, then add a cup of water. Then blitz again for a few minutes until the mixture is the consistency of a liquid.
7. Add the diced chicken breast to the wok with 2 tablespoons of olive oil, shallow fry on a medium heat for 3-5 minutes until seared.
8. Add the sauce back into the wok with the chicken, plus the green chillies (whole) if using.
9. Simmer on a low to medium heat for approximately 20 minutes with the lid on. Stir occasionally.
10. Once the chicken is cooked, it will be soft as it has absorbed some of the liquid. Add single cream and garam masala, the sauce will now start to thicken, cook for another 5-10 minutes then turn off and add the chopped fresh coriander if you wish.

100% VEGAN

NON-VEG CURRIES

Turkey Curry

⏳ **READY IN**
45 MINS

🍽 **SERVES**
3-4

Christmas is BIG in our family. Thanks to Bridget Jones, we also developed a Boxing Day feast, where turkey curry and sprouts became a massive hit!

If you have turkey left over, you can make the Indian "gravy" and add the cooked meat. Alternatively, you can use fresh turkey. This dish goes well with sprouts or any leftover veg that you want to cook Indian-style.

INGREDIENTS

2 tablespoons light olive oil

1 large onion, finely chopped

4 – 5 cloves garlic, finely chopped

4 – 5 turkey thighs, breast or leftover turkey (no stuffing please!)

½ tin tomatoes (200g)

2 medium potatoes, peeled and chopped into 1-inch chunks

2 tablespoons beaten natural set yogurt

1 cup water

2 or 3 small green chillies (optional)

SPICES

½ teaspoon jeera

1 teaspoon salt

¼ teaspoon haldi

¼ teaspoon paprika

1 teaspoon garam masala

METHOD

1. Using a medium heavy pan, add the oil on a medium heat, add the chopped onion and fry in the oil until pink, add the garlic, fry for a bit longer.

2. Then add the turkey and fry until cooked and well coated in the oil.

3. Add ½ tin of tomatoes, jeera, salt, haldi and paprika and cook until the tomato water has gone.

4. Add the potatoes with 1 cup of water, beat 2 tablespoons of yogurt in a cup with a fork then add this to the curry. Add the green chillies (whole) if you are using.

5. Put the lid on and turn the heat up until it boils, then down to simmer. Cook until the potatoes are done.

6. Add 1 teaspoon garam masala.

7. It is now ready to serve.

Note – You can also cook the turkey curry in a pressure cooker, the benefit of this is the meat will be very succulent. If you prefer to do this, follow the method as above; however, add only ½ cup of water and one steam of pressure.

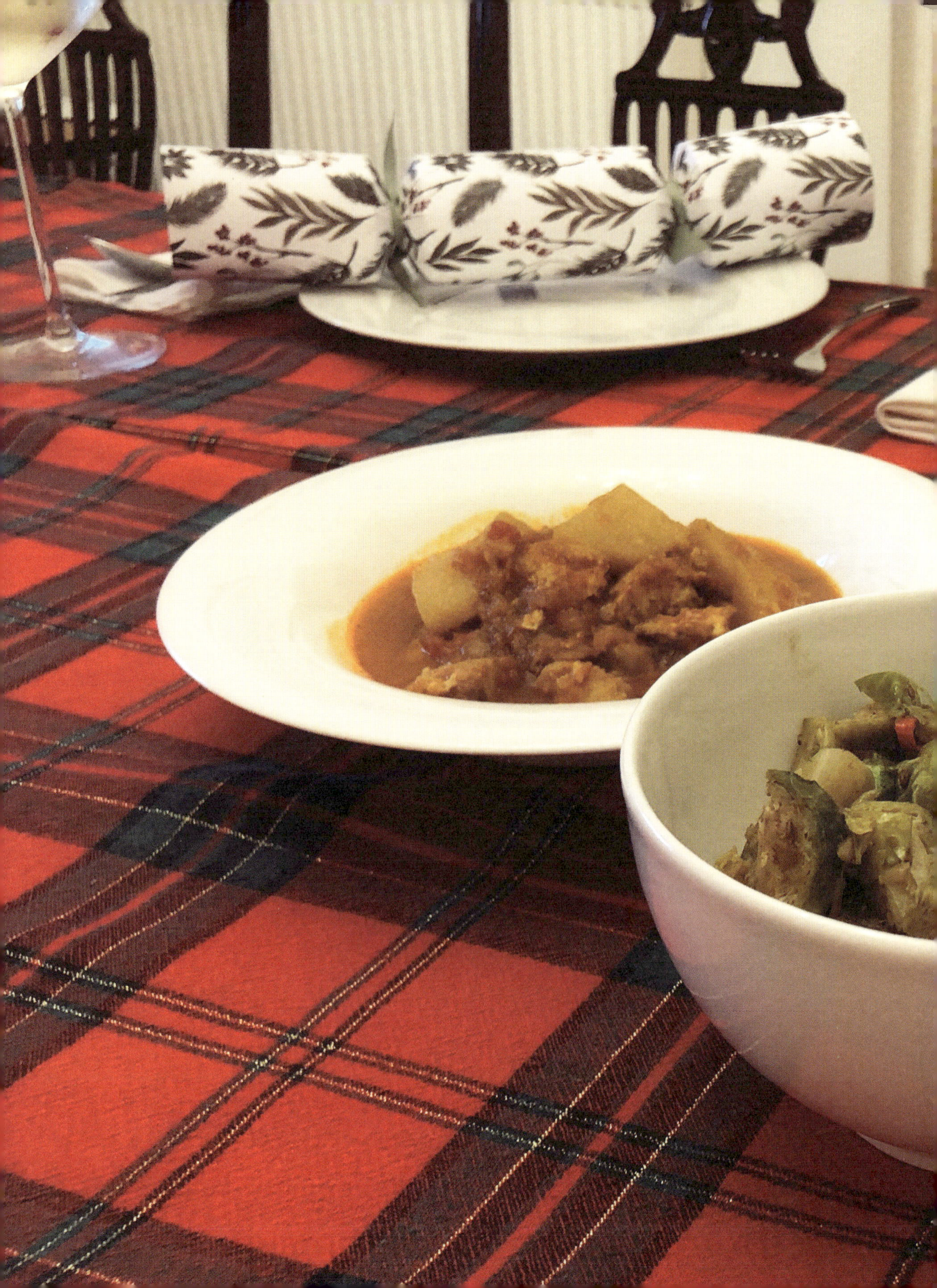

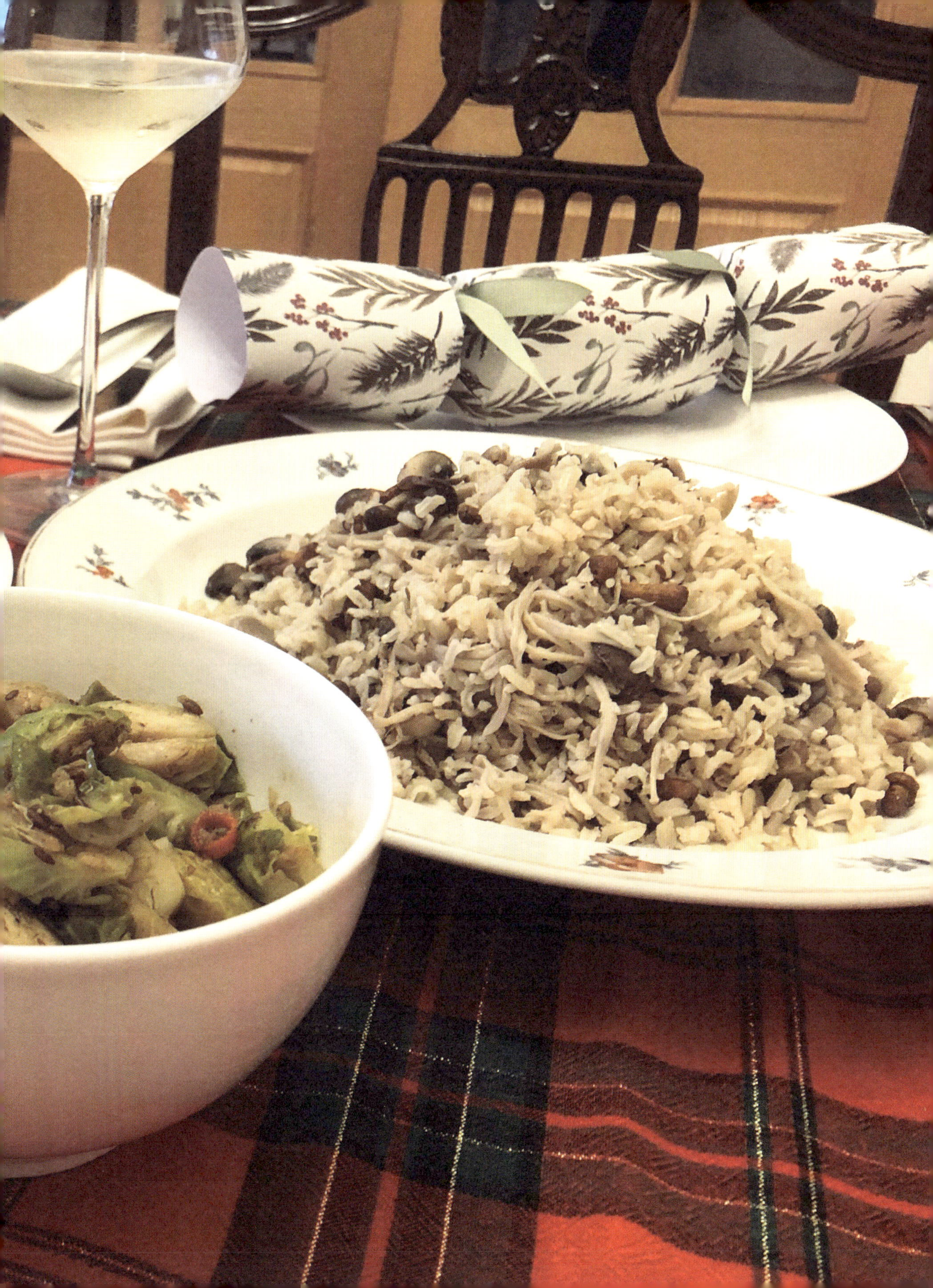

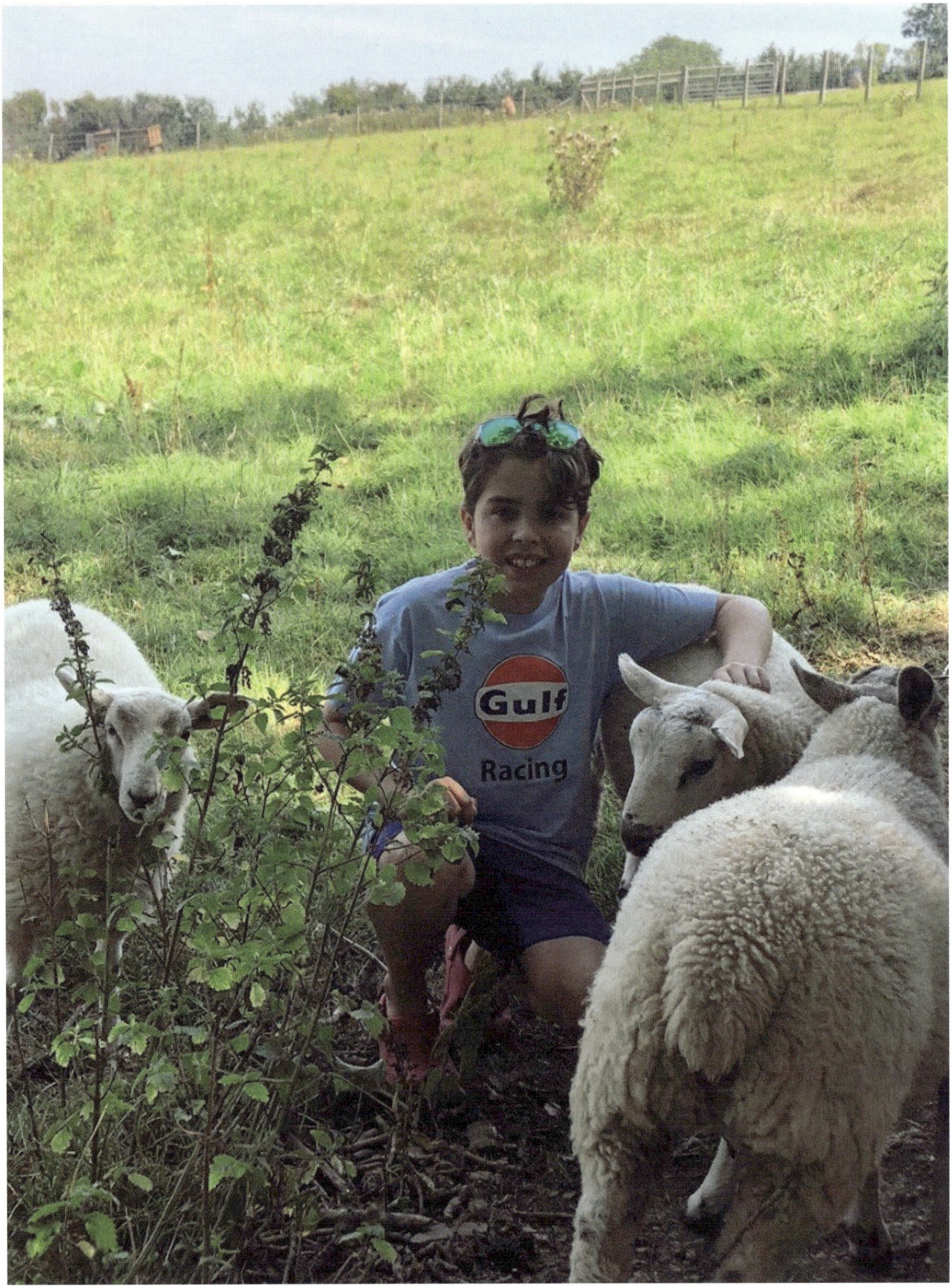
Gulf
Racing

NON-VEG CURRIES

Minced Meat

⏳ **READY IN**
45 MINS

🍽 **SERVES**
3-4

This is one of Big Dada's favourite meat dishes, Nadeem's too. Simple to cook and popular with the grandchildren. Because Hindus do not eat beef, this would be made with lamb mince; however, if you prefer beef, this recipe works well with beef.

Serve with a bed of rice, a spoon of natural set yogurt on the side and any dry vegetable dishes.

INGREDIENTS

1 large onion

2 tablespoons light olive oil

1 pack minced meat (500g)

2 tomatoes, chopped, or ½ tin chopped tomatoes (200g)

1 cup petit pois or peas

½ cup water

SPICES

1 teaspoon jeera

1 teaspoon salt

½ teaspoon haldi

½ teaspoon paprika

¼ teaspoon chilli powder

1 teaspoon garam masala

METHOD

1. Peel & finely chop the onion in a food processor then add to a medium heavy pan. Fry the onions in the oil on a medium heat, until the onions are a little darker than pink.

2. Add the mince and fry for 5 minutes.

3. Then add the tomatoes and continue to cook until the water has gone.

4. Add 1 teaspoon of salt, ½ teaspoon haldi, ½ teaspoon paprika and ¼ teaspoon chilli powder, stir and lower the heat.

5. Fry for a couple of minutes then add the peas and ½ cup of water.

6. Simmer on a low heat with the lid on for 15 - 20 minutes, then add 1 teaspoon garam masala, quick stir and turn off the heat.

Note: This dish can also be cooked in a pressure cooker, follow the method as above.

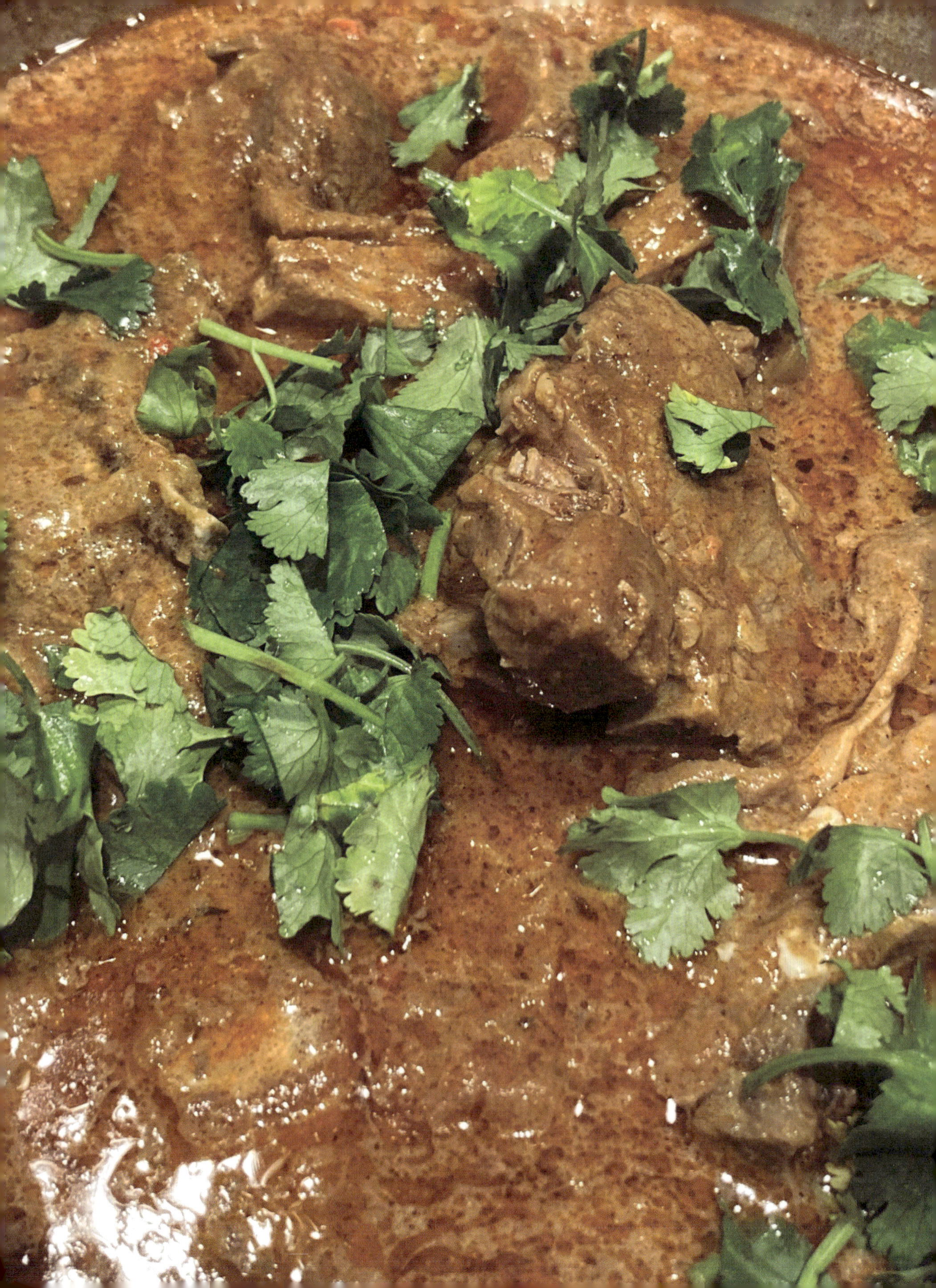

NON-VEG CURRIES

Lamb Chop Curry

READY IN 60 MINS
SERVES 4-6

This recipe was provided by Auntie Rita and Murray loves it! It uses some additions to the traditional 7 spices that we use in most of our cooking. Well worth giving it a go.

INGREDIENTS

- 3 – 4 tablespoons light olive oil
- 2 medium sized onions, peeled and finely chopped
- 1 inch ginger, peeled & finely chopped
- 1 fresh tomato, chopped
- 1kg lamb chops
- ½ tin chopped or plum tomatoes (200g)
- 4 cloves garlic, peeled & finely chopped
- 2 green chillies, chopped
- 1 ½ cups water
- Chopped fresh coriander to garnish
- Fresh cream or crème fraiche (optional)

SPICES

- 1 teaspoon jeera
- 1 ½ teaspoons salt
- 1 teaspoon coriander powder
- 1 teaspoon garam masala
- ¼ teaspoon haldi
- 1 teaspoon paprika powder
- ½ teaspoon ground cardamom
- ½ teaspoon ground cloves
- ½ teaspoon ground cinnamon
- ½-1 teaspoon chilli flakes

METHOD

1. Put the oil in a pan and heat, add the jeera. When the jeera starts to pop, add the ginger, garlic, green chillies and onions. Fry until the onions start to brown and then add the chopped fresh tomatoes. When this softens slightly, add the lamb chops.

2. Do all this on a fairly high heat as this sears the chops as well as removing any moisture. Once the chops are slightly brown, add the tinned tomatoes.

3. Continue cooking on the high heat for a few minutes and then lower the heat.

4. Now add the salt, coriander powder, garam masala, haldi and paprika powder. Stir and cook for a few minutes to infuse the spices. Add approximately 1 to 1 ½ cups of water.

5. Cover with a lid and allow the chops to simmer for about 45 minutes. When you feel the chops are cooked, add the cardamom, ground cloves and ground cinnamon. If you want extra spice add the chilli flakes now.

6. If you feel the chops are not soft enough, leave them to simmer till they reach the softness you want.

7. Take off the heat and let it stand for a while so the spices can infuse. Before serving garnish liberally with fresh coriander. If the gravy seems a bit thin you can add a dollop of crème fraiche or some fresh cream.

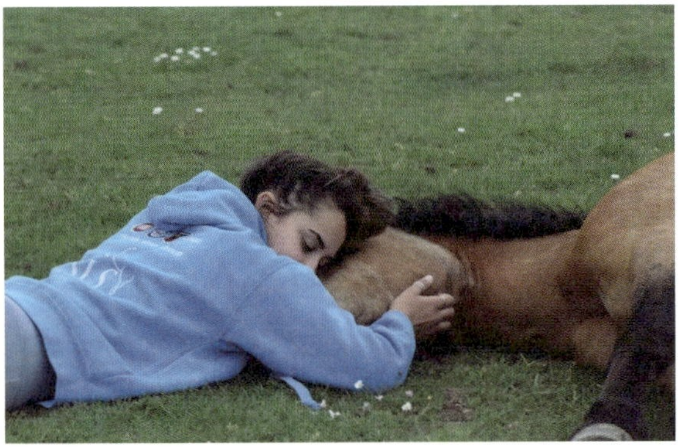
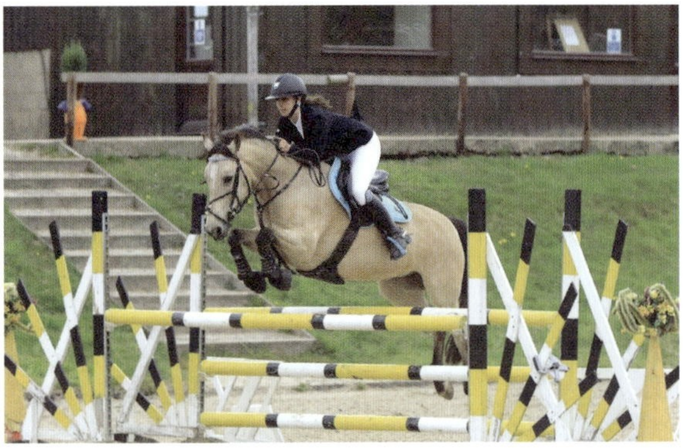
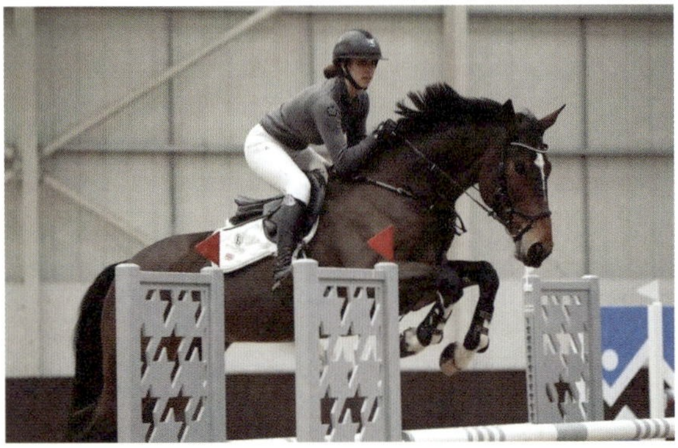
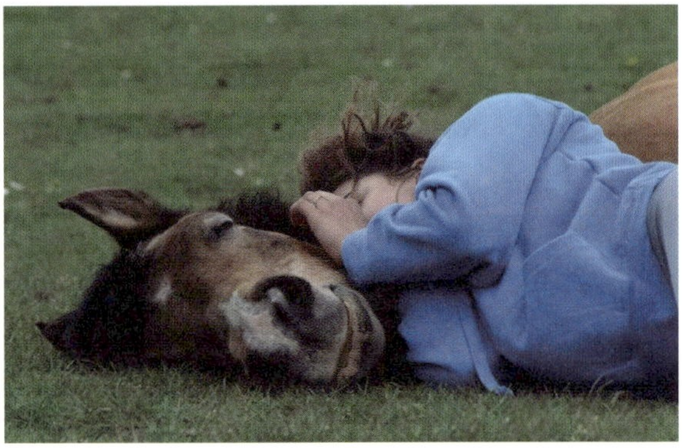
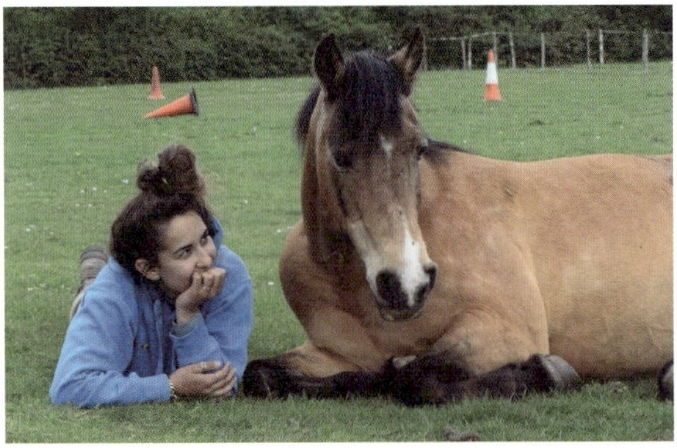
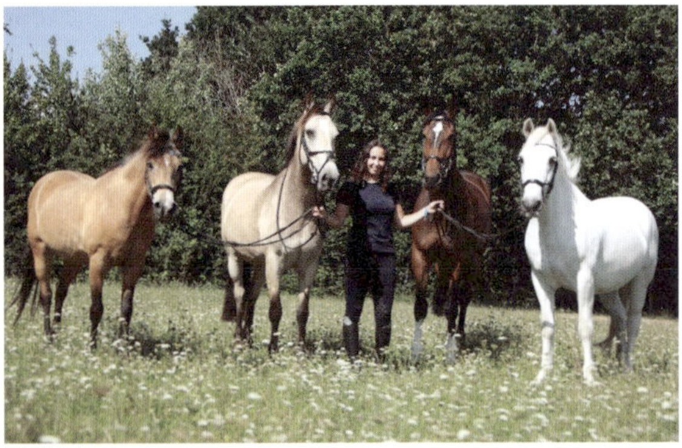
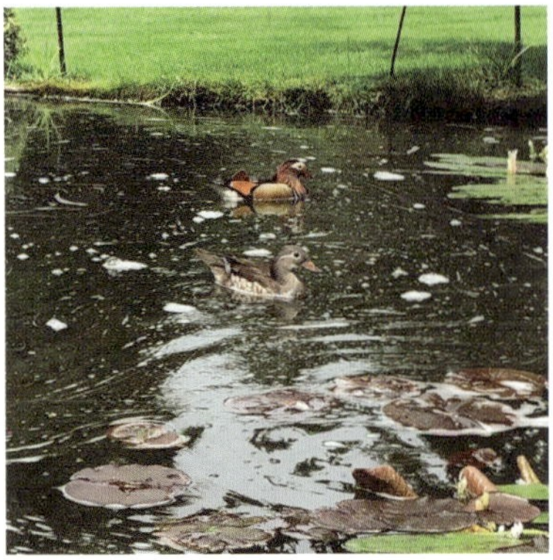
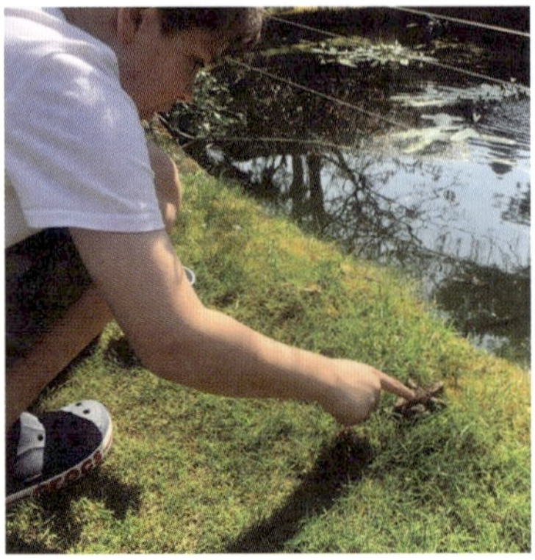
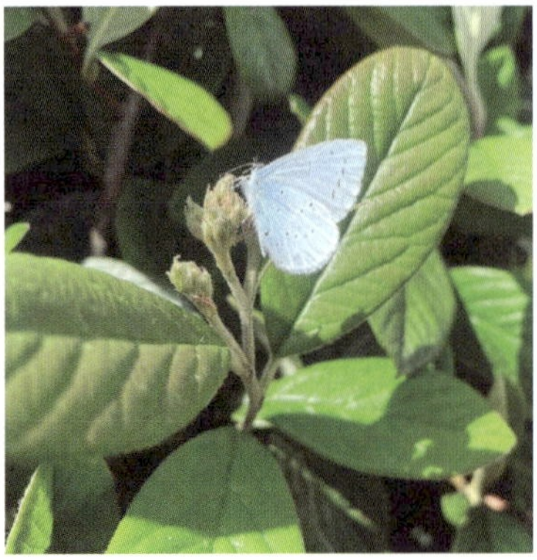

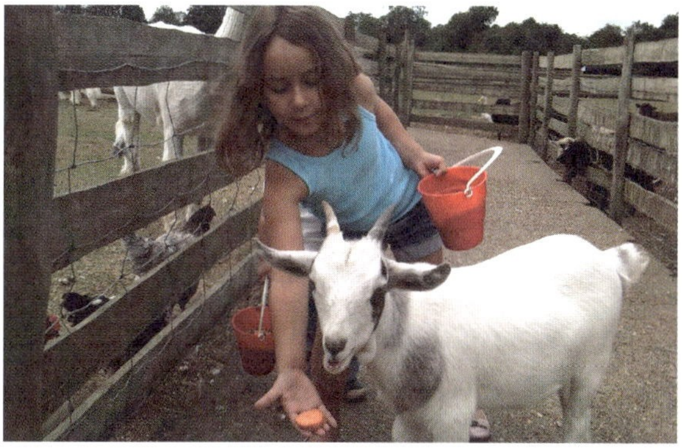
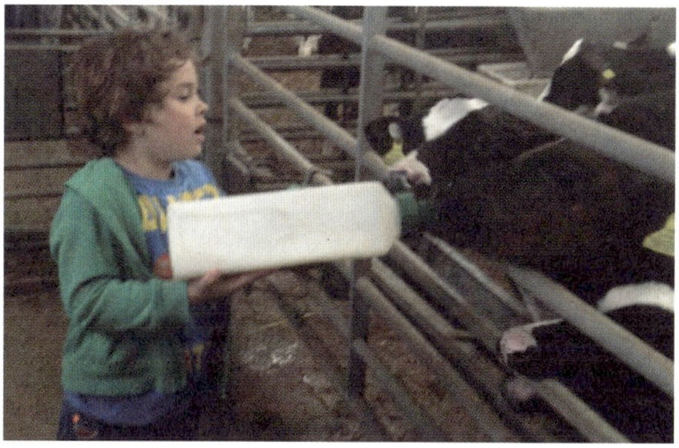
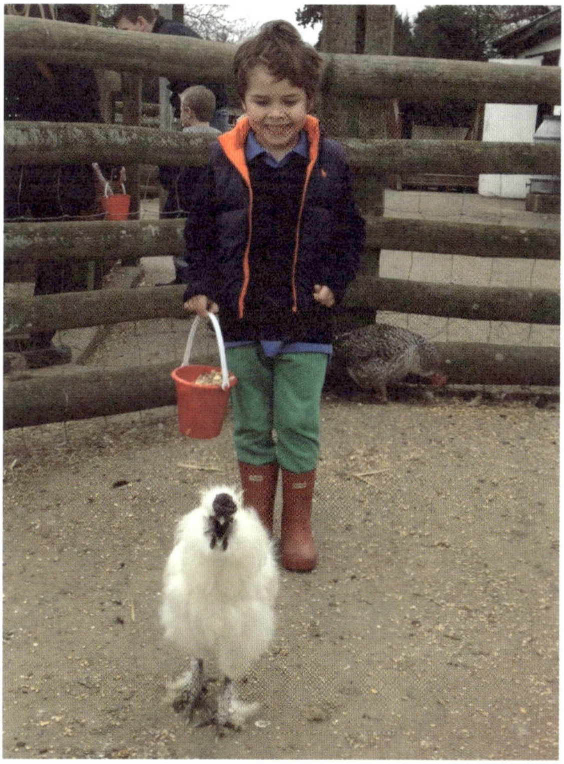
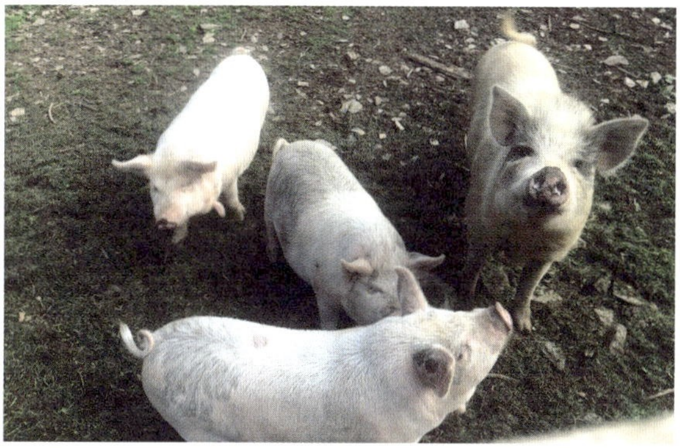
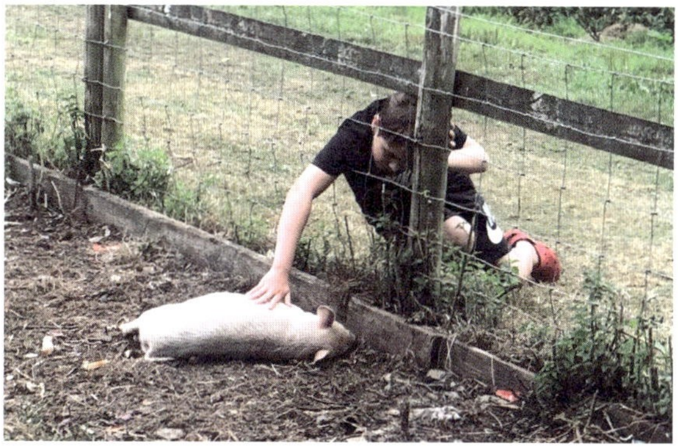
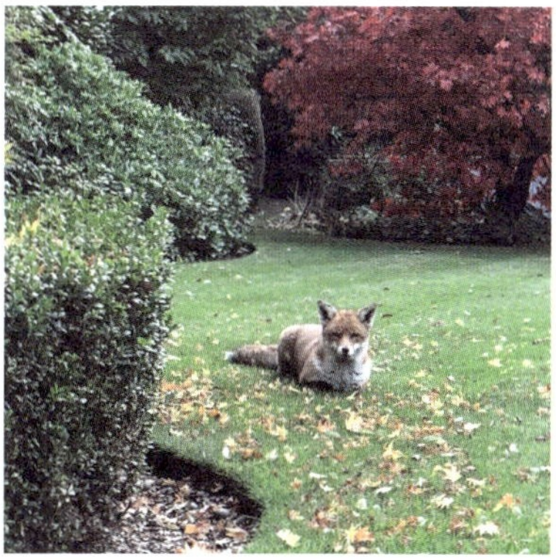
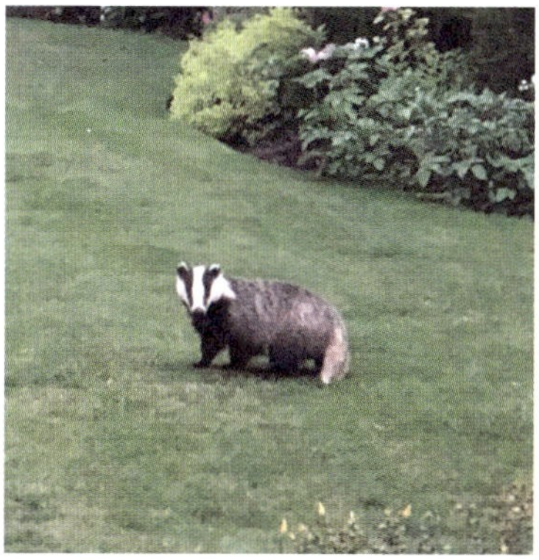
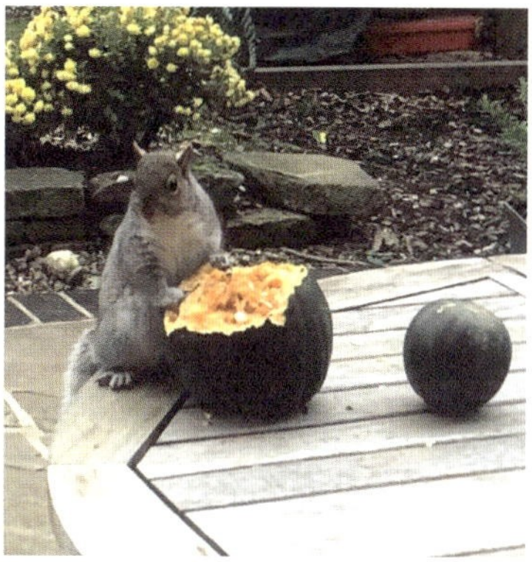

God,
Grant me the
Serenity to accept the things I cannot change,
the *Courage* to change the things I can,
and the *Wisdom* to know the difference.

The serenity prayer

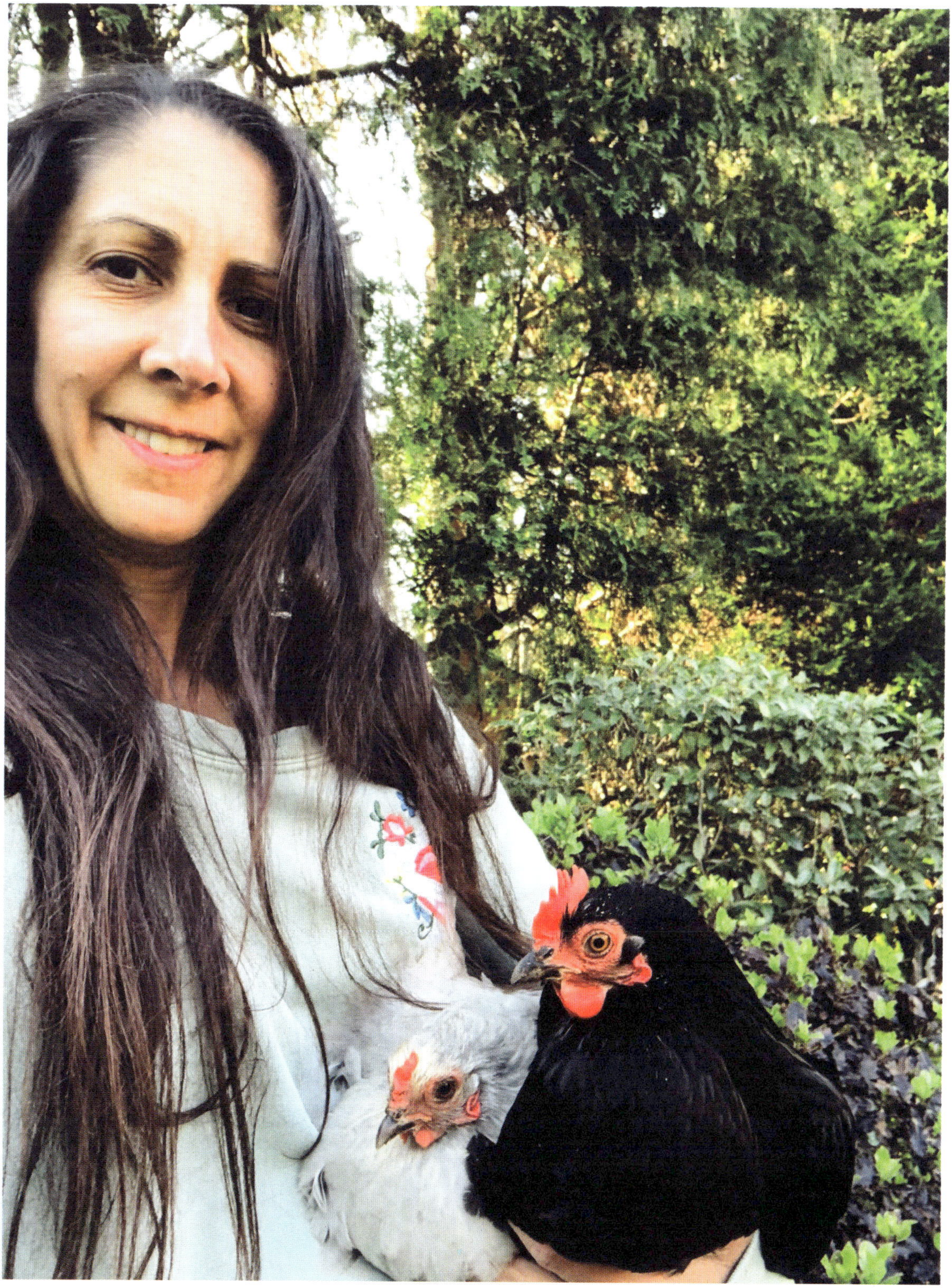

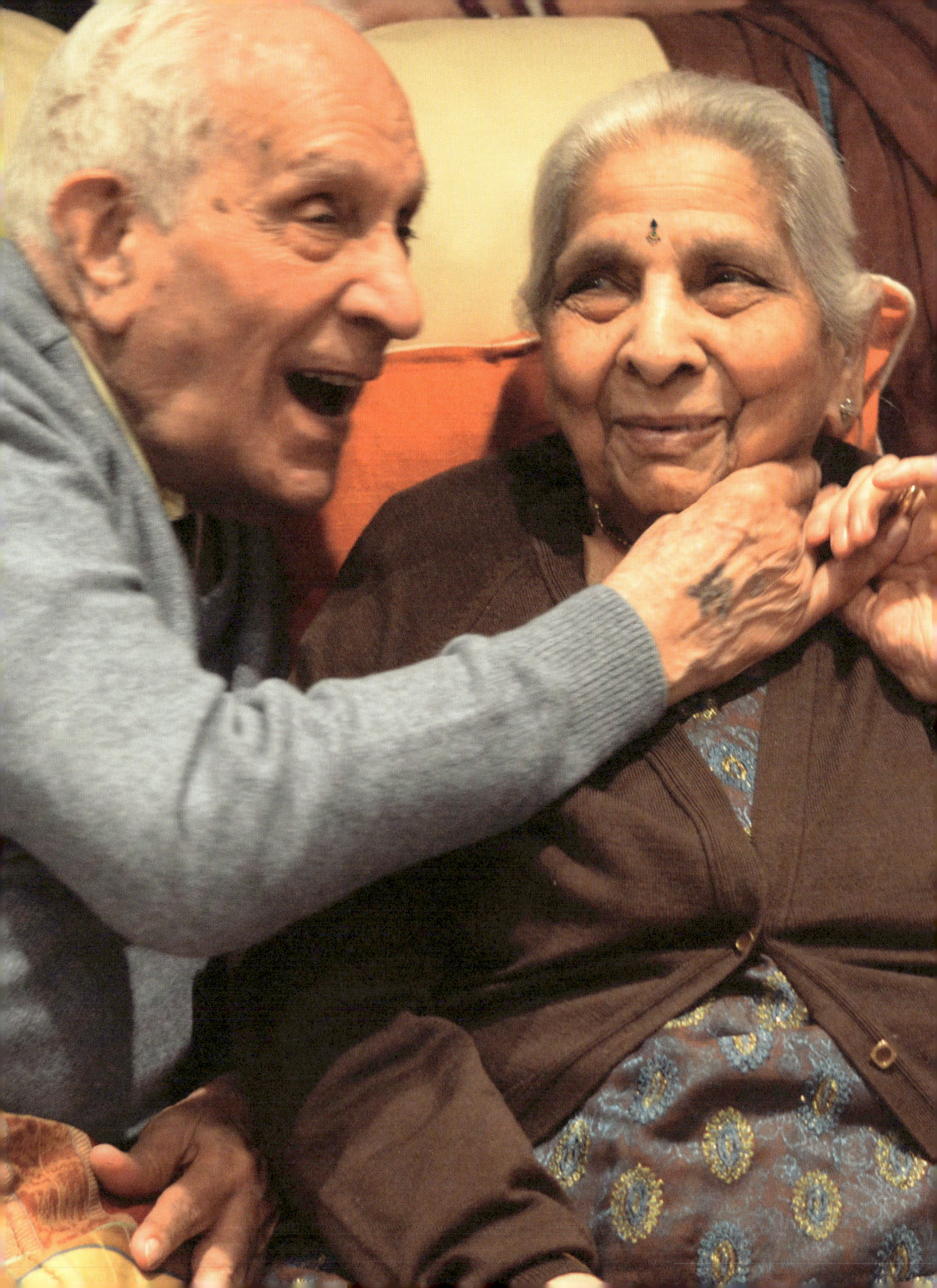

ACCOMPANIMENTS

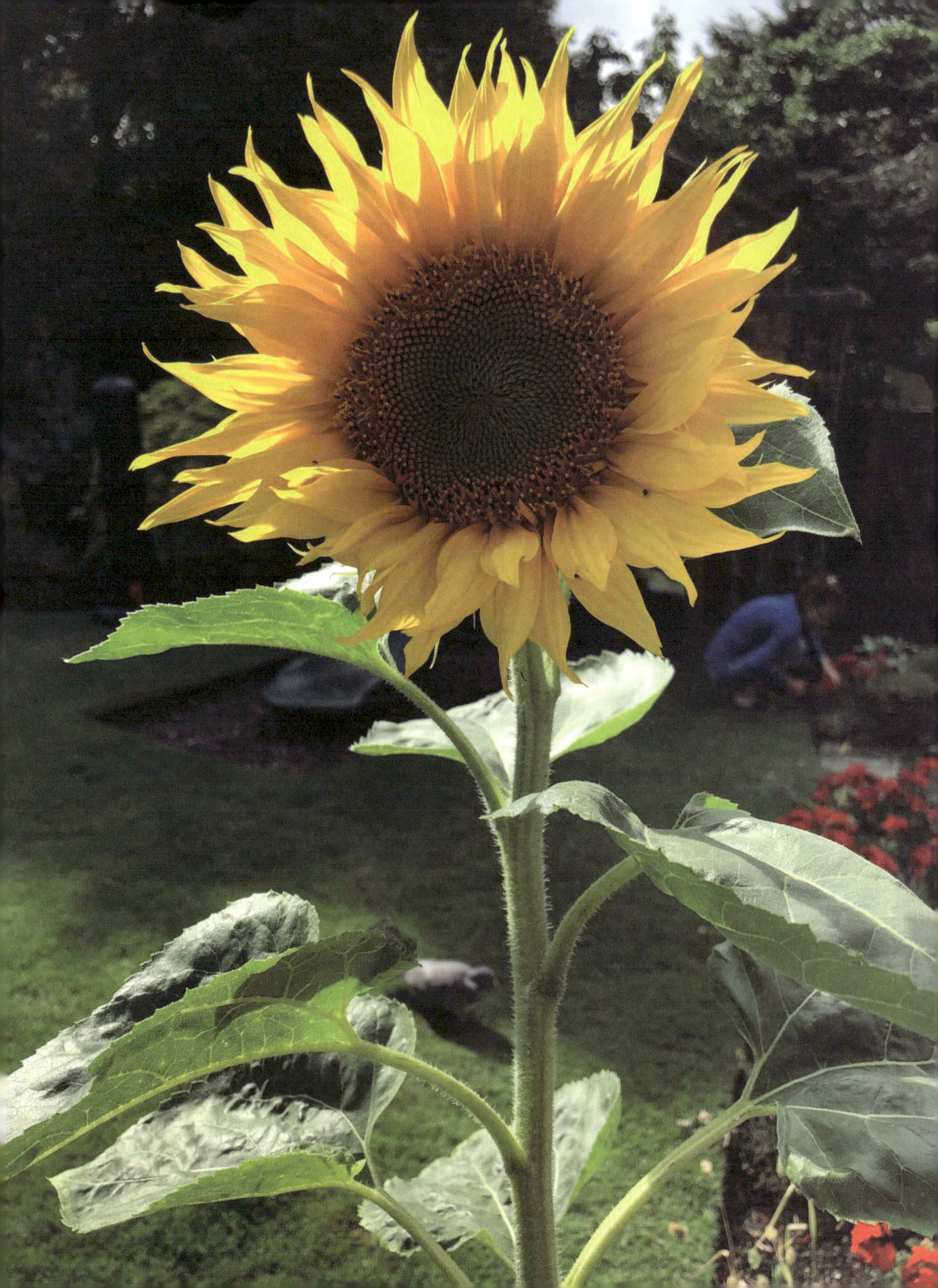

SAUCES & SIDES

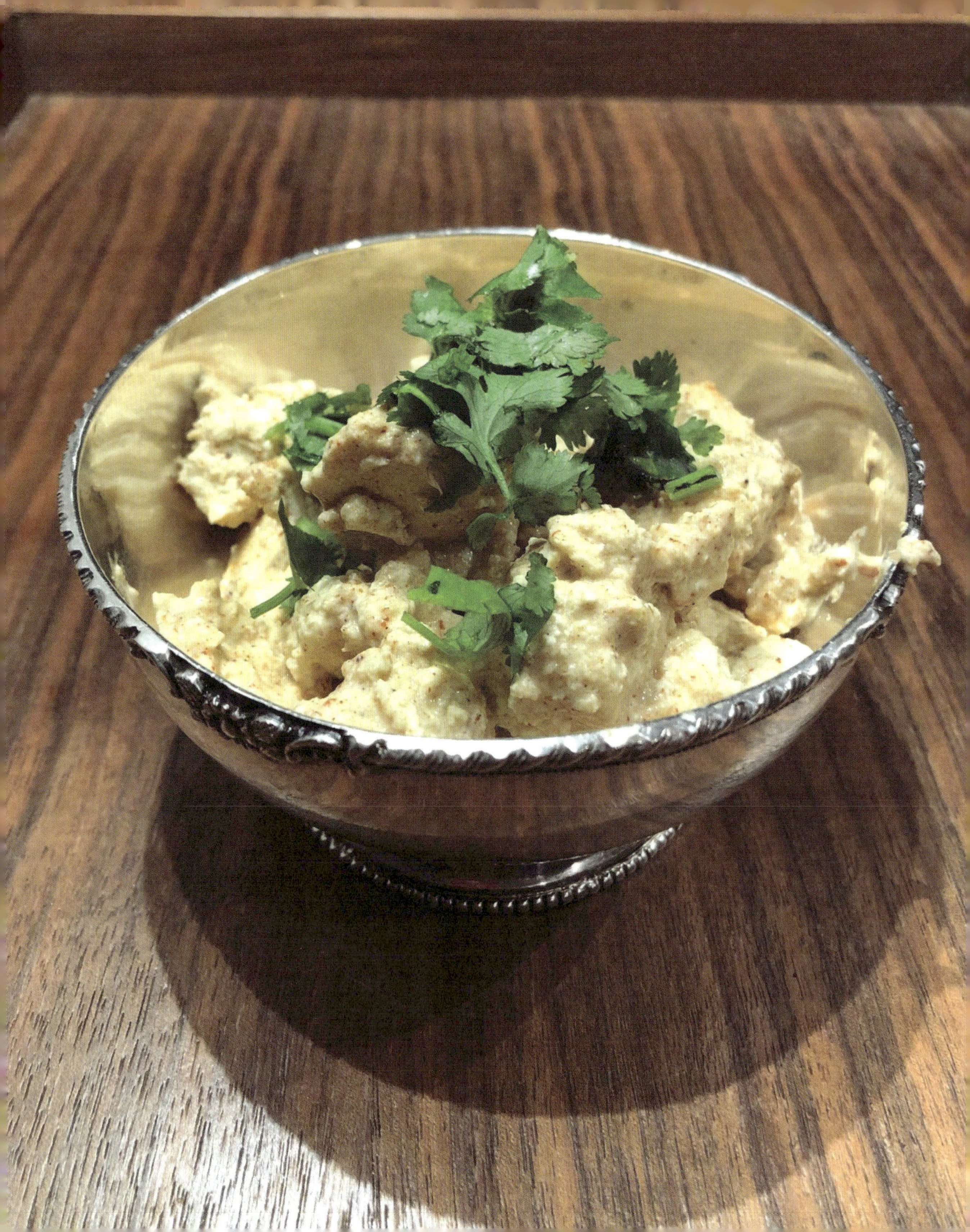

SAUCES & SIDES

Gigi Uncle's Marinade

READY IN
20 MINS
+ MARINATING

SERVES
3-4

This is an excellent marinade. I use it for tofu; however, it can also be used with paneer, lamb or chicken.

INGREDIENTS

1 lemon

1 teaspoon runny honey (optional)

1 large tablespoon unsweetened plant-based yogurt or plain set natural yogurt

300g tofu (1 packet)

Drizzle of oil

Coriander for decoration (optional)

SPICES

1 teaspoon salt (½ teaspoon if using paneer)

1 teaspoon tandoori masala

METHOD

1. Halve the lemon and squeeze the juice into a mixing bowl.
2. Add the salt and spices then mix with a fork.
3. Optional add the honey.
4. Then add the yogurt.
5. Add your choice of tofu, paneer or meat. If using tofu, I like to break it apart with my hands into small rough chunks.
6. Mix well and cover with clingfilm, leave in the fridge for a minimum of one hour or overnight.
7. Cook on the grill or barbecue on foil for about 15 minutes. Serve with a sprinkle of fresh chopped coriander.

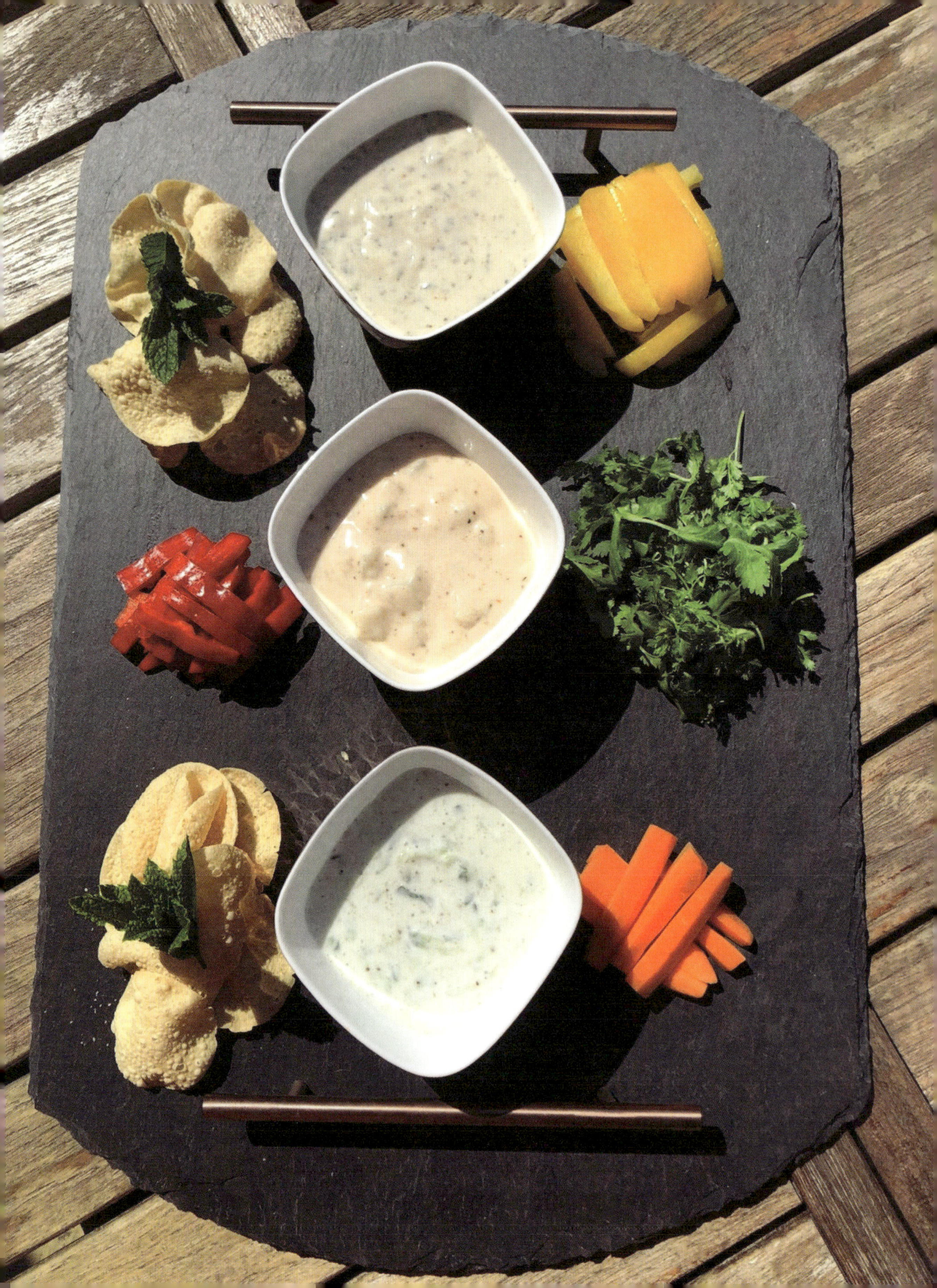

SAUCES & SIDES

Cucumber Raita

READY IN
10 MINS

SERVES
4-6

This is a famous yogurt served at most Indian parties, the cucumber adds depth and flavour. It's also great for cooling down one of Uncle Gigi's spicy curries! The kids love it and again, goes well with barbecue food. This is Indian Nanny's recipe.

I use oat yogurt and oat milk for an amazing vegan / dairy free alternative.

INGREDIENTS

¾ cucumber

1 x 500g pot natural set yogurt (we like Onken)

A little milk or dairy free alternative

SPICES

1 teaspoon salt

½ teaspoon coarse black pepper

½ teaspoon roasted ground jeera

METHOD

1. Grate the cucumber into a large bowl, gently squeeze the water out of the cucumber. Discard the water.
2. Add the yogurt and milk.
3. Whisk all ingredients gently together using a fork and add the spices.
4. Keep in the fridge until ready to serve, will keep for a day or so.

Nanny's tip – roast the jeera in the microwave for one minute. Then grind in a coffee grinder (or pestle and mortar); as an alternative you can use ground cumin.

SAUCES & SIDES

Potato Yogurt

READY IN 30 MINS   **SERVES** 4-6

Ok so it sounds unusual but believe me this is a very tasty yogurt dish. Goes well with Indian food. Auntie Veena's special recipe.

I use oat yogurt and oat milk for a tasty vegan / dairy free alternative, it comes out really well.

INGREDIENTS

5 small potatoes

1 x 500g tub natural set yogurt

A splash of milk if necessary

SPICES

1 teaspoon salt

½ teaspoon black pepper

½ teaspoon sweet red chilli powder or paprika powder

METHOD

1. Peel the potatoes and cut in half. Add them to a saucepan of water and bring to the boil. Simmer until you can get a sharp knife into the potatoes and they are cooked (about 10 minutes).

2. Once they are cooked, drain the water and let them cool.

3. Cut the potatoes into small pieces, approximately 1cm cubes.

4. In a bowl add 1 tub of yogurt, whisk it with an egg beater or fork; if it's really thick, add a splash of milk.

5. Add the potato pieces, 1 teaspoon salt, ½ teaspoon black pepper, ½ teaspoon chilli powder. Give it a gentle but good stir.

6. Keep in the fridge until ready to serve, will keep for a day or so.

SAUCES & SIDES

Mint Yogurt

READY IN
5 MINS

SERVES
4-6

This is great with a packet of pappadoms. Traditionally this is served with any of the starter or main dishes. A dollop on the side of your plate will cool down a hot, spicy curry!

Again, this can be made with oat yogurt and oat milk for a tasty vegan / dairy free option.

INGREDIENTS

2 tablespoons Colman's mint sauce

1 x 500g tub natural set yogurt

¼ pint full fat milk (or oat milk)

SPICES

1 teaspoon salt

½ teaspoon paprika

METHOD

1. Put all of the ingredients into a large bowl and whisk with an egg beater.
2. Keep in the fridge until ready to serve, will keep for a day or so.

SAUCES & SIDES

Boondi Yogurt

READY IN 10 MINS **SERVES** 4-6

Auntie Madhu taught me this recipe. Boondi are little "salted fried chickpea flour puffs", she says that Haldrirams brand is good as they are nice and crispy.

I use oat yogurt and oat milk for a tasty vegan / dairy free alternative.

INGREDIENTS

1 x 500g tub natural set yogurt

100g boondi

Splash of water (¼ cup)

SPICES

1 teaspoon salt

½ teaspoon black pepper

½ teaspoon paprika powder

METHOD

1. In a bowl add 1 tub of yogurt, whisk it with an egg beater or fork; if it's really thick, add a splash of water, you will need less than ¼ cup.

2. Add the boondi, 1 teaspoon of salt, ½ teaspoon black pepper, ½ teaspoon paprika powder. Give it a gentle but good stir.

3. Keep in the fridge until ready to serve however best made to serve.

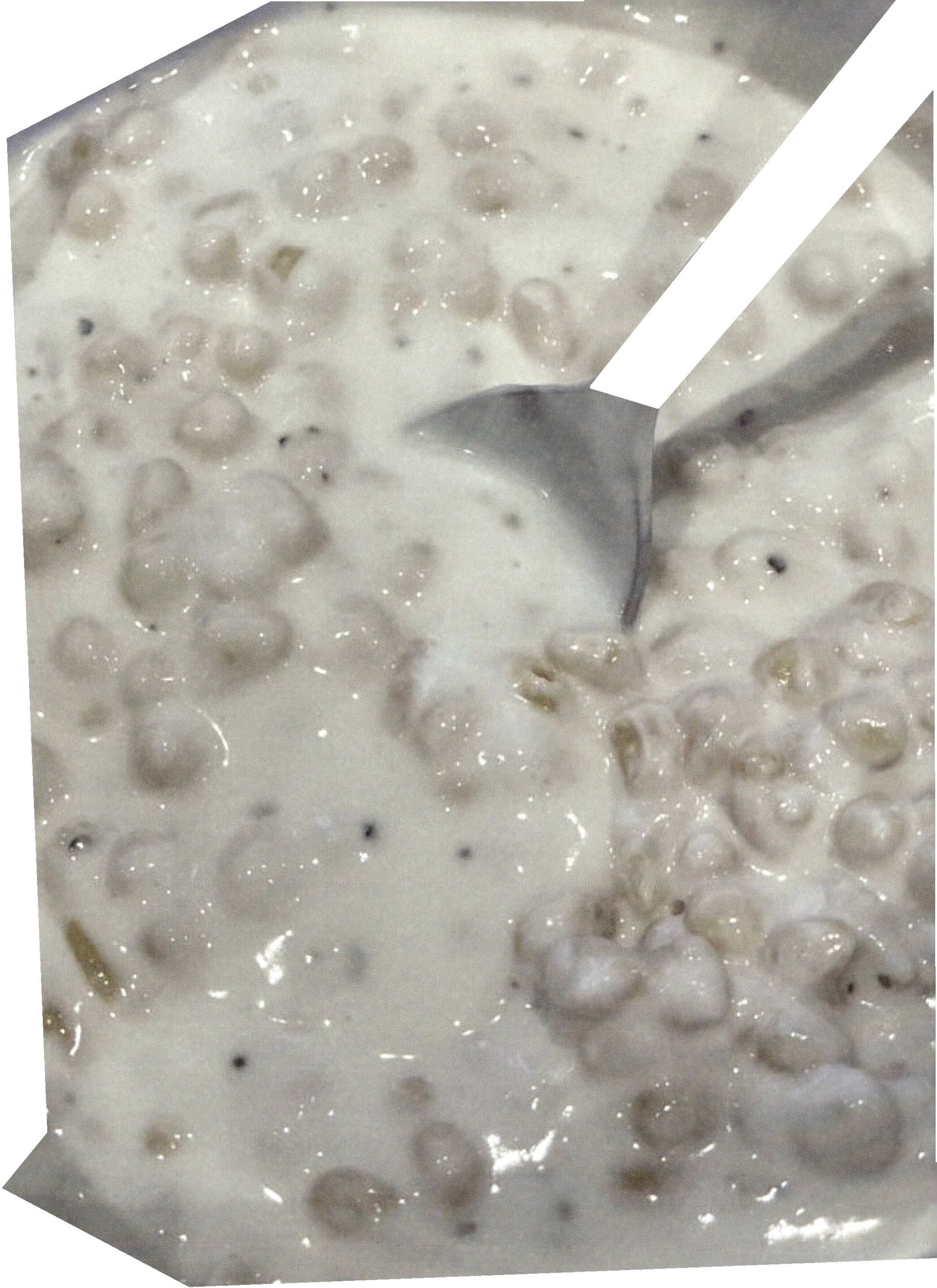

SAUCES & SIDES

Lemon Pickle

READY IN
20 MINS
+ PICKLING

MAKES
1 JAR

Indian Nanny taught me this recipe. My Swiss Uncle Sigi loved lemon pickle, so does my mum. A spoon on the side of an Indian meal adds wicked flavour.

INGREDIENTS

6 lemons

3x2 inches ginger (approximately 60g)

SPICES

6 dessert spoons salt

4 teaspoons chilli flakes

METHOD

1. Wash and dry the lemons thoroughly with kitchen towel.
2. Cut the top and bottoms off the lemons. Take off a bit of skin too if you like (if they have a thick skin).
3. Cut each lemon into 12 segments (lengthways twice and widthways twice). Put the segments into a bowl with the salt and chilli flakes, then mix.
4. Put the lemon segments into a jar with a tightly fitting lid, add all the salt and chilli on top. Put the jar in the sunlight or on the windowsill for 3 days. Rotate the jar once or twice a day so the lemons are soaking up the juice.
5. Once done, peel the ginger, wash and cut into matchsticks. It must be thoroughly dried, so I would suggest cutting it, then leaving overnight in kitchen towel.
6. Add the chopped ginger strips to the lemon pickle.

Notes – The ginger must be thoroughly dried or the pickle will go bad.

The lemon pickle will be ready to eat in 3-4 days and will last a few months in the fridge.

Really fresh chilli flakes are the best (red in colour rather than brown).

In Veena's recipe, she would put the ginger in at the same time and squeeze a few more lemons to make it juicier.

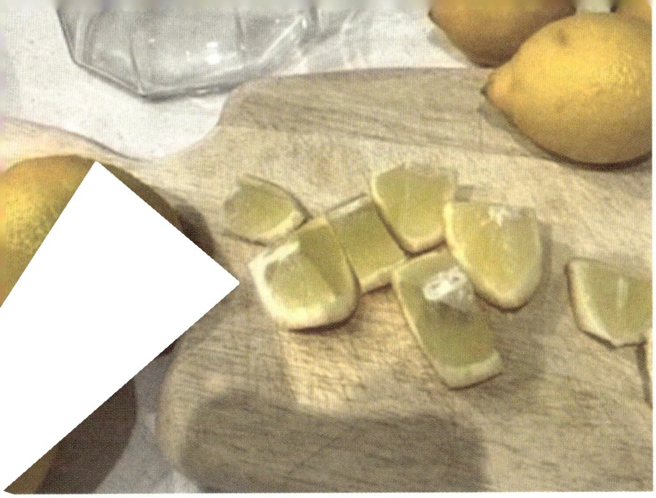
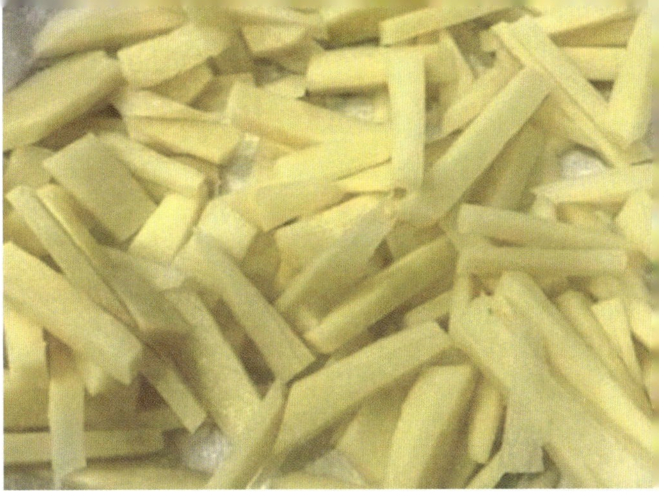
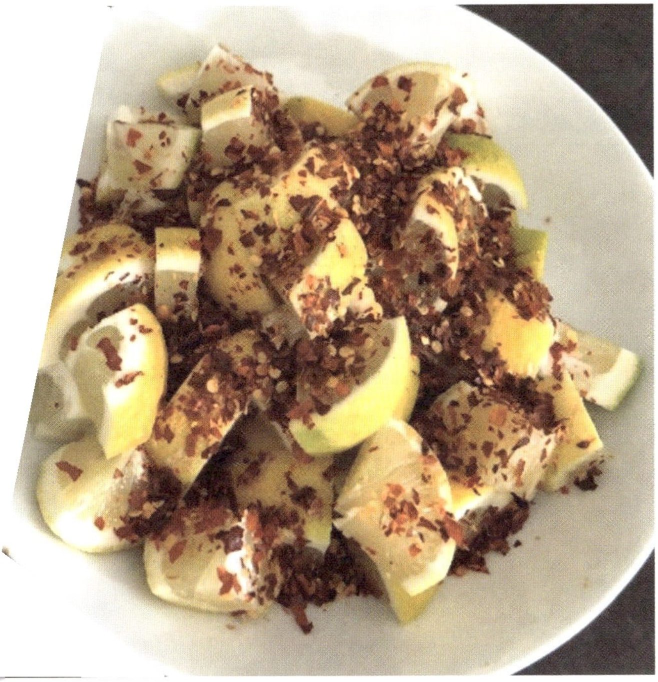
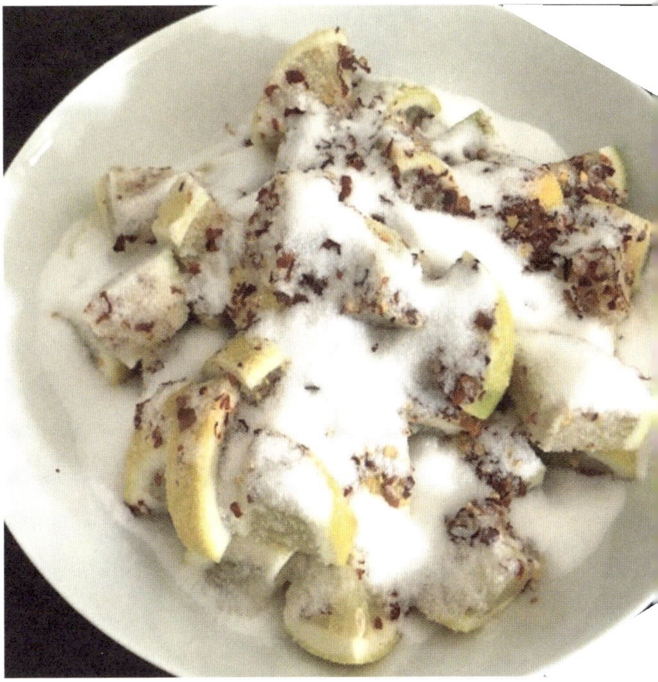
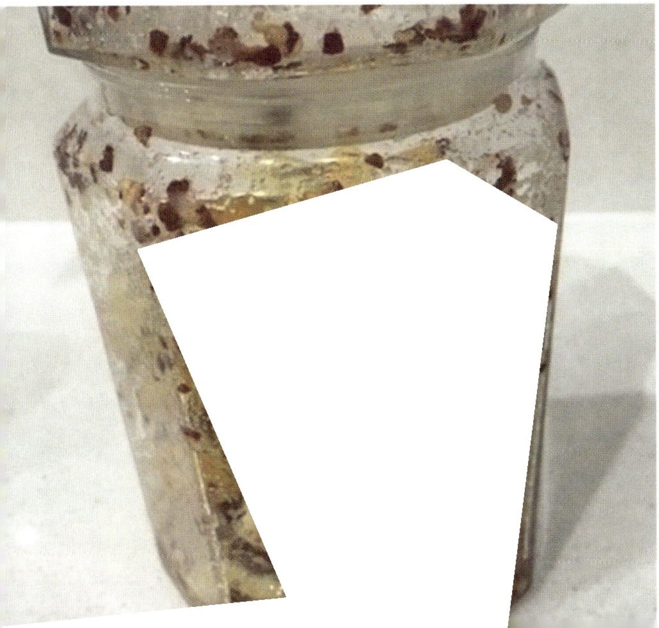
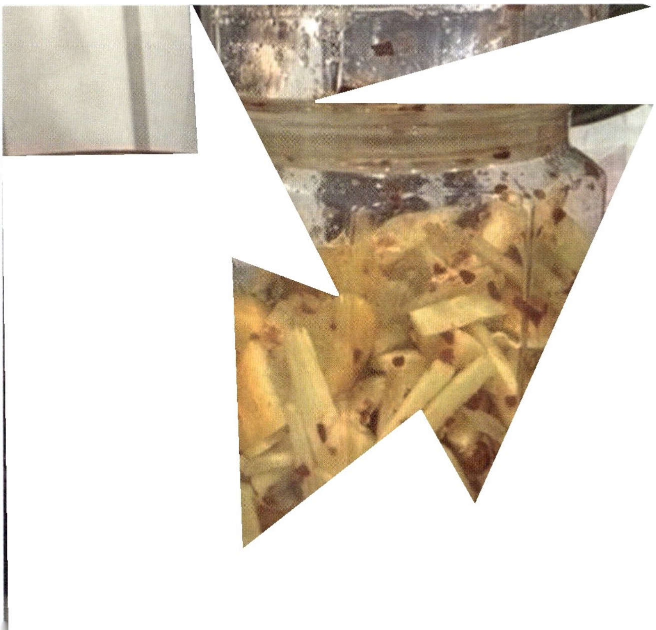

SAUCES & SIDES

Carrot Pickle

READY IN
20 MINS
+ PICKLING

MAKES
2 JARS

This is another one of Nanny's famous pickle recipes, she taught this to Rita. It's really simple to make and tastes delicious.

INGREDIENTS

1kg carrots

4 tablespoons malt vinegar

4 tablespoons oil (any)

½ cup water

SPICES

¾ teaspoon haldi

1 teaspoon chilli powder

1 tablespoon mustard seeds (blitz in the spice grinder)

¾ teaspoon salt

METHOD

1. Peel and cut the carrots into about 2-inch batons and parboil for a few minutes (in salty water says Indian Nanny).

2. Drain and put into a large mixing bowl.

3. Heat the oil in a wok, add the chilli powder and haldi. Then pour this over the carrots, add the mustard seeds and salt.

4. Add the water and vinegar. Stir well and mix all together.

5. Put into an airtight container and leave for 3-4 days, stirring now and then for everything to infuse.

6. Decant into sterilised jars and enjoy!

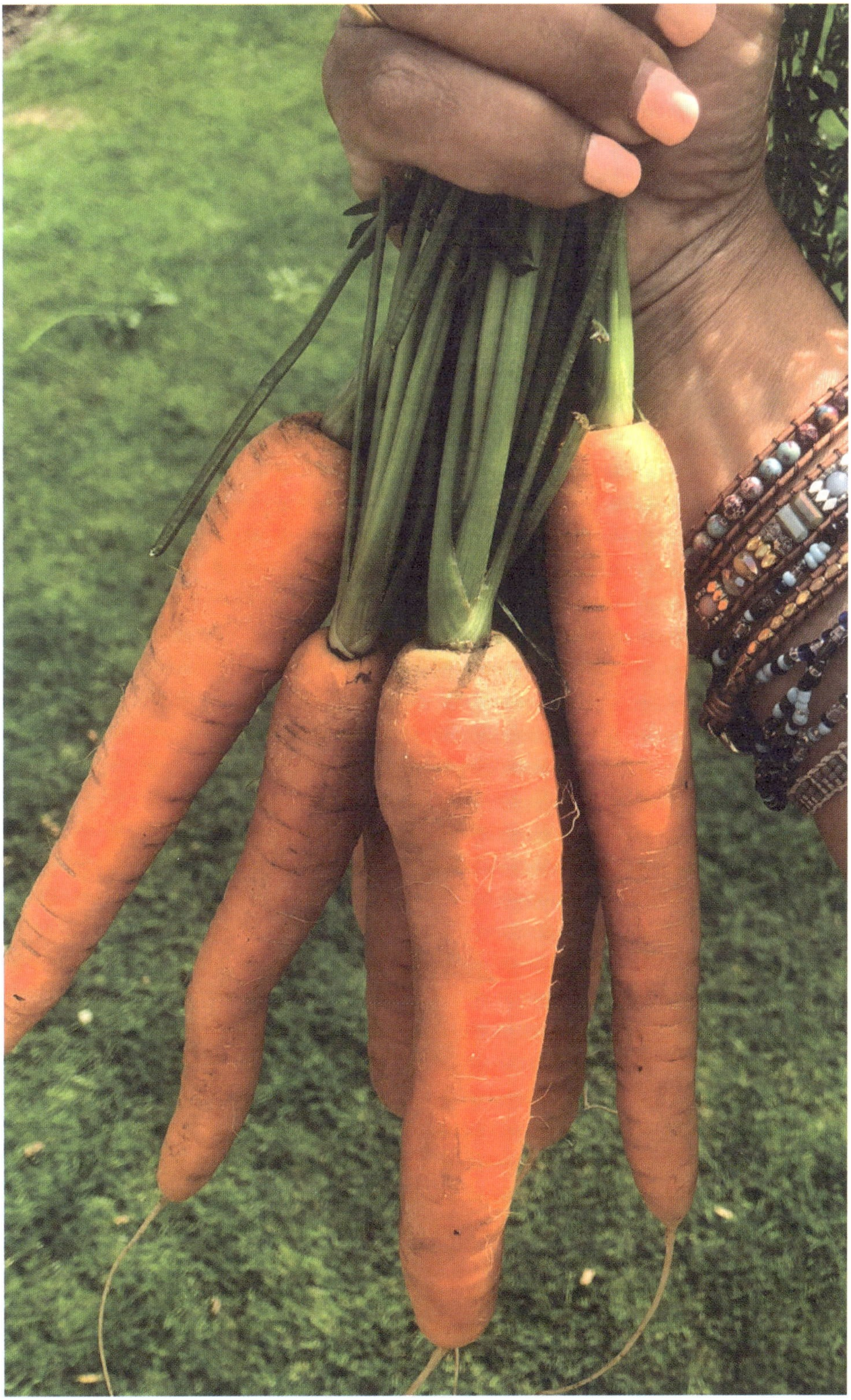

SAUCES & SIDES

Sweet No Chilli Dipping Sauce

READY IN
40 MINS

MAKES
3 JARS

INGREDIENTS

800g really ripe tomatoes

3x2 inches ginger (approximately 60g), peeled and finely chopped

2 cloves garlic, finely chopped

125ml rice vinegar

300g granulated sugar

This is a wicked dip, great with pappadoms, tortilla chips, pakoras, samosas, I'll even lick it off my fingers! Nice tangy taste. Easy to make. Give it a go!

Should store in a cool cupboard for few months. Once opened, refrigerate and use within a few weeks (if it lasts that long).

You will need a few jars for storing your sauce.

METHOD

1. Wash the tomatoes, then roughly chop. Blitz in the food processor until you have a coarse puree. Add the ginger, garlic and rice vinegar. Give it a good mix.

2. Pour into a saucepan and add the sugar. Bring to the boil, then turn down to simmer. Cook with the lid off on a low heat for about 30-45 minutes until it thickens.

3. While the sauce is cooking, wash your jars in hot soapy water then place on a baking tray top side down, lids off on the tray too. Pop into a preheated oven at 180°C for 15 minutes – this is to sterilise your jars.

4. Take care removing the hot jars from the oven. While the jars are still hot, pour the sauce into the jars, leave a couple of centimetres at the top of each jar and put the lid on. Make sure you wipe any sauce off the jar, screw the lid on tight, rotate the jar once to remove any air bubbles.

Note – If you would like to add a few red or green chillies, chop them up and add at the same time as the ginger & garlic.

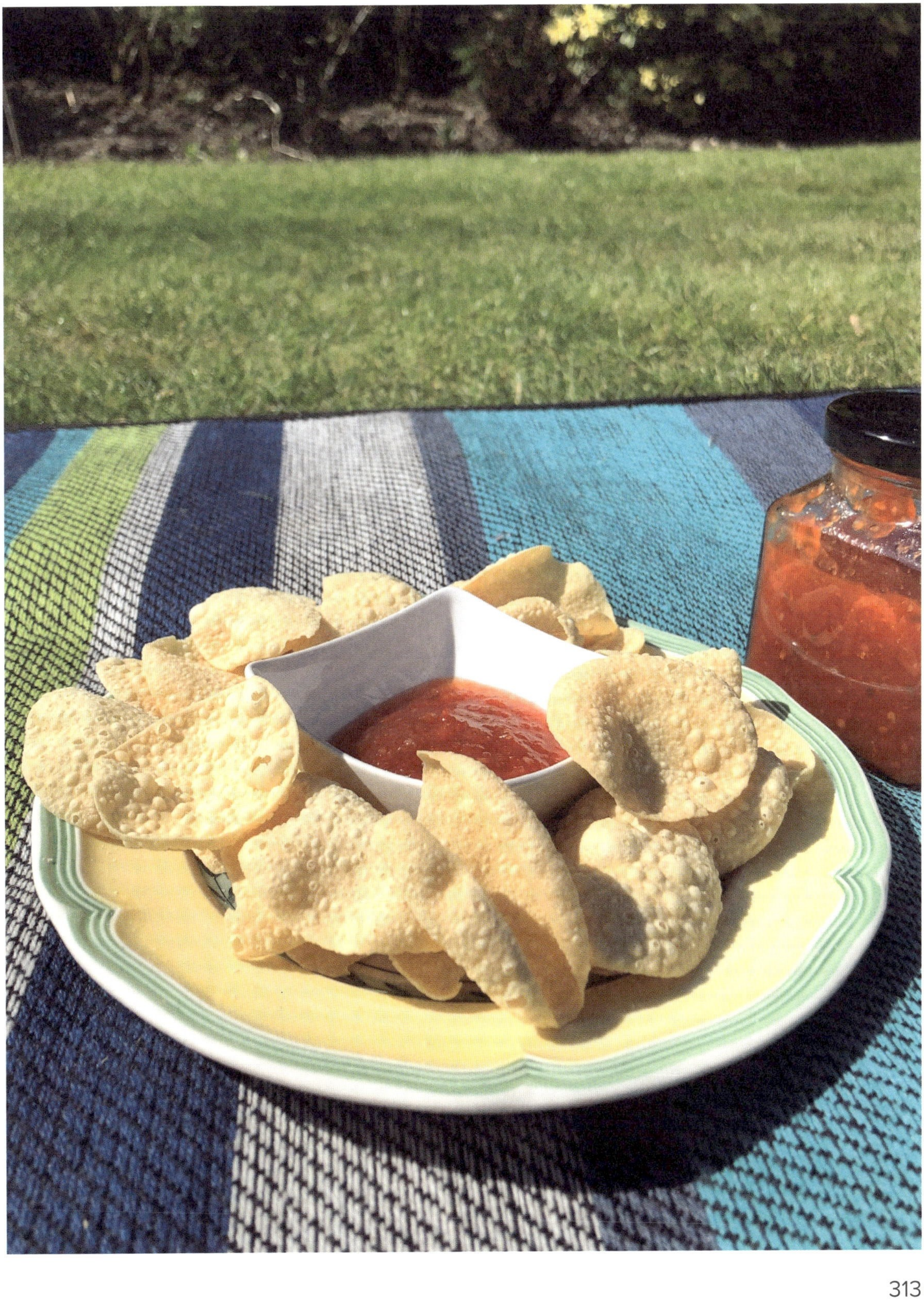

SAUCES & SIDES

Super Mango Salsa

READY IN
15 MINS

SERVES
3-4

We have to thank blonde Khanna's Mum – Anthea – for this beautiful salsa! She would bring it along to an Indian get-together and my Nan always commented on how tasty it was. It goes well with Indian food. We hope you enjoy Mummy Anthakis' super mango salsa too.

INGREDIENTS

2 ripe mangoes

½ red onion, peeled and finely chopped

10 cherry tomatoes

1 lime

Handful of fresh coriander, washed & chopped

SPICES

Good pinch of salt

Good pinch of chilli flakes

METHOD

1. Start by peeling and chopping the mangoes into bite size chunks, put them in a large bowl.

2. Then wash and chop the cherry tomatoes into quarters then half each quarter again, add to the bowl.

3. Add the finely chopped onion and chopped coriander. Add a good squeeze of the lime to the bowl as well as the chilli flakes and salt.

4. Mix gently and serve!

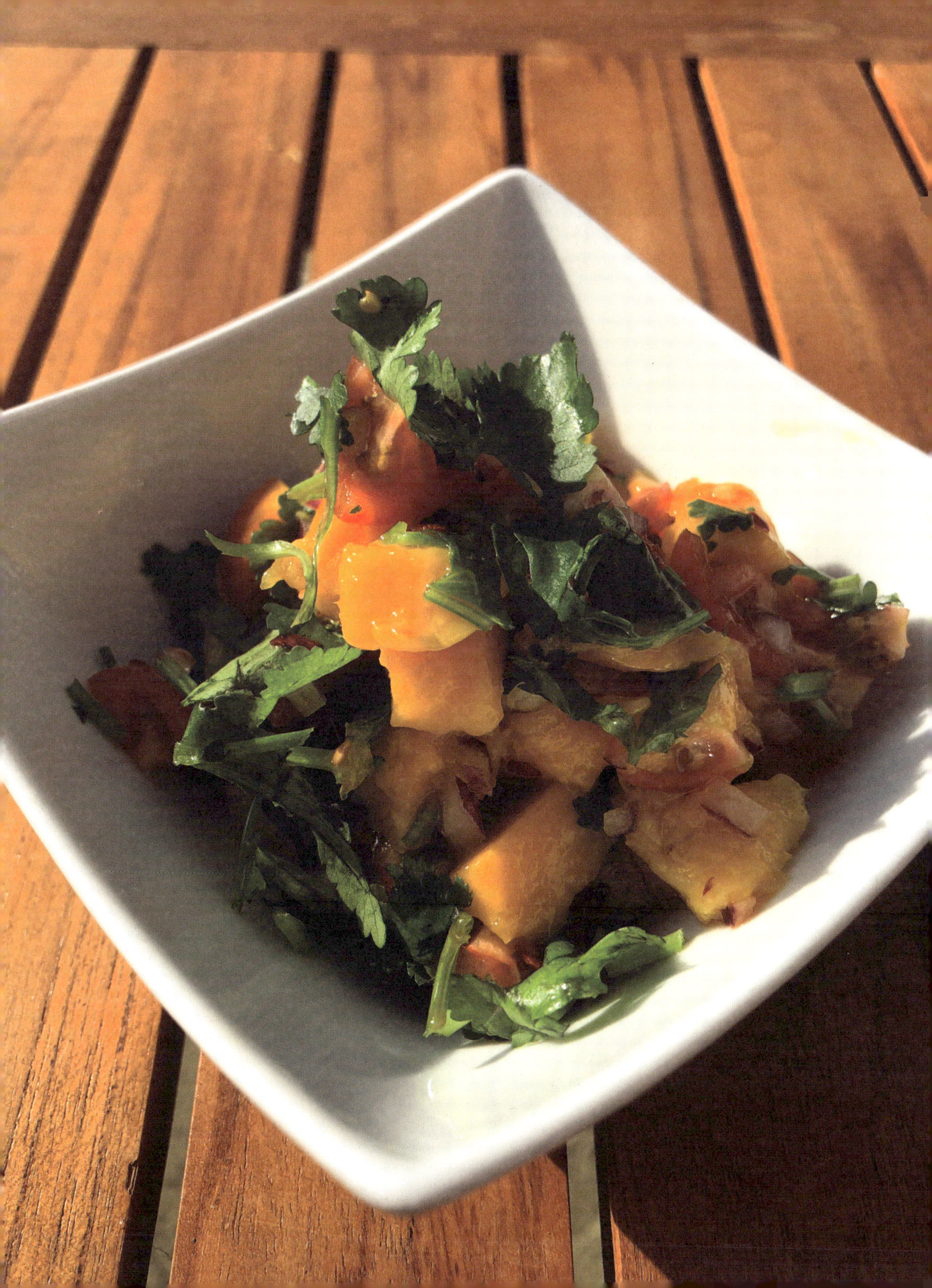

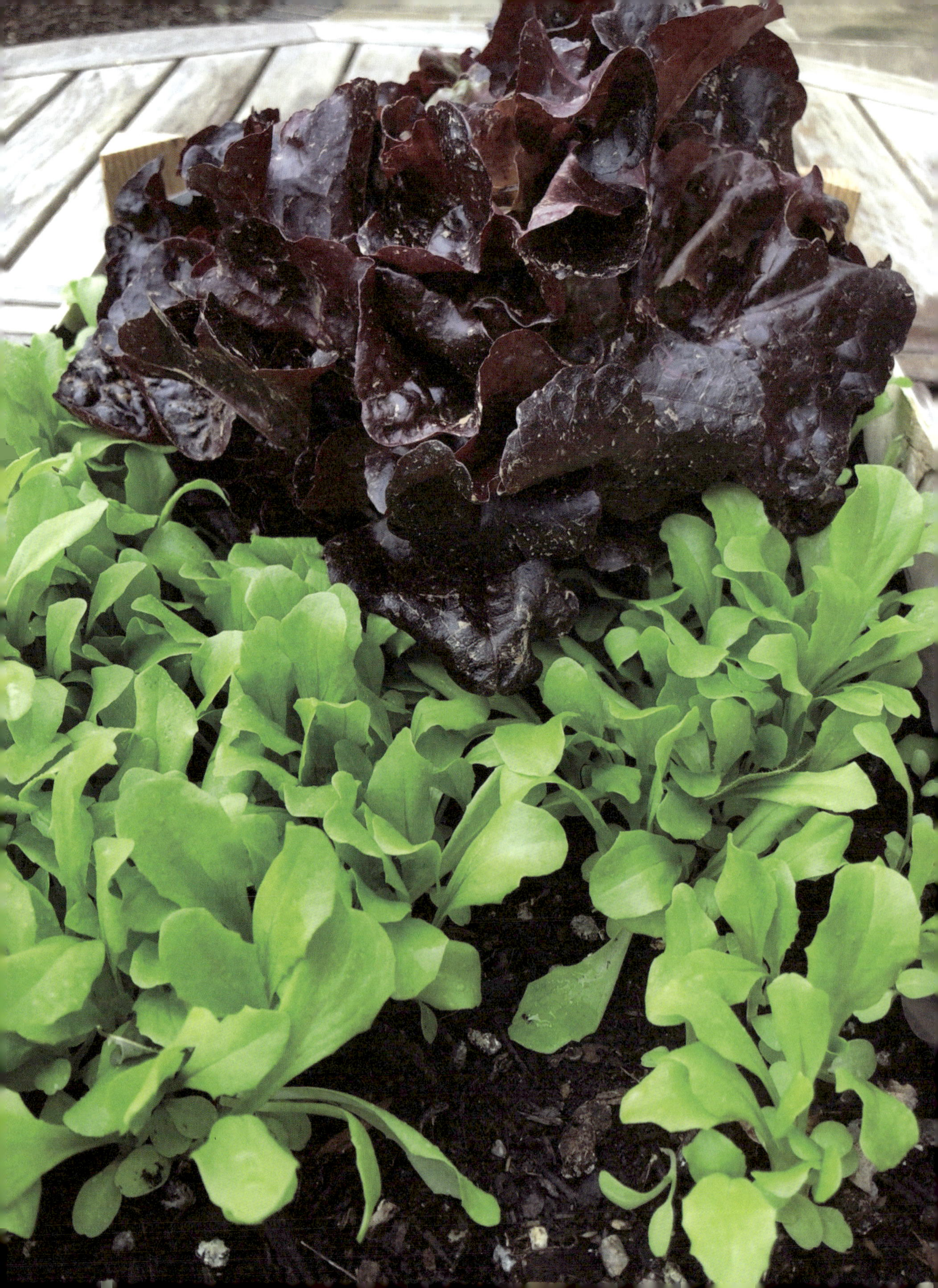

SALADS, SALAD AND MORE SALAD!

We always have a bowl of salad in the fridge. Would you believe me if I said, start with some fresh washed leaves at the bottom of a bowl then add whatever salad is in season / you have in your fridge?

I have added some classic favourites to this section until you grow in confidence to do the above. My daughter says I live on rabbit food, rabbits always look like they enjoy munching fresh greens too!

SALADS, SALAD AND MORE SALAD!

Simply Leaves

READY IN
10 MINS

SERVES
3-4

INGREDIENTS

Either 2 gem lettuce, 1 iceberg or 1 curly leaf salad

8 cherry tomatoes cut in half

Chopped chives / parsley / basil (optional)

METHOD

1. Wash the leaves and rinse to remove any dirt. My preference is to use a salad spinner – excellent piece of kitchen equipment!

2. Leave to dry for a while then chop into a large bowl.

3. Add the cherry tomatoes, then put the chopped chives, parsley or basil on top if you wish.

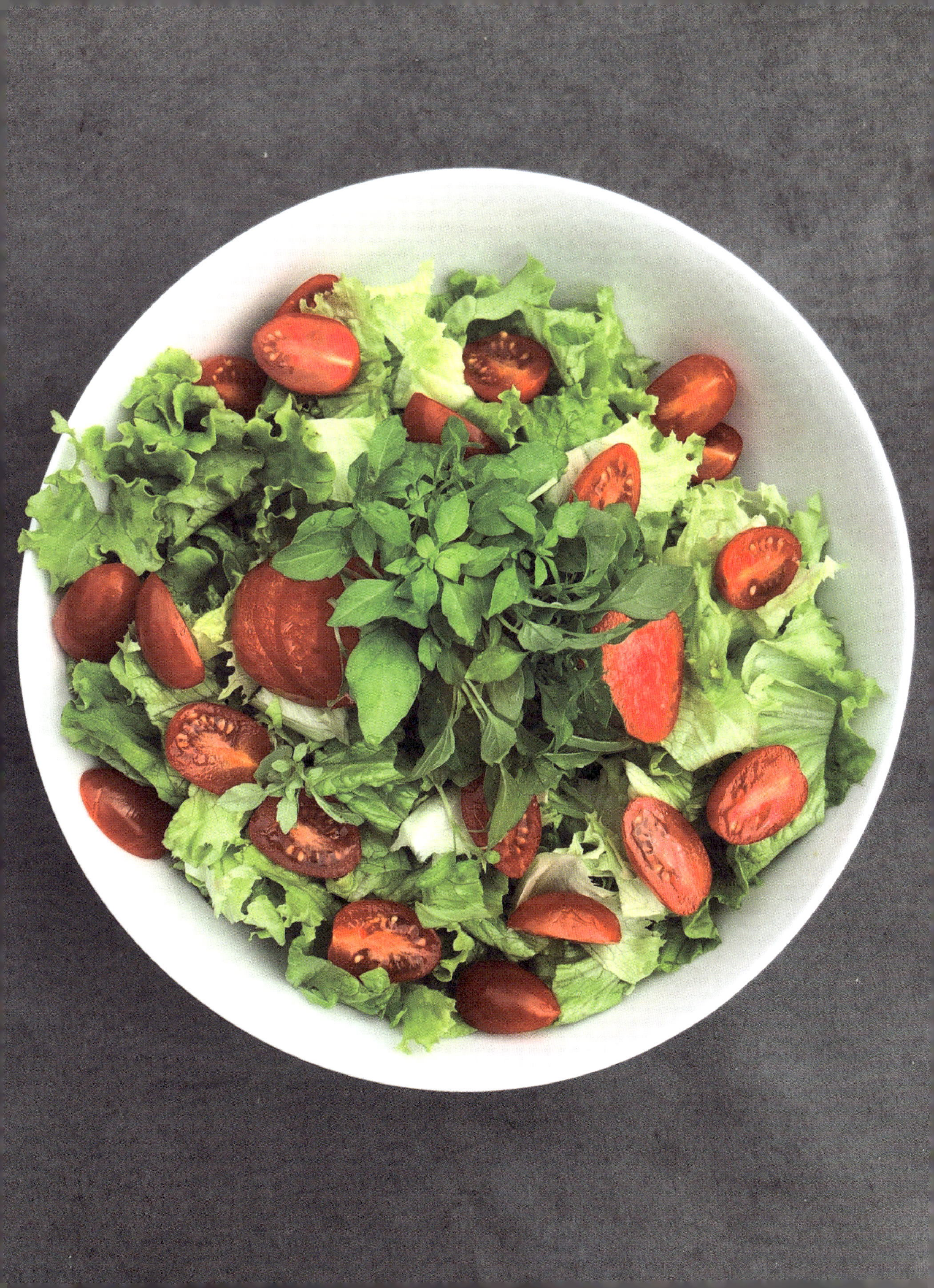

SALADS, SALAD AND MORE SALAD!

Super Salad

⏳ **READY IN**
45 MINS

🍽 **SERVES**
4-6

This is a great family salad. One to have in the fridge or as part of a main meal, in the middle of the table so everyone can dig in and help themselves to a large plateful.

INGREDIENTS

Either 2 gem, 1 iceberg or 1 curly leaf salad

½ bag Lambs lettuce

Tin sweetcorn (400g), rinsed and drained

Tin butterbeans (400g), rinsed and drained

Approximately 8 cherry tomatoes, cut in half, or a large tomato or two cut into 8 segments

1 carrot, peeled and grated

½ cucumber, thinly sliced

1 pepper, any colour, deseeded & sliced into matchsticks

6 radishes, sliced

½ red onion, thinly sliced, or 1 spring onion, thinly sliced, or some chopped chives

4 Boiled eggs (optional) peeled and cut in half. A dollop of mayo on top of each half and a little chopped parsley

Cheddar cheese cut in matchsticks

METHOD

1. Wash the leaves and rinse to remove any dirt. My preference is using a salad spinner – excellent piece of kitchen equipment!
2. Leave to dry for a while then chop into a large bowl.
3. Put the butter beans and the sweetcorn on top.
4. Add grated carrot, peppers, radishes, cheese matchsticks, then the cherry tomatoes and cucumber. Onions or chives go on top of the lot.
5. Carefully place the eggs round the side. Then put the chopped chives or parsley on top if you wish.
6. Enjoy!

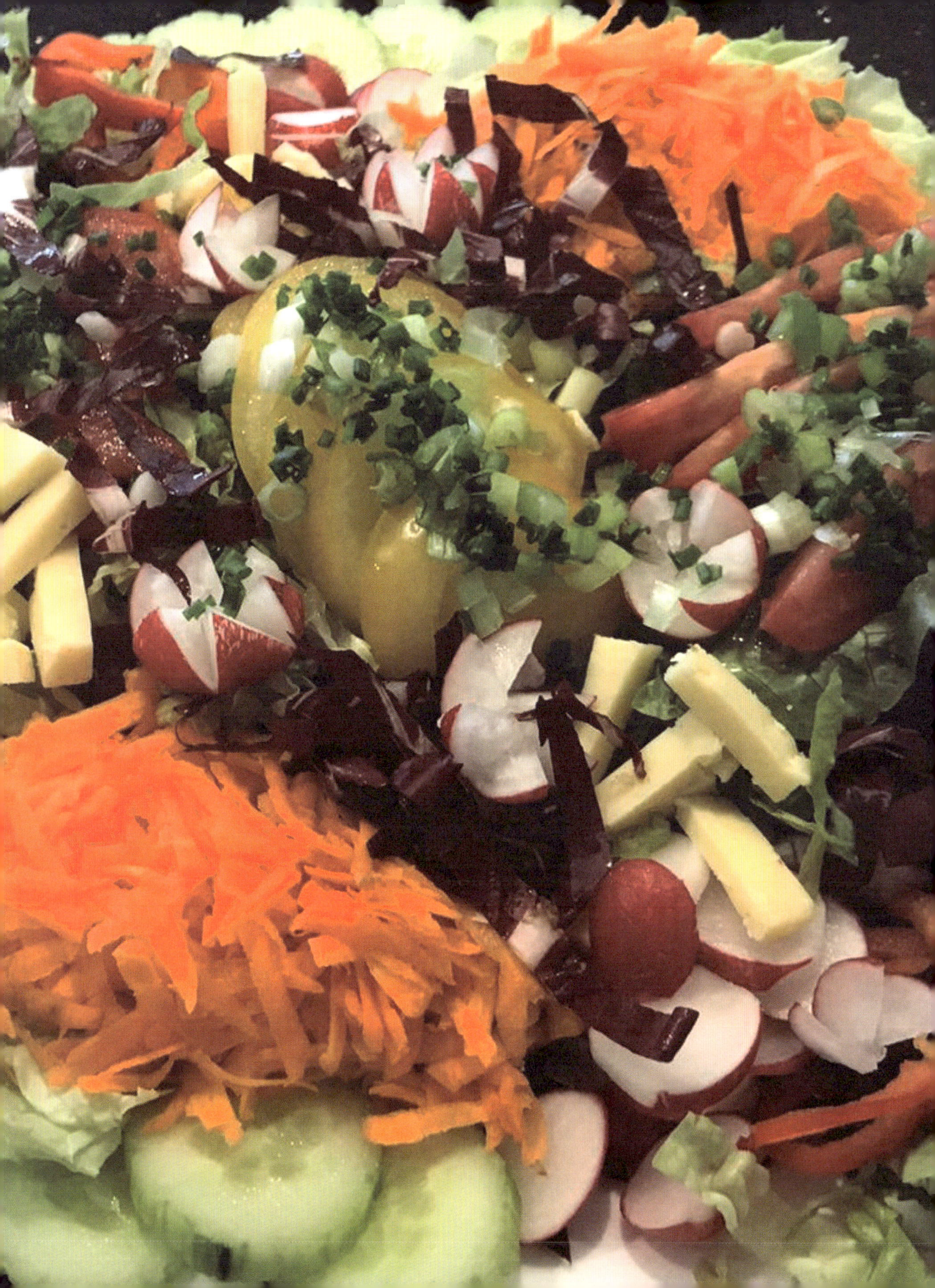

SALADS, SALAD AND MORE SALAD!

Rocket & Mixed Leaves

READY IN 10 MINS   **SERVES 3-4**

I love rocket. It's probably my favourite salad as it's quite peppery and strong in flavour. During my vegetarian days I loved tricolour on a bed of rocket. Watercress also works really well.

INGREDIENTS

Either a bag of rocket, watercress or mixed leaves

10 cherry tomatoes, cut in half, or tomatoes of your choice, cut as you prefer

2 ripe avocados

Basil washed and chopped or left as whole leaves

Fresh black pepper to serve

METHOD

1. Wash the leaves and rinse to remove any dirt. My preference is to use a salad spinner – excellent piece of kitchen equipment!

2. Leave to dry for a while then chop into a large bowl.

3. Add the cherry tomatoes.

4. Cut the avocados. The trick with this is halve them lengthways and remove the stone. Slice each lengthways 3 times then carefully remove the skin and place gently on the salad. If that doesn't go to plan, chop into chunks instead!

5. Then put the chopped basil on top and serve with the dressing of your choice and fresh ground black pepper.

SALADS, SALAD AND MORE SALAD!

Mooli Salad

READY IN 10 MINS

SERVES 3-4

Mooli is a white winter radish. It is milder than its siblings. A common Asian meal accompaniment.

INGREDIENTS

1 mooli

Fresh lemon juice

SPICES

½ teaspoon salt

½ teaspoon garam masala

½ teaspoon black pepper

½ teaspoon paprika

METHOD

1. Peel and grate the mooli.
2. Add the juice of one lemon, salt, garam masala, crack of black pepper and paprika.
3. Give it a good but gentle stir.

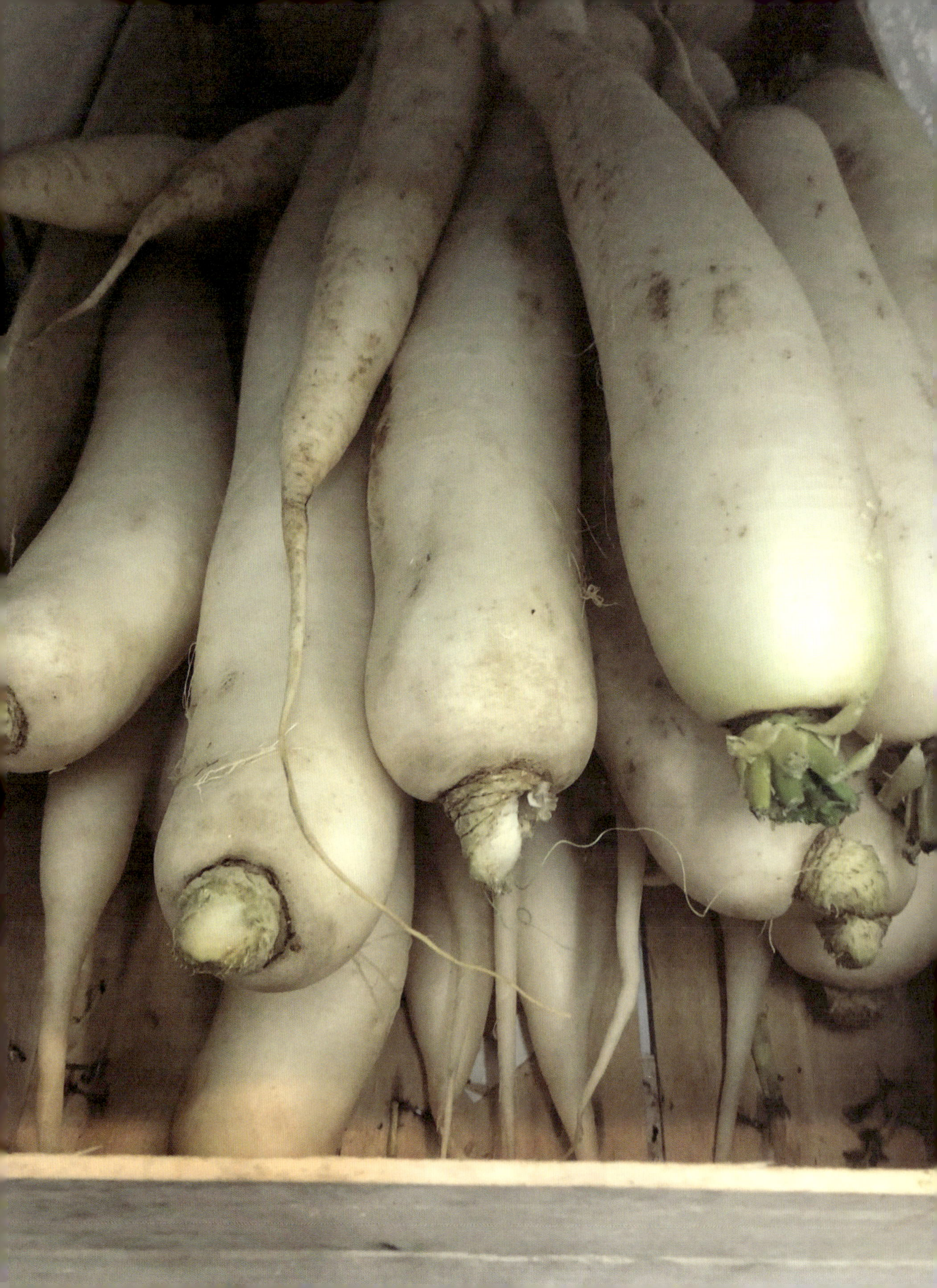

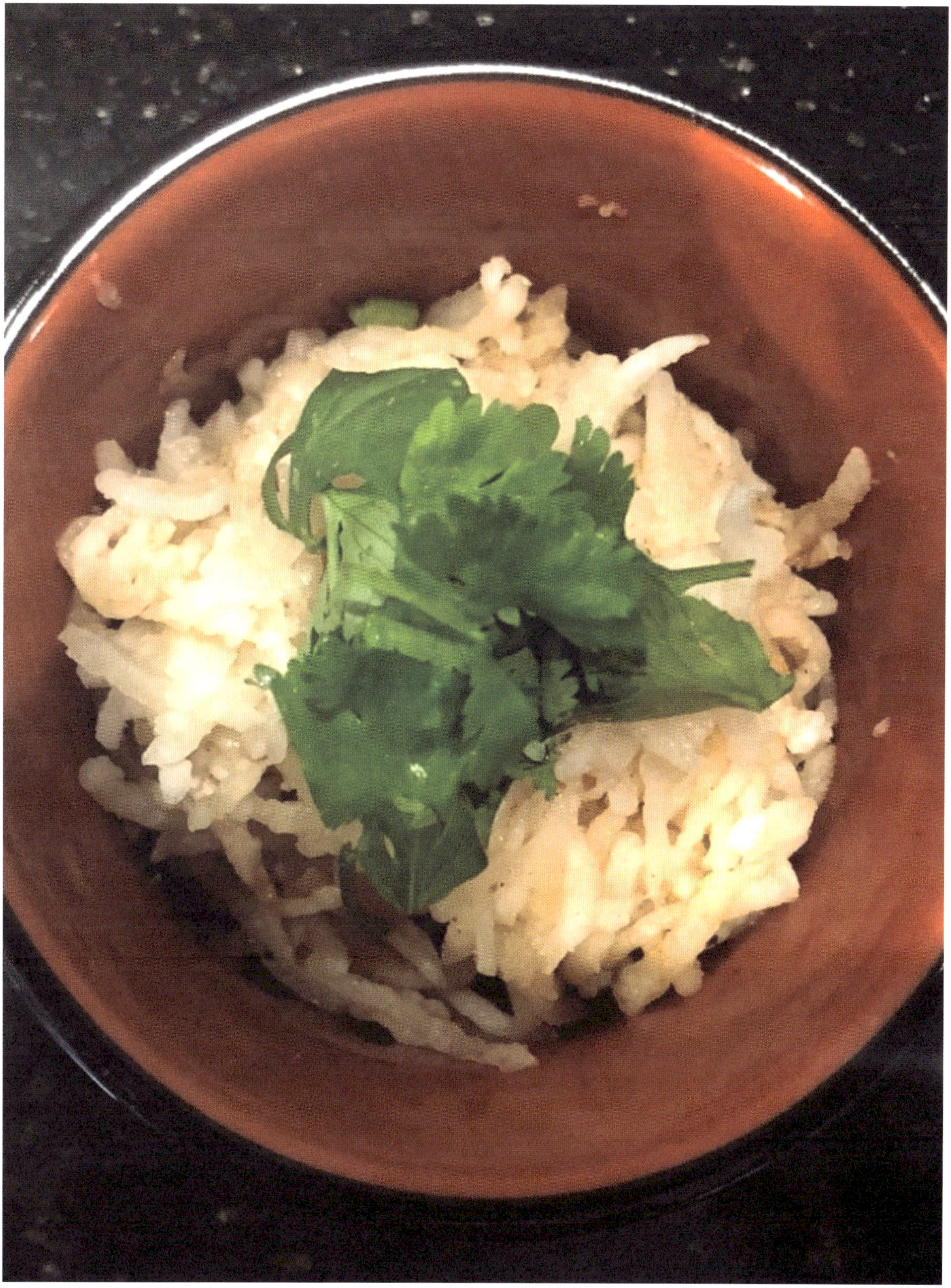

SALADS, SALAD AND MORE SALAD!

INGREDIENTS

1 cucumber

1 red onion

2 tomatoes

1 carrot

1 red pepper

Handful of fresh coriander

½ lemon

SPICES

½ teaspoon salt

½ teaspoon ground black pepper

Chopped Salad

READY IN 15 MINS   **SERVES 3-4**

A chopped salad works really well with an Indian meal. This is Auntie Veena's recipe.

METHOD

1. Wash the cucumber and dice, put it in a large bowl.
2. Skin the red onion, wash and finely chop by hand, add to the bowl.
3. Wash the tomatoes then dice and add to the bowl.
4. Peel and grate the carrot into the bowl.
5. Wash the red pepper, deseed and dice. Add to the bowl.
6. Wash and finely chop the coriander, add to the bowl.
7. Add a sprinkle of salt and a good crack of black pepper.
8. Squeeze ½ a lemon and add the juice to the salad.
9. Give a gentle but good stir to mix up the salad.

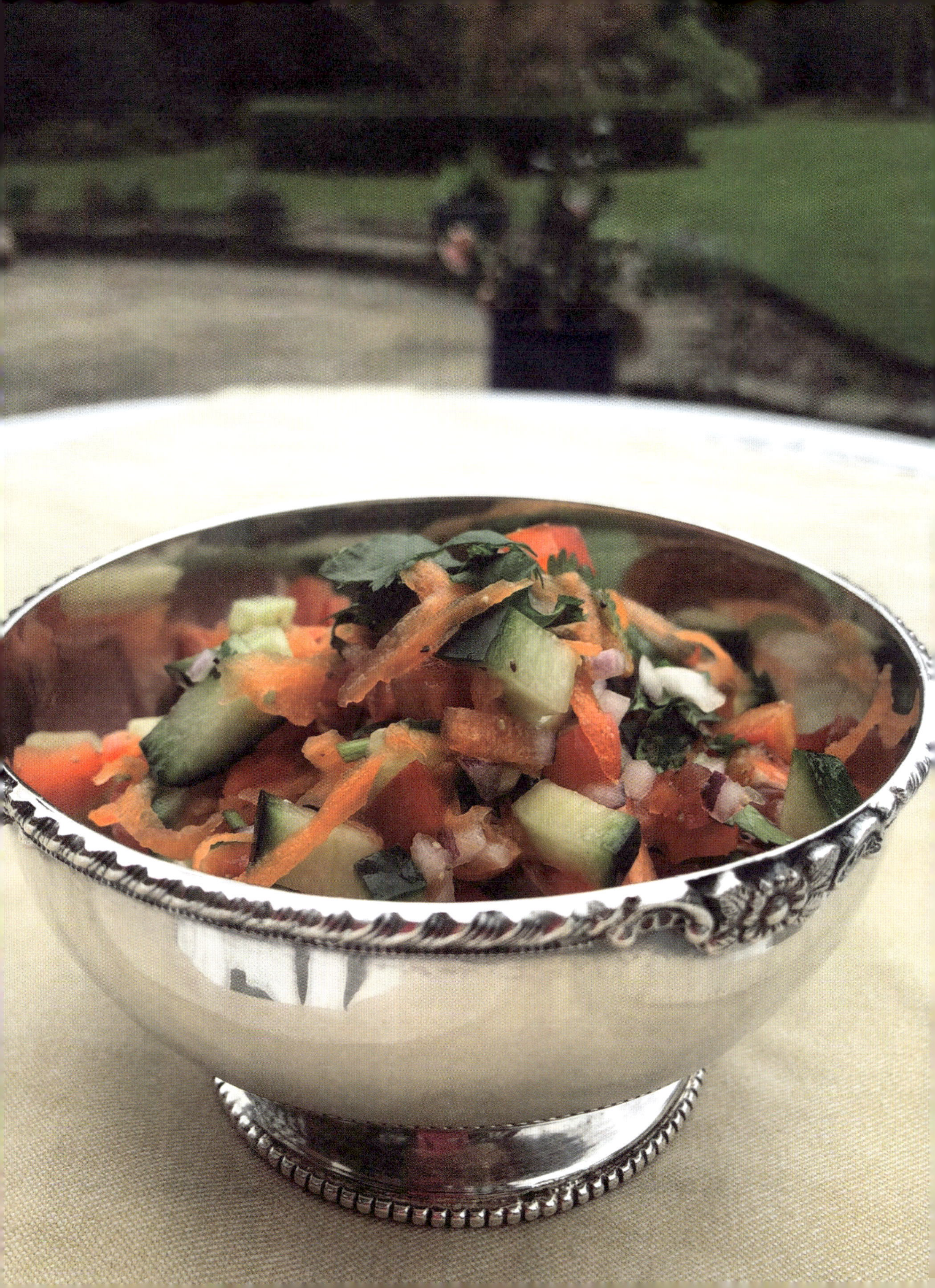

SALADS, SALAD AND MORE SALAD!

Chopped Salad with Paneer

READY IN 15 MINS **SERVES** 3-4

A chopped salad with a little crumbed paneer, tasty! This again is one of Auntie Veena's recipes.

METHOD

1. Wash the cucumber and dice, put it in a large bowl.
2. Skin the red onion, wash and finely chop by hand, add to the bowl.
3. Wash the tomatoes then dice and add to the bowl.
4. Peel and grate the carrot into the bowl.
5. Wash the red pepper, deseed and dice. Add to the bowl.
6. Wash and finely chop the coriander, add to the bowl.
7. Drain the paneer from the packet, dice and add to the bowl. This will mash up slightly when you stir it due to the texture.
8. Deseed and finely chop the green chilli.
9. Add salt and pepper, the juice of ½ lemon and the chopped chilli.
10. Give a gentle but good stir to mix up the salad.

INGREDIENTS

1 cucumber

1 red onion

2 tomatoes

1 carrot

1 red pepper

A handful of fresh coriander

125g paneer

½ lemon

1 green chilli

SPICES

½ teaspoon salt

½ teaspoon ground black pepper

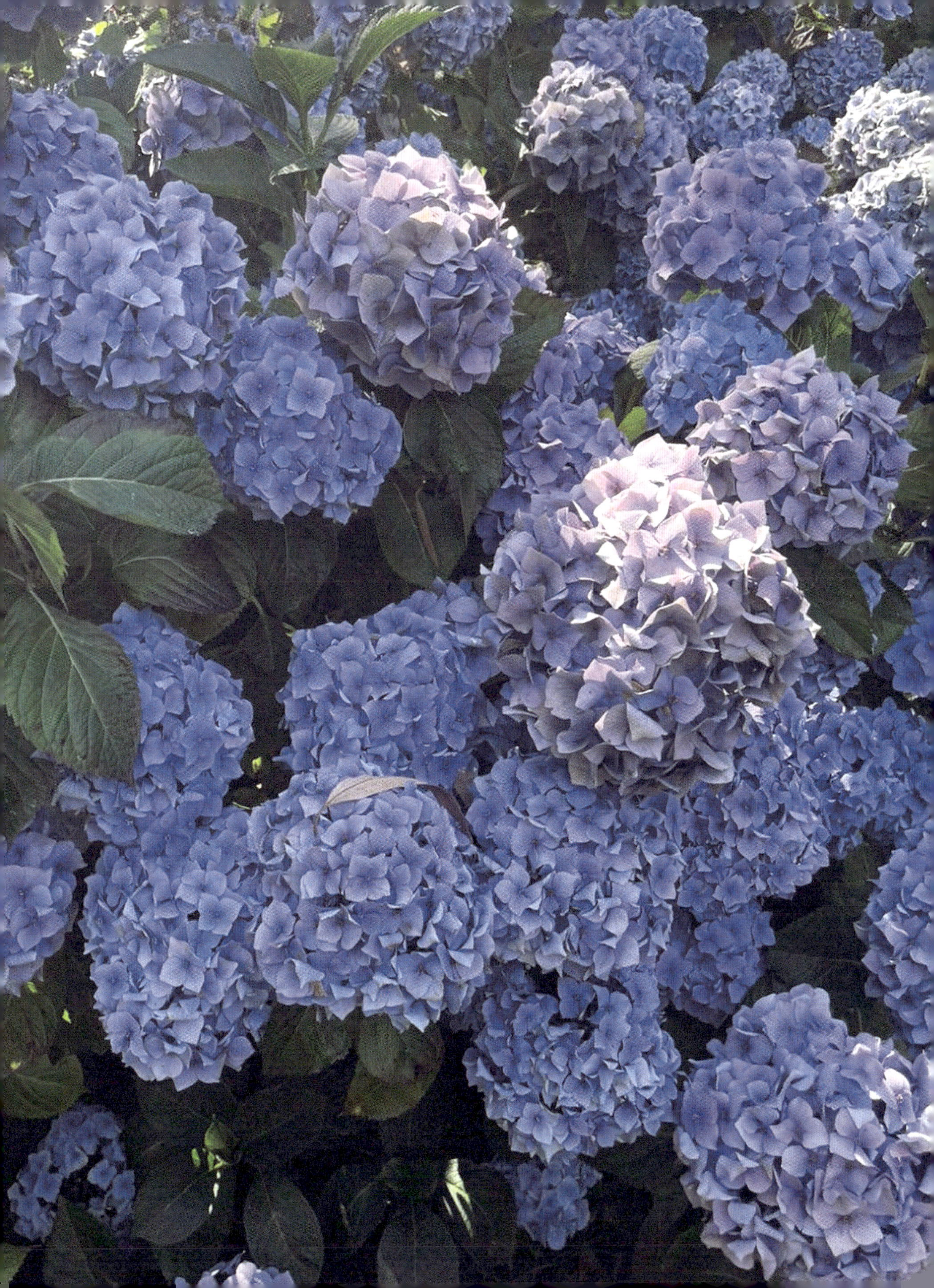

SALADS, SALAD AND MORE SALAD!

Chopped Salad with Tofu

READY IN 15 MINS

SERVES 3-4

Traditionally, a chopped salad is an accompaniment to an Indian meal. However, this is such a lovely salad, I'll happily eat it for lunch with a handful of salad leaves and a slice of sourdough! I like it best with smoked tofu.

METHOD

1. Wash the cucumber and dice, put it in a large bowl.
2. Skin the red onion, wash and finely chop by hand, add to the bowl.
3. Wash the tomatoes then dice and add to the bowl.
4. Peel and grate the carrot into the bowl.
5. Wash the red pepper, deseed and dice. Add to the bowl.
6. Wash and finely chop the coriander, add to the bowl.
7. Drain the tofu from the packet, dice and add to the bowl.
8. Deseed and finely chop the green chilli.
9. Add salt and pepper, the juice of ½ lemon and the chopped chilli.
10. Give a gentle but good stir to mix up the salad.

INGREDIENTS

1 cucumber

1 red onion

2 tomatoes

1 carrot

1 red pepper

2 handfuls of fresh coriander

225g smoked (or plain) tofu

½ lemon

1 green chilli

SPICES

1 ½ teaspoons salt

1 ½ teaspoons ground black pepper

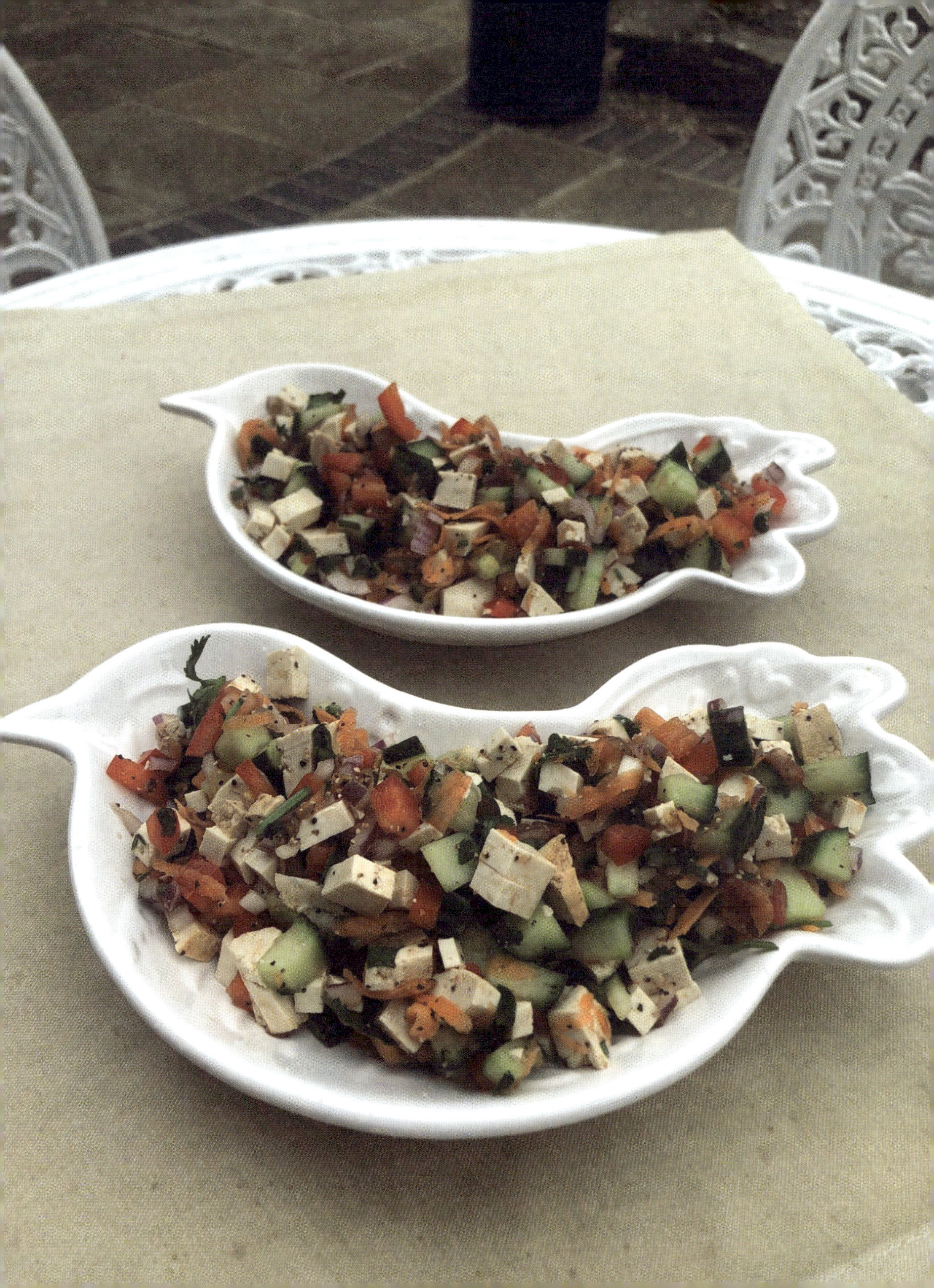

SALADS, SALAD AND MORE SALAD!

Onion Salad

READY IN 15 MINS

SERVES 3-4

A simple onion salad is a common accompaniment to an Indian meal. Strong in flavour and simple to make, a beautiful "pink" salad!

INGREDIENTS

1 small red onion

1 small white onion

Handful of fresh coriander

1 lemon

SPICES

½ teaspoon salt

½ teaspoon coarse ground black pepper

METHOD

1. Peel and wash both onions. Finely chop in a mini chopper, food processor or by hand, then put the onions in a large bowl.

2. Wash and finely chop the fresh coriander, add to the bowl.

3. Squeeze a lemon over this, sprinkle with salt and ground black pepper, give a gentle but good stir and serve.

Note: This will store in the fridge for a few hours, up to 24 hours; however, make sure it's in an airtight container or covered with cling film as it has a potent aroma!

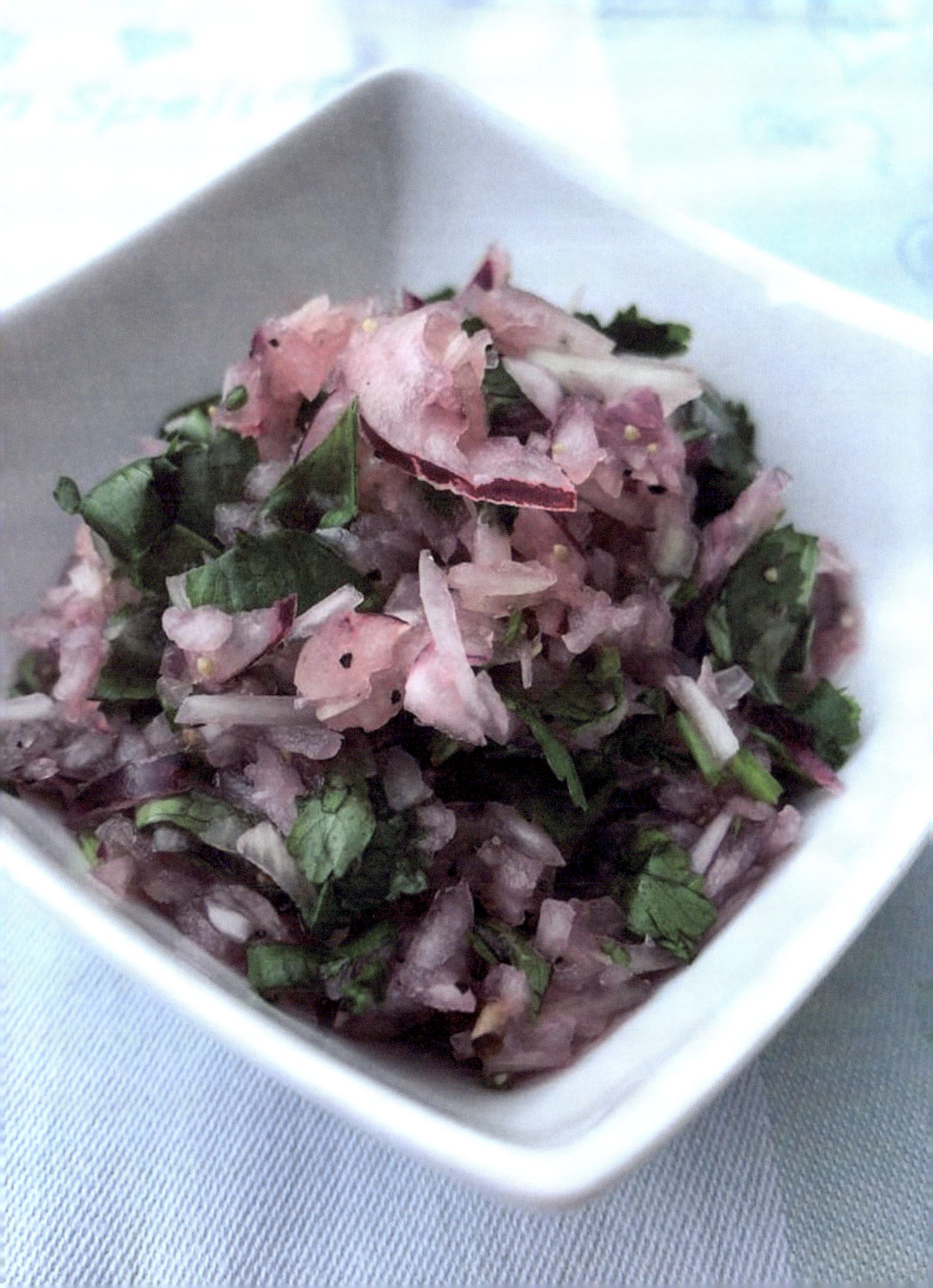

SALADS, SALAD AND MORE SALAD!

INGREDIENTS

1 cucumber

½ lemon

SPICES

½ teaspoon salt

½ teaspoon coarse ground black pepper

½ teaspoon chilli powder

½ teaspoon garam masala

Cucumber Salad

READY IN
15 MINS

SERVES
3-4

A classic salad, again very easy and quick to make. The fresh flavour can be cooling with a spicy curry.

METHOD

1. Wash and dry the cucumber. If you prefer the skin off, then peel it too.

2. Into a bowl, dice the cucumber into little squares or thinly slice if you prefer.

3. Add the salt, pepper, chilli powder, garam masala, a squeeze of lemon juice and give a gentle stir.

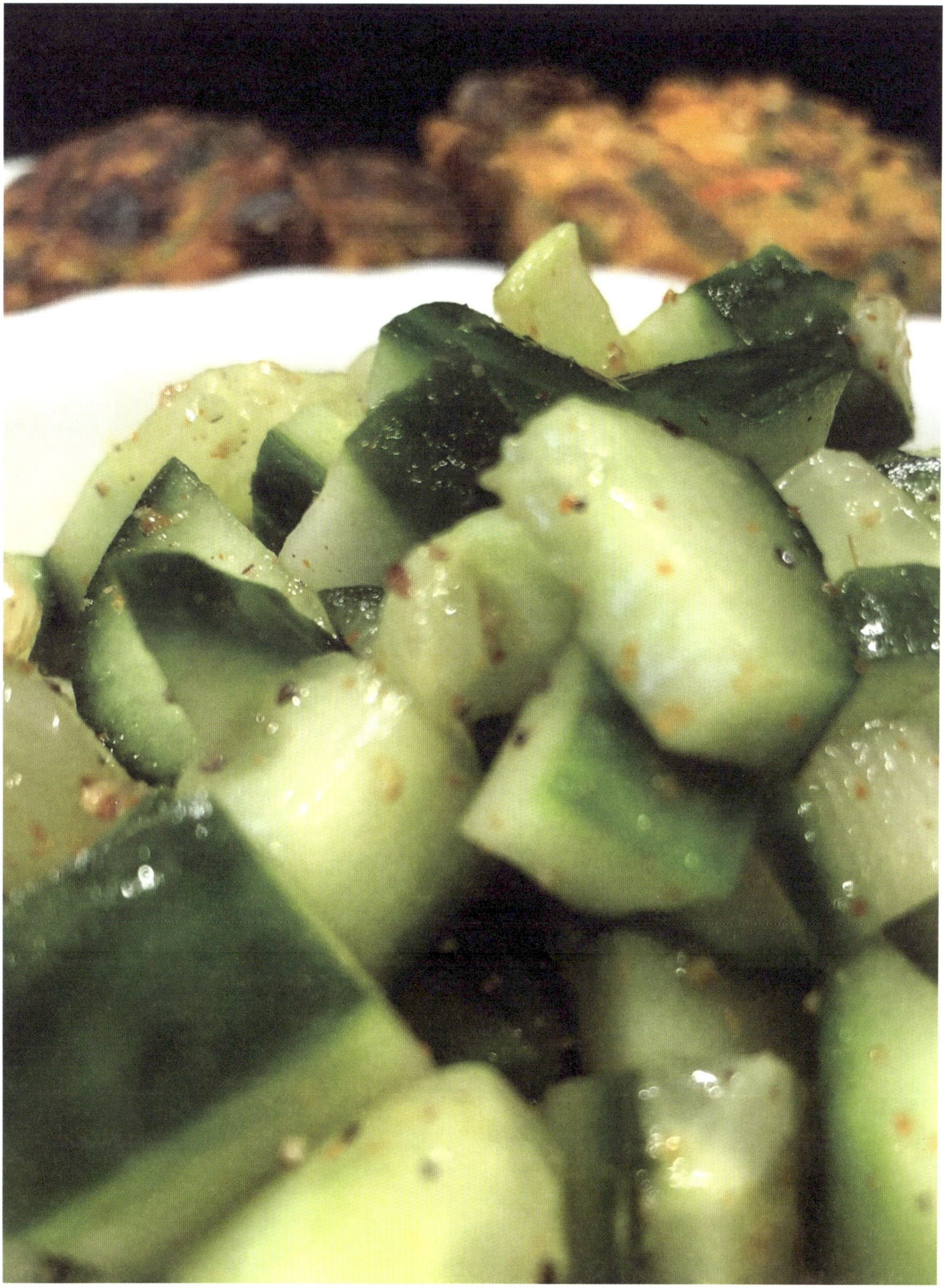

SALADS, SALAD AND MORE SALAD!

Junior Swiss Miss Salad Dressing

READY IN 5 MINS

MAKES 1 JAR

My mum is the salad queen and her dressing is highly sought after! She will happily make you a bottle but will not share her secret Swiss Miss Salad Sauce recipe with anyone.

I have developed my own salad dressing, clearly not as good as hers but I hope a close second! Once made will go in a jar in the fridge and store for about a week.

INGREDIENTS

- 10 tablespoons sunflower oil
- 5 tablespoons balsamic vinegar
- 1 teaspoon mild mustard
- 1 tablespoon mayo / vegan mayo

SPICES

- Pinch of salt
- Pinch of chilli flakes

METHOD

1. Add all of the ingredients to a jug, whisk until the mixture is smooth and creamy.
2. Decant into a bottle.
3. Store in the fridge, will last for about 7 days.
4. Shake before serving.

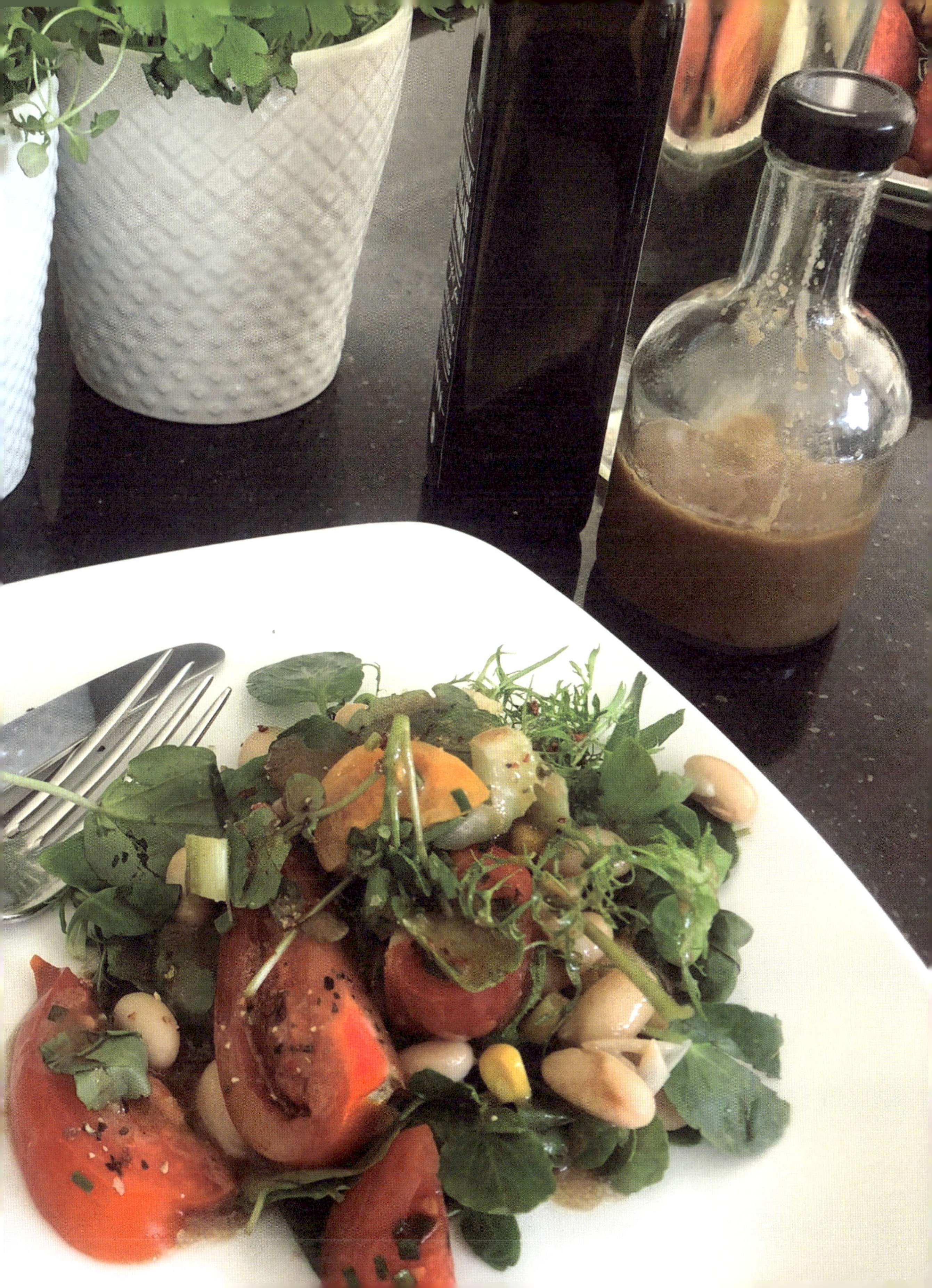

SALADS, SALAD AND MORE SALAD!

Asian Slaw

READY IN 25 MINS

SERVES 4-6

This is a fresh and tasty alternative to coleslaw. You can hand chop it all; however, if you use the slicing blade and grating blades in your food processor, it will take no time at all!

METHOD

1. Remove the outer leaves of the cabbage and discard. Finely chop the cabbage, red pepper and the red onion into a bowl.
2. Peel and grate the carrot into it.
3. Zest and squeeze the lime into the bowl, chop the chilli and add a tablespoon of sesame seeds.
4. Season with salt and pepper to taste.
5. Give it a good mix.

INGREDIENTS

1 pointed / sweetheart cabbage

1 red pepper

3 carrots

1 lime

½ red onion

1 red chilli

1 tablespoon sesame seeds

SPICES

Salt and pepper

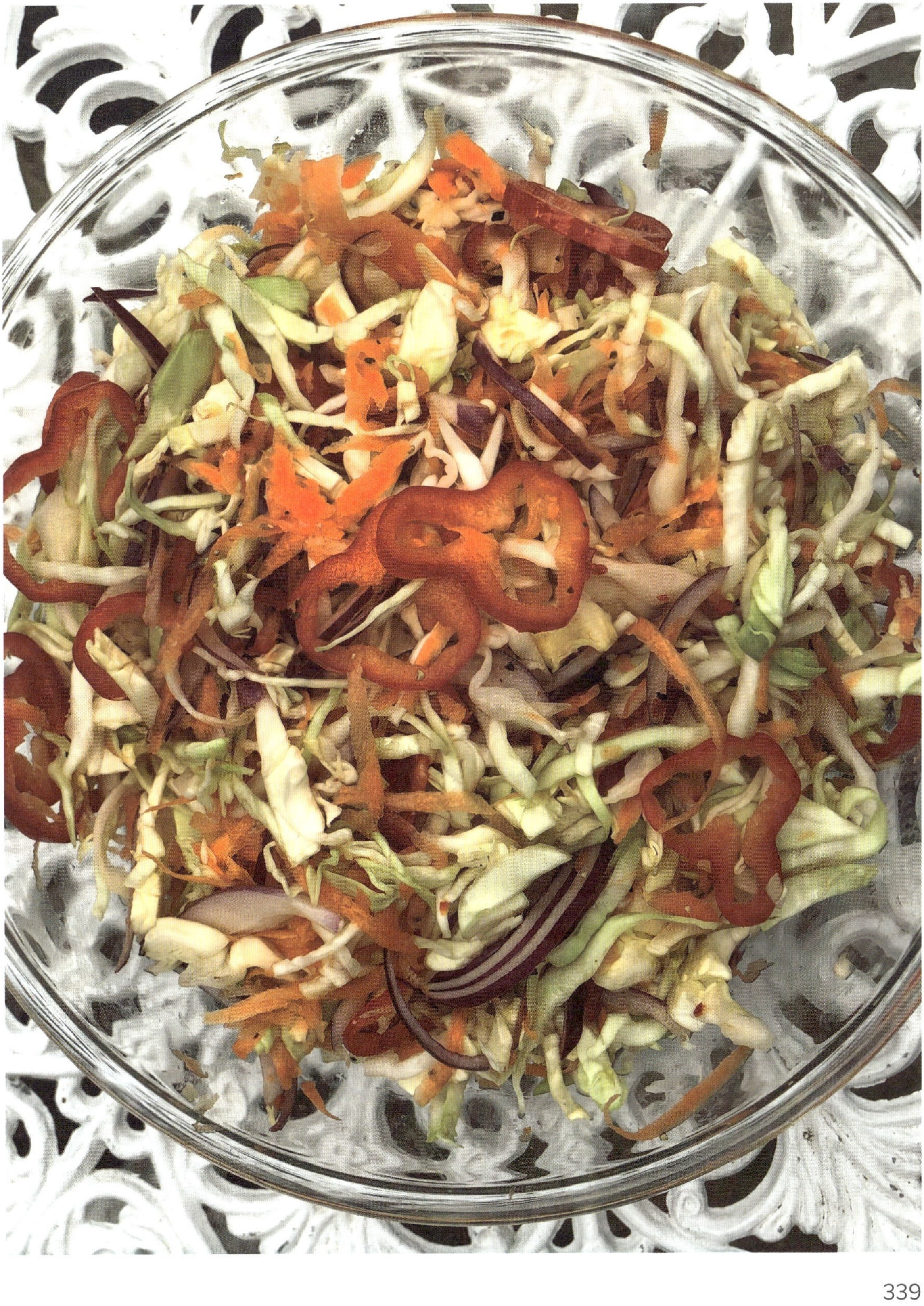

SALADS, SALAD AND MORE SALAD!

Riverford Coleslaw

READY IN 25 MINS **SERVES 4-6**

A good slaw goes well with a barbecue, fantastic with a salad or great in the fridge to snack on or add to a sandwich. This recipe was kindly given to me by someone we met at the Riverford shop on one of our many trips down to Devon. Indian Nanny used to go on holiday down there in the 70s and we followed her path from 2010 onwards.

Now in true West Country style there are no measurements, so you can make as much or as little as you like! It will drive one of my friends mad as he likes everything weighed!

INGREDIENTS

⅔ white cabbage – sweetheart is my favourite

⅓ red cabbage

A good amount of carrots (peeled)

Red onion, peeled & finely sliced

A good handful of fresh parsley or coriander or basil, washed and chopped

Squeeze of lemon

A good quality mayonnaise (vegan or standard)

SPICES

Salt and pepper

Chilli flakes (if required to spice it up!)

METHOD

1. Using the food processor slicing blade, slice both the white and red cabbage. Add to a large bowl. Then using the grating tool, grate the carrots and add to the bowl. Then using the chopping blade, finely chop the red onion and add to the bowl. Finally chop the herbs and add to the bowl.

2. Add a good squeeze of lemon, salt and pepper as well as a few large spoons of mayo.

3. Give it a gentle but good stir using a silicon spoon or equivalent.

4. Add more mayo, salt, pepper or chilli flakes to taste.

Note about mayo – the gentleman that gave me this recipe suggested that a good quality organic mayo is vital, he suggested "Ladylay". If you are lucky enough to be able to get Swiss "Tomy" that's Mum's favourite, or if you are like me, a good quality vegan mayo is really good (or you can make your own which is much easier than you think!)

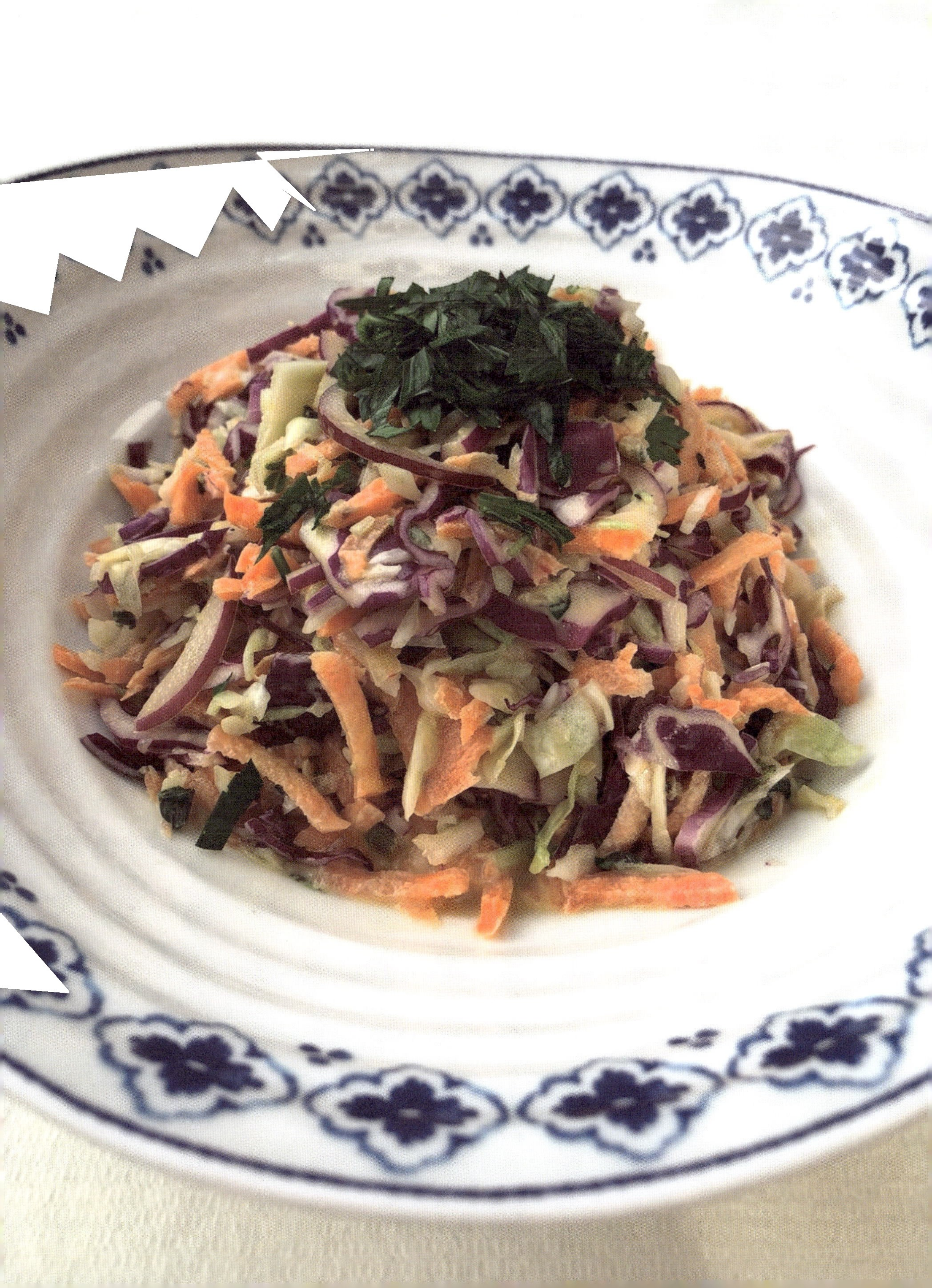

CARAVAN RULES
stay up late! BBQ's
Wake up smiling!
Look at the Stars
Have a drink or two! Make Memories!

Stokes

VISITOR CENTRE

78
BOBBY'S
Spirals
39p
PRAWN COCKTAIL
Spirals
39p

343

For BBQ tomo

Please don't eat!

x 1 John
x 2 Ernest
x 1 nan
x 1 Jude

→ rest for BBQ

DESSERTS

PLEASE KEEP A SAFE DISTANCE O
KEEP A SAFE DISTANCE OF 2 METRES

LITTLE CHEFS LOCKDOWN DESSERTS

During the 2020 coronavirus lockdown (number 1), my Auntie Rita kindly put on some Zoom cooking lessons for the children. The first one was the delicious aloo tikka recipe in the starter & snacks section of this cookbook. She then let the children choose, well, you guessed it – the lessons quickly turned to desserts!! We learnt all sorts.

This part of the book is dedicated to all the children for whom the lockdown will now form part of their childhood in efforts to protect the nation from this virus.

Thank you, little cousins!

DESSERTS

Chocolate Cake

Chosen by Mia

READY IN
1 HOUR

SERVES
6-8

INGREDIENTS

125g self-raising flour

200g caster sugar

65g cocoa powder

¾ teaspoon baking powder

½ teaspoon bicarbonate of soda

1 egg

60ml vegetable oil

1 tablespoon vanilla essence

125ml milk

125ml warm water

200g milk or dark chocolate

200ml double cream

You will need an 8-inch cake tin

This is Milly's special chocolate cake recipe.

METHOD

1. Preheat the oven to 160°C fan. Grease and line your cake tin.

2. Mix the flour, sugar, cocoa powder, baking powder and bicarbonate of soda together in a large bowl.

3. Then beat in the egg, oil, vanilla essence and milk. Beat for a good few minutes to ensure you have put air into the mixture. This will help it to taste light and fluffy. Then mix in the warm water gradually.

4. Transfer the mixture into the cake tin.

5. Bake in the oven for 30-40 minutes. Check the cake is cooked by inserting a knife into the centre and if it comes out clean the cake is ready. If the knife is not clean, leave it for a little longer until cooked.

6. Leave the cake to cool, then remove from the cake tin.

7. Once cooled – melt the chocolate in a microwave, remove and gently add the cream. Mix together well, then cover the cake with the chocolate cream. You can add any decorations if you wish.

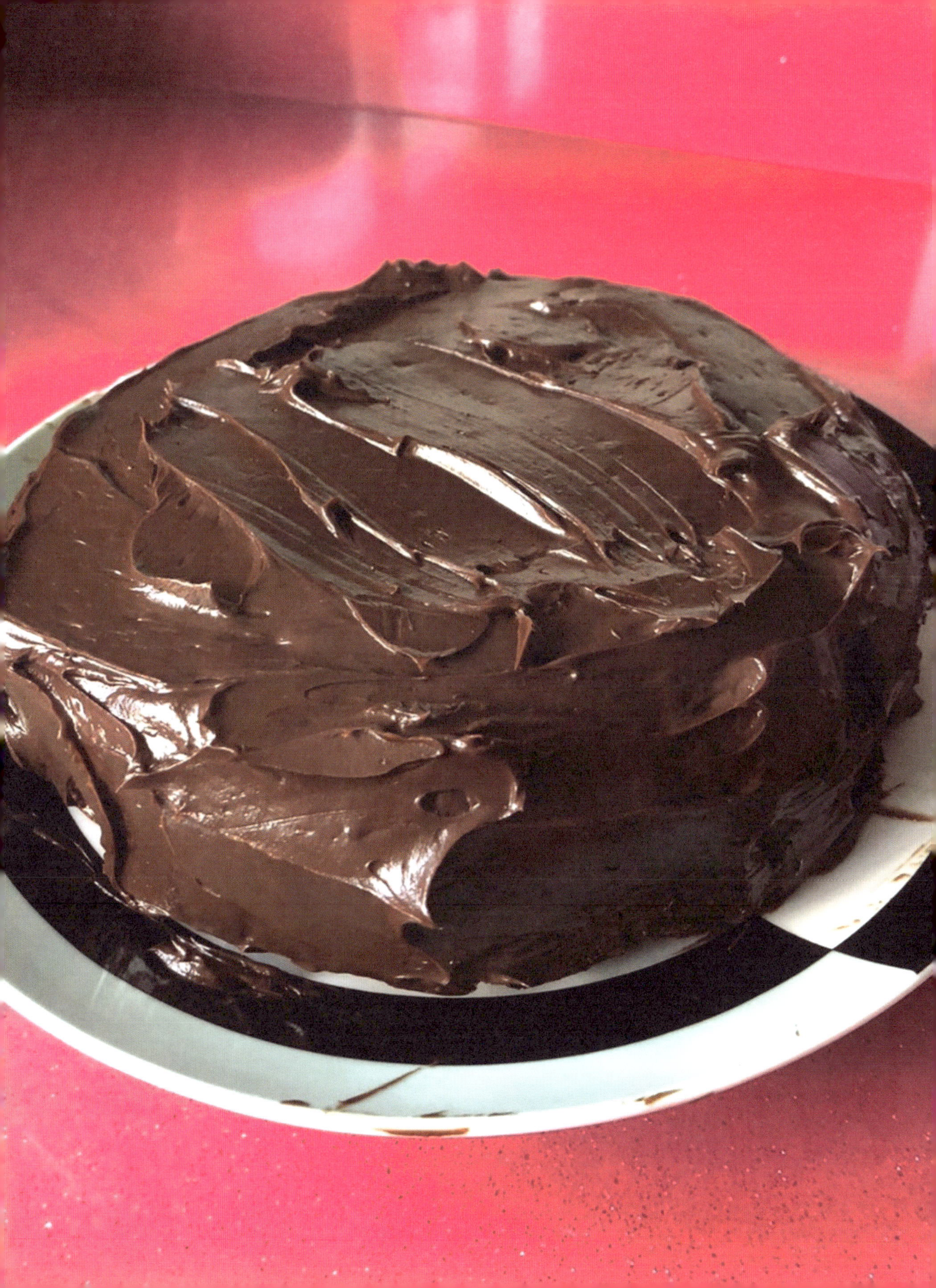

DESSERTS

Soft Cookies

Chosen by Micah

READY IN
40 MINS

MAKES
10 COOKIES

INGREDIENTS

150g salted butter

90g light brown sugar

90g caster sugar

1 tablespoon vanilla extract or orange extract

1 large egg

225g plain flour

½ teaspoon bicarbonate of soda

200g milk chocolate chips

METHOD

1. Preheat the oven to 180°C fan and line two baking trays with non-stick baking paper.

2. Put 150g softened salted butter, 90g light brown sugar and 90g caster sugar into a bowl and mix until creamy.

3. Mix in 1 tablespoon vanilla / orange extract and 1 large egg.

4. Sift 225g plain flour and ½ teaspoon bicarbonate of soda into the bowl and mix them together with a wooden spoon.

5. Add 200g milk chocolate chips and stir well.

6. Use an ice cream scoop or tablespoon to make balls of the cookie dough (this will create a cookie with a very soft centre), spacing them well apart on the baking trays. The mixture should make about 10 cookies.

7. Bake for 10-15 minutes until they are golden brown on their edges and soft in the centre.

8. Leave on the tray for a couple of minutes to set and then lift onto a cooling rack.

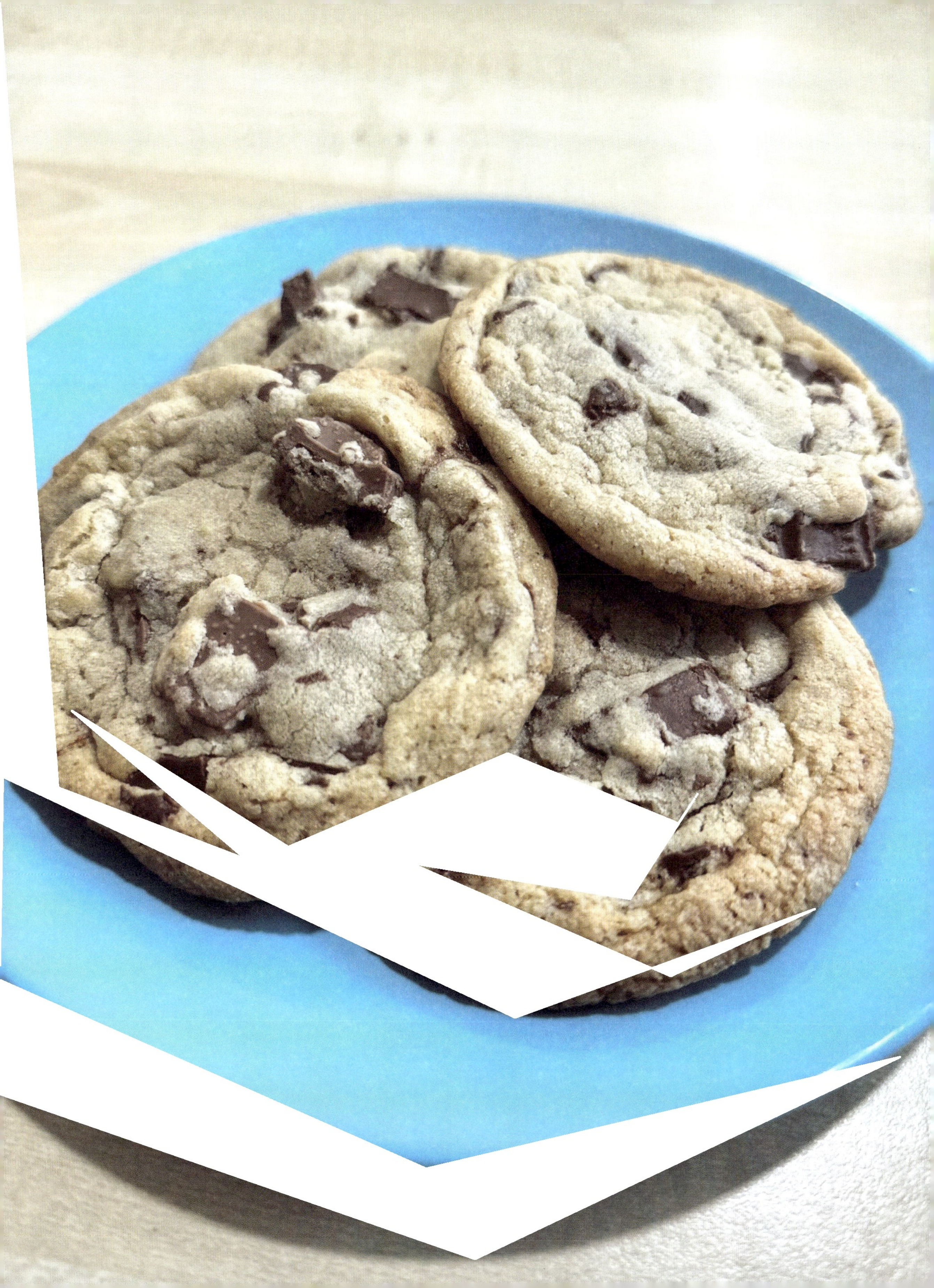

DESSERTS

Auntie Essie's Flapjacks

Chosen by Jude

READY IN 25 MINS

MAKES 9 FLAPJACKS

INGREDIENTS

Half a pack of butter (125g)

1 cup sugar

2 tablespoons golden syrup

2 ½ cups porridge oats

Pinch of salt

You will need a shallow sided baking tin lined with greaseproof paper

METHOD

1. Preheat oven to 180°C fan.
2. Gently melt half a pack of butter in a pan with 1 cup sugar and 2 tablespoons golden syrup.
3. Take off heat for 5 minutes.
4. Mix in 2 ½ cups porridge oats and a pinch of salt.
5. Pop mix into small, lined baking tin.
6. Cook in the oven for 12-15 minutes until the edges are slightly browner than the rest.

Allow to cool, cut into squares and demolish!

You can add chocolate chips, remove the golden syrup if you prefer

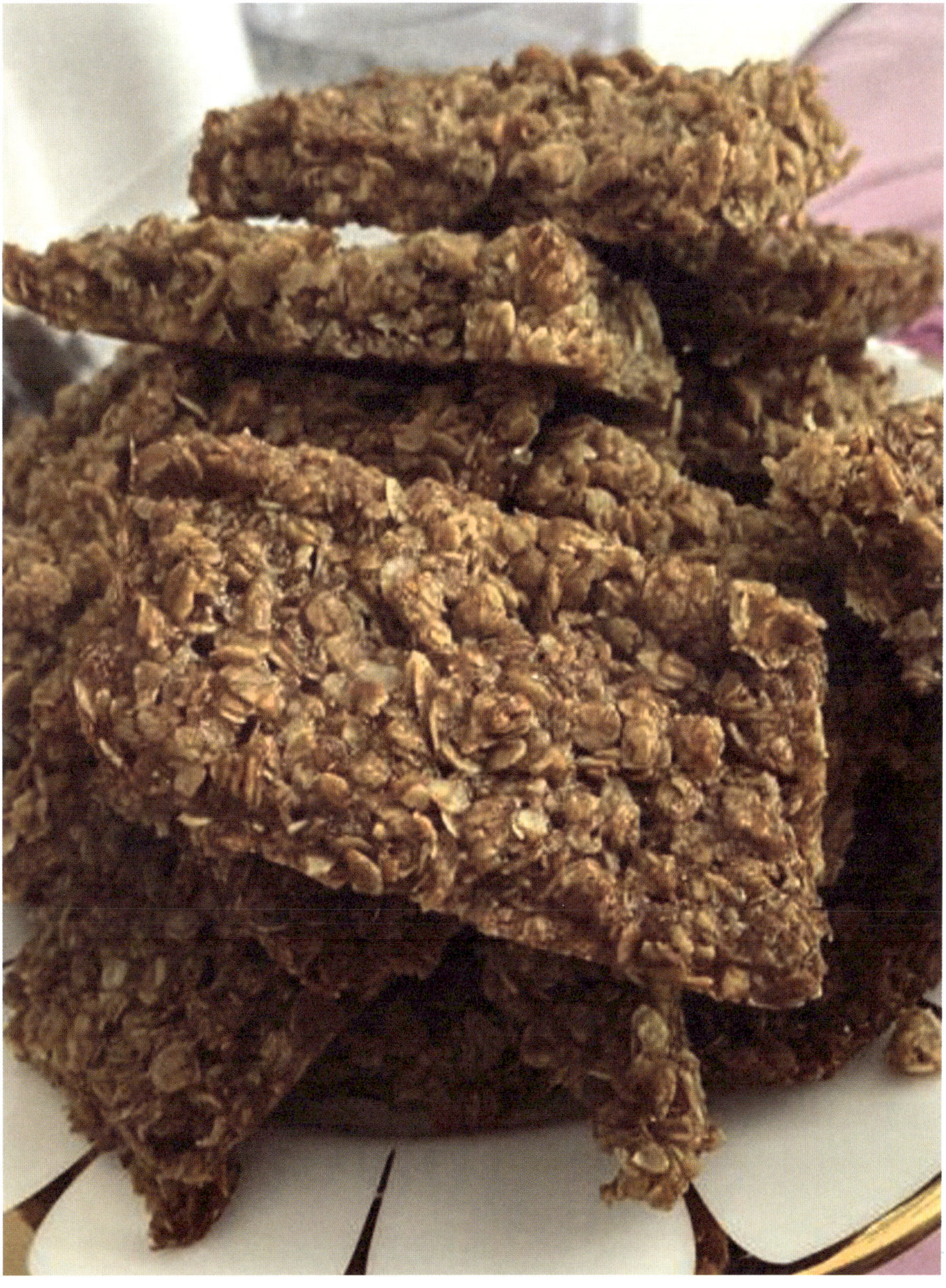

DESSERTS

Brownies

Chosen by Micah

READY IN
40 MINS

MAKES
9 BROWNIES

Hugo loves these!

INGREDIENTS

100g butter, cubed

200g milk chocolate, broken into pieces

4 eggs

250g caster sugar

100g plain flour

1 tablespoon baking powder

35g cocoa powder

100g white or milk chocolate chips

METHOD

1. Preheat the oven to 160°C fan.
2. Grease and line the tin with baking paper.
3. In a bowl, melt the butter and chocolate together in the microwave or over a pan of simmering water. Cool to room temperature.
4. In another large bowl, whisk the eggs and sugar together until the mixture is light and fluffy.
5. Add the chocolate mixture into the egg mixture and sift in the flour, baking powder and cocoa powder.
6. Give it a good but gentle stir to make a thick but smooth batter that is evenly blended.
7. Stir in the chocolate chips.
8. Bake for 25-30 minutes or until the top is cracked but the middle just set. Remove from the oven.
9. Cool completely. Then cut into 9 brownies while in the tin and remove. Or if you are like Milly, just cut straight away because you cannot contain your excitement!

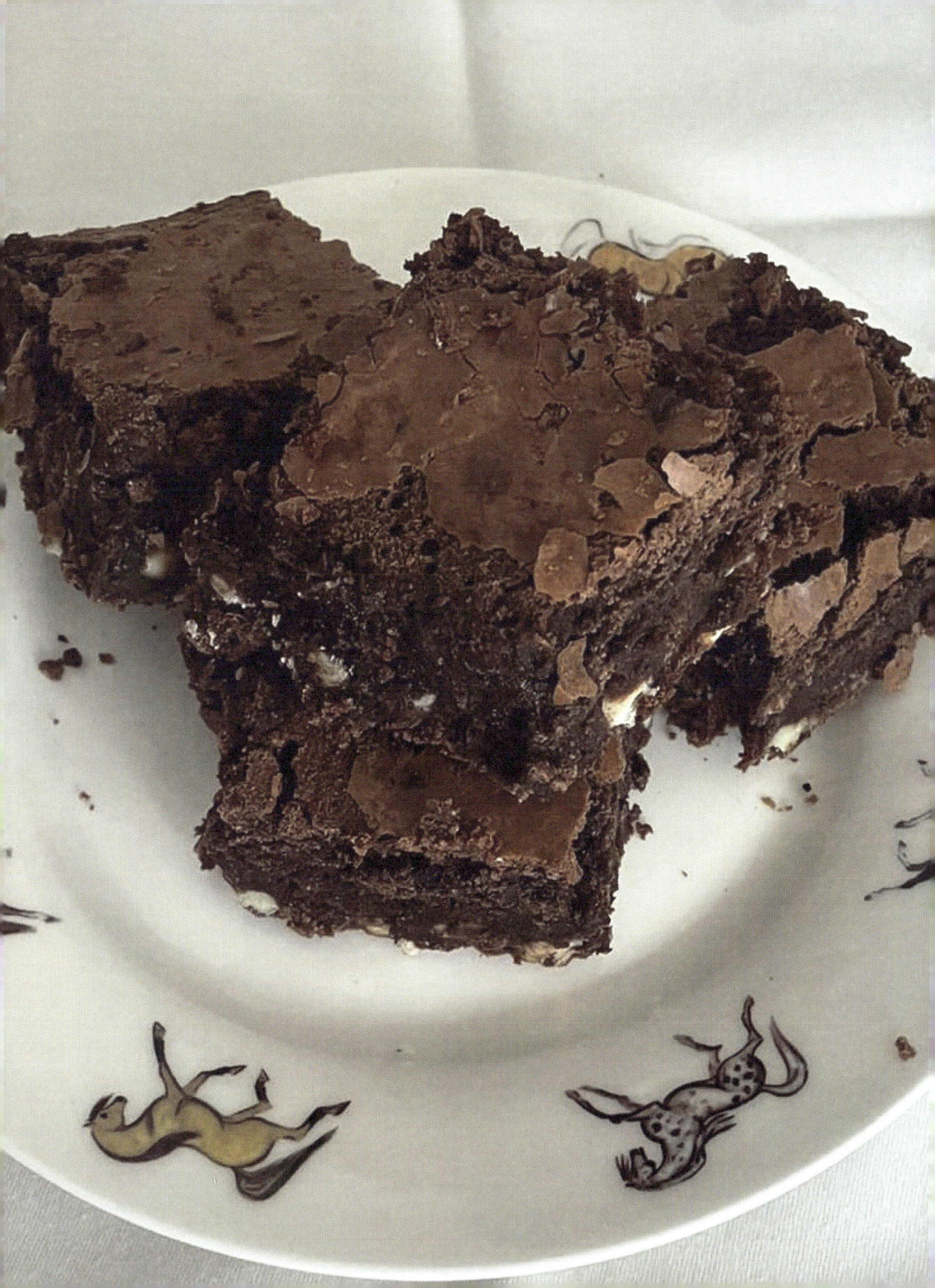

DESSERTS

Ginger Biscuits

Chosen by Saskia *(she wanted a gingerbread house but limitations on Zoom!!)*

READY IN **40 MINS**

MAKES **20-30**

INGREDIENTS

375g plain flour

1 teaspoon bicarbonate of soda

3 teaspoons ground ginger

120g unsalted butter (cold & cubed)

175g light brown sugar

5 tablespoons golden syrup

1 large egg

You will also need a cookie cutter, icing pen and any decorations you would like to use

METHOD

1. Preheat your oven to 180°C fan and line 3-4 baking trays with baking paper (or do it in two batches if you only have two trays).

2. In a large bowl, add the flour, bicarbonate of soda and ginger, then add the cold, cubed butter to the bowl.

3. Rub together with your fingers until it resembles breadcrumbs.

4. Add the sugar into the mixture, then add the golden syrup and the egg – mix with a spatula until it forms a smooth dough.

5. Knead the dough with your hands and then roll the dough out ½cm thick onto a lightly floured work surface.

6. Using your cookie cutter, cut out your desired shapes.

7. Place them on the lined baking trays and bake in the oven for about 10 minutes, cool on a wire rack fully and then decorate how you please!

You can use this recipe to make a gingerbread house; templates are available online. Use icing sugar and egg white mixed together to join the sides and of course any decorations you wish.

357

DESSERTS

Doughnuts

Chosen by Mia

READY IN
40 MINS
+ PROVING

MAKES AT LEAST
8

INGREDIENTS

300g flour

1 tablespoon dried yeast

2 tablespoons warm milk

2 eggs

2 tablespoons icing sugar

50g butter

1 teaspoon vanilla essence

¼ teaspoon salt

Oil to deep fry

2 tablespoons caster sugar for the coating and cinnamon powder if you want this flavour

You will also need a cookie cutter or lid to make the shape and a second smaller cutter – both round

Rolling pin and some extra flour for rolling out

METHOD

1. Sift the flour into a large bowl and make a little well in the middle. Put the yeast into the well and add a couple of tablespoons of the warm milk. Leave for about 5 minutes.

2. In another bowl, beat the eggs lightly, then add them with the icing sugar, butter, vanilla essence and salt to the flour mixture. Mix together until the dough starts leaving the sides of the bowl and the dough looks glossy. Cover the dough with cling film and leave it to prove for an hour.

3. After an hour, make small balls of equal size from the dough. Using a rolling pin, roll out each dough ball to about 1cm in thickness. With a round cookie cutter or small round lid cut out circles from the dough. Then cut out smaller circles in the middle to make a ring doughnut shape.

4. Using a heavy based pan, half fill it with oil and heat. Meanwhile place the caster sugar and cinnamon on a plate or into a bowl for the coating. When the oil is hot, place the doughnuts one at a time into the hot oil and turn fairly quickly. When they are golden brown remove and put them straight into the caster sugar coating on each side.

5. Enjoy!

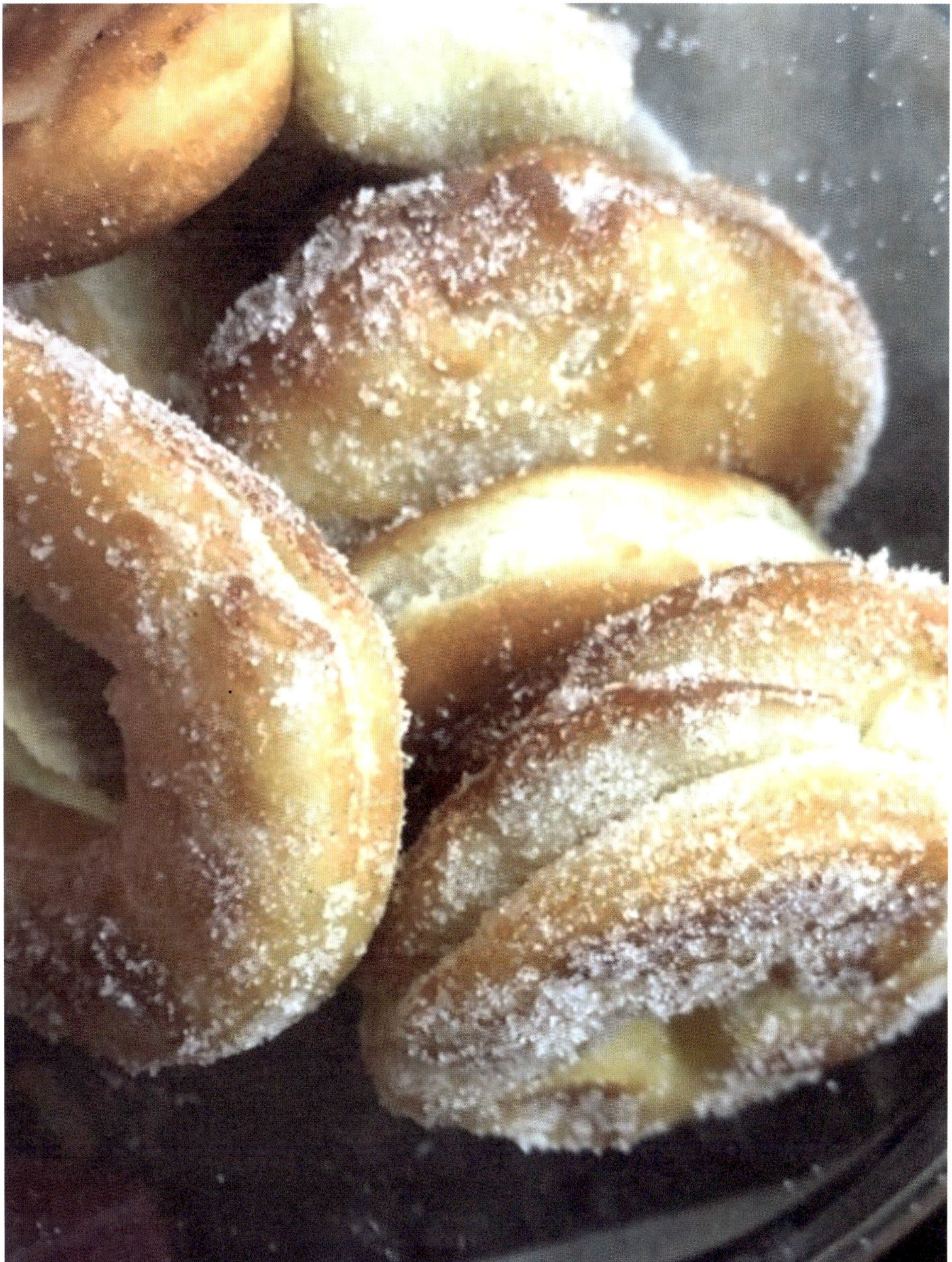

DESSERTS

Jelly & Ice Cream

READY IN
25 MINS
+ FREEZING
& SETTING

SERVES
4

It was Jude's week to choose and he chose jelly! So, Rita showed them how to make a jelly and ice cream dessert. Home-made ice cream is surprisingly easy to make and tastes awesome.

INGREDIENTS

Packet of Jelly

For the chocolate ice cream:

1 can (400g) sweetened condensed milk

3 tablespoons cocoa powder or icing sugar

1 teaspoon vanilla extract

1 litre double cream

200g chocolate chips and little bit extra if you want some for the topping

Tinned or fresh fruit (optional)

Little chefs will need individual moulds for the jelly & a container with lid for freezing the ice cream.

METHOD

1. Follow the jelly instructions on the back of the packet, pour into your moulds and put in the fridge to set.

2. Into a large bowl, put the cream, cocoa powder and vanilla extract. Using a food processor on high speed, whisk the mixture into soft peaks; this should take a few minutes. Melt the chocolate chips and set to one side. Fold the condensed milk into the mixture and then whisk again. At this point, add the melted chocolate chips or any other flavouring.

3. Place into an airtight container and freeze for a minimum of 8 hours.

4. When ready to serve, remove the jelly from the fridge, add a large scoop of ice cream from the freezer and some fruit topping.

Notes – If you prefer to make a different flavoured ice cream, it is simple to find out what you need to do this.

If you want a more intense flavour of chocolate, you will need an extra 200g chocolate, this will be melted and added to the ice cream.

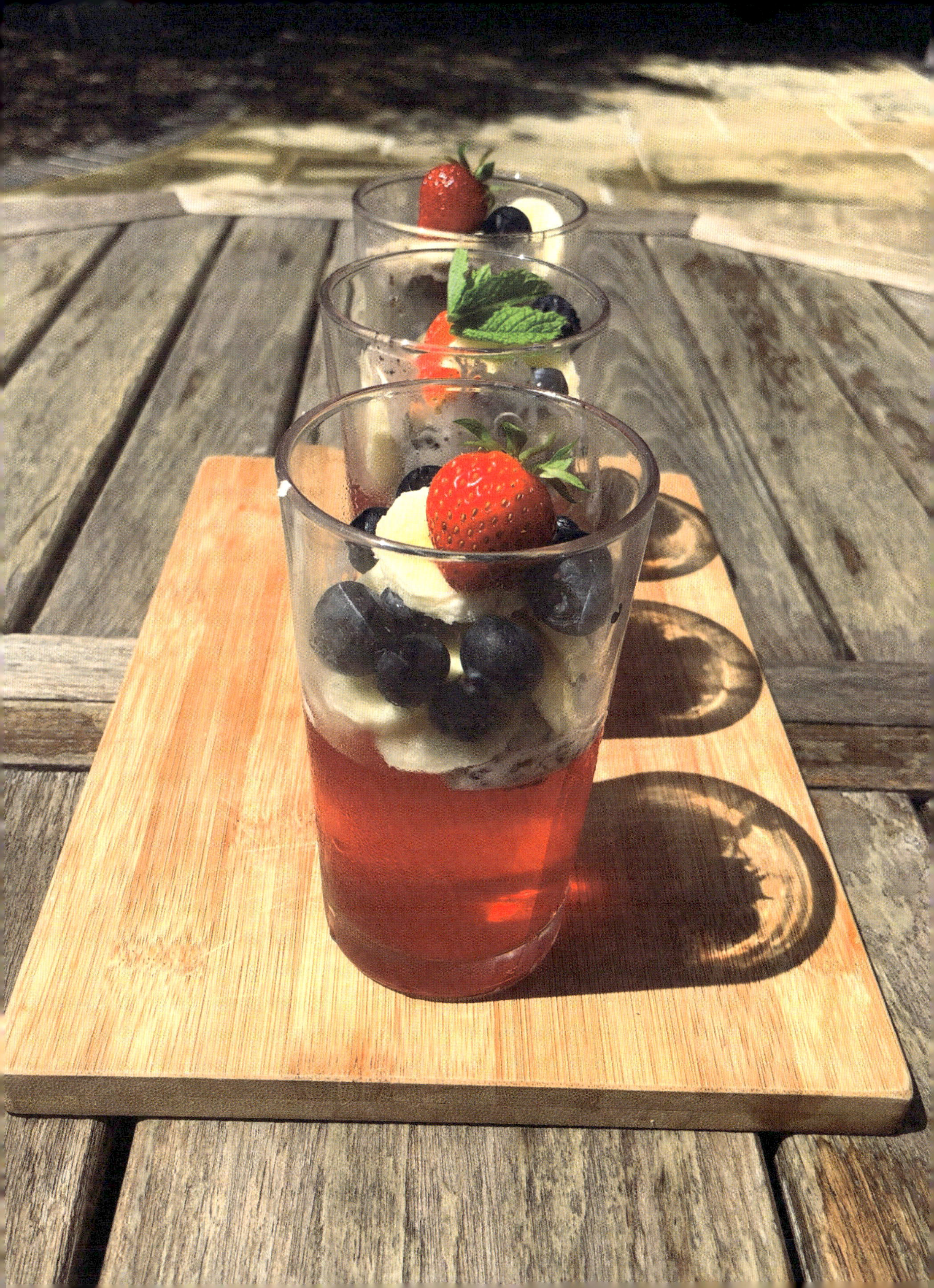

DESSERTS

Marble Cake

READY IN
1 HOUR 15 MINS

SERVES
8

So, Micah requested making a rainbow cake. An actual rainbow cake requires lots of time baking and cake tins but we made a marble cake, which is much easier. This recipe measures everything in cups, so if you use the same size cup for all ingredients, you should get the right proportions.

INGREDIENTS

¾ cup butter, softened

1 ¾ cups white sugar

4 eggs

1 teaspoon vanilla extract

1 cup full fat milk

3 cups plain flour

2 teaspoons baking powder

4-7 food colourings of your choice (you literally need a couple of drops of each)

ICING INGREDIENTS

400g butter, softened

600g icing sugar

You will also need an 8-inch cake tin, lined

METHOD

1. Preheat the oven to 170°C fan.

2. Cream the butter and sugar together in a large bowl. Add the eggs, one at a time and then the vanilla essence, beat until light and fluffy. Add the milk and mix all together. Slowly fold in the flour and baking powder.

3. Divide the mixture into small bowls, equal to the number of colours you will be using, so for instance if you use 7 colours divide into 7. If you use 4 colours divide into 4.

4. Add a few drops of a colour into each. So red in one, blue in another and so on. Fold in the colour very gently so you do not knock any air out of the mixture.

5. Put each coloured cake mixture one by one into the cake tin, then swirl around with a wooden skewer, this will give you the marble effect.

6. Place in a preheated oven for about 40-50 minutes. When the cake is cooked, take out and allow to cool.

7. In a bowl, mix the icing sugar with the butter. When the cake is cool, cut it in half horizontally, cover the top of one half with the buttercream icing and put the other half of the cake on top to make a sandwich. Then, cover all the cake with the rest of the buttercream icing.

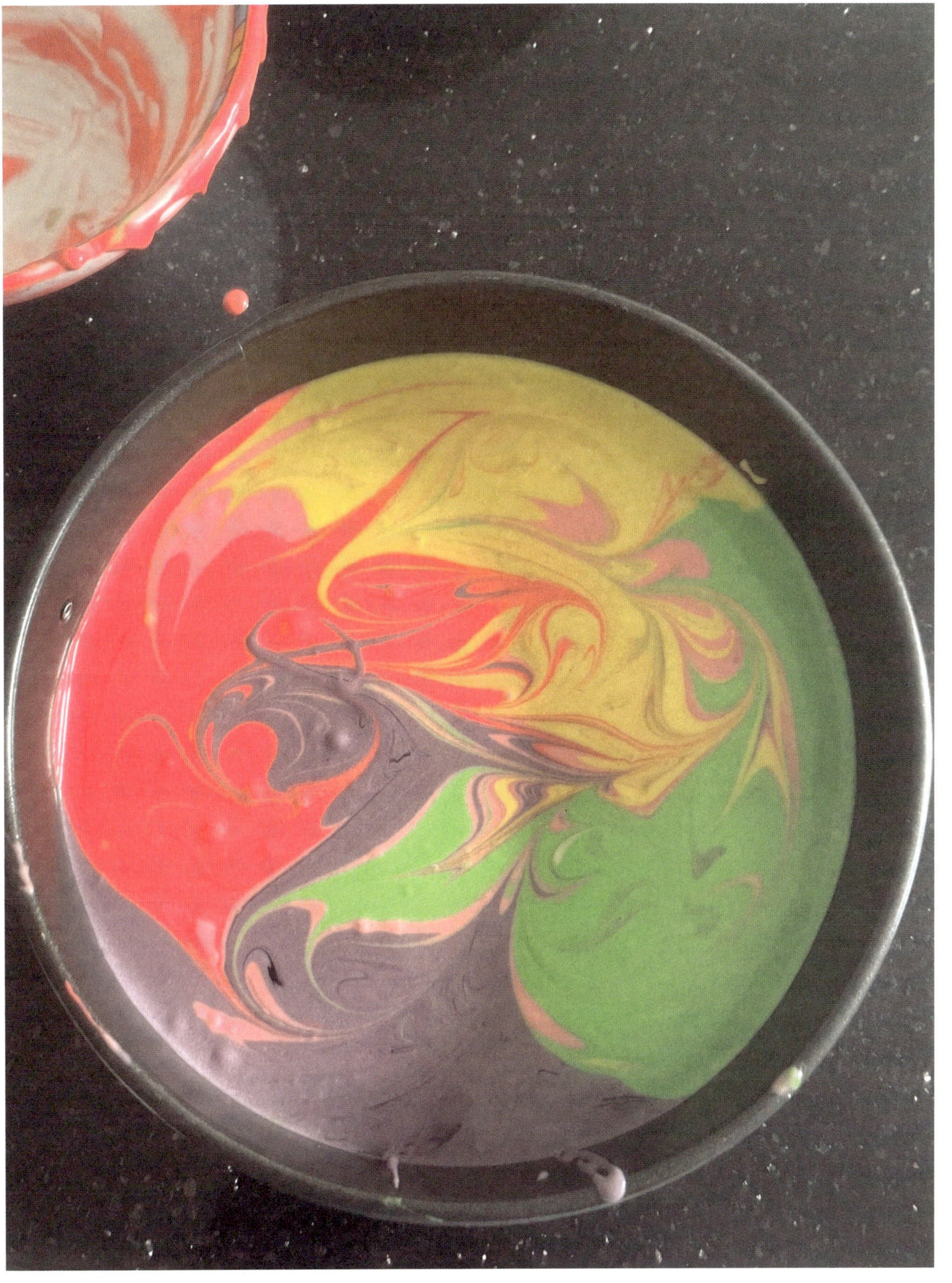

DESSERTS

Cheesecake

READY IN
40 MINS
+ SETTING

SERVES
8

INGREDIENTS

200g digestive biscuits

100g unsalted butter

600g cream cheese

100g icing sugar

1 teaspoon vanilla extract

½ lemon, finely grated, zest only, and juice

200ml double cream

100g white chocolate chips

400g strawberries

You will need an 8-inch round cake tin preferably with removable bottom

The lovely Mia chose cheesecake. We added strawberries as they were in season, but if you prefer to make a plain cheesecake just omit the fruit, or you can make any other flavour of your choice.

METHOD

1. Grease and line a loose-bottomed cake tin with baking paper.

2. To make the base, put the digestive biscuits into a food processor and blitz until crumbed, alternatively put them in a plastic food bag and crush using a rolling pin. Melt the butter in a pan or microwave. Put the crumbs in a bowl and pour over the melted butter. Mix thoroughly, then tip into the cake tin and press down firmly to create an even base. Chill in the fridge for 1 hour to set.

3. Into a food processor, put the cream cheese, icing sugar and vanilla extract, then beat until smooth. Pour in the double cream and continue beating until the mixture is completely combined and fairly firm. Add the lemon zest and juice.

4. Now spoon the cream mixture onto the biscuit base, it works well if you start from the edge and work towards the middle, flatten any air bubbles. Make the top of the cheesecake smooth with a spatula. Put in the fridge to set for about 6 hours.

5. Remove the cheesecake from the fridge about 30 minutes before serving. Run a knife round the edge to loosen it and then to remove it from the cake tin, you can place the base on top of a can and gently pull the sides of the cake tin down. Transfer the cheesecake onto a large plate, removing the lining paper and cake tin base.

6. Cut the strawberries in half and decorate the cheesecake with these and white chocolate chips. Or flavour with any topping of your choice.

365

DESSERTS

Madeira Cake

READY IN
1.5 HOURS

SERVES
8

Indian Nanny loved a madeira cake. Perfect for a teatime treat, really easy to bake. I've made madeira cake since I was the kids' age!

INGREDIENTS

225g self-raising flour

175g caster sugar

175g butter, cubed

3 eggs

1 teaspoon vanilla essence

You will need a loaf tin.

METHOD

1. Preheat the oven to 150°C fan.
2. Grease and line a loaf tin.
3. Sift the flour into a bowl then add all other ingredients.
4. Whisk until smooth, I prefer to do this using the steel blade in the food processor.
5. Use a scraper to remove batter from the bowl and put into the cake tin.
6. Bake for about 1 - 1¼ hours.
7. Check the cake is cooked by inserting either a wooden skewer or knife – if it comes out clean then it's cooked.
8. Remove from the tin and cool on a wire rack.

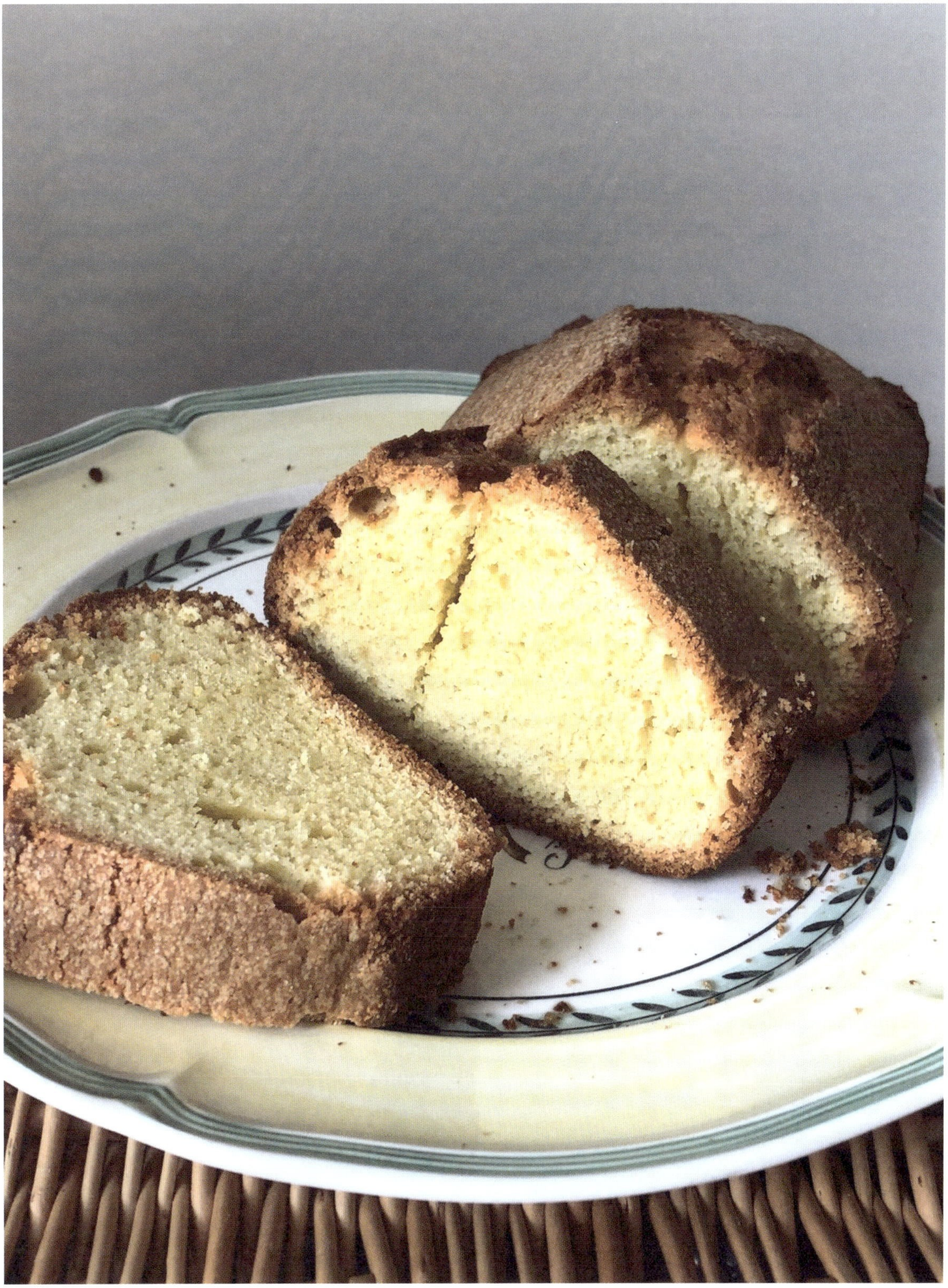

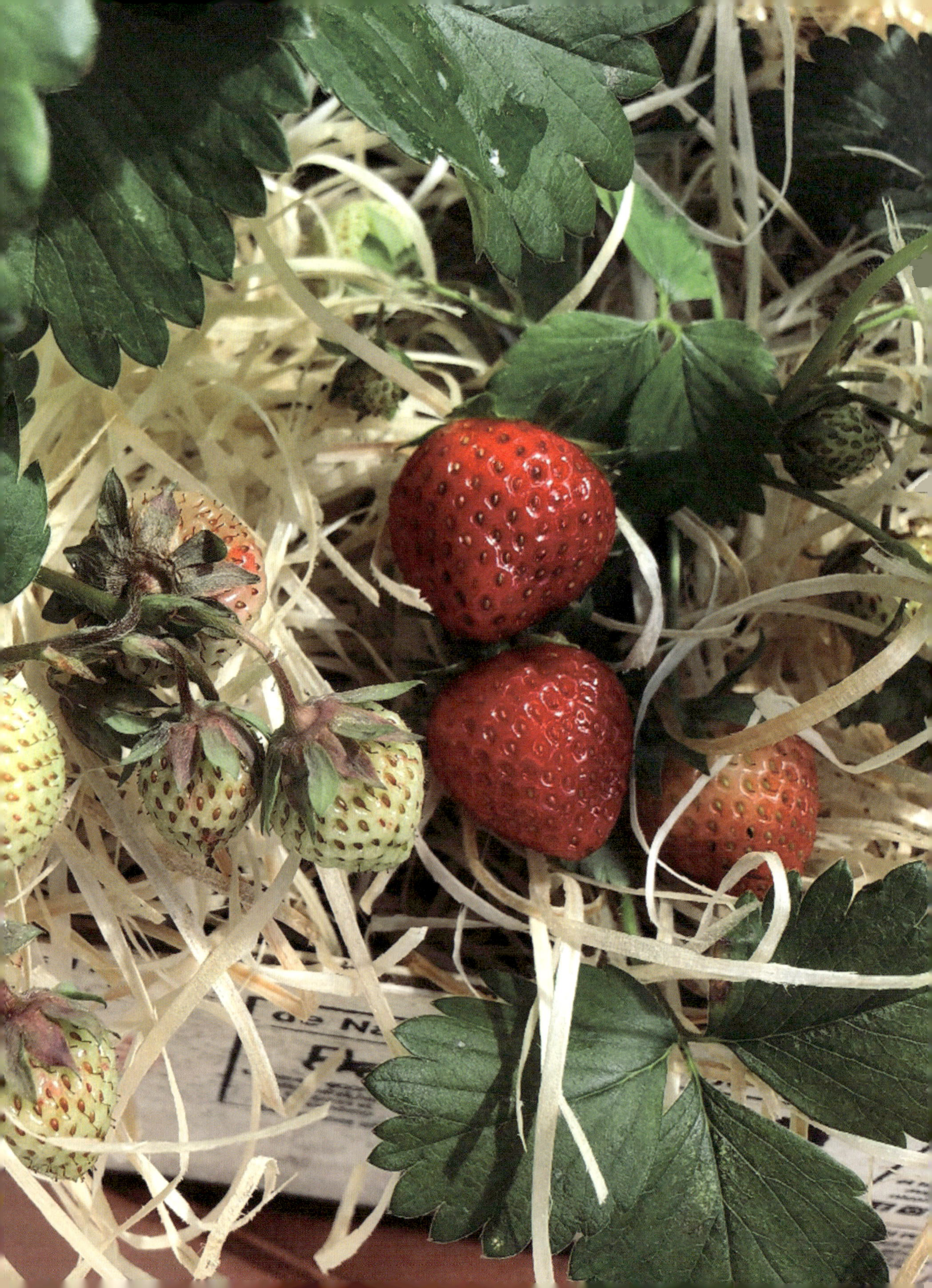

FRUIT DESSERTS

DESSERTS

Fresh Fruit Salad

READY IN
45 MINS

SERVES AT LEAST
15

As I said earlier, we love a salad! My mum is renowned for making an excellent fruit salad. Fruit salad with a scoop of vanilla ice cream makes a great dessert after an Indian meal. Any fruit nicely chopped will work, you can choose whatever's in season. This is my mum's special recipe which she would use for a party sharty!

You can make this in the morning and store in the fridge.

INGREDIENTS

3 oranges or 1 glass fresh orange juice

1 tin pineapple chunks 425g (cheat!) optional

2 apples – one red and one green

2 pears

3 bananas

500g red and green grapes (1 punnet)

2 kiwis

400g strawberries (1 punnet)

150g blueberries (1 punnet)

150g raspberries (1 punnet)

1 mango

½ melon

2 tablespoons caster sugar

METHOD

1. Into a very large bowl, squeeze the 3 oranges. Add the tinned pineapple & juice if using.
2. Wash and dice the apples and pears, add to the bowl.
3. Wash the grapes, halve and add to the bowl.
4. Skin the bananas and kiwis, slice and add to the bowl.
5. Skin and deseed the melon, dice, add to the bowl.
6. Skin, de-stone and cut the mango, chop and add to the bowl.
7. Wash the blueberries and raspberries, add to the bowl.
8. Lastly, wash the strawberries, take off the green tops, then cut into quarters, add to the bowl.
9. Sprinkle 2 tablespoons of sugar over the fruit and very, very gently mix.

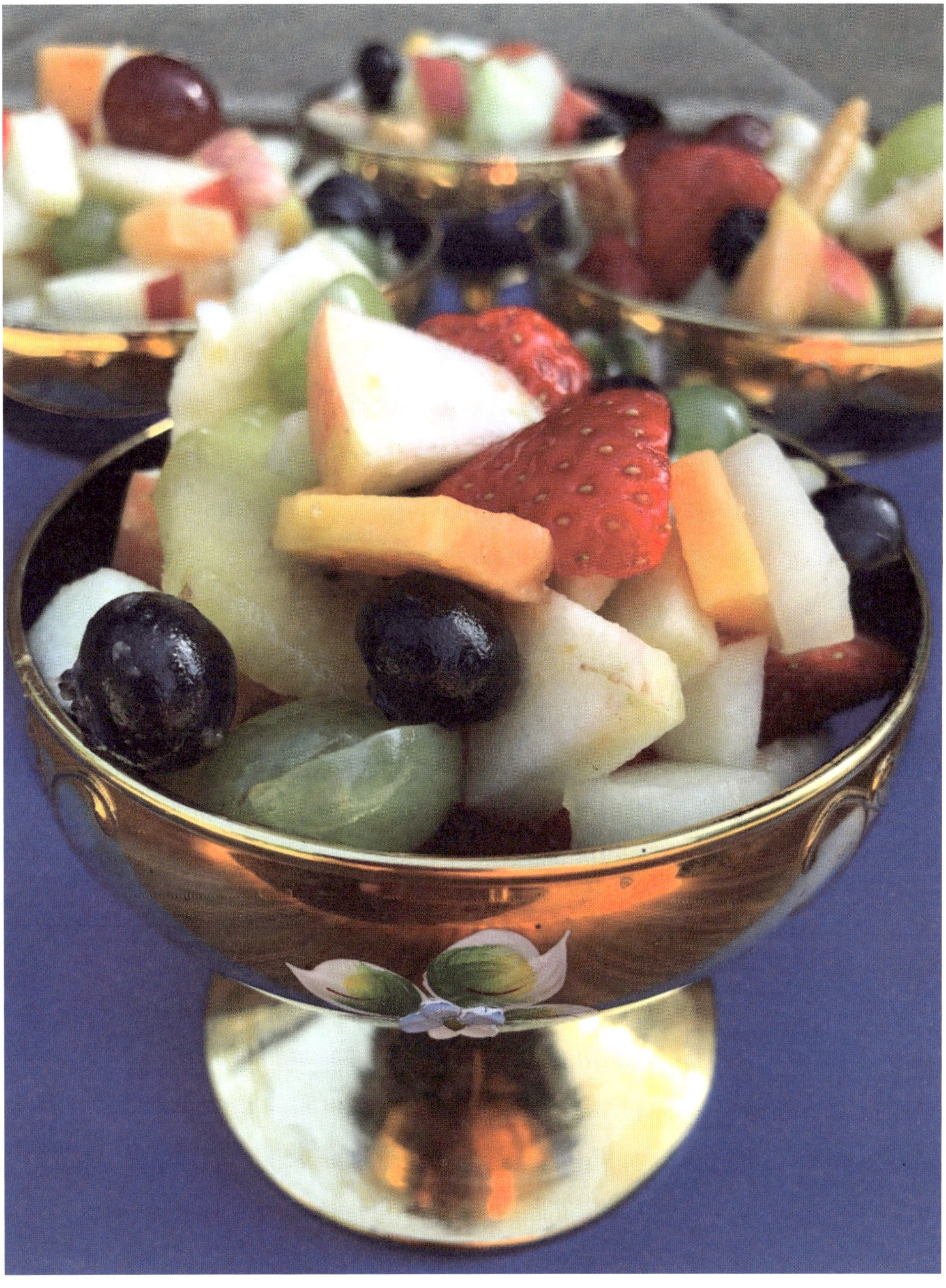

Lychees

Veena remembers picking these on a fruit farm in Dehradun where they used to go on holiday in Northern India. These strange-looking little fruits are an Asian beauty. They bear a small stone in the middle, sweet strawberry-tasting flesh. We call them eyeballs!

You can place them in a bowl and everyone can peel their own.

DESSERTS

Mangoes

Mangoes, mangoes and more mangoes!! Alfonso mangoes are probably our favourite. The season is short but it's well worth a trip to the Indian shop to get a box.

Mangoes need to be cut when ripe and again make an excellent snack anytime of the day or for dessert.

DESSERTS

Milly's Mangoes

READY IN 5 MINS

SERVES 2

My Dad taught Milly how to cut a mango, this is how!

INGREDIENTS

2 mangoes

Raisins and raspberries (optional)

METHOD

1. To check if a mango is ripe, give it a bit of a squeeze – if there's give, it's ripe.
2. Wash the mangoes.
3. Hold the mango with the stem facing upwards.
4. Using a sharp knife slice the mango downwards, either side of the stem, avoiding the hard stone in the middle.
5. You will end up with the two mango ends and the middle section which has the stone in it.
6. Place the stone section to one side. With the other 2 pieces, score the flesh lengthways and widthways, creating a crisscross pattern. Being careful not to cut through the skin.
7. Invert by pushing in the middle of the skin side.
8. Use in a fruit salad, lassi or eat with a teaspoon straight away.
9. Add 2 raisins for eyes and a raspberry for the nose if you wish to make a mango hedgehog!
10. The stone section can also be enjoyed, just use your knife to cut away the skin, then suck the juice and flesh from the stone. It may be messy but it's delicious!

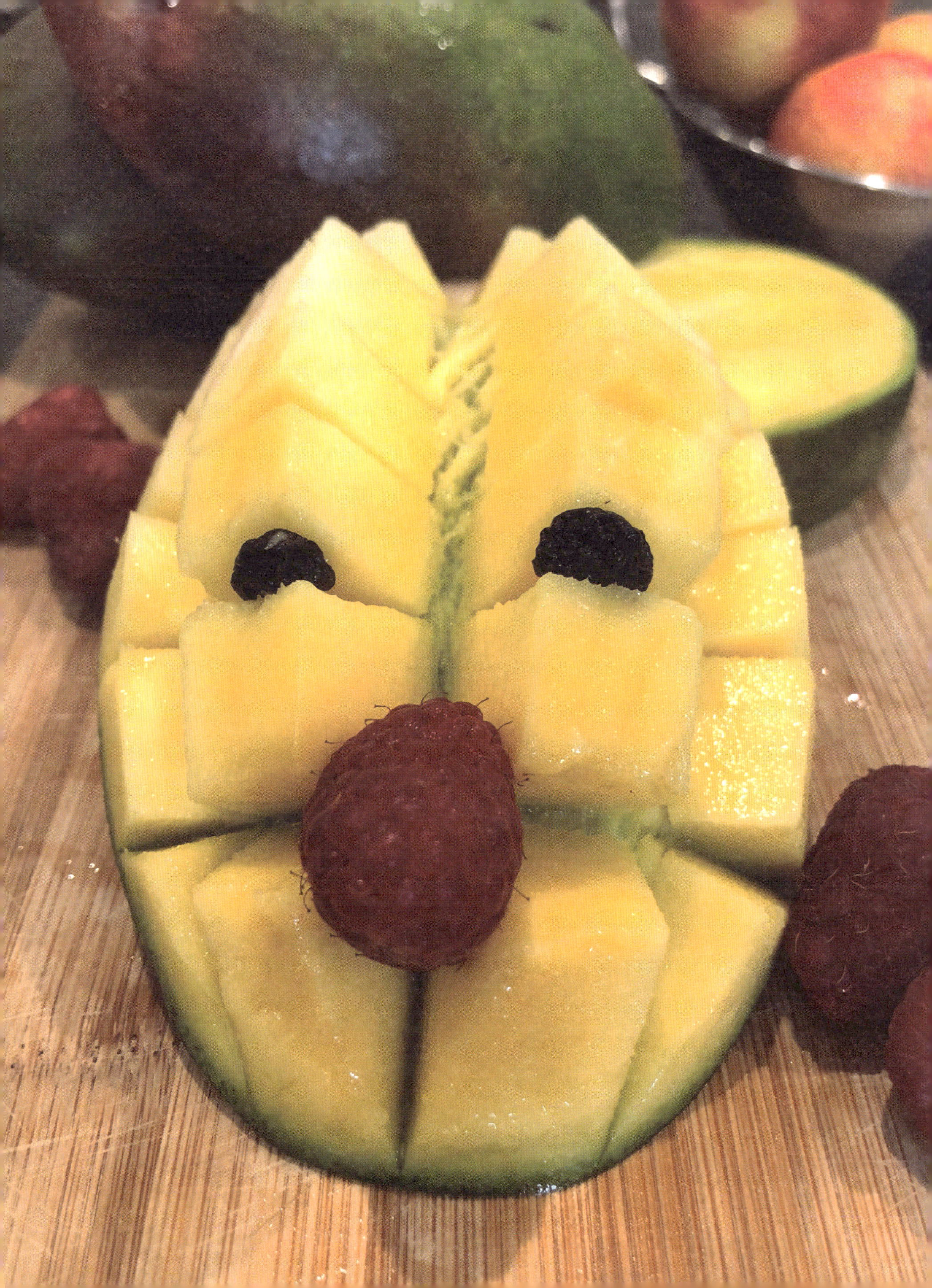

376

377

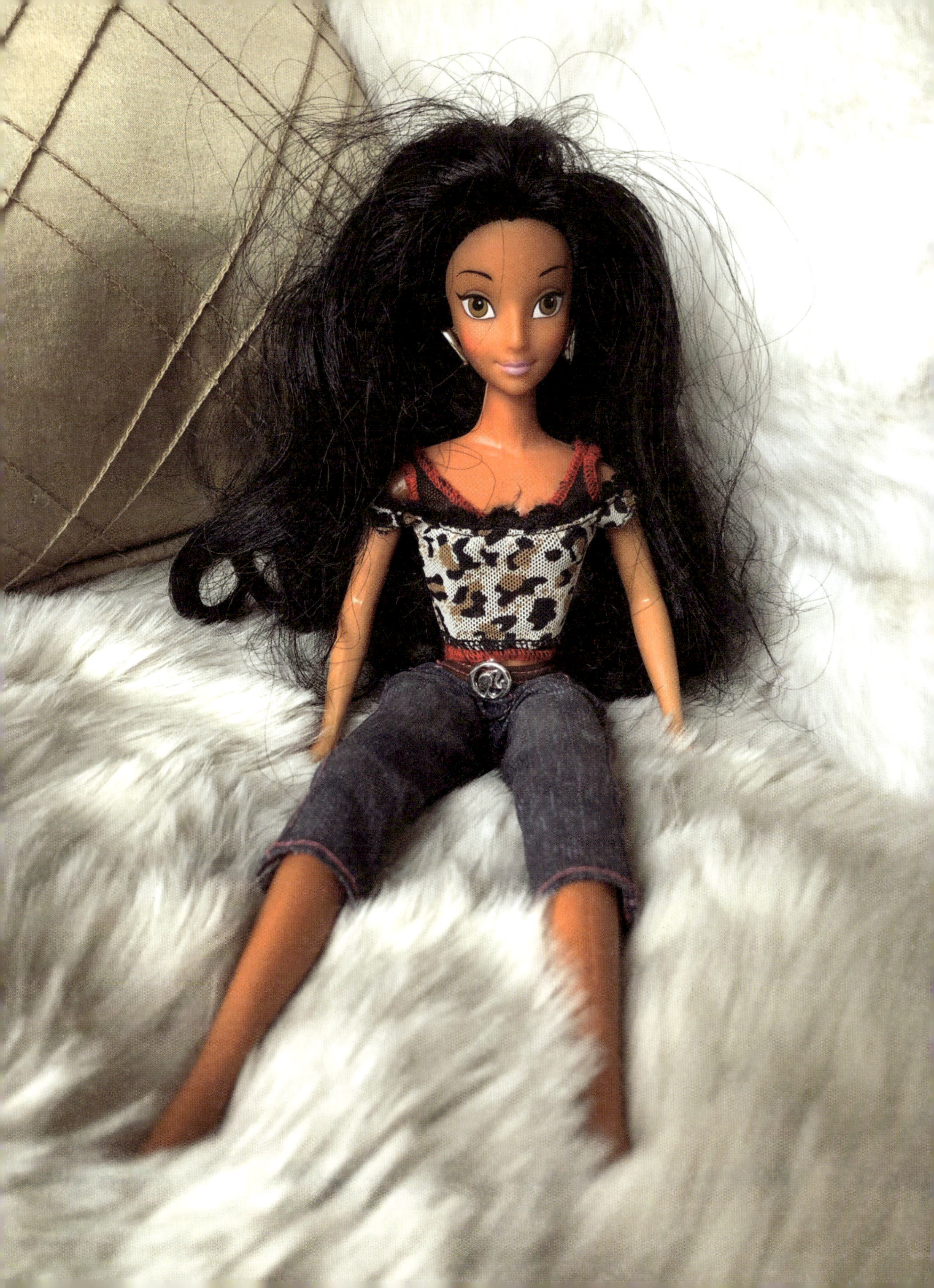

DRINKS

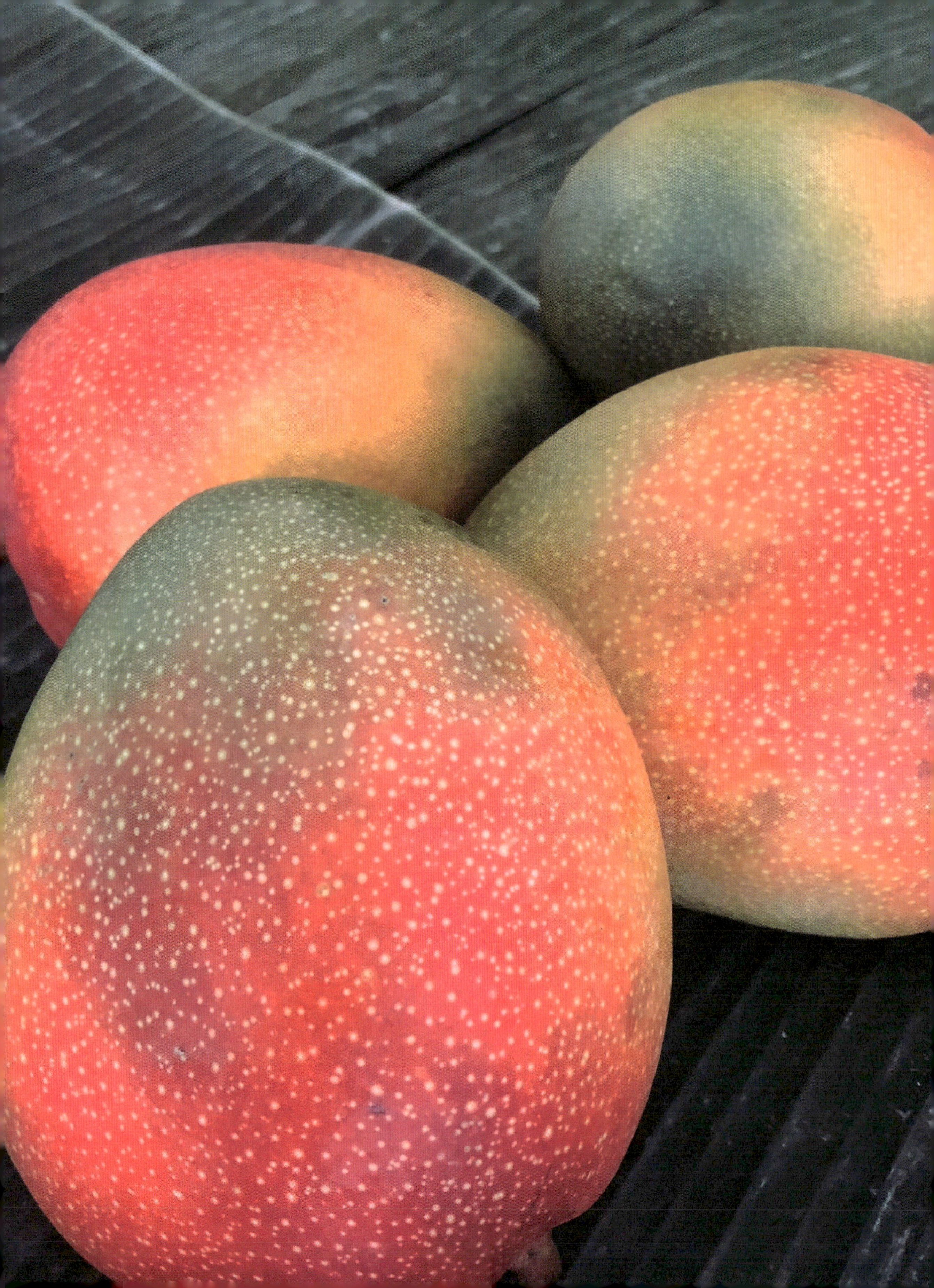

DRINKS

Lassi

⏳ **READY IN**
5 MINS

🍽 **SERVES**
2

My Nanny used to make these. They go really well with a pronti or as a refreshing drink.

INGREDIENTS

500g natural full fat yogurt

500ml water

5 tablespoons sugar

METHOD

1. In a blender, add the yogurt and the sugar.
2. Whisk for a few seconds until smooth.
3. Add the water and whisk again so you see a little froth at the top.
4. Serve immediately, pouring over ice cubes.

Mango Lassi

⏳ **READY IN**
5 MINS

🍽 **SERVES**
2

Now this is a good one! Milly loves a mango.

INGREDIENTS

1 mango, peeled, stone removed

500g natural full fat yogurt

500ml water

5 tablespoons sugar

METHOD

1. In a blender, blitz the mango to a pulp.
2. Add the yogurt and the sugar.
3. Whisk for a few seconds until smooth.
4. Add the water and whisk again so you see a little froth at the top.
5. Serve immediately, pouring over ice cubes.

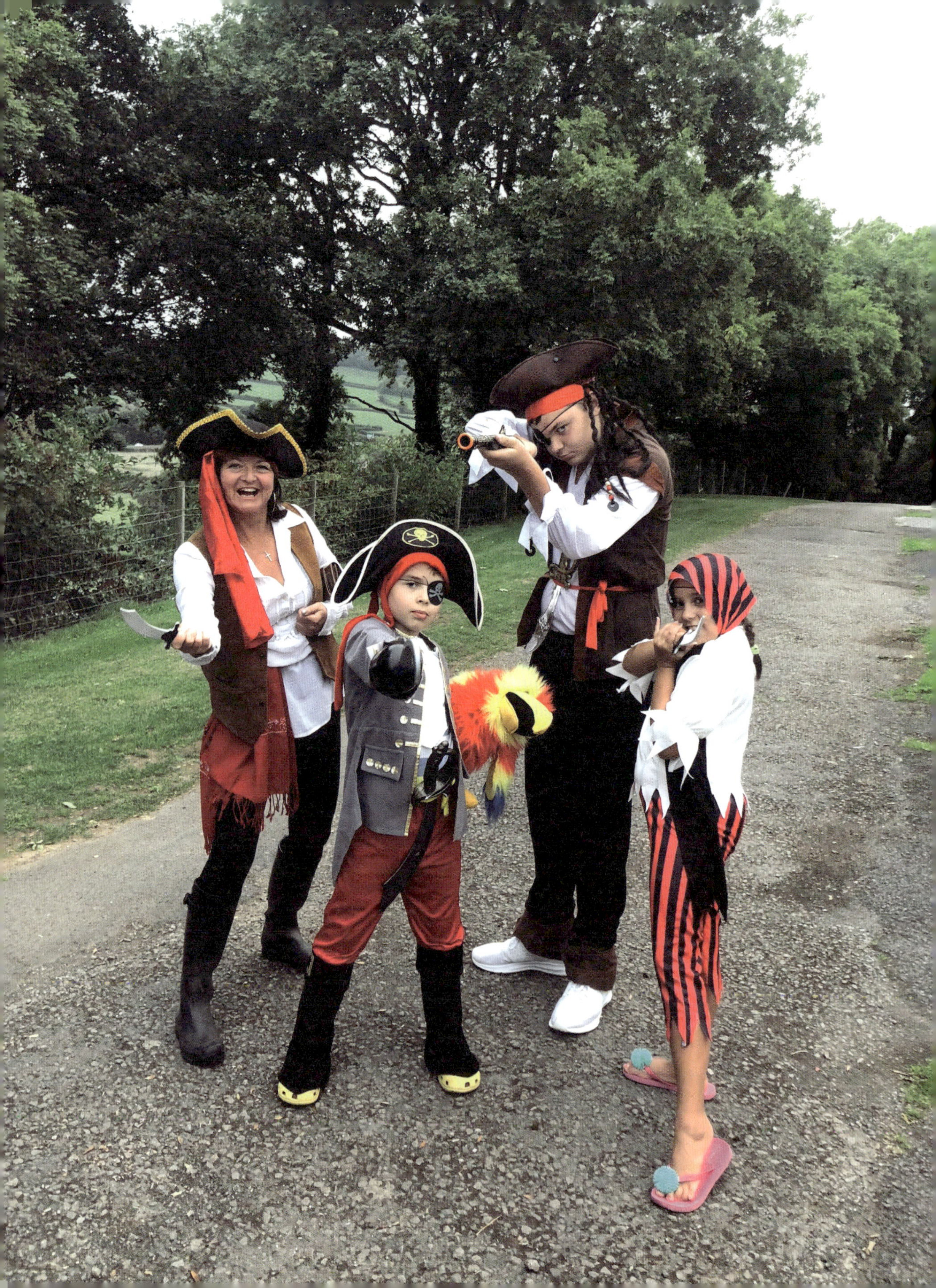

Jack and Julie's Cocktails

Jack and Julie like to have a cocktail party when we are at the caravan in Devon! They put a few family favourites on the cocktail menu.

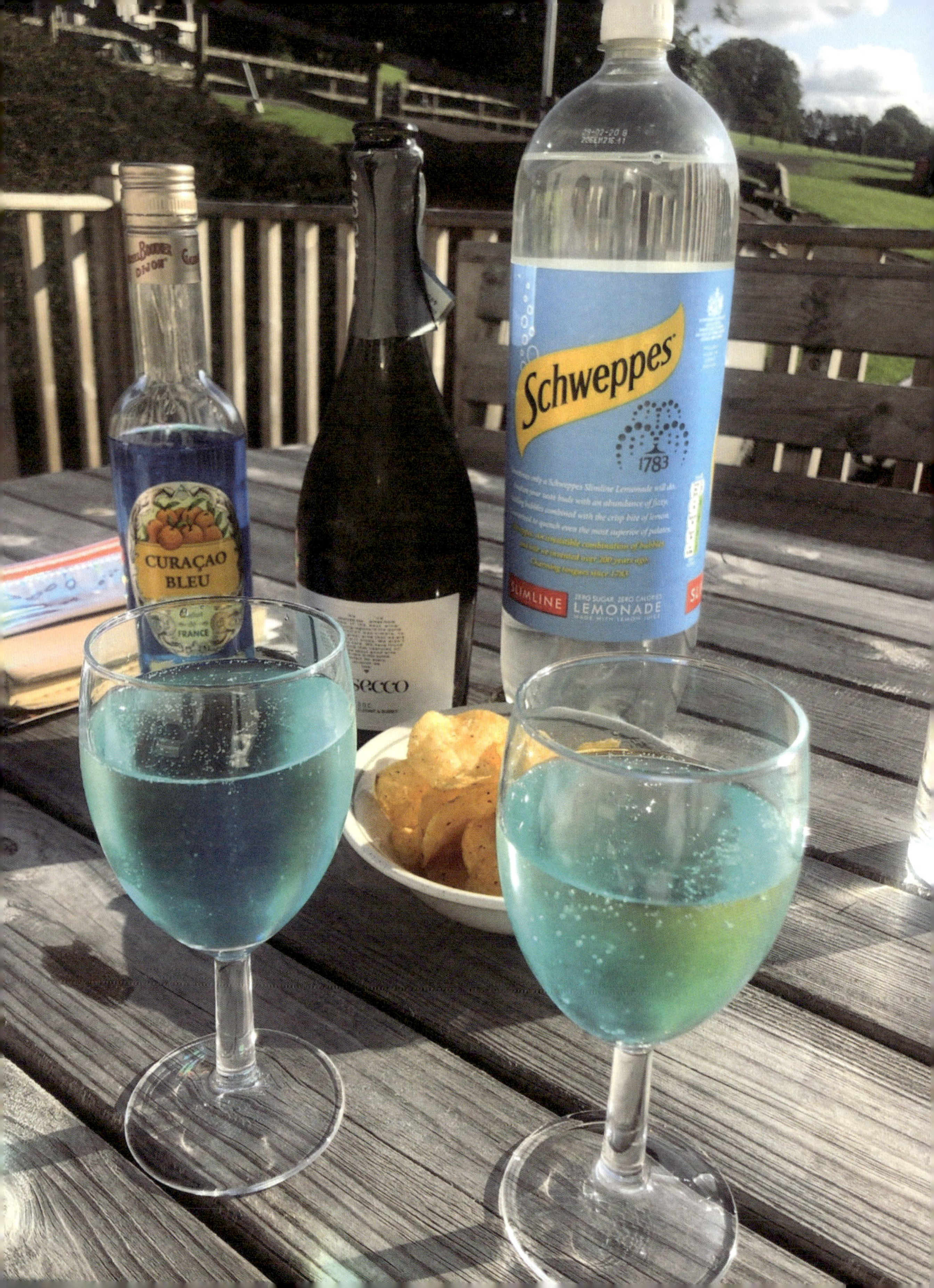
CURAÇAO
BLEU
FRANCE
Schweppes
1783
SLIMLINE
LEMONADE

DRINKS

Parkers Porn Star Martini

The porn star martini originates from the Lab bar in Soho but was reinvented at Parkers in 2017!

You can buy vanilla vodka ready-made; however, Julie likes to "brew her own" by popping a vanilla pod in a bottle of vodka for a few days.

INGREDIENTS

2 passion fruits, cut in half

50ml vanilla vodka

100ml passion fruit juice (Rubicon is good)

Shot glass of your favourite fizz (Prosecco / Champagne / Cava)

METHOD

1. Mix the vodka and passion fruit juice with ice, give a good shake in a cocktail mixer.
2. Pour into a martini glass (triangle style) and garnish with half a passion fruit.
3. Serve the shot of fizz on the side… sip it, drink it in one or pour it into the cocktail… the dryness of the fizz complements the sweetness of the cocktail.
4. Serve immediately and enjoy!

Big Dada's Blue Drink

During the 80s all the cousins remember the adults drinking a "blue drink". We also celebrated Big Dada's 100th birthday with a blue drink toast. Then, on our family holiday to the Chateau in France in 2019, would you believe they served it there as an aperitif! It's always on Julie and Jack's cocktail menu.

If you prefer something sweeter, add a dash of lemonade.

INGREDIENTS

Your favourite fizz chilled (Prosecco / sparkling wine / Champagne /Cava)

60ml Bols Blue Curacao Liqueur (French orange flavour liqueur)

METHOD

1. Using a champagne flute, add the Blue Curacao
2. Top up with fizz.
3. Raise your glass and toast the legend!

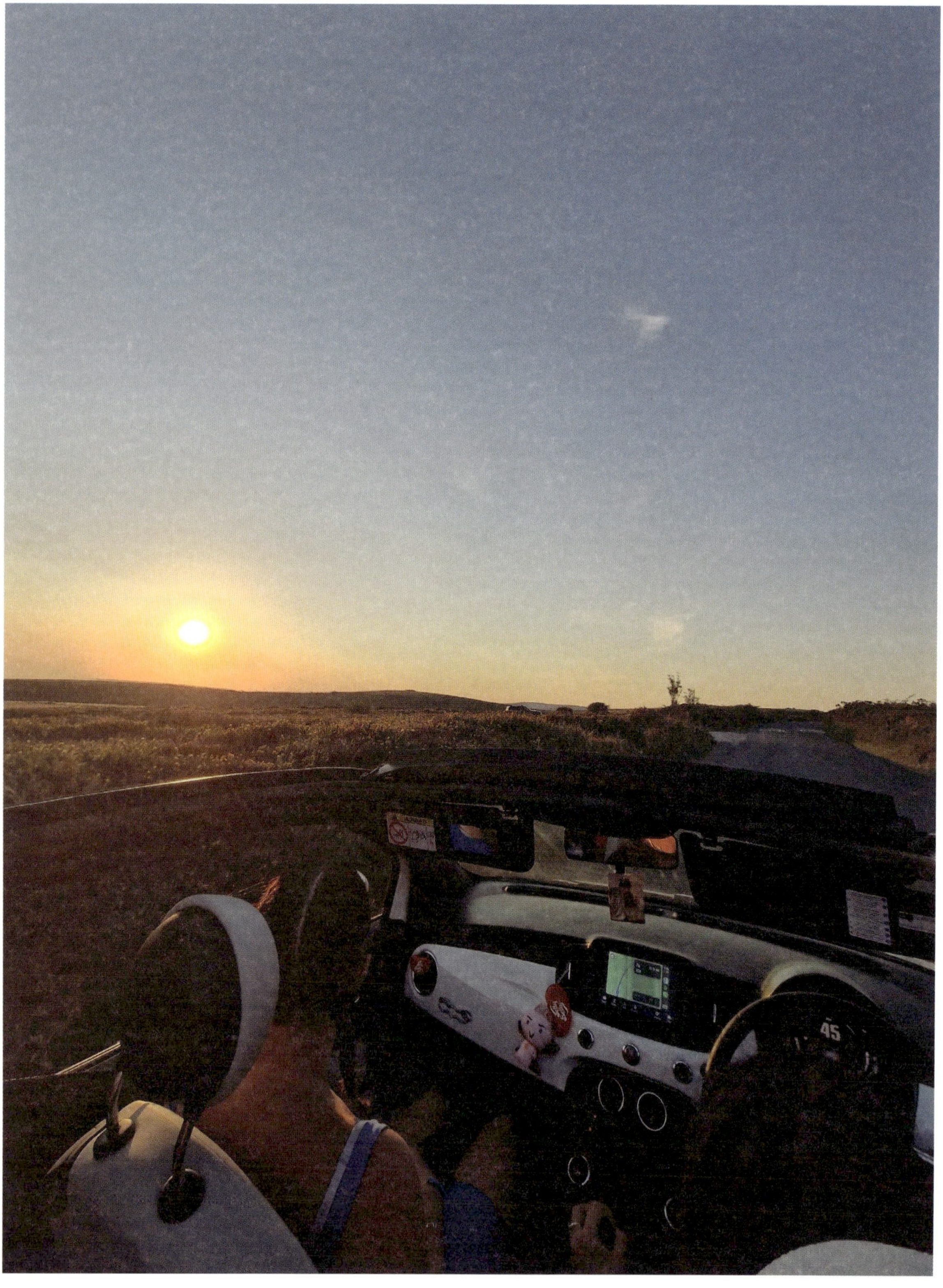

DRINKS

Katy's Cocktail

READY IN 5 MINS **SERVES** 2

When the girls got their own van, they started mixing cocktails too! Katy introduced them to Sex on the beach. Here's her recipe.

INGREDIENTS

- Vodka
- Peach schnapps
- Orange juice
- Cranberry juice
- Ice

METHOD

1. Into a wine glass fill with a good measure of vodka, then the same of peach schnapps.
2. Add some orange juice and finish with cranberry juice.
3. Add a few cubes of ice if you have it and enjoy with karaoke!

Milly's Santa Maria

READY IN 5 MINS **SERVES** 2

Milly's caravan cocktail, made with her favourite spirits and the signature blue liqueur.

INGREDIENTS

- Peach schnapps
- Malibu
- Passion fruit juice
- Blue Curacao Liqueur

METHOD

1. Into a large wine glass add equal amounts of peach schnapps & malibu (either 25ml or 50ml).
2. Add the passion fruit juice, as much as you like.
3. Using the back of a tablespoon, press it against the inside of the glass and pour a drizzle of blue curacao liqueur.
4. Allow to settle for 30 seconds and see the beautiful gradient from blue to yellow!
5. Enjoy!

Calories

FEVER-TREE
Refreshingly Light

INDIAN
TONIC
WATER

MADE WITH NATURAL FLAVOURS
INCLUDING NATURAL QUININE

Delicious and low in calories
500ml

DRINKS

Gigi's Whisky

READY IN 5 MINS **SERVES** 2

Indians are whisky drinkers!!

METHOD

1. Into a tumbler add an inch or two of Whisky.
2. Add a handful of ice.
3. Top up with water or soda.
4. Serve immediately.

INGREDIENTS

Black Label whisky

Water or soda

Dad's Famous G&T

READY IN 5 MINS **SERVES** 2

Gin has become trendy and easy to drink. Funnily enough while Big Dada was drinking blue drink in the 80s, the Aunties were having a G&T!

METHOD

1. Into a gin glass (very similar to a large red wine glass) add an inch of Gin.
2. Handful of ice and either the cucumber or lemon.
3. Top up with tonic.
4. Serve cold and immediately.

INGREDIENTS

Hendricks Gin

2 slices of cucumber or lemon

Good quality tonic, e.g. Fever-tree (chilled)

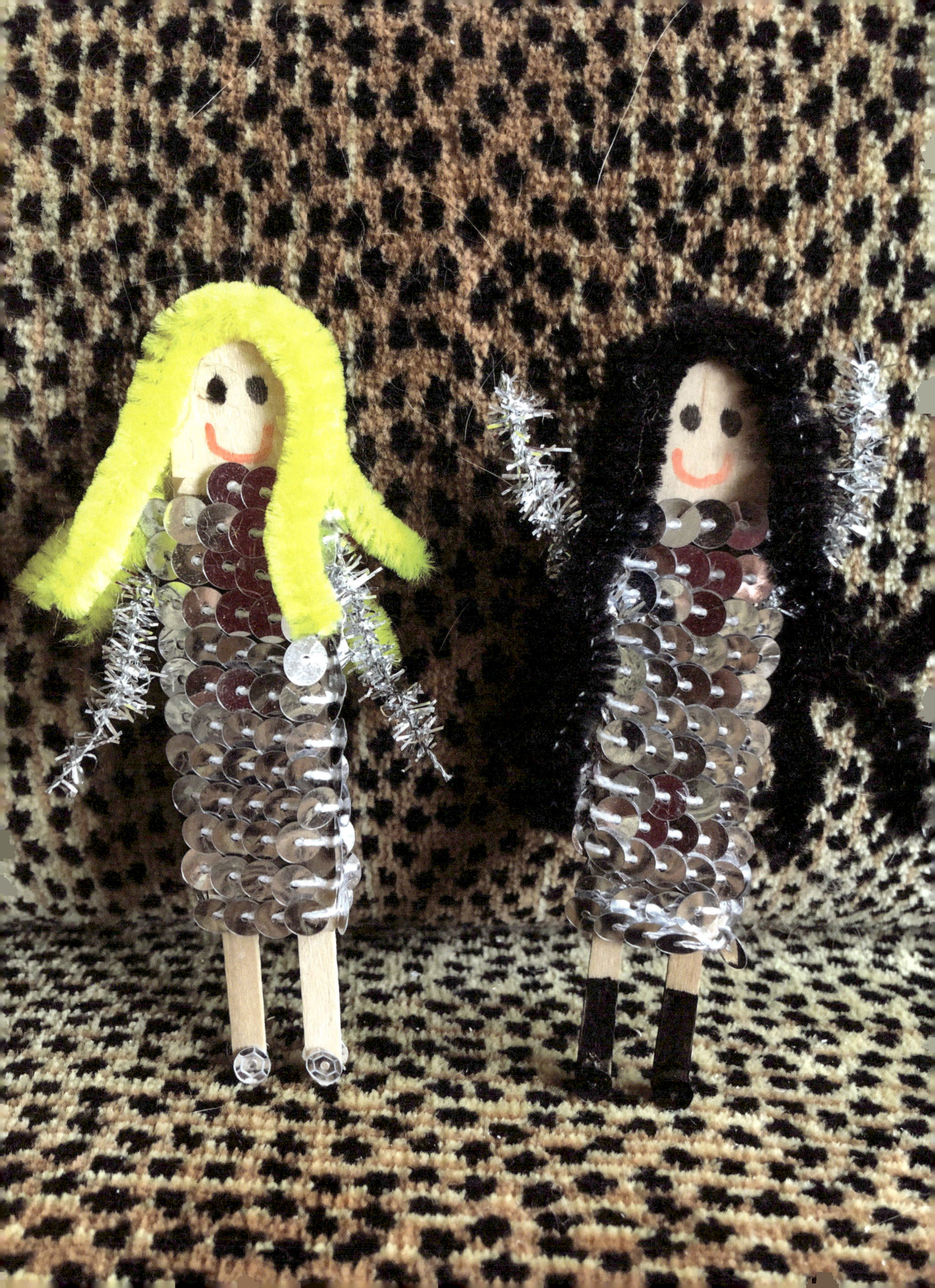

Mocktails & Juices

These are awesome for a "dry" spell. Here are a few of my favourites...

DRINKS

INGREDIENTS

Elderflower cordial

Sprig fresh mint

Sparkling water

Essie's Elderflower Cordial

READY IN 5 MINS **SERVES** 2

When Esme moved to the country, she found the country girl somewhere within the heart of a city girl! On exploring her land she found she had elderflower trees and made some wicked cordial. Elderflower trees are actually pretty easy to find in season. Or you can buy it ready-made in the supermarket.

METHOD

1. In a large wine glass or tumbler add an inch of elderflower cordial.
2. Add some ice.
3. Fill up with cold sparkling water.
4. Add a sprig of mint and enjoy!

Lime and Soda Spritz

READY IN 5 MINS **SERVES** 2

Is what it says on the tin.

METHOD

1. In a large wine glass, squeeze ½ lime.
2. Slice ¼ lime and add this to the glass too.
3. Fill up with cold sparkling water.

INGREDIENTS

Sparkling water

1 Lime

DRINKS

Apple and Ginger Fizz

READY IN 5 MINS **SERVES** 2

The flavour in this is incredible.

METHOD

1. In a tall glass add an inch of cordial over lots of ice.
2. Mix 50% apple juice and 50% ginger beer, then serve with a straw.

INGREDIENTS

- Bottlegreen ginger and lemongrass cordial
- Cloudy apple juice
- Fever-tree light ginger beer

Posh Squash

READY IN 5 MINS **SERVES** 2

Fresh and fruity!

METHOD

1. Put a large glug of the grenadine in a glass with ice and top up with cold still or sparkling water.
2. Decorate with a handful of berries if you wish.

INGREDIENTS

- Teisseire Le Sirop Fruity Flavour Grenadine
- Ice
- Sparkling or still water
- Handful of berries

Milly & Jude's Juices

We got given a juicer, I think by Uncle Kevin! You can literally juice any fruit; the kids love making fresh juices. You can also buy frozen fruit which is great for juicing or if you do not have a juicer, you can make these mixed juices from cartons too.

INGREDIENTS

Pineapple

Mango

Strawberries

Pineapple, Mango and Strawberry

READY IN 5 MINS

SERVES 2

An Abama Hotel favourite!

METHOD

1. This looks best layered. So, start with the pineapple and juice it with ice so it's slightly thicker in consistency.

2. Do the same with the mango.

3. Then the strawberries.

4. Add equal quantities of juice to a tall glass.

5. Serve with a straw.

DRINKS

INGREDIENTS

Pineapple

Mango

Orange

Pineapple, Mango and Orange Juice

READY IN
5 MINS

SERVES
2

METHOD

1. Add equal quantities of juice over ice with a splash of water.
2. Serve with a straw.

Pineapple and Watermelon Juice

READY IN
5 MINS

SERVES
2

This is my favourite juice of all time. An Aussie juice.

METHOD

1. Juice the pineapple and watermelon.
2. Serve over ice.

INGREDIENTS

Pineapple

Watermelon

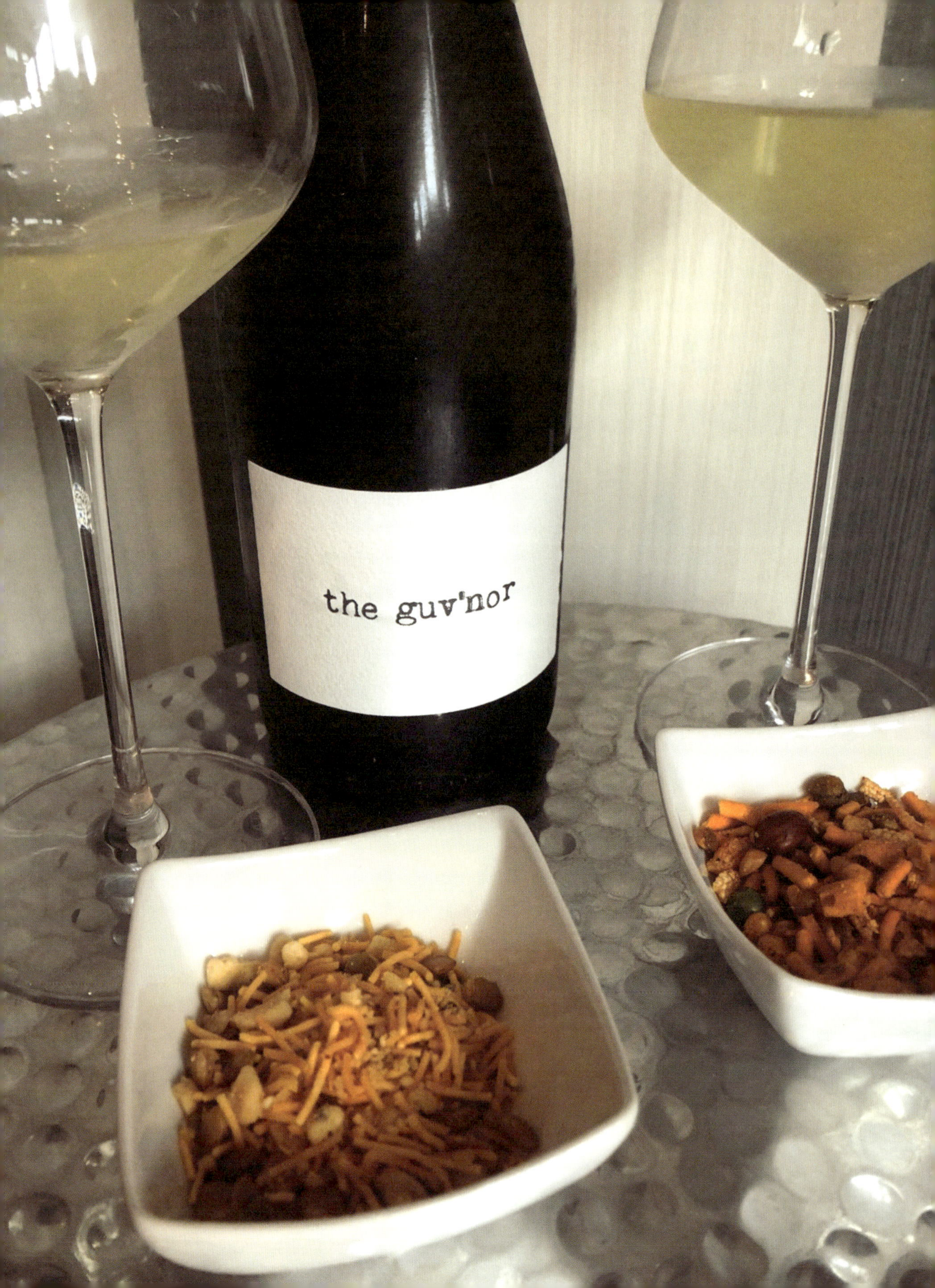
the guv'nor

Wine & Beer

We are (and I'm not scared to admit) great wine drinkers. Here is Dad's special wine list.

CHAMPAGNE
Laurent Perrier Rosé
Bollinger – both White and Rosé
Taittinger

WHITE WINE
Macon – France
Chablis – France
Alberino – Spain
Verdejo – Spain
Chenin Blanc – Stellenbosch, Cape Town
Chardonnay – Aussie (that's mine!)

ROSÉ WINE
Cote de Provence – France

RED WINE
Châteauneuf-du-Pape – France
Burgundy – France
Bordeaux – Claret – France
Malbec – Argentina
Rioja – Spain

BEER!
The cousins love a beer, perfect accompaniment to Indian dishes. Beck's is a firm family favourite. Cobra and Tiger are Indian beers, which we love. They also do a zero-alcohol version, which is really nice too.

Chilli Art by Georgiana Cooper & Elodie Larsson

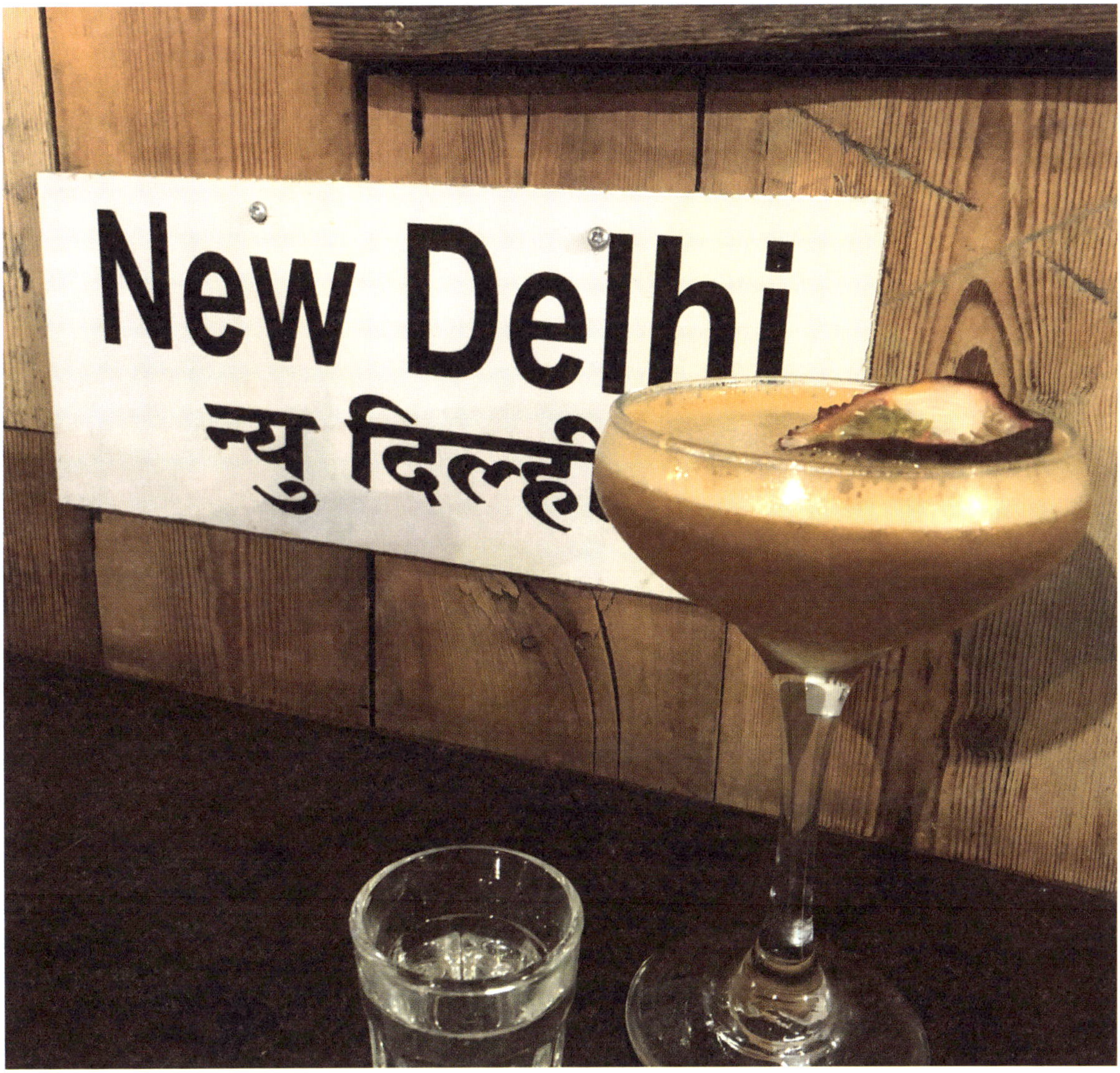
New Delhi

Thank you!

Thank you so much for reading, cooking and eating!

I hope you, your family and friends enjoy Indian Nanny's simple home cooking as much as we do x

A massive thank you to Nanny and Big Dada
Mum and Dad
Milly and Jude
Gigi, Rita, Veena, Madhu, Mishi, Ravi
Helena, Nisha, Tina, Kevin & Carly
Nick, Esme, Rols, John & Rosemary, Julie & Jack, Sarah, Jane, Sue & Bill, Chris
Ginger, Petal, Rosie, Bella, Connor, Lacey and Candy
The Indian Shop, Riverford & Parkers

The majority of cookery photos in this book have been taken using my iPhone 8, the dishes were cooked by me, photographed by me and eaten by many! Thank you to Rohit, Seema, Rax, Emma, Nick, Anna, Victoria, Jill, Peter, Megan Blake Photography, Martin, Friends, Cousins and Aunties for their photography contributions.

All my marvellous family, friends and colleagues who have unconditionally supported me by helping, eating the food and trying the recipes (you know who you are!)

Freepik for the high-quality illustration & Ruth and the team at ukbookpublishing.com

Cooking lessons both online and face-to-face are available from Ma Pushpa Kitchen contact Rita ritamehra17@hotmail.com M: 07956 417035

Famine and poverty in India is vast. Proceeds from this book sale will be donated to Indian Nanny's favourite charities.

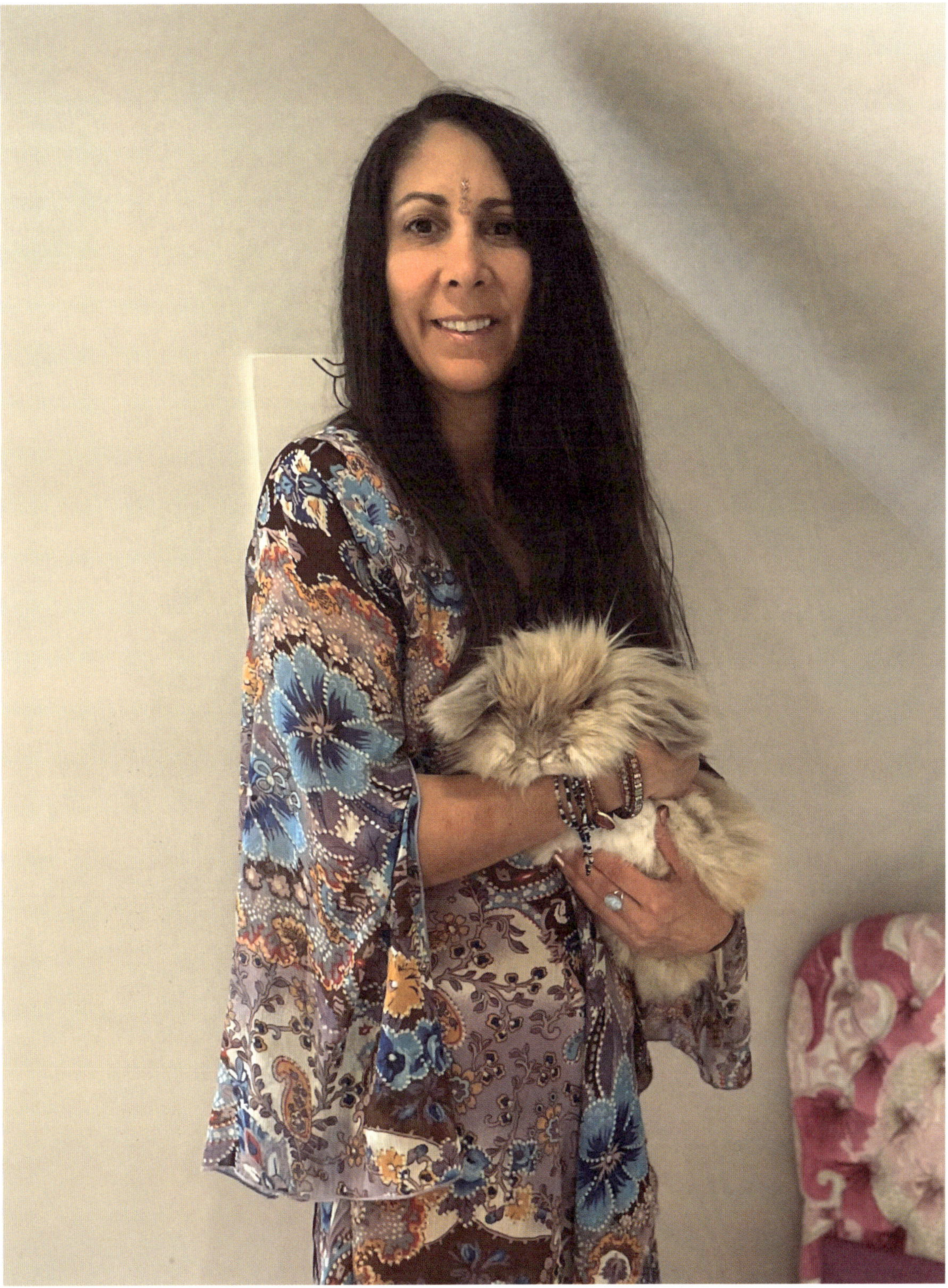

350/2
හබරාදූව
ஹபராதுவ
HABARADUWA
ගාල්ල
காலி
GALLE
SPRPTA
GQ-
5817
SPRPTA